Thomas Hardy and Desire

Also by Jane Thomas

THOMAS HARDY, FEMININITY AND DISSENT: Reassessing the 'Minor' Novels

THE WELL-BELOVED WITH *THE PURSUIT OF THE WELL-BELOVED*,
Thomas Hardy (*editor*)

A CHANGED MAN AND OTHER STORIES, Thomas Hardy (*editor*)

LIFE'S LITTLE IRONIES, Thomas Hardy (*editor*)

Thomas Hardy and Desire

Conceptions of the Self

Jane Thomas

Senior Lecturer in English, University of Hull, UK

First published 2013 by
PALGRAVE MACMILLAN

Palgrave Macmillan in the UK is an imprint of Macmillan Publishers Limited, registered in England, company number 785998, of Houndmills, Basingstoke, Hampshire RG21 6XS.

Palgrave Macmillan in the US is a division of St Martin's Press LLC, 175 Fifth Avenue, New York, NY 10010.

Palgrave Macmillan is the global academic imprint of the above companies and has companies and representatives throughout the world.

Palgrave® and Macmillan® are registered trademarks in the United States, the United Kingdom, Europe and other countries.

ISBN 978–0–230–22463–6

This book is printed on paper suitable for recycling and made from fully managed and sustained forest sources. Logging, pulping and manufacturing processes are expected to conform to the environmental regulations of the country of origin.

A catalogue record for this book is available from the British Library.

A catalog record for this book is available from the Library of Congress.

10   9   8   7   6   5   4   3   2   1
22 21 20 19 18 17 16 15 14 13

Contents

Preface

Things are not all as graspable and sayable as on the whole we are led to believe; most events are unsayable, occur in a space that no word has ever penetrated, and most unsayable of all are works of art, mysterious existences, whose life endures alongside ours, which passes away.

Rainer Maria Rilke (1903; 2011) *Letters to a Young Poet*: 6

My only desire's a desire
to be free from desire.

'Desire's a Desire', Selima Hill, *Gloria: Selected Poems*
(Newcastle-upon-Tyne: Bloodaxe Books, 2008: 117)

Acknowledgements

Much of this book was written during two periods of research leave from the University of Hull for which I am deeply grateful. A British Academy Overseas Conference Grant and awards from Hull University's Faculty of Arts and Social Sciences Research and Staff Development funds enabled me to participate in seminal Hardy conferences in Dorchester, UK, and New Haven, Connecticut. My thanks go to Rosemarie Morgan, Angelique Richardson and Richard Nemesvari for the opportunity to be a part of 'Hardy at Yale' 2010 and 2012. I owe a large debt of gratitude to the Thomas Hardy Society of Great Britain and to its dedicated and hard-working Council of Management. I particularly appreciate the practical and scholarly support and the friendship of Mike Nixon, Helen Gibson, Brenda Parry, Sue Clarke, Sue Theobald, Furse and Rosemary Swann, Dee and Patrick Tolfree, Helen Lange, Andrew and Marilyn Leah, Mary Kinsey and, above all, the Society's indefatigable Chairman, Tony Fincham, for inviting me to companion him on some wonderful walks through the landscape of Hardy's novels in Dorset and Cornwall and for his matchless enthusiasm for and knowledge of all things Hardyian. It has been a pleasure and a privilege to be the Academic Director of the International Thomas Hardy Conference and Festival of 2010 and 2012. I have greatly appreciated the opportunity to test out my ideas in such an engaged and richly informed environment of new, established and independent scholars.

The national and international community of Hardy scholars is wide and generous and I have benefitted from discussions with Mary Rimmer, Angelique Richardson, Richard Nemesvari, Roger Ebbatson, William Greenslade, Bill Morgan, Dennis Taylor, Hillis Miller, Penny Boumelha, Sanae Uehara, Neil Sargent, Linda Shires, Kari Nixon, Rebecca Welshman and Jacqueline Dillion. I am grateful to Phillip Mallett for his unfailing support and encouragement, to Keith Wilson and Barrie Bullen who read and commented incisively on draft sections of this book and to Simon Gatrell who did this and more, talking and walking me through Hardy's vision of Wessex and indulging my mild obsession with Dorset cream teas on the way. My thanks also go to Philip Davis for generously providing references over the years.

William T. Flynn of the Institute for Medieval Studies, University of Leeds, assisted with Latin translations as did my colleagues David Bagchi and Veronica O'Mara. My thanks also go to James Booth, David Kennedy, Martin Goodman and especially Paul Gilbert for their readiness to engage in discussions about Hardy, Lacan and desire. Kathy Mills and Frances Kelly kept me going when my own interest and enthusiasm flagged, and Dan Bryan enlivened many an hour with his own take on desire.

I thank Paula Kennedy of Palgrave Macmillan for commissioning this book, Ben Doyle for his patience and good humour in seeing it through and Devasena Vedamurthi and the production team at Integra India, for their assistance in preparing it for publication. I am particularly grateful to Tim Armstrong and Hillis Miller for their willingness to engage with and comment on the typescript, to Kirsten Simister and Caroline Rhodes at the Ferens Art Gallery, and Hull Museums for permission to use Herbert J. Draper's *Ulysses and the Sirens* and to Suzanne Fairless-Aitken and Bloodaxe Books for permission to quote Selima Hill.

I owe most to John Osborne, without whom I would not have got this far, and to Rhiannon, Aeronwy and Carys who I hope will never give way on their desire. This book is for them.

Abbreviations

AL	*A Laodicean* (1881; 1997), ed. John Schad (London: Penguin).
BE	*A Pair of Blue Eyes* (1873; 2005), ed. with notes by Alan Manford, introduction by Tim Dolin (Oxford: OUP).
CL	*The Collected Letters of Thomas Hardy* in 7 vols., ed. Richard Little Purdy and Michael Millgate, 1978–1988 (Oxford: Clarendon Press), vol. 1: 1840–1892 (1978); vol. 2: 1893–1901 (1980); vol. 3: 1902–08 (1982); vol. 4: 1909–1913 (1984); vol. 5: 1914–1919 (1985); vol. 6: 1920–1925 (1987); vol. 7 1926–1927 (1988).
'DP'	'The Distracted Preacher' in *Wessex Tales* (1888 (1912); 1998).
DR	*Desperate Remedies* (1871; 2003), ed. with introduction and notes by Patricia Ingham (Oxford: OUP).
FMC	*Far from the Madding Crowd* (1874; 2002), ed. with notes by Suzanne B. Falck-Yi, introduction by Linda Shires (Oxford: OUP).
'FoR'	'The Fiddler of the Reels' in *Wessex Tales* (1888 (1912); 1998).
HoE	*The Hand of Ethelberta* (1876; 1997), ed. with introduction by Tim Dolin (London: Penguin).
Hynes	*The Complete Poetical Works of Thomas Hardy* in 5 vols., ed. Samuel Hynes (1982–1995) (Clarendon Press: Oxford); vol. I (1982); vol. II (1987); vol. III (1985).
ILH	*An Indiscretion in the Life of an Heiress and Other Stories* (1878; 1994), ed. Pamela Dalziel (Oxford: OUP).
'IW'	'An Imaginative Woman' in *Life's Little Ironies* (1894; 1999).
JO	*Jude the Obscure* (1895; 1998), ed. Patricia Ingham (Oxford: OUP).
LLI	*Life's Little Ironies* (1894; 1999), ed. Alan Manford, introduction by Norman Page (Oxford: OUP).
LN I	*The Literary Notes of Thomas Hardy*, ed. Lennart Björk (1984), vol. I (Basingstoke: Macmillan).
LN 2	*The Literary Notes of Thomas Hardy*, ed. Lennart Björk (1985) vol. 2 (Basingstoke: Macmillan).
LW	*The Life and Work of Thomas Hardy by Thomas Hardy*, ed. Michael Millgate (1984) (Basingstoke: Macmillan).
'MH'	'The Melancholy Hussar of the German Legion' (1890), pub *Wessex Tales* (1888 (1912); 1998).
MoC	*The Mayor of Casterbridge* (1886; 2004). ed. with notes by Dale Kramer, introduction by Pamela Dalziel (Oxford: OUP).
PW	*Thomas Hardy's Personal Writings*, ed. Harold Orel (1967) (London: Macmillan).

RoN   *The Return of the Native* (1878; 2005), ed. Simon Gatrell, notes by
Nancy Barrineau, introduction by Margaret Higonnet.

Td'U   *Tess of the d'Urbervilles* (1891; 2005), ed. Juliet Grindle and Simon
Gatrell, introduction by Penny Boumelha, notes by Nancy
Barrineau (Oxford: OUP).

TM   *The Trumpet Major* (1880; 1991), ed. Richard Nemesvari (Oxford:
OUP).

ToT   *Two on a Tower* (1882; 1996), ed. Sally Shuttleworth (London:
Penguin).

TW   *The Woodlanders* (1887; 2005), ed. with notes by Dale Kramer,
introduction by Penny Boumelha (Oxford: OUP).

UGT   *Under the Greenwood Tree* (1872; 1999), ed. with introduction and
notes by Simon Gatrell (Oxford: OUP).

WB   *The Well-Beloved* (1897; 1986), ed. with introduction by Tom
Hetherington (Oxford: OUP).

WT   *Wessex Tales* (1888 (1912); 1998), ed. with introduction and
notes by Kathryn King (Oxford: OUP).

Introduction – Thomas Hardy and Desire: Conceptions of the Self

In May 1882, Hardy noted an obituary for Ralph Waldo Emerson in the *Spectator* which compared Emerson and Carlyle as 'transcendental' thinkers. He extracted the following quotation:

> Carlyle showed us how small a proportion of our life we can realize in thought; how small a proportion of our thoughts we can figure forth in words; how immense is the difference between the pretensions of human speech & the real life for which it stands; how vast the forces amidst which the human spirit struggles for its little modicum of purpose ... how, in spite of this array of immensities the Spirit whose command brings us into being requires of us the kind of life which defies necessity....
>
> (*LN*, I: 1274)

The obituarist's distinction between 'the pretensions', or false claims, of human speech and the 'real life for which it stands' anticipates in simpler terms Lacan's linguistic theory of the unconscious, its relationship to the 'Real', or the realm that is unassimilable to language, and to the constraining, 'pretentious', but productive realm of the symbolic order (or 'reality system') itself. It is in the 'difference', or gap, between the two that Lacan locates desire. Because the symbolic order is sustained by the continuous activity of those who locate themselves within it, it is never entirely stable or fixed, although it can appear so to the frustrated and resistant subject who struggles to make conscious his or her desire within and in spite of 'this array of immensities', and at times it appeared so to Hardy. In 'The Function and Field of Speech and Language in Psychoanalysis', Lacan describes it thus:

> Symbols in fact envelop the life of man in a network so total that they join together those who are going to engender him "by bone and flesh" before he comes into the world; so total that they bring to his birth, along with the gifts of the stars, if not with the gifts of the fairies, the shape of his destiny; so total that they provide the words that will make him faithful or renegade, the law of the acts that will follow him right to the very place where he is not yet and beyond his very death; and so total that

1

through them his end finds its meaning in the last judgement, where the Word absolves his being or condemns it – unless he reaches the subjective realization of being-towards-death.

(2006: 231)

Desire describes the energy of the human spirit as it struggles for recognition, to attain 'its little modicum of purpose', in relation to the impossibility of the Real, and necessity of the 'Word'. To live the kind of life approved of by Emerson's obituarist – one which defies this necessity – is to reject the satisfaction of compromise: to refuse in Lacan's terms, to 'give way' on one's desire.[1] However, as Lacan reminds us, 'there is nothing that is anything but outer darkness to us beyond [the] wall' of language.[2] Speech is merely that which 'echo[es]' off it (260). At the same time these walls and networks long precede us, and in that respect they represent what is 'Other' to us. Thus our desire can only find its meaning in the other's desire, 'not so much because the other holds the keys to the desired object, as because [the subject's] first object(ive) is to be recognised by the other' (222). The subject speaks but only because language has made him or her a subject – subject, in fact, to the desire of the other. In this way, Lacan claims, 'the subject [...] loses his [sic] meaning in the objectifications of discourse' (233).

Desire, then, is driven by the need for recognition and sometimes results in what Lacan terms in 'The Freudian Unconscious and Ours', the 'discovery' or 'surprise': 'that by which the subject feels himself [sic] overcome, by which he finds both more and less than he expected – but, in any case, it is, in relation to what he expected, of exceptional value' (1977b: 25). However this 'discovery' – when desire appears to cohere with its object – is fugitive and transitory: as soon as it occurs it becomes a recognition or 'rediscovery' and 'furthermore, it is always ready to steal away again, thus establishing the dimension of loss' (25). The symbol (by which Lacan means the 'sign') manifests itself in the absence, or 'killing of the thing, and this death results in the endless perpetuation of the subject's desire' (2006: 262). Although desire may be defined as the energy that pushes on to fulfilment, it cannot itself be satisfied. However, this is not to deny the potentiality of desire in 'creative subjectivity' which 'has not ceased in its struggle to renew here the never-exhausted power of symbols in the human exchange that brings them to light' (2006: 234). This book is an exploration of desire in relation to that 'discovery' which, for Hardy's characters, may be equated with falling in love and, for Hardy the writer, with the struggle of the creative subject to achieve 'its little modicum of purpose'.

Thomas Hardy and Desire offers in-depth, text-centred studies of a broad selection of Hardy's novels, poems and shorter fiction in relation to a concept of desire informed by poststructuralist theory. Desire is understood here as an essential yearning that defines the human condition, as the energy that drives individuals to seek recognition in relation to a social and symbolic order which pre-exists them. The central thesis of my study is that Hardy's work offers a sophisticated and sustained exploration of the role of desire in relation to the constitution of the human subject, that anticipates and supplements some of the defining elements of Lacanian theory, which we may summarise as: the persistent, obsessive, frustrating and essentially narcissistic nature of desire; its necessary objectification in forms that ultimately fail to satisfy the desiring subject; and its fundamental importance as the energy behind creative endeavour. While my understanding of desire is influenced by Lacan's psychoanalytical theories and his conception of the 'lack' that is inscribed in language, I have chosen to use his ideas strategically rather than systematically, not to suggest that Hardy was a Lacanian *avant la lettre* but to demonstrate how Hardy's fiction and poetry express a modern understanding of the role of desire in the conception of the self. While aspects of his texts can be seen to anticipate poststructuralist conceptions of desire by almost half a century, this book is not intended as a Lacanian reading of Hardy or his work. Indeed, my approach to Lacanian theory is necessarily selective, and the main focus of this study is insistently on the works of Thomas Hardy and the relationship between desire and the formation of subjectivity as it is presented there. Any comparison between Lacan and Hardy will invariably find in favour of the latter, not least in terms of clarity, readability and the capacity to please and move the reader. The chapters of this book are arranged thematically and, taken together, they describe an arc that spans the trajectory of the human life from birth to death and from ontological lack and nostalgia to creative fulfilment and the establishment of presence in the future through the medium of art.

J. Hillis Miller's *Thomas Hardy, Distance and Desire* (1970) was the first full-length treatment of desire in Hardy's work. Miller demonstrates how Hardy's characters imagine 'a distant source of radiance for their lives' which may be a place or a thing but which is more often someone different from the person to whom they have already committed themselves: 'even if they have never loved before, they have an unsuspected susceptibility to a sudden crystallization of desire around someone they encounter' (115–16). Desire is generated by 'distance, unfamiliarity, inaccessibility, connection with something more distant' (120) and expressed as love.

> The experience of an "emotional void" within, a distance of oneself from oneself, drives [Hardy's] characters to seek possession of another person. To possess the beloved would be to replace separation by presence, emptiness by a substantial self.
>
> (Miller, 1970: xii)

My reading of desire in Hardy's work is inevitably influenced by Miller's study. I have, however, sought to extend some of his insights into new areas and into different texts.[3]

In particular I explore the concept of the ego-morphic dimension of sexual or romantic desire in Hardy's novels: the way that the beloved exists not simply in his or her own right but as the signifier of something else that reveals itself as necessary to the lover's conception of him or her self. More recent studies of desire in Hardy's work, such as Terry Wright's *Hardy and the Erotic* (1989) and Judith Mitchell's chapter on Hardy in *The Stone and the Scorpion* (1994), have focussed almost exclusively on its erotic dimension and its manifestation as (hetero)sexuality. However, as Felix Guattari insists, 'once desire is specified as sexuality, it enters into forms of particularized power, into the stratification of castes, of styles, of sexual classes' (Guattari, 1979: 57). Desire (or 'libido' in its Latin form) is not just sex but the psychic energy that drives the process of subjectivity, and finds its expression in a variety of objects. While acknowledging the extent to which desire is structured by the sexual economy, my aim here is to address the concept of desire in its broadest terms in relation to nostalgia, yearning, narcissism, aspiration and aesthetic fulfilment. Lacan locates the origin of desire in the undifferentiated realm beyond the symbolic: the realm of the impossible out of which we strive to produce the possible. As Hardy's texts so insistently demonstrate, desire cannot be assimilated to any one object, and this is particularly the case when that object is the focus of erotic or romantic yearning.

A further distinguishing feature of this book is its reference to texts from across the range of genres with which Hardy engaged, including novels, poetry, shorter fiction and the essay, in order to demonstrate the tenacious and sustained nature of his thinking about desire. Following the general critical consensus, Judith Mitchell's study of sexual desire focuses on Hardy's 'four best-known novels', which she claims 'also happen to be his most erotic', by which she means most directly concerned with heterosexuality (Mitchell, 1994: 156): *Far from the Madding Crowd*, *The Return of the Native*, *Tess of the d'Urbervilles* and *Jude the Obscure*. Terry Wright likewise devotes most of his compact and revealing study of erotic desire to only four of Hardy's novels: *The Mayor of Casterbridge*, *Tess of the d'Urbervilles*, *Jude the Obscure* and *The Well-Beloved*.

In *Hardy's Fables of Integrity, Woman, Body, Text* (1991) Marjorie Garson acknowledges the extent to which both *Far from the Madding Crowd* and *The Woodlanders* 'lend themselves almost uncannily to a Lacanian reading, which alone seems to make sense of their otherwise anomalous details', and that 'some of Hardy's most celebrated individual scenes have a power which Lacan's theories can help to explain'. She cites the 'Great Barn' as an example of 'the fortress or stadium which Lacan identifies as often expressing, in dream and fantasy, the illusion of wholeness', the 'enduring and capacious female body' with which Gabriel Oak aligns himself (1991: 3). Her concern, however, centres more specifically on bodily than on psychic wholeness in Hardy's novels, and what she terms 'somatic anxiety', namely 'anxiety about bodily integrity, fear of corporeal dissolution' (1). Nevertheless, my own study of desire in relation to ontological concerns in Hardy's fiction and poetry has profited from her insights. Although 'impressed by recent arguments about the construction of the Hardy canon', and what might be at stake when that canon is uncritically endorsed, Garson likewise admits that her choice of texts 'has been thoroughly canonical'. Her rationale is that Hardy's more marginal, less 'great' novels are 'less canny in masking their concerns' and therefore less open to a critique of 'how that masking takes place' (Garson, 1991: 5). My own selection of Hardy's novels is not determined by his retrospective classification of them in the 'General Preface' to the 1912 Wessex Edition, which was conceived in relation to the dominant conception of realism that his own aesthetic pronouncements seem deliberately to undermine.[4] I have also ignored the vexed boundary between the so-called 'major' and 'minor' novels drawn by those critics who almost invariably neglect over half of his novelistic output.[5]

This book is also concerned to explore the challenge Hardy's novels offer to Lacan's assumption that women cannot function as active desiring subjects in their own right, and Hardy's insistence on women as subjects of desire rather than as imaginary sites for the satisfaction of the desires of men. Judith Mitchell claims that Hardy's novels privilege 'male language and male desire' (1994: 170) and that he 'is seemingly able to imagine but not to condone female desire' (182).[6] My reading of Hardy's female characters reveals, on the contrary, his sympathetic understanding of the ways in which women's desire is mediated and frustrated by a patriarchal heterosexist social and symbolic order.

Marjorie Garson rightly defines Jude Fawley as 'constituted in lack' (Garson, 1991: 152), a description that may be equally applied to all of Hardy's tragic characters. Hardy's texts can be seen to mediate between a belief in what Joan Copjec defines as 'a surplus existence that cannot be caught up in the positivity of the social' (Copjec, 1994: 4) and a productive, aspirational conception of desire as the energy behind positive individual and social change.[7] As Copjec suggests, Lacan's theory of desire is predicated on 'permanent self-questioning' (5), a constant inducement to express our desire in ever more satisfying forms. The ideal life that the subject yearns for is an imaginary state of wholeness in which the self is fully enabled and wholly fulfilled within an idealised social and symbolic order. This potentially transformative relationship between the self and language, language and the material world, is an effect of desire.

A central concern of this book is to demonstrate in Hardy's novels, shorter fiction and poetry the presence of a more affirmatory concept of desire than has hitherto been recognised. As an artist himself, indeed as a writer, Hardy was acutely aware of the constraining and productive dimension of the 'reality system' and of the language through which we make our desires known in relation to it, which offers us the necessary illusion of control and integrity, without which we could not function. His work recognises the ways in which the subject is impelled and frustrated by the systems that bring him or her into being and explores this dynamic, productive relationship between desire and language and the systems language helps to reify. Hardy's work locates desire in the gaps and fissures between the energy of being and the psychic, linguistic and aesthetic structures available to its articulation.

As previous critics have indicated, Hardy's understanding of desire was influenced by his reading of various philosophers, including Plato, Spinoza and Schopenhauer.[8] *The Well-Beloved* (1897) was his last novel and the culmination in fiction of his ideas on art, aesthetics and desire. In a letter to *The Academy* on 3 April 1897, which he extracted for *Life*, Hardy claimed that the novel 'was sketched many years before' its serial publication 'when I was comparatively a young man, and interested in the Platonic Idea' (*LW*: 304). This suggests that theories of desire were of fundamental concern to him from early in his career and that they developed out of his interest in Platonism. However, as an agnostic with a serious interest in philosophical ideas, Hardy is ambivalent with regard to the existence of an agency or realm wholly exterior to human consciousness. He recognised that individuals carry their lives forward in what Matthew Arnold, in an essay on Heinrich Heine, described as 'an immense system of institutions, established facts, accredited dogmas, customs, rules which have come to them from times not modern' and which is 'not of their creation' (*LN*, I: 1017). Superadded to this is Hardy's sense that individual consciousness develops in a potentially transformative, ameliorative relation to an unconscious, amoral 'Scheme of Things', which he variously apostrophised as 'Necessity', 'Law', the 'First Cause', the 'Unconscious Will' and the 'Immanent Will'.[9] Lacan likewise insists that the dimension of the unconscious has nothing 'unreal or dereistic' about it. It simply designates 'neither being nor unbeing but the [as yet] unrealized' (1977b: 30). The goal of the analyst, therefore, is not the successful socialisation of the patient but 'to bring the patient to confront the elementary coordinates and deadlocks of his or her own desire' (4). The 'religious dream of plenitude' that Judith Butler charges Lacan with (Butler, 1987; 1999: 240) would seem to link back to 'the Platonic Idea', that the visionary artist Jocelyn Pierston and 'all men are pursuing'- the 'shadow, the Unattainable' (*LW*: 304). However, in 'Of the Network of Signifiers', Lacan insists that subjectivity is a process of remembering or recollection wherein the subject is continually called upon to 're-enter himself in the unconscious'. He adds:

Recollection is not Platonic reminiscence – it is not the return of a form, an imprint, a *eidos* of beauty and good, a supreme truth, coming to us from the beyond. It is something that comes to us from the structural necessities, something humble, born at the level of the lowest encounters and of all the talking crowd that precedes us, at the level of the structure of the signifier, of the languages spoken in a stuttering, stumbling way, but which cannot elude constraints.

(1977b: 47)

In this respect, 're-membering' or 're-collection' describes how subjectivity is a constant process of testing or measuring desire against the productive constraints of signifying practices.

Hardy's notion of the centrality of desire to the human condition was also influenced by the ideas of Schopenhauer, who conceived the foundation of existence as essentially 'unceasing *motion* without any possibility of that repose which we continually strive after'. Life is 'a process of disillusionment':

> As things are, we take no pleasure in existence except when we are striving after something – in which case distance and difficulties make our goal as if it would satisfy us (an illusion which fades when we reach it).
>
> (Schopenhauer, 1851; 1970: 54)

He contends that happiness is not possible 'where nothing occurs but Plato's "continual becoming and never being" ' and where life 'has consisted merely of a succession of transient present moments' (52). Schopenhauer's is the quintessential philosophy of transience, loss and nostalgia for what can only be recognised and valued in retrospect. The moments of which our life is constituted usually only appear as whole and beautiful from a distance:

> That is why to attain something desired is to discover how vain it is; and why, though we live all our lives in expectation of better things, we often at the same time long regretfully for what is past. The present, on the other hand, is regarded as something quite temporary and serving only as the road to our goal. That is why most men discover when they look back on their life that they have the whole time been living *ad interim*, and are surprised to see that that which they let go by so unregarded and unenjoyed was precisely their life, was precisely that in expectation of which they lived. (53)

This nostalgic desire for a life lived whole in the past, and the subject's alienation from him or herself in the present moment, is registered by Hardy in poems such as 'He Wonders About Himself', 'Self-Unconscious' and, as I discuss more fully in Chapter 1, 'The Self-Unseeing' (Hynes, I: 206).

In 'He Wonders About Himself' Hardy's narrator imagines himself 'like some fantocine' or puppet 'tugged by a force above or under' (Hynes, II: 256). The circumlocutory 'much I wonder/What I shall find me doing next' implies not just a duality of self but a self that is triply alienated: the narrating self speculates upon a future state of self-division. These lines enact the meaning of the poem's title, in its literal and homophonic sense, implying self-alienation and a kind of self-perambulation: 'won-dering/wandering' about the space around which self coheres. In 'Self-Unconscious' (Hynes, II: 40) the narrator laments the possibility of fully grasping the self in the present moment and expresses nostalgia for a perceived lost moment of plenitude that was unregarded at the time.

> Along the way
> He walked that day,
> Watching shapes that reveries limn,
> And seldom he
> Had eyes to see
> The moment that encompassed him.

The imagined shapes and thoughts that preoccupy him are 'limned' ('embel-lished with gold or bright colour') in his mind, but he is blind to the beauty of the 'bright yellowhammers', the 'flashes of white' and the 'metal shine' of the distant sea in the moment that 'contains' him, so that 'himself he did not see at all'. Many years later 'that self/As he was, and should have been shown, that day' is revealed to him, prompting nostalgic desire for that lost moment of perceived integrity and regret that the vision to see – not just the moment as it was then but 'the whole' at a 'clear-eyed distance' – was denied to him. The poem sets up a complex relationship between the younger self projecting 'his' desires into the future and the older, wiser self looking back from the vantage point of that future with the benefit of hind-sight, 'conning' not just the moment but everything that it presaged. The title is teasingly ironic, for the narrating self remains 'unconscious' of the present moment except as one in which he looks back to a lost past. He lives his life *'ad interim'* between the transient moments of the present and the lost moment of the past: always, as Proust coined it in his famous novel of 1913, *'à la recherche du temps perdu'*. Tim Armstrong suggests that Hardy's narrators frequently 'achieve understanding, only at the cost of the death of an earlier innocent self' (Armstrong, 2000: 18). The definition of the term 'self-conscious' as specifically an awareness of one's actions and intentions entered the language in 1860, supplementing the older, broader definition of being 'inwardly sensible or aware' (*OED*). Hardy's title puns on the term while suggesting that the self can never be wholly aware of its actions and intentions except retroactively.

Chapter 1 of *Thomas Hardy and Desire*, 'House and Home: Nostalgic Desire and the Locus of the Self', examines how the lost moment of plenitude and self-propriety can be equated with Lacan's notion of the *'manque-à-être'* (Lacan, 2006: 524) and how it is desired and imagined nostalgically in the trope of home: particularly the lost childhood home which many of his poetic narrators yearn for but find themselves unable to return to or shut out from. The adult house – the present constitution of the self – offers a placed condition for meaningful interaction with others but constrains, inhibits or traps its dweller or tenant. Many of Hardy's 'unhoused' fictional characters are dispossessed men from the labouring classes (Giles Winterbourne, Jude Fawley), or women forced to inhabit their father's or husband's house, and who are attracted to the house of a male lover, which offers them an equally unsatisfactory habitation for the self. Hardy explores this fruitless ontological yearning or ontological 'homesickness' more generally through the character Matthäus Tina in the poignant story of 'The Melancholy Hussar of the German Legion'. In giving voice to the 'true' story of the much maligned Matthäus and his lover Phyllis, the narrator strives to resolve his own nostalgic desire for wholeness.

Chapter 2, 'Desire, Female Amity and Sapphic Space', describes the strategies employed by Hardy's dissenting female characters in their desire to live, or gain recognition, outside the patriarchal domestic space. In Hardy's novels, the childhood home or domestic space signifies what Lacan and others have defined as woman's double-alienation from desire. The female characters discussed here are 'unhomed' by their subjection to the symbolic order and also the ways in which its signifying systems are regulated and given meaning by patriarchy. Through the establishment of what I have designated the 'sapphic space', characters such as Cytherea Aldclyffe, Paula Power, Elizabeth-Jane, Grace Melbury and Tess Durbeyfield seek to establish what Judith Butler defines as 'more inclusive conditions for sheltering and maintaining life that resists models of assimilation' (Butler, 2004: 4). The opportunity to create or inhabit a sapphic space is denied to the modern, isolated Sue Bridehead who rebels against the oppressive weight of 'old houses' only to find herself metaphorically and ontologically 'homeless', and driven back to the sheltering oppression of the church and the marital home.

On a midnight drive through Hintock Forest, an unwitting Edred Fitzpiers treats his rival, Giles Winterbourne, to his Spinozan theory of love:

> Human love is a subjective thing – the essence itself of man, as that great thinker Spinoza says – *ipsa hominis essentia*; it is joy accompanied by an idea which we project against any suitable object in the line of our vision, just as the rainbow iris is projected against an oak, ash, or elm-tree indifferently'.
>
> (*TW*, 2005: 106)

It is not 'human love' exactly that Spinoza designates as the essence of man, but desire: 'Desire is the very essence of man; that is, the conatus [striving] whereby man endeavours to persist in his own being' (Spinoza, 1677; 1991: 141). However, as Michael Della Rocca explains, Spinoza makes little if any distinction between desire and human appetite, insisting that 'by the word *desire*, I understand any of a man's strivings, impulses, appetites, and volitions' (Della Rocca, 2008: 154). For Spinoza, the desire to 'persist in [ones] own being' describes both the impulse towards self preservation and the will to increase one's power of acting: 'Desire, on the part of the mind, is simply the mind's tendency to go from one representation to another' [....] As Spinoza says [...]."The mind, insofar as it can, strives to imagine those things that increase or aid the body's power of acting" ' (Della Rocca, 2008: 157). Fitzpiers's regards his appetite for three different women as an enactment of Spinoza's pattern of desire.

For Lacan, desire is the unconscious made conscious through its objects: the 'objets a', or signifiers of desire, that the subject's 'true' desire is distracted by (Lacan, 1977: 198). These also represent the means through which she or he strives towards the illusion of self-presence. Because desire can never be wholly represented or satisfied by or in its objects, the subject is condemned to move along an endless chain of libidinally charged signifiers, none of which is able to satisfy him or her at the ontological level. Chapter 3, 'The Lure of the Erotic', examines Hardy's male and female characters in the grip of the compelling power of the sexual drive and 'lured' on, or distracted by, erotic signifiers of desire. In this I have followed Terry Wright definition of the erotic as 'a "fiction", a cultural phenomenon, a product of human perception and distortion of the biological "facts" of sex' (Wright, 1989: ix).

Chapter 4, 'Poor Men and Ladies: Aspirational Desire', examines Hardy's 'Poor Man and Lady' plots and how the Poor Man sees in the Lady a narcissistic self projection: an object in which he recognises and loves himself, as well as the means of increasing his own power of acting. The stories of Ethelberta Petherwin and Viviette Constantine reverse this paradigm to show, in Viviette's case, the Lady's self-investment in the Poor Man's youth and opportunity and, in Ethelberta's, her determination to act out her own desire rather than be a mirror for his.

If houses and homes offer a placed condition for the self, albeit one whose space contains and constrains, dress offers another form of inhabitation or (literal) self-investment, especially for women. Chapter 5, 'As You Like It: Cross-Dressing and the Gendered Expression of Desire', investigates the potential of various forms of 'crossing over' into an interdicted 'masculine' realm, which offers these rebellious or dissenting female characters the opportunity to explore new forms of self-conception outside the rigid prescription of gender. As Judith Butler suggests, the fantasy of cross-dressing allows women to move beyond the constraints of the real, 'it points [...] elsewhere, and when it is embodied, it brings the elsewhere home (Butler, 2004: 217). These attempts at self-embodiment through and against the available signs of class, gender and race harness the creative potential of language – in its broadest sense – to produce new and radical articulations of women's desire. Using Marjorie Garber's concept of the 'third space', I argue that Hardy's cross-dressed women create new spaces of possibility

outside the recognised forms of gendered subjectivity. This 'third space' constitutes a liminal position *between* the genders – a form of performative
hermaphroditism – from which they are able, however temporarily, to experience, articulate and sometimes elicit desires which threaten and undermine
the acceptable sexual codes.

Hardy's last novel, *The Well-Beloved*, is his most concise statement on
desire in its various manifestations and is the sole text under discussion in
Chapter 6: 'Art, Aesthetics and Masculine Desire'. In July 1926, less than two
years before his death, Hardy noted:

> It appears that the theory exhibited in *The Well-Beloved* in 1892 has been
> since developed by Proust still further:
>
> Peu de personnes comprennent le caractère purement subjectif du
> phénomène qu'est l'amour et la sorte de creation que c'est d'une personne
> supplémentaire, distinct de celle qui porte le même nom dans le monde,
> et dont la plupart des éléments sont tirés de nous-mêmes (*Ombre*, i. 40.)
>
> Le désir s'élève, se satisfait, disparait – et c'est tout. Ainsi, la jeune fille
> qu'on épouse n'est pas celle dont on est tombé amoureux (*Ombre*, ii.
> 158, 159.)
>
> (*LW*: 466–7)[10]

The 'theory' that Hardy recognised in Denis Saurat's article on Proust (Taylor,
1981: 23) is of 'the transmigration of the ideal beloved one, who only exists
in the lover, from material woman to material woman'. Hardy describes his
novel as a 'fantastic tale of a subjective idea' (*LW*: 303), 'a fanciful exhibition
of the artistic nature' (*CL*, 2: 159).

The Well-Beloved is Hardy's most concentrated interrogation of a gendered
model of desire in which Woman is constituted as the lost or missing element of a masculine desiring subject which he embodies, and seeks to
assimilate to himself, in the real and idealised form of his 'Well-Beloved'.
Pierston's 'Well-Beloved' is a narcissistic or 'supplementary' projection of his
own desire for romantic, erotic and creative fulfilment: the embodiment of
'her who was the World's desire' (*WB*: 95); the Ideal of Beauty and the 'Eternal Feminine'. She is 'a sign or token of the forbidden maternal, an ideal
or fantasy which can never be fully appropriated, [but] only "believed in" '
(Butler, 1987; 1999: 203).[11]

As Hardy's extract from Proust registers, Pierston's quest is essentially
narcissistic. His 'Well-Beloved', his erotic and artistic muse, is his own supplement; she has little relation to any of the actual women who appear to
embody her, except for Avice Caro: the one woman whose death has placed
her forever beyond his reach and whom he resurrects or 're-members' as
a fantasy or phantom of his own conceit. Pierston's failure is aesthetic as
well as erotic and romantic. As an artist and a desirous man he is trapped

at the level of the signifying systems of a mid-to-late Victorian social order and is thus condemned endlessly to move along conventional libidinally charged signifiers of the 'Eternal Feminine'. Rather than create something new, Pierston's art merely reproduces existing recognisable forms, 'hitting a public taste he had never deliberately aimed at, and mostly despised' (*WB*: 52).

Judith Butler notes that while Deleuze and Foucault 'accept Lacan's decentering of the Hegelian subject, and his postulation of the cultural construction of desire', they challenge, in different ways, Lacan's formulation of desire as prohibition and negativity, 'arguing that not negation but *affirmation* characterises primary human longings' (Butler, 1987; 1999).[12] Writing to thank Swinburne for his 'kind words' about his last and, in the author's view, unfairly maligned novel, Hardy was reminded of his own attempt to 'strike out a better equivalent [...] than the commonplace "Thou, too, shalt die" ' for the Sappho fragment 68 in Henry Thornton Wharton's edition of *Sappho, Memoir, Text, Selected Renderings and a Literal Translation* (*LW*: 305). The narrator of the fragment commits the addressee to oblivion for failing to dramatise his or her testimony in the form of art:

> Thee too the years shall cover; thou shalt be,
> As the rose born of one same blood with thee,
> As a song sung, as a word said, and fall
> Flower-wise, and be not any more at all,
> Nor any memory of thee anywhere;
> For never Muse has bound above thine hair
> The high Pierian flowers whose graft outgrows
> All Summer kinship of the mortal rose.
>
> (Wharton, 1895: 114)[13]

The 'few words' of the first line of this rendering by Swinburne Hardy claimed as 'the finest drama of Death and Oblivion, so to speak, in our tongue' (*LW*: 305). Implied in Swinburne's poem is the recognition that the artist, unlike the carping reviewer (or even the admiring critic), may secure a presence in the future as well as the present through what Martin Amis, commenting on the poetry of Philip Larkin, has called the 'achieved' work of art (Amis, 2011: xi). In Chapter 7, ' "Scanned Across the Dark Space": Poetry, Desire and Aesthetic Fulfilment', I explore the paradox that this productive conception of the aesthetic, especially as demonstrated in 'Poems of 1912–13', offers an affirmative, positive notion of desire. J. Hillis Miller suggests that the decision to be a writer opposes the desire for oblivion with the desire for immortality. Hardy's writing 'cooperates with the impersonal mind of the Void by keeping [his characters'] fugitive moments of experience alive in the new form his words give them' (Miller, 1970: 239).[14] Life passes into the realm of death and is 'rescued by art' and, as I endeavour to prove in the final chapter, nowhere is this more so than in Hardy's elegiac poems. My focus is on how Hardy discovers and also rescues human experiences, not only by reimagining them in poetic form but also by giving them a sublime immediacy in language, especially through the device of the poetic symbol. Tim Armstrong notes that

> the self is always for Hardy a supplement, the marker of an absence in life which is replaced by his writing. The self, as Derrida says in his discussion of the supplement 'can accomplish itself, only by allowing itself to be filled through the sign and proxy'.
>
> (Armstrong, 2000: 145)

The possibility that the self can be 'filled', that desire can be satisfied through the production (and indeed the consumption) of 'achieved' art, is implicit in Lacan's theories. Hardy writes of his love of 'the art of concealing art' (*LW*: 322), his constant attempt to close up the gap between signifier and signified through the polysemic effect of poetic language and the symbol. He recognised analogies between poetry and architecture in that both sought to bring new forms, new accommodations, of desire into being (*LW*: 323). This understanding of the potential and capacity of art to offer satisfaction and fulfilment for both writer and reader, even when the art in question is focussed on loss, frustration and despair, demonstrates the presence of a creative, affirmative concept of desire. To quote Martin Amis: 'Achieved art is quite incapable of lowering the spirits. If this were not so, each performance of *King Lear* would end in Jonestown' (Amis, 2011: xi). My test case for this includes Hardy's magisterial 'Poems of 1912–13'. As Jeanette Winterson so aptly puts it in her autobiographical memoir, a poem such as Hardy's 'The Going' 'finds the words that finds the feeling' (2011: 187).

My methodology is text-centred and informed by the conviction that any attempt to psychoanalyse the author through his writings is imprudent, impertinent and based on a persistent disregard for the profoundly self-conscious textuality of Hardy's art.[15] Poststructuralist critics of Hardy, from Miller to Julian Wolfreys, have registered the warning offered by Jacques Derrida and others that we should exercise caution in using biography or history to ground or stabilise meaning in literary texts. As Miller reminds us:

> If the distinction between 'real' and 'fictive' is a false one [...] if things in the real or historical world are already human interpretations of some physical substratum, and if things in the fictive world are no more unreal or imaginary than any other significant things, then the 'real world' (that of a historical time or that of the author's experience of life) cannot constitute a base or origin, an unmoving centre which will immobilize the

ambiguous interplay among meanings in the text and give it a stable, spatialized meaning.

(Hillis Miller, 1970: 35–6)

The effect of Hardy's textual strategies is to challenge and unsettle the conventions of realism and, in the poetry in particular, to resist the flattening out or elision of the subtleties of his thought by the simplifying, and often distorting, lens of biographicalism.[16]

In Hardy's texts, desire is transgressive and potentially transformative. It is the force behind change and progress and motivates the subject's recognition of the discrepancy between her or his fundamental energy and the forms that exist to express but also to contain it. While Hardy conceives of desire as 'lack', he is also aware of its positive transformative potential in both the political and the aesthetic realm. The vital force that remains unexpressed, the excess or residue that pushes the subject beyond his or her symbolic function, and thus carries with it the threat of disempowerment, psychosis and non-recognition, is the energy of desire. For Slavoj Žižek, Lacan's bitter lesson is that we must accept the fundamental inconsistency that 'it is desire itself that sabotages its own liberation' (2006: 39), in that in pushing through to recognition and fulfilment of desire in language we inevitably betray it. At the same time, however, the phantom [or fantasy] of personal liberation resides precisely in this compulsion to 'break the vicious circle of my alienated desire and learn to formulate my desire in an autonomous way' (Žižek, 2006: 15). This is also Hardy's bitter lesson and, to this critic's mind, his achievement. The final aim of this book is to offer an alternative to the commonly held perception of Hardy's work as the unalloyed expression of unfulfillment, lost chances and unassuaged desire. To read his work in this way is to ignore his appreciation of the potential of the imagination and the creative act itself as a means towards the attainment of a satisfaction and fulfilment that will outlast the originating artist.

1
House and Home: Nostalgic Desire and the Locus of Being

> O Giles, you've lost your dwelling-place, And therefore, Giles, you'll lose your Grace.
>
> *(TW*, 2005: 99)

Over a century before Lacan formulated his theory of the *'manque-à-être'*[1] Thomas Hardy was engaging directly with a modern sense of alienated being. The nostalgia for a lost plenitude, a satisfaction of ontological yearning, is most poignantly expressed in the poetry and fiction through the trope of homes and homelessness, in particular the lost childhood home which functions as a powerful metaphor of desire or the 'want-to-be' for the adult self. Hardy's work demonstrates how the alienated modern subject strives to create a 'vital space': a sense of harmony or an imagined integrity and security within the self. Being at home is equated with 'being-at-home' and nowhere is this more poignantly realised than in the remembered or oneiric childhood home.[2] For the nostalgic Hardy subject, however, this past or childhood home is often closed or else, as Julian Wolfreys notes, inhabited by an alien or spectral element that renders it *'unheimlich'* (Wolfreys, 2009).

This chapter will explore the conceit of 'home' – in particular the lost childhood home – in a selection of Hardy's poems; his first published essay 'How I Built Myself a House' (1865); *The Woodlanders* (1887); *Jude the Obscure* (1895) and the short story 'The Melancholy Hussar of the German Legion' (1889–90). In each of these texts, 'home' can be seen to function as a signifier of yearning for an illusive plenitude that is permanently lost to the nostalgic adult, one in which desire is endlessly displaced. The corollary of this is the image of the house built, occupied or relinquished by the adult seeking to realise his or her desire for an actual and metaphysical dwelling for the self in the present.

In Hardy's work, houses are revealed as structures of desire: temporary, contingent dwellings or 'vital spaces' that shelter but also constrain, subject as they are to the rules and signifying systems that dictate not only their shape and function in a particular place and time but also the nature and duration of the tenancy of their occupants. Homes, homesickness and homelessness function as plot devices and also as metaphors for ontological yearning and the desire for a lost sense of being-at-home that so many of Hardy's modern subjects experience.

The son of a master mason and a builder, in the 'old-established' sense of a constructor of dwellings,[3] Hardy trained and practiced as an architect from the age of 16 until his marriage to Emma Gifford at 34, after which he embarked on life as a professional author. He designed a number of dwellings including his own – Max Gate – in 1885, whilst also overseeing the 'restoration' of various religious edifices.[4] Significant among these was the crumbling church of St Juliot in the parish of Boscastle where he met Emma Gifford, the woman who was to share that home with him after more than a decade of married life spent in temporary accommodation in and around Dorset and London. Throughout his career as a writer, Hardy was intellectually and personally intimate with the theory, practice and metaphorical significance of built space. He was an avid reader of Ruskin and Pater, turning to the former for his thoughts on architecture, church restoration and the art of Turner and taking from the latter a heightened interest in 'the deeper reality', and the imperative that drives the artist towards the perfect embodiment of idea in form.[5] In common with both writers, Hardy establishes a close, metaphorical relationship between the house or home, the self, and that which is 'other' to it and from which the dwelling appears to offer shelter.

Hardy broke into publishing in 1865 with a humorous sketch in *Chambers' Journal* entitled 'How I built myself a house' in which the narrator describes how he and his wife moved from an inconvenient dwelling in the suburbs of London: 'the sort of house called a Highly-Desirable Semi-detached Villa', to a residence of their own design and construction, which 'was to be right and proper in every respect' and 'of some mysterious size and proportion, which would make us both peculiarly happy ever afterwards' (*PW*: 159). Despite their determination to the contrary, the narrator and his wife find themselves at the mercy of architects, builders and surveyors to the point where their own house, when built, bears little or no resemblance to their original plans. Among other things, the house can be read here as a metaphor for the subject driven by the desire to establish and shape the appearance and function of its inhabited space but constrained and frustrated by the systems or signifying systems that bring it into being. The house offers the illusion of control and integrity necessary to the sense of self. The move to the 'Highly-Desirable-Semi-detached Villa' demonstrates the energy of desire as it impels the subject into new and more commodious modes of being. It signifies the subject's place in the present and the past and also offers a model of the self within the constraints of the Other. It signifies 'home', and yet, it is something the subject feels the constant need to reassess and sometimes reject or escape from. This is particularly true when the subject is 'dispossessed' either by gender, class or national origin.

Hardy's adult 'habitations' are provisional loci of being which offer substance and structure to mental constitution and disposition but which fail to
satisfy the deeper yearning at the heart of the self. His work is suffused with
ontological desire for the oneiric or remembered childhood home, which
represents an imagined space that is unconstrained by a consciousness of
cultural proscription, moral sanction and human suffering.[6] Remembering or revisiting the childhood home becomes an impossible attempt to
re-member, recall or re-collect the culturally innocent self that existed before
'the birth of consciousness'[7] An important exception to this is Jude Fawley,
information on whose childhood home in or near Marygreen is withheld
from the reader and whose sojourn at the home of his waspish and begrudg-
ing Aunt Drusilla (to which he moves at the age of ten) is defined by rejection
and disappointment.[8] It is hardly surprising then that Jude is Hardy's most
intensely alienated and self-alienated character.[9] In adulthood, Jude, Sue and
Tess Durbeyfield experience a modern rootlessness and homelessness, as they
strive against the odds to develop new ways of dwelling and being in structures that long predate them. It is Sue Bridehead – Hardy's most pessimistic
presentation of the limited powers of the self under the constraints of history and patriarchy – who experiences most acutely the oppression of the
'houses of the past'.

Hardy's early poem 'Domicilium', composed sometime between 1857 and
1860, begins with a description of the narrator's birthplace: the first house
to be built in an isolated spot between wild uncultivated heath and a
managed landscape of gardens and copse (Hynes, III: 279–80). The poem's
latinate title, however, is richly suggestive of something more profound
than simple nostalgia for a childhood home first settled by the narrator's
paternal grandparents.[10] Hardy chooses 'Domicilium', meaning 'habitation';
the place of dwelling, or 'abode' rather than 'Domus': more specifically
the house or building in which one dwells.[11] For Uli Knoepflmacher this
early home represents a specifically female place of origin: 'the voice of
the grandmother that finishes the narrative undercuts the cultivation of
the would-be-poet who has given the name "domicilium" to what she, far
more simply, calls "our house" ' (Knoepflmacher, 1990: 1057). However, the
grandmother's voice has no independent existence outside the narrator's
imagination, and the place is more than 'simply' 'our house'. It represents
the impossible desire to give material substance to both the place of origin
and the place of being: in Lacanian terms the pre-linguistic *jouissance* that
precedes individuation but to which the adult narrator can never return.

The opening words of the poem – 'It faces west' – delineate not a house
but a space of dwelling defined by an immaterial 'veil of boughs'. The 'roof'
and 'walls' of the dwelling materialise only in the third and fourth lines and
even then are swiftly displaced by the vigorous 'Wild honeysucks' that climb
up and over them. The narrator makes at least three attempts to 'settle' this
wild space in both the present and the past, each time failing effectively to

colonise or even realise the dwelling itself in words. The perspective of roof and walls, shrouded and smothered by trees and shrubs, swiftly gives way to the untrained, flourishing garden of 'hardy plants', a field and distant cottages with trees, before being lost in the 'distant hills and sky'. In the third stanza the narrator returns to the house a second time, only to move immediately 'behind' it in both space and time. Here 'the scene is wilder', solely composed of 'heath and furze' on unlevelled ground, some 'stunted' thorn trees and an oak sprung from a seed dropped by a bird a century before.

Uli Knoepflmacher notes how, at the exact mid-point of the poem, 'Hardy' turns to a female mediator, his paternal grandmother, to help him 'explore his own origins' (Knoepflmacher, 1990: 1057) and to return him to the 'original maternal envelope' (1056). However, this third attempt to settle the space of his origins is as much a failure as the first two. Not only does the grandmother take the child speaker away from the house, and 'out to walk', her gaze likewise moves beyond the house to the 'uncultivated slopes', the 'narrow path shut in by ferns' that leads away from it and the wild ponies on the hills. Even an act of 'narrative transvestism' (Osborne, 2008: 10) fails to grant the narrator access to what Knoepflmacher terms the 'lost and obliterated [...] *heimisch* [...] maternal place' (1056). Eschewing, for now, the gender essentialism and biographicalism of Knoepflmacher's Cixousian reading of 'Domicilium', it is clear that the poem's narrator remains outside and alienated from the desired homespace. The experience of the imagined child 'in days bygone – / Long gone' is subsumed in, and displaced by, the narrative of the imagined grandmother, which is itself placed back half a century: even before the child's birth. Each attempt to approach and penetrate the interior of 'our house', through this 'youthful discourse of desire' (Knoepflmacher, 1990: 1058) – actually and metaphorically – further distances the narrator in spatial and temporal terms. Both grandmother and house are figurations that succeed only in dis-locating the ontological desire they are deployed to satisfy. Neither manages to retain its presence in the face of the 'Real', symbolised here by encroaching nature: the 'wilder heath', the unreachable hills and unfathomable sky. If, as Lacan claims, the signifier is the subject's way of achieving presence in desire (Lacan, 2006: 508) this presence is insinuated 'against a background of absence, just as it constitutes absence in presence' (496–7). Indeed, *human* presence is barely insinuated in 'Domicilium' except perhaps in the invitation to the reader to conspire in the fanciful anthropomorphising of the trees and plants, which 'seem to sprout a wish / (If we may fancy wish of trees and plants) / To overtop the apple-trees hard by', and even here it is placed in parenthesis. The fancied 'passer-by' on the 'narrow path' is obscured by ferns: precursors of the 'tall firs / And beeches' that now obscure the house. In addition, the narrator is twice dispossessed of the imagined grandmother in her own right. Not only is she introduced as 'my father's mother', she is also, now 'Blest with the blest'.

The bedrooms, are entered vicariously through a 'child' narrator conceived in the imagination of the remembered grandmother, who sees there not her younger self and her siblings but only snakes, efts and bats, and heathcroppers who formed 'our only friends'. Four generations of the narrator's family have failed wholly to 'settle' the wild otherness in which they seek to build a homespace. The precarious yet impermeable space of primal desire – the 'domicilium' – shapes itself in what Lacan calls 'a synchrony of signifiers' that comes together in a space of 'subornation' or unlawful bribery (Lacan, 2006: 495). The subject is subordinated to, bribed by, the signifier (the childhood home), which offers itself as a means of filling or colonising the fundamental space at the heart of being, only to lead away from its interior and on along the endless chain of further signification to the 'heath', 'and last / The distant hills and sky'.

Julian Wolfreys notes how the poem's latinate title 'marks and remarks itself with distancing irony, historical anachrony and untranslatability (the loss, or breakdown, of communication)'. There is 'something foreign' at the heart of home, something 'always unassimilable, irrecuperable, and other'. ' "Domicilium": 'a title in another's tongue remains on the page as a boundary resistant to domestication, as well as a threshold one will never cross' (Wolfreys, 2009: 6).[12] We might also note how the voice of the narrator's long-dead paternal grandmother registers the impossibility of ever returning to the original, simple, 'wild' place of origin, for 'change has marked the face of all things'. The familiar lineaments of home are challenged and redrawn by the imagined grandmother's reminiscences which disrupt and displace the narrator's experience of the place. The lost childhood home offers a fragile and finally intangible refuge from the unregulated potentiality of the Real which threatens the constitution of the self in the regulated world in which it seeks recognition.[13]

A companion poem to 'Domicilium' is 'The Self-Unseeing' in which the narrator 'revisits' a past dwelling either in reality or in the imagination, and conjures up a vision or memory of the inhabitants of the old homestead.[14]

> Here is the ancient floor,
> Footworn and hollowed and thin,
> Here was the former door
> Where the dead feet walked in.
>
> She sat here in her chair,
> Smiling into the fire;
> He who played stood there,
> Bowing it higher and higher.
>
> Childlike, I danced in a dream;
> Blessings emblazoned that day;
> Everything glowed with a gleam;
> Yet we were looking away!

(Hynes, I: 206)

Whilst the poem is open to a biographical reading,[15] and one in which the revisited house is a material entity, it can also be read as another figuration of nostalgic, ontological desire. No walls are specified for this homestead. The 'ancient floor' suggests that of an actual dwelling, or the outlines or floor plan of one now demolished or merely imagined, which seems to offer the narrator a base or stage for the imagined dancing child-self. Access to, or through, this 'dwelling' is gained by means of a 'former door': one which no longer exists – except in memory – and which allows only the 'dead feet' to walk in.[16] This line suggests that access to this past moment, and all it signifies in the present, is denied to the narrator. The woman who 'sat here in her chair' and the violin-playing man who 'stood there' are spectral presences. They do not acknowledge, or 'see' the 'self' who narrates the poem who, though inside the boundary of the house, remains outside this self-enclosed and self-sufficient figuration of the past and, indeed, outside and unacknowledged by his own spectral 'childlike' dancing other. The undefined walls of the dwelling and the ghostly door leave open the speculation that the 'here' and 'there' – which seem to give it a material presence – like the woman, the man and the dancing child, function only in the narrator's memory or imagination.

The 'Self-Unseeing' of the title includes in its compass the smiling woman and the violin-playing man, enfolded with the child in this brief moment of domestic harmony, all of whom 'unsee', in the sense of looking away from or failing to take due note of its 'gleam' of significance at the time. The word 'gleam' is suggestive here of both the faintness and brevity of the moment of wholeness. It also suggests the transfigurative power of art: its ability to bring forth new manifestations of desire into the realm of knowledge. In 1877, early in his writing career, Hardy wrote: 'I think the art lies in making [Nature's] defects the basis of a hitherto unperceived beauty, by irradiating them with "the light that never was" on their surface, but is seen to be latent in them by the spiritual eye' (*LW*, 1989: 118). The 'gleam', then, represents 'the light that never was', but which becomes apparent later to the 'spiritual eye', or the imagination, of the artist/poet.[17]

The title also includes the older self – who revisits the ghostly outlines of that moment with a new, if ill-timed, visionary awareness, – and the spectral self who is described not as a child but only 'childlike': a self whose identity cannot be grasped by the future 'I' who now looks to it for confirmation of the possibility of ontological wholeness.[18] The narrating self remains decentred, unable to 'see' or grasp itself as a stable, integrated entity, even in this nostalgic memory or reconstruction of the past.[19] The lost moment of plenitude appears even more desirable because that loss is irrevocable. The choice of the verbal substantive 'blessings' is suggestive here, as it effectively denies the possibility of a *willed* ontological plenitude: 'blessings' are petitioned for and dispensed by a higher authority.

The title 'The Self-Unseeing' is multivalent, implying that the self only recognises the significance of the moment of wholeness when it is past and also that it can never fully apprehend or grasp itself at any point, past or present. The narrator cannot learn from this belated appreciation of the past and embrace a sense of wholeness in the present: only though nostalgia can he or she gain perspective on the moments of the past and see them as whole and true, if irrevocably lost. In this sense the 'self', for Hardy, is always 'un-seeing'. The image of the dwelling self, even when recalled from the past of childhood, carries with it only the illusion of wholeness and freedom. The walls which contain and protect the 'free' childhood self have disappeared, leaving only the trace of a ground plan and a spectral door. The dancing, visionary, impercipient, childlike self is wholly absorbed in the dance of desire, unable to look out or forward into its future.

One of Hardy's last poems, 'Concerning His Old Home', collected in *Winter Words* and published posthumously in 1928, offers a mature response to 'Domicilium'. Here the narrator charts his/her changing response to a previous dwelling (or the memory of it) from disdain, to nostalgia, to desire and finally to an obsessive revisiting – a 'haunting' – of that memory, or the place itself, as the self strives to situate itself in relation to its own presence in the past and present, and to the unbearable thought of its absence in the future. The 'Moods' of each of the short quatrains suggest the stages of life: youth; middle age; old age; and finally death, when the relationship between the self and its 'dwelling' is imagined as wholly spectral. Each quatrain successively explores the narrator's desire to 'see' the place, in all senses of regarding, perceiving, apprehending and experiencing: 'to see it never'; 'to see it once'; 'to see it often'; and to see it always. In this sense the poem enacts the vexed and changing relationship between the self and its place in the Other in which the 'I' struggles to apprehend the notion of being in, being independent from and being nostalgic for what defines or shapes it in the face of its own absence or inevitable extinction. This poem also suggests the impossibility of the self ever truly grasping the locus of its being while demonstrating how it is, nevertheless, obsessively compelled and drawn to do so, even more so perhaps as life draws to a close. The initial rejection and the subsequent growing allure of the 'old home', metaphoric or actual, also functions as a model of the contrapuntal forces of desire – a yearning outward and away balanced by a nostalgic yearning to return and merge – that suffuse Hardy's poetry and fiction. The old home is at once dismal and memoried, despicable and loveable, rejected and incessantly desired. It both 'haunts' and is the 'haunt' of the self: where the self has its being or 'home'; what brings it into being and what constrains it; and what it yearns for nostalgically as a perceived locus of wholeness, of being-in-the-moment, 'being-at-home':

I'll haunt it night and day –
That loveable place,
With its flowers's rich store
That drives regret away!

(Hynes, III: 194)

In August 1878 Walter Pater published his essay 'A Child in the House' in *Macmillan's Magazine*. In March of the same year Hardy and Emma left the 'idyll' of Riverside Villa, Sturminster Newton – a newly built 'villa' which they may have been the first to occupy (Millgate, 2004: 171) – and signed a three-year lease on a house at Upper Tooting, a move demanded by 'the practical side of [Hardy's] vocation as a novelist' (*LW*: 121). It was here that they began to feel 'that "there had passed away a glory from the earth" ' and in this house, we are told, 'their troubles began' (*LW*: 128).

In 'A Child in the House' Pater explores the concept of what he calls '*chez-soi*' (Pater, 1878: 315), which translates literally as being 'at the home of oneself'. The essence of the childhood home, he argues, 'constitutes our ideal, or typical conception, of rest and security'. This early habitation becomes 'a sort of material shrine or sanctuary of sentiment' and the origin of 'a system of visible symbolism [that] interweaves itself through all our thoughts and passions' thereby becoming part 'of the great chain where-with we are bound' (315). For his protagonist, Florian Deleal, the childhood home is the 'body and earthly tabernacle' of the wandering soul, where the harmony between self and its external environment 'is like perfectly-played music, and the life led there singularly tranquil and filled with a curious sense of self-possession' (316). The 'instinct' of home generates in Florian a strong sense of 'yearning and regret' in later years 'towards he knew not what', but which swiftly resolves itself as 'sensibility—the desire of physi-cal beauty' (319) that functions as a kind of antidote to the 'soul-subduing' thought of his own death.

As Catherine Maxwell suggests,

for Florian the remembered house in which he lived as a child becomes a container for part of his nascent identity [...] the child is in the house but the house is also inside the child and he will carry it with him when he leaves its physical walls and makes his journey into the adult world.

(Maxwell, 2008: 79)

This consolatory sense of 'being-at-home' is denied to Hardy's nostalgic char-acters and poetic speakers, whose yearning for the home of their childhood is unassuaged, and whose desire for physical beauty is inevitably overwhelmed or negated by the realisation of their own impending dissolution.[20] Like Pater's Florian Deleal, the subject of 'A Child in the House' (1878), Hardy's nostalgic speakers look back to the lost homes of the past for a sense of who they were then, who they are now and how, if at all, they may dwell in the present. However, where the childhood home – the 'early familiar' – constitutes for Pater 'our ideal, or typical conception, of rest and security' and offers a delightful sense of *chez-soi* which is carried through into adulthood, the houses of the past offer Hardy's nostalgic characters little solace or respite from their ontological angst.

Julian Wolfreys sees Hardy as a writer who 'dwells on dwelling', and here the terms 'dwell' and 'dwellings' are understood in the Heideggerian sense of how one lives on the earth (as opposed to how one might 'simply exist') and in relation to history and the past. Consciousness of one's material existence on earth is contained in this sensitivity to one's relationship and interaction with past lives, now extinct, but whose presences can be sensed in the silence 'that is the signifier of a present haunted by memory' (Wolfreys, 2009: 4). Thus 'dwelling' means here 'to orientate oneself with regard to one's being, and the historicity of being' (5). For Wolfreys the present home, the present sense of self,

> is always troubled by a communication from some other time, some other place, which has fallen into partial or complete ruin and untranslatability, and yet which is intimately bound up in that which gives identity a home, and which makes us who we are. (6)[21]

John Ruskin believed that buildings were living, organic things, having a language and a life that was 'gifted' to them through the years by their inhabitants whose deeds and experiences permeated their fabric and gave them 'significance'.[22] This 'gifting' was a type of sanctification, much like that of a church or cathedral, but a secular one (Ruskin, 1849: 8.225). Ruskin's 'gifting' is a symbiotic process in which the house not only bears the record of its past inhabitants – discernible in part in what he calls the 'golden stain of time', it also sees 'and almost seem[s] to sympathize' in everything the inhabitant does and feels. The walls of the house, like those of the self, are semi-permeable membranes through which there is an exchange of influences in which each is modified in perceptible and imperceptible ways. The language of continuity in a house is composed of memories and associations that communicate themselves to the current dweller, linking him or her to the past and to past generations. Old houses are saturated with the lives and acts of previous inhabitants, – a percolation palpable to those who are sensitive to it. Good men, says Ruskin, forced to exchange the commodiousness of their earthly abode for the 'room made for them in the grave' would be grieved by the thought that the former was to be swept away after their death (Ruskin, 1849: 8.225).[23] A man's house and his living body are the 'earthly abodes' of his spirit and a dying man feels acutely the severing of the connection between himself and his 'house', and is troubled by the thought of its destruction or decomposition.

Hardy's late poem 'Silences', published posthumously in *Winter Words* (1928), explores different degrees and states of silence and concludes that

> the rapt silence of an empty house
> Where oneself was born,
> Dwelt, held carouse
> With friends, is of all silences most forlorn!

(Hynes, III: 201)

There is no sense here of Ruskin's notion of symbiotic gifting or the 'golden stain of time'. So many of Hardy's characters and poetic narrators experience great difficulty orientating themselves in relation to this historicity of being. For Wolfreys, the silence of the empty house 'is the most strident in its call; for it brings to the poet's mind the human past, of lost songs, "music-strains", the sounds of friends – all in fact that constitutes for Hardy the experience of what it means to dwell' (Wolfreys, 2009: 4). However, a different reading of this poem suggests that nothing can stimulate or release that sense of past or other lives that Ruskin believed permeated and was ever present in the fabric, contained space and memory of old houses. The roof, rafters and window panes of this empty home are closed against the narrator. They are 'absent-thoughted, tranced, or locked in prayer'. Its space is torpid 'like a tomb's'. The speaker cannot link the 'remembered songs and music-strains' of the past to his later experience of the physical space in which they happened: 'It seems no power on earth can waken it / Or rouse its rooms'. The return to the actual home of the past literally 'displaces' that past – pushing it beyond the grasp of the present. This silence is not, as Wolfreys suggests, 'strident' but 'rapt' which, with its homophone of 'wrapped', offers another deeply suggestive metaphor of self-alienation which reveals the subject as haunted by a libidinal memory that it cannot access or articulate. The house of the past is a signifier haunted by the surplus of meaning that it cannot adequately express or release. It stands as a barrier to what Judith Butler terms 'the affective memory of a pleasure prior to individuation' whilst functioning as a signifier of 'that pleasure's irrecoverability' (Butler, 1999: 186–7). The poem's title enacts this very conundrum. The title 'Silences' challenges the assumption that silence can be specifically defined or that it exists in only one form. At the same time, if 'silence' designates a condition resulting from an absence of speech or utterance (*SOED*), then the poem is itself an attempt to 'utter', quite literally, this very condition.[24]

The image of the self-enclosed house that fails, or refuses, to communicate its past – even the more immediate past of the speaker who was born there – challenges Ruskin's notion of historical 'gifting' and Wolfreys' sense of Hardy's relationship to the historicity of being. In 'The Tenant-For-Life', published in *Poems of the Past and Present* (1901), as in 'Silences', Hardy severs Ruskin's comforting link between the 'home' which endures and the body which decays. Neither 'lives' without the spirit that inhabited it and, instead of giving the access to its vibrant, immortal past, the empty house merely serves to recall the narrator to his own mortality. The sun emphasises the tenant's temporary purchase on the house and garden insisting that 'new hands' will alter the lineaments of the garden just as strangers will inhabit the house and, while they might wonder how it came about, 'They'll talk of their schemes for improving it, / And will not mention your name'. Neither will they care for the yearnings or the sad and happy experiences of the current lessee who may 'feel more in an hour of the spot / Than they will feel in a year'. The continuation of a house offers little comfort to its current inhabitant who will join past inhabitants as one of the many 'dead men out of mind!' (Hynes, I: 200).

In a later poem 'The Two Houses' (*Late Lyrics and Earlier*, 1922) Hardy examines the significance of the human history of a dwelling not just in terms of physical alterations but also the permeation of its walls by its former inhabitants. Again, Hardy's notion of the symbiotic influence of the past is less comforting and enabling than Ruskin's. A dialogue between an old dwelling and a 'smart newcomer' establishes Ruskin's notion of how 'men's lives, deaths, toils, and teens' 'print [...] their presences' on older houses:

> Where such inbe.
> A dwelling's character
> Takes theirs, and a vague semblancy
> To them in all its limbs, and light, and atmosphere.

> (Hynes, II: 363)

However, the experiences of the past have cracked the hide and furrowed the face of the older house, turning its 'gear' gray, yet it possesses a 'substance' – an 'inbeing' (to borrow Hardy's coinage) – that is yet to be 'gifted' (in Ruskin's sense of the word) to the smart new dwelling. Hearing the old house list the 'sylph-like surrounders' that throng its rooms, the new one asks if the day will come 'When I shall lodge shades dim and dumb – / And with such spectral guests become acquaint?' The old house confirms that this will indeed happen:

> Such shades will people thee,
> Each in his misery, irk, or joy,
> And print on thee their presences as on me.

However the mood of 'The Two Houses' is less celebratory than in Ruskin. At the start of the poem the new house has boasted of its airy, well-ventilated and well-serviced modernity:

> Modern my wood,
> My hangings fair of hue;
> While my windows open as they should,
> And water-pipes thread all my chambers through.

The old house, by contrast, is crowded with the spectres of 'men's lives, deaths, toils, and teens' and seems to 'mourn' the loss of that unmarked newness that its brother displays. The old house laments that it is aged and furrowed by the history of its past inhabitants, and the anticipation of such a 'gifting' leaves the new house 'awestruck, faint' at the prospect.[25]

This poem establishes a dialectic between the necessity of the shaping discourse of history, the historical accretions of language and their inevitable constraints. The new 'living dwellers', like those of 'The Tenant-For-Life', are 'blind' to the spectral forms that 'pack' the old house's rooms; they 'come and go/ [...] with souls unwoke'. While this blindness to the historicity of their own placement is to be deplored, the very 'substance' of the old house threatens to stifle the living dwellers, to elbow them, almost literally, out of their own home. While this poem enacts the relationship of the subject to history in a way that challenges Ruskin's comforting metaphor of symbiosis, it offers no viable alternative.

In Hardy's work, modern subjectivity appears constrained and stifled by the structures of inevitability, and the systems and dead weight of historical and linguistic accretion. Nevertheless it is this that provides the medium in which each 'dweller' has his or her being.[26] We might remind ourselves here of another, older meaning of the word 'dwell' which perfectly captures its provisional and its constraining aspect. The Old Saxon 'bi-dwellian' means 'to hinder' while the later Middle Dutch signifies 'to stun or perplex' and the Old High German 'twellen' carries the sense of to 'delay' or 'harass', with the Middle English translation being 'to abide for a time in a state, place or condition'. By 1667 'dwell' indicates 'to cause to abide' (*SOED*). In each example, the word retains the sense of a temporary, contingent condition *imposed* upon a subject rather than chosen as an act of freewill. The more archaic, but nevertheless significant, meanings of the term are useful for the exploration of the relationship between desire, selfhood and the intimate space of dwelling in Hardy's work. These connections are explored in Hardy's novel *The Woodlanders* (1887) which is, among other things, a developed meditation on the nature of human *being* and an exploration of the relationship of 'home' to the formation of the self – especially when that self is dispossessed, or 'unhomed', from patriarchal structures by gender or class.

George Melbury's house, Grace's birthplace, is 'of no marked antiquity; yet of a well-advanced age', an irregular block of buildings' which reverberates with 'queer old personal tales [...] yet audible if properly listened for; and not, as with those of the castle and cloister, silent beyond the possibility of echo' (*TW*, 2005: 22). The door jambs of the house bear witness to the generations that have literally inscribed their presence both in and on the fabric of the place in the shape of 'certain time-worn letters [...] initials of byegone generations of householders who had lived and died there' (42). Grace, who has been displaced from Hintock by her elaborate education, returns to her childhood home after an absence of some years. Wandering pleasurably through it, she encounters both the reassurance of the past and its duplicity, its familiarity and its unsettling, alien or *unheimlich* nature:

> Each nook and each object revived a memory, and simultaneously modified it. The chambers seemed lower than they had appeared on any previous occasion of her return, the surfaces of both walls and ceilings standing in such near relations to the eye that it could not avoid taking microscopic note of their irregularities and old fashion. Her own bedroom wore at once a look more familiar than when she had left it, and yet a face estranged. The world of little things therein gazed at her in helpless stationariness, as though they had tried and been unable to make any progress without her presence. (43)

Even the reassuring 'brown spot of smoke' indicating where her candle used to stand has been artificially preserved by her doting father and thus belongs more to his reality than to hers. The hidden and unsettling knowledge that is revealed to her here is her own alienation from her past and her present self. Home, however longed for and nostalgically desired, can no longer give her that vital sense of 'being-at-home'. It is unsurprising then that no sooner has she settled into her old room than she is almost immediately attracted by the magical colour-changing light from Edred Fitzpiers's cottage, shining like a beacon in the liminal space or 'meeting-line' between the shade of the dim tree-tops and the light of the sky on a nearby hill: 'the house had been empty when she was last at home, and she wondered who inhabited the place now' (44). Grace's fancy constructs a personality to complement what she imagines to be the pursuits of 'the man behind the light', and this becomes the lodestar of her desire (43). From the start then Fitzpiers and his dwelling, or Grace's idea of them, are revealed as self-projections emanating from her own sense of ontological lack, a lack intensified by Grace's position as a woman in a set of patriarchal systems that shape desire and its expression.

Throughout the novel Grace moves from dwelling to dwelling constantly seeking somewhere to belong that will express who she is and give her a sense of self-possession. For her there is literally 'no place like home' in that each successive dwelling – her father's house, Fitzpiers's cottage, his hotel room and, eventually, his 'little furnished house' in the Midlands – is saturated with and regulated by patriarchal configurations of desire related to class consciousness and normative heterosexuality. Each house has been constructed by and belongs to a man and thus offers her only a provisional shelter and one that undermines rather than enhances her sense of self-possession. Grace's desire for self-possession can only be expressed in terms of her sexual desire for the men who will take over custody of her from, and briefly return her to, her father. Trapped in the liminal zone of the deserted wife, and unable to regain the status of a single woman because of the inadequate divorce laws of the time, Grace looks to her father 'to come home and [...] let me know clearly what I am' (262) before finally settling for the unsatisfactory 'home' offered by the errant Fitzpiers. Grace Melbury exemplifies the profound self-alienation experienced by Hardy's women characters, who are sheltered and shaped by patriarchal structures of gender, sexuality and language that do not feel 'homely'.

Escaping the possibility of renewed sexual attention from her unfaithful husband Grace obeys 'a Daphnean instinct' and (not for the first time) flees into the dark depths and the uncanny, unsettling weirdness of the ancient plantations. If Hardy's earliest poem 'Domicilium' can be seen to offer the arbitrary and 'untrained' vigour of the natural world as a metaphor for the 'Real' that threatens to encroach upon the self and its 'dwelling', then *The Woodlanders* intensifies its signifying power to the point of surrealism:

The plantations were always at this hour of eve – more spectral far than in the leafless season, when there were fewer masses and more minute linearity. The smooth surfaces of glossy plants came out like weak lidless eyes; there were strange faces and figures from expiring lights that had somehow wandered into the canopied obscurity; while now and then low peeps of the sky between the trunks were like sheeted shapes, and on the tips of boughs sat faint cloven tongues. (268–269)

Defined by André Breton in 1924 as a new mode of expressing thought 'in the absence of any control exercised by reason, exempt from any aesthetic or moral concern', surrealism sought to reveal and explore the creative potential of the unconscious mind (Breton, 1924). This description of Hintock wood in late summer – with its disembodied, lidless eyes, strange faces and figures – appears to anticipate the movement by some 40 years. The 'faint cloven tongues' that sit on the tips of the boughs suggest, the 'cloven tongues of fire' that sat upon each of the apostles at Pentecost, symbolising the descent of the Holy Spirit and the ability to preach eloquently in several languages simultaneously, so that they were understandable by all.[27] This ideal notion of language, expressing not only a seamless connection between signs and an extra linguistic reality, but also a universal understanding of that connection, is rendered surreal by the context in which these cloven tongues appear to hover suggestively, but only 'faint[ly]', on the 'tips of the boughs'. The surrealist project was founded on the exposure and whole-sale rejection of spoken or written language, which Breton regarded as an example of 'the laws of an arbitrary utility' (Breton, 1924).

Grace's fear of the threatening, '*unheimlich*' otherness of the wood is, the narrator informs us, not 'imaginative or spiritual' but moral and practical. The plantation offers her no reassuring sense of security in her element but threatens her with the exposure of the purely arbitrary nature of all 'laws of utility', including the moral law and thus threatens her 'integrity' in every sense of that word. In his exploration of the function of signification, Lacan resorts to the metaphor of the 'phlogiston': 'the hypothetical essence that exists in all combustible bodies that is discharged or disengaged in the com-bustion process or flame: something that is both there and yet not there: perceivable but intangible'. Signification, he concludes, 'no more emanates from life than phlogiston escapes from bodies in combustion'. On the con-trary it is to be understood as 'the combination of life with the 0 atom [the zero at the heart] of the sign' (Lacan, 2006: 495–7). The indistinct cloven tongues on the tips of the boughs in Hintock forest offer a surreal vision of this imaginary phlogiston and demonstrate how the subject is double-crossed – 'suborned' – by language, and yet, deprived of the 'arbi-trary utility' of such structures, he or she becomes 'unhoused', exposed to the meaninglessness of the Real.

Seeking refuge from the 'expiring lights' of the 'canopied obscurity' of the woods, Grace is attracted by another light from a window, one which was 'so very small as to be almost sinister to a stranger, but to her it was what she sought. She pushed forward and the dim light of a dwelling was disclosed. It was the place she sought' (*TW*: 269). The narrator's repetition of 'she sought' emphasises Grace's desire for a 'place' of shelter even if it is the shelter of another man's house. Initially intending only to profit from Giles's help in reaching the sanctuary of a friend's house in Exonbury, Grace is forced by the oncoming storm to abide in his hut: her temporary sense of security being increased by Giles's scrupulous behaviour:

> Without so much as crossing the threshold himself he closed the door upon her, and turned the key in the lock. Tapping at the window he signified that she should open the casement, and when she had done this he handed in the key to her.
>
> 'You are locked in,' he said; 'and your own mistress.'
>
> (*TW* 2005: 272)

Although Grace, quite literally, makes herself at home in Giles's hut, putting it in order 'and making little improvements which she deemed that he would value when she was gone' it represents only a provisional dwelling, an imagined integration of herself. Stunned and harassed by Fitzpiers's infidelity and her own confused and illicit sexual feeling for Giles, Grace is 'caused to abide' (in the seventeenth-century sense of the word 'dwell') in a borrowed and provisional shelter which comes under fierce attack from the external elements. This fatal storm takes on an anthropomorphic quality, it is both palpable and 'an invisible colourless thing', and embodies the threat of the Real that would undo Grace, ontologically speaking, and Giles, quite literally, in that it brings about his death. The crude construction of hurdles which his moral scruples drive him to, offers him insufficient protection from its destructive force.

> It was difficult to believe that no opaque body, but only an invisible colourless thing, was trampling and climbing over the roof, making branches creak, springing out of the trees upon the chimney, popping its head into the flue, and shrieking and blaspheming at every corner of the walls. As in the grisly story, the assailant was a spectre which could be felt but not seen. She had never before been so struck with the devilry of a gusty night in a wood, because she had never been so entirely alone in spirit as she was now. She seemed almost to be apart from herself – a vacuous duplicate only. The recent self of physical animation and clear intentions was not there. (277)

Contrary to her expectation, Grace is neither healed nor made whole by her sojourn in the shelter of Giles's hut. In a complex example of pathetic fallacy, her 'dwelling' is both assailed and haunted by the spectre of the Real which seems to emanate from the plantation outside the hut and which reduces the 'arbitrary utility' of language (Breton: 1924) to incoherent 'shrieking and blaspheming'. Under such duress Grace herself becomes 'cloven': seeing the self that signifies as a 'vacuous duplicate' only, exposing what Lacan defined as the 'zero' at the heart of the sign (Lacan: 2006: 495–7).

The death of Giles, and her misguided erotic identification with him as the pastoral ideal, leads to the death of her questing spirit and the metaphorical burial of her heart in his grave. However, even this is a temporary abode for, despite Fitzpiers's conjecture, Grace was not, and indeed could never be, 'One who lived where [Giles] lived' (*TW*:300) and Fitzpiers notes that, despite her protestations, she 'wilfully keeps open the grave' so as to effect her eventual escape from the lost bucolic self that it symbolises (307).

Following Giles's death Grace abandons the woods which are now 'uninteresting' (309) to her and remains inside her father's house, a 'dwelling' whose precincts are literally 'haunted' by her estranged husband and which she eventually abandons for the neutral space of a room at 'that newly done-up place the Earl of Wessex' before finally taking up residence in her husband's 'little furnished house' in the Midlands. (323) Grace's brave excursion to the threatening, but potentially liberating, indeterminacy of the wood ends in the reassuring, because familiar, 'man trap' of her husband's arms.

Grace Melbury's 'self-possession' is continually undermined and reconfigured by prevailing class and gender discourses, which shape and direct her desire in relation to the conventional and legal constraints of the patriarchal heterosexual imperative. Giles Winterbourne, though similarly assailed, is even less securely housed as a result of his class subjection. Hardy's extreme sensitivity to the rural labourer's sense of *chez-soi* was sharpened by his direct experience of the tentative nature of their tenure in real life.[28] Giles is a leaseholder of his own cottage and those of his tenants, the rent from which contributes to his livelihood. Unlike George Melbury, Giles's possession of his birthplace hangs on the life of another (John South) and his tenure is subject to the whim of 'a practised woman' (Felice Charmond), who is the permanent owner of the houses by inheritance from her husband. Unlike Grace's, Felice's house is not written over by its former inhabitants but by the 'letterings and shoe-patterns' scored into the lead work of its roofs by those who built it (53).

The loss of Giles's cottages and his eviction is made even more significant by the fact that 'by those houses hung many things', not least his success in securing Grace as his wife, for 'Melbury's doubt of the young man's fitness to be the husband of Grace had been based not a little on the precariousness of his holdings in Little and Great Hintock' (91). Giles's cottages represent not only his practical shelter but also his means of economic and social survival. They also symbolise the 'language of continuity' that registers his historic right to dwell on that spot, and the space of his 'dwelling' itself. His failure to secure possession of them by payment of a simple fine is evidence not only of his impracticality but also the injustice of a social, and for Hardy a cosmic, system that declares, as Giles puts it so presciently, 'houses should be *leased* for lives' (32) [my emphasis]. Everything that is essential to Giles's 'self-possession', everything that he desires – in the broadest sense of the term – is embodied in those dwellings, which are central to the realisation of his heart's desire: Grace. As the faithful, if somewhat insensitive, Robert Creedle declares:

> ye've lost a hundred load of timber well seasoned; ye've lost five hundred pounds in good money; ye've lost the stone-windered house that's big enough to hold a dozen families; ye've lost your share of half-a dozen good wagons and their horses: – all lost – through your letting slip she that was once yer own!
>
> 'Good God, Creedle, you'll drive me mad!' said Giles sternly. 'Don't speak of that any more!' (159)

The loss of his property leaves Giles 'discomposed': disarranged, unsettled, undone. Creedle's blunt resumé of the wholesale demolition of everything that Giles represents, and indeed represents him, is tellingly summed up in Marty South's charcoal graffiti on the whitewashed, rough cast of the front of his house:

> O Giles, you've lost your dwelling-place, And therefore, Giles, you'll lose your Grace. (99)

Giles loses his chance to marry Grace Melbury, but in a deeper, theological sense of the word 'grace', he forfeits his entitlement to dignity, favour and peace of mind: he is utterly dispossessed. In losing his home he loses the very fabric of his identity and his ability to endure, regenerate and progress. Like Michael Henchard and Jude Fawley, the irretrievable loss of what he desires results in the demise of desire itself and eventually the demise of the self that was constituted in and by those desires.[29]

There is a poignant political, as well as an ontological, message in the demolition of Giles's paternal home to widen the road for Felice Charmond's carriage. Inscribed in the clearing in the wood are the traces of Giles immediate and historical tenure of the land. As in 'The Self-Unseeing', the floor-plan of Giles's and his paternal ancestors' home persists in the gloom:

> He could trace where the different rooms had stood; could mark the shape of the kitchen chimney-corner, in which he had roasted apples and potatoes in his boyhood, cast his bullets, and burnt his initial on articles that did and did not belong to him. The apple trees still remained to show where the garden had been. (167)

The silence of this once inhabited space is even more profound than the silence of the wood, in that it offers a place where meaning was once inscribed, and it is here that Giles confronts his own impending extinction. As he sits 'lost in his thoughts as usual', the space or 'piece of sky' once blotted out by the comforting outlines of his roof, walls and chimneys is slowly replaced by the lights of stars which were extinguished long before. In contemplating these, Giles contemplates the sign of the extinction of his own being.[30]

If Giles is drawn to the spot by the silent space that designates the absence of his home, it is fitting then that Felice Charmond, the architect of this destruction, is herself overturned, quite literally, by the space she has made and left 'sitting on the heap of rubbish that had once been his dwelling' (168). Felice's eviction of Giles is a pyrrhic victory, rather like Marty's revenge upon the lady for the 'rape' of her locks and the sexual damage that lady has caused by wearing them as her own. This silent space, redolent with memories, and bearing the traces of those who once inhabited it, signifies the dispossession of those who worked the land by those who inherited it, as well as the inevitable demise of the individual who had 'first seen the day' there (167). Giles then is doubly displaced, twice dispossessed of his home and his sense of *chez-soi*: firstly by his class inferiority, signified by the caprice of an inconvenienced landlady, and secondly by his sexual subjection to Grace Melbury, who charges Marty to tell her father the truth about her compromising position in Giles's modest hut: 'Go and tell him [...] what you saw – that he gave up his house to me' (292). Giles gives himself up to the elements, as Jude will later do. Unable to 'fence against the storm' in his crude shelter of hurdles (273) he becomes even more 'de-composed' until, like the extinct stars he glimpsed in the newly exposed piece of sky where his home was once, 'his soul seemed to be passing through the universe of ideas like a comet; erratic, inapprehensible, untraceable' (282). Finally, all that remains of him is 'the unadorned stone that marked [his] last bed', tended for now by Marty South but eventually itself to sink without trace.

Marty South is the one exception to the personal narratives of alienation traced here. Hintock Forest can also be read as a metaphor for the interaction between the 'Real' and 'Other' – described by Lacan as 'the locus of speech and, potentially, the locus of truth' (Lacan, 1977: 129) Hintock Forest is a mediating space within which the woodlanders build their dwellings and establish their sense of *chez-soi*. Despite its 'primeval' appearance much of the forest is the product of human management, although this is a management that is, as Gaston Bachelard terms it, 'before-me, before-us' (Bachelard, 1994: 188). Its ancient oaks and yews enclose copses, glades, clearings and plantations where, as Marty sees it, new saplings 'sigh because they are very sorry to begin life in earnest – just as we be' (59). This primeval forest is a primitive witness to how human beings might interact with the symbolic structures in which they have their being. As the architect or builder shapes the intimate spaces of living, so Giles (like those who pre-date him), 'with a gentle conjurer's touch' initiates 'the soft musical breathing' of trees that will be felled 'long after the two planters had been felled themselves' (59). Like the town or the city, the forest is the product of culture; a work of art on 'nature's canvas', its seasonal changes from summer to winter demonstrating what the narrator – with characteristic Victorian imperialism – calls 'a retrogressive step from the art of an advanced school of painting to that of the Pacific Islander' (48). The forest is not a space outside culture but a 'primitive' cultured space and it is in the productive interaction between the outer immensity of the forest and the inner immensity of developing subjectivity that the woodlander establishes his or her 'dwelling'. The interaction of the two immensities has the potential to shape the construction and the constitution of the intimate space in which being abides. This interaction is symbolised at the start of the novel by the image of Marty South's irradiated cottage, which is both a dwelling within the forest and the place in which she fashions its products – straight, smooth hazel rods called spargads (9) – into pointed sticks to fix thatch on the roofs of other dwellings. It is the work of protecting the dwellings of others that will ensure that she retains a roof over her own head and that of her sick father. By the end of the novel this symbiotic relationship with the 'Real'/Other of Hintock Forest takes on a symbolic significance, illustrating how one might be truly at home in a culturally mediated environment, although this seems to require the reorientation of sexual desire along more general, altruistic lines – a possibility that is briefly considered in the earlier novel *Two in a Tower* (1882). *The Woodlanders* closes with an idealised image of Marty South in which the signifiers of gender and class are absent:

> As this solitary and silent girl stood there in the moonlight, a straight slim figure, clothed in a plaitless gown, the contours of womanhood so undeveloped as to be scarcely perceptible in her, the marks of poverty and toil effaced by the misty hour, she touched sublimity at points, and looked almost like a being who had rejected with indifference the attribute of sex for the loftier quality of abstract humanism. (331)

This 'accommodation' is denied to Giles, whose desire is poorly deployed, baulked and depleted by his love for Grace Melbury and the vicissitudes of his class position. It is also denied to Grace herself and to Felice Charmond whose desire is shaped by the imperative of patriarchal heterosexuality.

Hardy's story 'The Melancholy Hussar of the German Legion' is one of his most moving studies of nostalgic desire.[31] The traces of the camp of the King's German legion, which can still be discerned beneath the undisturbed sod of the downs after 90 years, represent an even more provisional dwelling than the outlines of the house in 'The Self-Unseeing' and the remains of Giles Winterbourne's cottage. Nevertheless they retain the 'silent' echoes of their former inhabitants: 'the old trumpet and bugle calls, [and] the rattle of the halters'. These are caught at night time by the 'attentive ear' of the narrator, as they mingle with 'the scourings of the wind over the grass-bents and thistles'.[32] He sees in his mind's eye the 'spectral tents and the *impedimenta* of the soldiery' within the distinct traces of banks and midden-heaps, and from these spectral forms issue the 'guttural syllables of foreign tongues, and broken songs of the fatherland' ('MH': 45). These echoes and traces of national history move the narrator to tell the 'truth' about a far more local story that happened almost a century before, which he has heard from the lips of one now dead and buried nearly 20 years ago. He has kept it secret until prompted by these visual and aural traces of the past. Now he will disinter the repressed fragments of cultural memory to give a different version of Phyllis Grove's story from those that 'got abroad' and were kept alive but which 'are most unfavourable to her character' ('MH': 40).

'The Melancholy Hussar' was written at the time of the re-ignition of British interest in the Transvaal due to the discovery of gold and diamonds there, which led to the second Boer War of 1899–1902. On the surface, it appears to be a nostalgic recreation of the Napoleonic Wars during which Britain held the Cape Colony against the French. Then, declares

the narrator, soldiers were 'monumental objects', kingship was still associated with 'divinity' and 'war was considered a glorious thing' (9). However,
just as the landscape carries hidden traces of its historical past, the threat
of invasion and the spectral echoes of foreign inhabitation or 'occupation',
so the narrator is haunted by and burdened with the story of the execution
of Matthäus Tina and the discrediting of Phyllis Grove's good name. This
is a further example of what Julian Wolfreys refers to as the 'foreign guest
[...] an apperception of [...] what haunts the familiar, of what disturbs in
the most familiar location, home' (Wolfreys, 2009: 6). However, in giving
voice to Matthäus's story, the narrator is also struggling to articulate his own
homesickness, his own nostalgic desire for a sense of belonging.

Linda Hutcheon has described how, during the nineteenth century, the
condition of nostalgia underwent a semantic shift 'from being a *curable*
medical illness to an *incurable* indeed unassuageable condition of the spirit
or psyche' (Hutcheon, 1998: 2–3). It no longer described a simple yearning to return to a place, 'but to a *time*, a time of youth', and the term
became the expression of the melancholic recognition of the 'irrecoverability' of the past.[33] This not the past of actual experience, however, but 'the
past as idealized through memory and desire'. Nostalgia operates through
Mikhail Bakhtin's notion of 'historical inversion' in which an unattainable
ideal is 'memorialized' as past, 'crystallized into precious moments selected
by memory, but also by forgetting, and by desire's distortions and reorgani-
zations'. An idealised, partial and irrecoverable past is invoked in response
to the dissatisfactions of the present (Hutcheon, 1998: 3). Hutcheon quotes
Susan Stewart's definition of the 'social disease' of nostalgia as 'the repetition
that mourns the inauthenticity of all repetition'. As such, nostalgia is deeply
implicated in all failed attempts to recover the 'soul of truth', whether that
is located in the past or in the constant struggle to articulate the present.

> The argument is that in denying or at least degrading the present as it
> is lived, nostalgia makes the idealized (and therefore always absent) past
> into the site of immediacy, presence, and authenticity.

In this respect nostalgia is ' "prelapsarian" and indeed utopian' (4).

The buried traces of the temporary home of the 'Melancholy Hussar',
and the traces of Matthäus's own 'home-woe' or '*heimweh*' for his 'dear
fatherland' and his lonely mother, become a cipher for the narrator's own
nostalgic desire for a sense of belonging and a lost sense of self-possession or
integrity. Like the poorly parented, motherless, non-native Phyllis Groves,
the narrator is 'infected' with Matthäus's 'own passionate longing' (48) as
are Matthäus's fellow soldiers who are depressed by a 'dreadful melancholy, a
chronic home-sickness' to the point where they are no longer able to attend
to their drill.

Ironically, the exotic foreign soldier, having 'none of the appurtenances of
an ordinary house-dweller', represents an ideal notion of 'home' for Phyllis

also (46). Like Matthäus Tina, Phyllis is not a native of the village, neither is she 'at home' in the house of her father – a 'small, dilapidated, half-farm half-manor-house', which seems to embody her father's growing sense that 'he had wasted his time in the pursuit of illusions' (40). She is happier perched on top of the garden wall which forms a boundary between the enclosed, highly-regulated space of her home and the path across the broad, open down, which will bring the homesick German Hussar to her. However, their plan to elope together back to Matthäus's homeland and to the welcoming arms of his mother is subject to the prohibition of others, and he is caught and shot as a deserter. Evicted from their coffins after their execution, in order to provide an example for others, Tina and his companion Christoph are finally buried in unmarked graves which are now sunken in and neglected. But the narrator and the older villagers still recollect where they lie, with Phyllis nearby, a constant reminder – like the traces of the German soldiers' camp upon the English Downs – of the foreignness at the heart of home.[34]

Hardy's dwellings then, unlike those of Pater or Ruskin, rarely manage to provide the subject with an abiding sense of *chez-soi*. His texts repeatedly feature homes imperfectly realised, lost or demolished on a whim; towers that fall; houses and castles which burn to the ground, are threatened by the elements or whose walls press down upon their inhabitants with the weight of history and custom. Of all of Hardy's characters, Jude Fawley is perhaps the most unhoused. He is trapped in what Lacan calls 'the defiles of the signifier' and the signifying systems that engender him, shape his destiny and condemn him and absolve him at his death (Lacan, 'The Function and Field of Speech', 2006: 231). As a child, he experiences this sense of entrapment in the vast concavity of the 'harrowed' field in which he scares the crows, and which constrain his subjectivity at the level of a rural labourer. All that is visible is 'the brown surface' which extends 'right up towards the sky all round, where it was lost by degrees in the mist that shut out the actual verge, and accentuated the solitude' (*JO*, 2002: 8). The horizon line, or edge, of the distinct 'channelings' of the field is lost to the eye, offering the boy no apparent means of egress from obscurity to self-definition.

It is significant that the catalyst for the development of his relationship with Arabella is the spectacle of a cottage on fire which they run, hand in hand, to see:

> The conflagration had been got under by the time they reached it, and after a short inspection of the melancholy ruins they retraced their steps – their course lying through the town of Alfredston.
>
> Arabella said she would like some tea. (43)

The 'lonely roadside cottage that is their first marital home, situated between the Brown House close to where Jude's parents parted and Marygreen where part of his loveless childhood was spent, expresses how this 'was not the sort of life he had bargained for' (57). After the breakdown of his marriage, Jude's life is reduced to a pile of effects auctioned off at the house of his father-in-law. All that remains is a photograph of himself framed in bird's-eye maple, given to Arabella as a wedding present, which he finds 'in a dingy broker's shop [...] amid a heterogeneous collection' of household effects: 'saucepans, a clothes-horse, rolling pin, brass candlestick, swing looking-glass'. He buys it only to burn it along with its frame (72). Though he rescues an image of himself from the remains of his marital home, it has no real substance and he destroys it. In this way, the disintegration of his first marital home, unsatisfactory though it was, mirrors the incipient disintegration of Jude himself. Wandering to the upland 'whereon had been experienced the chief emotions of his life' he strives to regroup his scattered ambitions into a vehicle for the forward trajectory of his life, which only '*seemed* to be his own again' (73; my emphasis).

It is no coincidence that his desire for Christminster, which will be subject to the constraints of class, and his sexual desire – 'that new and transitory instinct' which is defined by the prevailing discourses of heterosexual morality – are both experienced on almost the exact spot where his own parents parted and his conventional childhood ended. On this very spot, despite his maturity and his past experiences – scholarly and marital – Jude finds that 'he could not realise himself' and turns to a bold but ultimately meaningless act of self-assertion, carving his name into the back of the milestone pointing to Christminster: 'Thither J. F.' (73). This material 'utterance' (see note 24) of his ambition helps to re-ignite his desire for self-actualisation:

> The sight of it, unimpaired, within its screen of grass and nettles, lit in his soul a spark of the old fire. Surely his plan should be to move onward through good and ill – to avoid morbid sorrow even though he did see ugliness in the world? Bene agree et laetari – to do good cheerfully – which he had heard to be the philosophy of Spinoza, might be his own even now.
>
> He might battle with his evil star, and follow out his original intention (74).

However, Jude escapes from the indeterminate mist of the harrowed field, and the fog of Marygreen, only to enter the bluer, moister atmosphere of the strange, flat landscape beyond it from which the 'topaz points' of Christminster are 'faintly revealed [...] or miraged in the peculiar atmosphere' (17). Once there, he remains caught in the margin between town and gown, wandering under walls and doorways and down 'obscure alleys, apparently never trodden now by the foot of man, and whose very existence seemed to be forgotten'. In these newer, more indistinct and blurred 'channelings', Jude becomes even more dispersed and dis-integrated as a self: 'a self-spectre, the sensation being that of one of who walked, but could not make himself seen or heard' (80). It is in Christminster – the desired destination – whose ancient mouldy walls cannot offer a home for him and his family that his existential impulses are finally thwarted.

Unlike the narrators of Hardy's 'domicilium' poems, unlike Grace and Matthäus Tina, Jude has no childhood home to be nostalgic for. His bedroom at Aunt Drusilla's reminds him only of his failures. A wanderer through the countryside and towns of Wessex, Jude moves from one house to another but he is never at home except in his own grave. At the novel's close, Arabella lures him back to her father's house and an inevitable remarriage by reminding him that 'not having a home of your own' leaves one vulnerable to being left out on the street. It is significant that the befuddled Jude believes that he is back 'in our old house by Marygreen' and thus begins the final stage of his life, trapped once again by Arabella's machinations and the patriarchal demands of her father, who informs him:

> You and my daughter have been living here together these three or four days, quite on the understanding that you were going to marry her. Of course I shouldn't have had such things going on in my house if I hadn't understood that. As a point of honour you must do it now (402).

In Hardy's work, then, the house can be read as a symbol of how we strive to construct a 'homespace': a sense of vital space within the signifying structures that bring us into consciousness as subjects. As Hardy was well aware, architecture shapes and contains space. As such, it functions metaphorically for the interpretive framework that mediates desire. 'Dwellings' house the self – metaphorically as well as actually – and offer a 'placed condition', allowing it to address and interact with that which is perceived as outside it. At the same time, architecture represents the regulatory practices of the time in which the original impulse of desire is both enabled and constrained. In this respect, it is poignantly significant that Jude Fawley is a mason: skilled in patching up the ancient buildings of others but unable to design and construct a dwelling of his own.

For Hardy the home or childhood house represents a fugitive security – a provisional structure of desire for the childhood self but one that can only be apprehended at a distance, located as it is in the nostalgic recreation of the past in memory. For the adult self, the domestic space, shaped by the patriarchal, heterosexual discourses of gender, class and sexuality, becomes the constraining mould that hampers flexibility and growth: the 'gin which would cripple [...] for the rest of a lifetime' (*JO*, 1998: 61). Where Ruskin and Pater's male dwellers are conscious of a nourishing, symbiotic relationship between exterior and interior space, Hardy's characters and narrators experience the constraints and the almost unbearable weight of the contingent forces that give shape and shelter to the conscious self. This is especially true of his female characters. Where Ruskin and Vernon Lee write of the sense of being 'companioned by the past, of being in a place warmed for our living by the lives of others' (Lee, 1892; 2006: 3) Sue Bridehead, the would be pioneer of the modern spirit, feels 'crushed to earth' by the weight of previous lives lived in ancient dwellings such as 'Old-Grove Place'. Hardy's novels engage with the vexed issue of how one might bring into being new conceptions of self within the enabling constraints of language and other signifying systems. Having expressed a preference for the provisionality of the railway station, which symbolises 'the centre of the town life now', over the ancient and massive presence of the cathedral, 'which was a very good place four or five centuries ago; but is played out now' (139), we find Sue, by the novel's close, subjugated to 'a heap of black clothes beneath the symbol of the imposing Latin cross of St Silas church' (368–9). Sue's modern belief that one might make or support a life of one's own, isolated from the contingencies of past and present, is ill-founded and naive. Not even she can live outside 'the social moulds civilization fits us into' (*JO*, 1998: 215).

As with Grace Melbury, the modern sense of alienation and homelessness drives Sue back to the apparent shelter of conventional, conservative and restrictive practices and regulations, particularly those of normative heterosexuality within marriage, sanctioned by the established church. Immediately before she is caught in the mantrap set by the cuckolded Tim Tangs for Fitzpiers, Grace re-reads the marriage service and becomes 'quite appalled at her recent offhandedness' with her husband 'when she discovered what awfully solemn promises she had made him at Hintock chancel steps not so very long ago':

> She became lost in long ponderings on how far a person's conscience might be bound by vows made without at the time a full recognition of their force. That particular sentence, beginning, 'Whom God hath joined together,' was a staggerer for a gentle woman of strong devotional sentiment. She wondered whether God really did join them together.
>
> (*TW*, 2005: 319)

The next chapter will examine how women are doubly dispossessed of vital space, in that the childhood and domestic home is shaped by the regulatory practices of patriarchy and normative heterosexuality through which women are offered vital recognition in Judith Butler's sense of the socially articulated and changeable terms 'which confer or withhold humanness' (Butler, 2004, p. 2). Hardy's resistant female characters, who find themselves both constituted by and dependent upon this recognition are also critical of and seek to transform the norms which determine it. This desire to live critically and in a transformative relationship to these regulatory practices I read as the desire to create an alternative space of being: a 'sapphic space'.

2
Desire, Female Amity and Sapphic Space

> I may feel that without some recognisability I cannot live. But I may also feel that the terms by which I am recognized make life unlivable. This is the juncture from which critique emerges, where critique is understood as an interrogation of the terms by which life is constrained in order to open up the possibility of different modes of living; in other words not to celebrate difference as such but to establish more inclusive conditions for sheltering and maintaining life that resists models of assimilation.
>
> (Butler, 2004: 4)

A close examination of houses and homes as metaphors for the locus of being in Hardy's work reveals how the modern subjectivity of so many of his female characters is oppressed by the houses of the past or constrained by those of the present.[1] Hardy's critique of the ways in which female desire is confined, or refused houseroom, resides in his exploration of how domestic space is shaped by the regulatory practices of patriarchy and normative heterosexuality. These practices offer women vital recognition, in Judith Butler's sense of the socially articulated and changeable terms 'which confer or withhold humanness' (Butler, 2004: 2), that is deeply problematic. The childhood home or domestic space in Hardy's work signifies what Lacan and others have defined as woman's double-alienation from desire. The female characters discussed here are doubly dispossessed: firstly, by their individuation by and in the symbolic order, and secondly, by the ways in which its signifying systems are regulated and given meaning in the service of patriarchy. Woman's relationship to the symbolic order is particularly conflicted in that, constituted or recognised as an object of exchange, 'the symbolic order literally subdues her, transcends her' (Lacan, 'Sosie', 1988: 262). Her desire can only be expressed through what Judith Butler describes as 'the full appropriation of femininity, that is in becoming a pure reflector for male desire, the imaginary site of [his] satisfaction' (Butler, 1999: 203). In the following chapter, I will argue that, for these characters, the desire to live critically and in a transformative relationship to such regulatory practices is expressed in the desire to create or inhabit an alternative space for dwelling and being; not just as a refuge from the homelessness that attends non-recognition but also as a new accommodation for the self.

Close female companionship – the 'sapphic space' – provides an alternative to the existing regulatory structures of patriarchal and erotic exchange that characterise the domestic space and the heterosexual and reproductive confines of marriage.[2] It also offers Hardy's female characters the opportunity to express desire in radically new ways that challenge the accepted signifiers of femininity in the later decades of the nineteenth century. Amative or companionate relationships with other women constitute a place apart, however temporary or short-lived, for psychic self-examination and development marked by the interrogation of the conventional orientation of desire along gendered and erotic lines. This is briefly considered in Hardy's first published novel *Desperate Remedies* (1871) and presented in more developed ways in *A Laodicean* (1881) and *The Woodlanders* (1887). However, the establishment of the sapphic space in each of these texts is compromised and undermined from the start because it cannot exist outside the rules of recognition that regulate the signification of femininity. Abandoning the domestic space of home leaves the resistant female character with a stark choice between an as yet unregulated realm, in which subjectivity and selfhood are threatened with dissolution, or an alternative dwelling space which reveals itself to be already shaped by the very regulatory practices she seeks to avoid. Rejecting this compromised sapphic space leaves her with no alternative but to re-enter a new patriarchal home established by a husband or lover or, as in the case of Tess Durbeyfield, face the consequences of ontological homelessness or 'unbeing'. Close female relationships are undermined from the start by the regulatory effect of the heterosexual imperative, which reveals itself in the chosen female companion or is exemplified in the incursion of a desiring or desired male figure. In the case of *Jude the Obscure*, there is no place for companionate female relationships or sapphic spaces. Sue's relationship with Arabella is sexually competitive and the women-only communities, such as the ecclesiastical establishment where Sue initially works and the Teacher Training College at Melchester, are heavily implicated in the proscription of female desire.

Sharon Marcus identifies the period from 1830 to 1880 as 'the heyday' of sentimental friendships between women, 'legitimated in terms of affection, attraction and pleasure and federated into marriage and family ties'. During this period, the 'discourse of female amity' remained relatively uninfluenced by *fin de siècle* sexology (Marcus, 2007: 28). Although marriage remained the primary viable and legitimate outlet for female erotic and social energy female friendships, while functioning largely within the status quo as far as gender roles and social status were concerned, provided women with socially permissible opportunities to engage in behaviour commonly seen as the monopoly of men: competition, active choice, appreciation of female beauty, and struggles with religious belief. (26)

For Marcus, the emphasis placed within queer studies on secrecy, shame, oppression and transgression has masked the extent to which these same-sex bonds were acknowledged within the bourgeois liberal public sphere in powerful and enabling ways (13). Far from being antagonistic to the courtship and marriage plot, the relative stability of female friendships provides the necessary space within which the heroine can undertake an exploration of her psyche and develop 'the emotional disposition necessary for companionate marriage' (82). Marcus suggests that Bathsheba Everdene's retroactive friendliness towards her unfortunate rival Fanny Robin

germinates the compassion that flowers in her marriage to the aptly-named Gabriel Oak, which the narrator assesses as a happy union because it realizes the 'good-fellowship' – camaraderie – [. . .] seldom superadded to love between the sexes. (87)

However, Bathsheba's marriage to Oak has also been read not so much as a companionate refiguring of marriage but as the capitulation of a headstrong woman broken by the exigencies of sexual passion.[3] Similar reservations pertain to other marriages which succeed or displace close relationships between women, such as the union of Grace Melbury and Edred Fitzpiers in *The Woodlanders,* and Paula Power and George Somerset in *A Laodicean.* In the earlier novel, the close companionate relationship between Paula Power and Charlotte de Stancy clearly offers Paula an enabling space within which to undertake activities normally considered outside the feminine sphere: in particular, a personal struggle with religious belief and an active engagement with the architectural design of her own dwelling place – Stancy Castle. However, her lack of a sense of real entitlement to her home, despite her plans to sympathetically rebuild and redesign it, reflects her insecure identity as a prototype New Woman. As a result, Paula's desire finds its legitimate recognition as a wife rather than as a companion to another women, while the destruction of her castle by fire symbolises the dangers of unregulated desire as well as the need to break free from the suffocating, if historically compelling, regulatory structures of the past that so oppress Sue Bridehead.

Hardy's novels are ambiguous on the potential for close relationships between women to form an alternative space for the expression of female desire. In *Desperate Remedies* (1871), female companionship is inflected with the lurid glare of gothic sensationalism, apparently confirming Elaine Mark's observation that, in texts by men, the older seductive/corrupting woman is often portrayed as 'intense and overtly hysterical' (Marks, 1979: 357).[4] The fiercely possessive claim of Cytherea Aldclyffe on her younger name-sake Cytherea Graye is imbued with vampiric elements similar to those found in Coleridge's *Christabel* (1815), in Baudelaire's *Les Fleurs du Mal* (1857), Swinburne's *Poems and Ballads* (1866) and in Sheridan Le Fanu's 'Carmilla', published the year after *Desperate Remedies*.[5] Sapphic nuances and echoes supercharge the gothic atmosphere of Hardy's first published novel with a destructive and cloying sensuality, linking Cytherea Aldclyffe's affec-tion for her young maid with that of Swinburne's Sappho for Anactoria or Tannhäuser's for Venus in 'Laus Veneris'.[6] Swinburne presents Sappho's desire as all-consuming, insatiable and destructive, expressible only in pos-sessive, vampiric or even cannibalistic and murderous forms.[7] Swinburne's Sappho asks her beloved 'Why wilt thou follow lesser loves? Are thine / Too weak to bear these hands and lips of mine?' and charges her

> To crush love with thy cruel faultless feet,
> [...] keep thy lips from hers or his,
> Sweetest, till theirs be sweeter than my kiss:
>
> (McGann and Sligh, 2004: 94)[8]

This is echoed in Miss Aldclyffe's rather more demotic and gender-specific exhortation: 'Cytherea, try to love me more that you love him – do. I love you better than any man can. Do, Cythie; don't let any man stand between us. Oh, I can't bear that!' (*DR*: 82). Miss Aldclyffe's passion upsets Cytherea with its fiery vehemence and imperiousness; it is 'in one sense soothing, but yet it was not of the kind that Cytherea's instincts desired. Though it was generous, it seemed somewhat too rank, sensuous, and capricious for endurance' (83). The use of 'rank' here, somewhat undermines the mater-nal aspect of Miss Aldclyffe's feelings for Cytherea, typifying it instead as excessive, coarse, overly luxuriant perhaps even licentious or indecent.[9] The term 'sensuous' infuses this unwanted invasion of a young maid's bed by her older female employer with an erotic sensuality that Hardy was later clearly embarrassed by. Changes to the 1912 edition of the novel empha-sise the maternal nature of Miss Aldclyffe's desire for Cytherea indicating, as Patricia Ingham suggests, that between 1871 and 1912 Hardy became sensitive to the 'Sapphic' (as in the erotically 'lesbian') overtones of this pas-sage (Ingham, 2003: 396, note 79).[10] As with Sue Bridehead, the character of Cytherea Aldclyffe is edited and rewritten in response to the pathologising language of sexology, which specified close relationships between women as morbid and perverse.[11]

Hardy had encountered the sensual, if not the erotic, potential of amative relationships between women in Swinburne's *Poems and Ballads* and in reviews in periodicals such as the *Saturday Review*.[12] Whilst praising his 'bountifulness of imagination' and the 'music of [his] verse', his 'passages of rare vigour' and 'exquisite phrases', John Morley castigates Swinburne for 'grovelling down among the nameless shameless abominations which inspire him with such frenzied delight' and laments his 'attempt to glorify all the bestial delights that the subtleness of Greek depravity was able to contrive (Morley, 1866: 144). Morley takes comfort in the observation that 'such a piece as "Anactoria" will be unintelligible to a great many people, and so will the fevered folly of "Hermaphroditus," as well as much else that is nameless and abominable' (145). This stands as a corrective to the view that Sappho's lesbianism is only reasserted after Henry Thornton Wharton's edition of *Sappho* and 'only though the pen of "Michael Field" ' (Thain, 2007: 52).

Wharton's *Sappho* (1885/95), which Hardy owned and read extensively,[13] with its flexibility and openness regarding the restoration of the female pronoun, where grammatically appropriate, in many of the translations and renderings it featured, extended the scope of desire beyond the realm of the heterosexual, opening up distinctly homoerotic readings of the relationships between Sappho and her female companions. Wharton insisted upon Sappho's as the voice of desire in its various and complex forms (Wharton, 1895: 43). This broader understanding of the work was emphasised in the poetic renditions of the fragments by 'Michael Field', Swinburne and John Addington Symonds. Bradley and Cooper appear to have chosen to mediate their lyric voice through Sappho because of the deliberately ambiguous gender identity of the speaking subjects of Sappho's fragments and of the Sapphic voice itself (Thain, 2007: 45).[14]

Critics, including Mary Rimmer and Patricia Ingham, have demonstrated that *Desperate Remedies* is suffused with classical references, as in the names of the major characters: the anti-hero Aeneas Manston and the two Cythereas.[15] Despite the lurid, sensationalist touches to the portrayal of what appears to be a blatantly libidinous relationship between two women, for which Hardy may have drawn from Gothic texts, Swinburne's 'Anactoria' and possibly the experiences of his sisters Mary and Kate at the Salisbury college for women where they had trained to be teachers, there are aspects of *Desperate Remedies* which indicate that he was aware of the broader significance of Sapphic desire beyond the lesbian erotic. The mirroring of the two Cythereas is significant here and is a device that will feature in the portrayal of the relationship between Elizabeth-Jane and Lucetta in *The Mayor of Casterbridge* and Grace and Felice Charmond in *The Woodlanders*. The two Cythereas are linked by more than their Christian names. Cytherea Graye is roughly the same age as Cytherea Aldclyffe was when she met and lost Ambrose Graye, who subsequently named the child from his marriage to another woman after her. Cytherea Graye can be seen as a more complex object of desire for Cytherea Aldclyffe than the simply sexual. She represents lost love, lost youth, lost innocence and the lost opportunity for happiness for the older woman, and the narcissistic mirroring of the two women suggests that each Cytherea becomes a 'symptom' of the other: a sign of her ego-morphic desire.

Cytherea is the addressee in Sappho's 'Fragment 62': 'Delicate Adonis is dying, Cytherea; what shall we do? Beat your breasts, maidens, and rend your tunics' (Wharton, 1895: 109).[16] This fragment has been identified as Sappho's version of the dirge or lament for the death of the annually-renewed, youthful vegetation god Adonis, traditionally sung before sacrifices were offered to the muses. The cult of the dying Adonis was a particularly female one, allowing for the collective expression of unbridled emotion by women confined by the rigid order of the polis and the family, and is said to have been fully developed by Sappho and her young female disciples on Lesbos around 6000 BCE. It is founded on the notion of threnody, or lamentation for its own sake. The object of that passionate grief remains unspecified or, at best, could be said to encompass loss and transitoriness in all its manifestations, as symbolised by the passing of the fertile seasons. As a lamentation for what is lost, the dirge expresses desire in its purest form. In Sappho's fragment, Cytherea appears as a member of this ancient sorority, and her name was also interchangeable with that of Aphrodite the Greek goddess of beauty and love. This suggests a reading of 'sapphic' desire, especially in relation to the older Cytherea, that incorporates the longing for all things transitory – youth, beauty, pleasure and life itself – embodied in the younger woman.[17]

On one level, Cytherea Graye appears as Miss Aldclyffe's erotic object of desire; but in a broader sense, she embodies all the metonymic objects of desire that the older woman yearns for in her demand for completion. Cytherea Graye is a clear example of Cytherea Aldclyffe's narcissistic, or what Henry Staten terms 'ego-morphic', object (Staten, 1995: 175). In loving her, the older woman loves a phantom or fantasy image of herself. As she declares to the younger woman: 'I can't help loving you – your name is the same as mine – isn't it strange?' (80). Miss Aldclyffe requests Cytherea to say her prayers adding 'It would seem like old times to me – when I was young, and nearer – far nearer Heaven than I am now. Do, sweet one' (81). Cytherea represents for the older woman her younger, unspoilt self: as she might have been before she was 'cruelly betrayed' by her 'wild' officer cousin (372); hence, Miss Aldclyffe's disappointment at Cytherea's admission that she has already been kissed. Consequently, Cytherea becomes instead a version of Miss Aldclyffe's postlapsarian self: yet another girl 'whose mouth and ears have [...] been made a regular highway of by some man or another! Whose heart has [...] been had!' (82). Following this bitter exchange, Miss Aldclyffe dreams of her own death:

'Oh such a terrible dream!' she cried, in a hurried whisper holding to Cytherea in her turn; 'and your touch was the end of it. It was dreadful.

Time, with his wings, hour-glass, and scythe, coming nearer and nearer to me – grinning and mocking: then he seized me, took a piece of me only. [...] But I can't tell you. I can't bear to think of it. How those dogs howl! People say it means death.' (88)

The 'piece' stolen by 'dreadful Time' can be seen to represent the older Cytherea's younger, innocent self, which is the true subject of her narcissistic desire.

Desperate Remedies demonstrates the two-way nature of sapphic desire. The disempowered Lady's Companion also identifies with her female benefactor, who becomes the focus for erotic and ambitious wishes in a reconfiguration of Hardy's 'Poor Man and Lady' plots.[18] Cytherea Graye forms a romanticised image of the older woman, who represents power and female authority to this wholly disempowered, would-be Lady's Companion. At their first meeting Cytherea Aldclyffe appears 'like a tall black figure standing in the midst of a fire' (54) and offers a pointed contrast to the young woman's father Ambrose Graye, whose fall from the phallic spire of Hocbridge Church she witnessed just a few months earlier, and also her brother Owen and her would-be lover Edward Springrove. Indeed, Richard Nemesvari reads Owen Graye as symbolically castrated by his mysterious oedipal lameness, and Edward Springrove as 'a stagnant man' who has failed to advance himself or his suit for over 15 months (Nemesvari, 2011: 44). Christina Parish has suggested that Cytherea Graye identifies with Cytherea Aldclyffe not as a maternal figure but as 'the mother's exotic, adventurous other'. Cytherea forms a romanticised image of Miss Aldclyffe 'predicated upon male impotence and female authority to which female companions aspire' (Parish, 2006: 6).

In *Desperate Remedies*, *The Mayor of Casterbridge* and *The Woodlanders*, the 'Poor Woman's' identification with the 'Lady' is presented as negative not least because of the manifestation of feminine subjectivity the older woman represents. Here the sapphic space (the houses of Miss Aldclyffe, Lucetta and Felice Charmond) is severely compromised and the 'Poor Woman' eventually abandons it for the more familiar, reassuring confines of the marital home. The relationship between the Lady and the Lady's Companion takes on a further complex dimension in these novels. Rather than posing a 'threat' to or refuge from patriarchal heterosexuality, the companionate relationship between women offers only an intermediate space or, as Scott Herring terms it, an 'indifferent terrain', in which the heroine indulges in self-examination before proceeding to marriage or, in the case of Grace Melbury, to a reconciliation with an estranged and inconstant husband (Herring, 2007).

The Mayor of Casterbridge likewise exploits the device of doubling in which the object of the heroine's desire appears as an elevated or perfected image of herself.[19] Lucetta Le Seur's name suggests her limited capacity for female bonding and support. The 'sisterly' implications of 'S[o]eur' are negated by the masculine 'le': a negation that is compounded by her later adoption of the surname Templeman. Although Lucetta is initially an ego-morphic projection for Elizabeth-Jane, the younger woman eventually rejects her as a debased and compromised female other. Elizabeth-Jane's first meeting with Lucetta takes place at Susan Henchard's grave in a context of sexual competition. Elizabeth-Jane attends the grave as a dutiful daughter, Lucetta has gone there, armed with some sort of guide book, to confirm the death of the woman whose arrival in Casterbridge prevented Henchard from honouring his promise to marry her and restore her reputation. Elizabeth-Jane is immediately struck by the apparent similarity between herself and the stranger:

> This figure, too, was reading; but not from a book: the words which engrossed it being the inscription on Mrs Henchard's tombstone. The personage was in mourning like herself, was about her age and size, and might have been her wraith or double, but for the fact that it was a lady much more beautifully dressed than she.
>
> (*MoC*: 125)

Harassed and rejected by the 'uncultivated' Henchard, who imagines himself humiliated by her use of dialect, her 'round hand' and her 'lowering' of herself by waiting on Farfrae at the Three Mariners, Elizabeth-Jane transfers her desire to the figure of Lucetta, who represents an elevated and gentrified image of herself. She is attracted by 'the artistic perfection of the lady's appearance' which seems to suggest a higher evolutionary stage than her own: 'it was a revelation to Elizabeth that human beings could reach this stage of external development – she had never suspected it'. However, the narrator is at pains to emphasise the superior qualities of the younger woman, who feels her 'freshness and grace' leeched away by Lucetta's vampiric influence and heterosexist competitiveness. The gothic image of a veiled woman 'of curious fascinations' in a churchyard 'old as civilization', who 'vanishes behind the corner of the wall' (125), suggests 'some devilry' to the impressionable girl, but she is quick to dismiss this for the advantages of refinement and study that a place in Lucetta's household might offer (133). Initially Elizabeth-Jane relates to the older woman 'almost with a lover's feeling' (130) and the narrator's reference to Lucetta as 'the lady of her fancy' combines the romantic, the erotic and the phantasmic, demonstrating Elizabeth-Jane's misguided libidinous investment in a debased and meretricious self-projection.

Sharon Marcus contends that companionate, desirous relationships between women help the heroine to develop 'the emotional disposition necessary for companionate marriage' (2007: 82); but in this case, Elizabeth-Jane's maturity, and the reward which accompanies it, are consequent upon the critical perception and rejection rather than the acknowledgement of her rival and what she represents. Initially, Lucetta effaces Elizabeth-Jane and this is consolidated with the transference of Farfrae's affections from the younger to the older woman, which renders Elizabeth-Jane 'invisible in the room': 'Lucetta had persisted in dragging her into the circle; but she had remained like an awkward third point which that circle would not touch' (163). The effect is to transform the younger woman from an admiring companion to a 'discerning, silent witch'. Elizabeth-Jane has already imagined herself as Lucetta meeting Farfrae in the early stages of their relationship: 'A seer's spirit took possession of Elizabeth, impelling her to sit down by the fire, and divine events so surely from data already her own that they could be held as witnessed' (160). The arrival in the room of Lucetta herself, as if conjured up from nowhere, echoes the earlier scene in the graveyard where the older woman materialised as if in response to the lonely girl's supernatural bidding. This serves to emphasise Lucetta's function as Elizabeth-Jane's 'ideal-I', one which must be subdued or banished in order for the younger woman to prosper (Lacan, 'Mirror Stage', 2006: 76). The narcissistic doubling of the women is suggested here, as it is in *Desperate Remedies* and *The Woodlanders*, by a literal mirror scene. The process of Lucetta's banishment begins as Elizabeth-Jane holds up a mirror in which the older woman anxiously surveys her own face for signs of wear. This scene, with its echoes of the wicked stepmother in 'Snow White', extends the association of Elizabeth-Jane with witchcraft in that the witch's 'speculum' or 'scrying mirror' was commonly believed to reveal the future. It also anticipates the reversal of roles between the two women: Elizabeth-Jane's eventual triumph over her rival and the 'false' accomplishments and desires Lucetta represents:

'Bring me a looking-glass. How do I appear to people?' she said languidly. 'Well – a little worn,' answered Elizabeth-Jane, eyeing her as a critic eyes a doubtful painting; fetching the glass she enabled Lucetta to survey herself in it, which Lucetta anxiously did.

'I wonder if I wear well, as times go,' she observed after a while.

'Yes – fairly.'

'Where am I worst?'

'Under your eyes – I notice a little brownness there.'

'Yes. That is my worst place, I know. How many years more do you think I shall last before I get hopelessly plain?'

There was something curious in the way in which Elizabeth, though the younger, had come to play the part of experienced sage in these discussions. 'It may be five years,' she said judicially, 'or, with a quiet life, as many as ten. With no love you might calculate on ten.' (161–2)

The admirably artful Lucetta now assumes the status of 'a doubtful painting', possibly even a forgery, for the younger woman and the deliberate use of the adjective 'judicially' emphasises Elizabeth-Jane's move from supportive companion to judgmental critic. The final deposition of Lucetta is effected in the public humiliation and debasement of the skimmity-ride in which the older woman and her desires are embodied in the crude effigy, the sight of which quite literally kills her.

The psychic exploration that Elizabeth-Jane undertakes in the space provided by her relationship with Lucetta involves learning to let go of the 'false' desires and aspirations that Lucetta represents and rejecting the conventional aspirational image of herself she has projected onto the older women. Elizabeth-Jane's amative desire is not for Lucetta, but for herself in Lucetta's place, which is where, in fact, she finds herself at the novel's close. Maturity and fulfilment for Elizabeth-Jane involve the movement from a split to a more integrated sense of self, something that Hardy's more tragic and demanding characters fail to achieve, but only within the confines of marriage. Lucetta changes for Elizabeth-Jane from the object of fascinated desire to an artwork of dubious value, a debased effigy and finally to a corpse 'borne along the churchyard path' to the graveyard where Susan Henchard's dust 'mingled with the dust of women who lay ornamented with glass hairpins and amber necklaces' (125). The narrative comes full circle, back to the first meeting place of all three women. Lucetta is now no longer associated with the living, youthful Elizabeth-Jane but with Susan Henchard whose grave had so fascinated the older woman and where Lucetta's 'two footprints distinct in the soil' beside her rival's grave had signified 'that the lady had stood there a long time' (125).

The narrator describes Elizabeth-Jane's early feelings for Lucetta as 'almost [...] a lover's' (130). In identifying with her older, socially superior female mentor, the younger woman desires, initially, to assimilate her to herself. In this respect, Hardy's sensitive portrayal of the relationship between the two women would appear to support Lacan's theory of woman's double-alienation from desire. Elizabeth-Jane's desire can only be resolved through what Judith Butler describes as the full appropriation of a recognised femininity as Farfrae's wife. At the same time, it does show women as subjects of desire in their own right and that ego-morphic desire is not exclusive to heterosexual men. Hardy's heterosexual women can also 'eagerly consume images of desirable femininity' (Marcus, 2007: 19).

In *The Woodlanders* (1887) the libidinous investment by the younger woman in her older companion is more overt than in the slightly earlier *The Mayor of Casterbridge*, and the relationship of desire to its object is similarly complex. Melbury is a paternalistic version of Hardy's aspirational poor man. His love for his daughter is as much mercantile as filial, and deeply rooted in the pragmatic, aspirational rural culture of Little Hintock, which, despite being 'one of those sequestered spots outside the gates of the world', is driven by surprisingly worldly concerns. Personal relationships are motivated by the cash nexus and individuals are commodified: Marty South to her glorious, saleable hair; Giles Winterbourne to his specimen apple tree which he held 'like an ensign' in Sherton market (*TW:* 67); Grammer Oliver to her 'large organ of brain' (80); and Grace to 'a mere chattel' (119), 'an article' (52) and 'a gift' her father seeks to make 'as valuable a one as it lay in his power to bestow' (49). Initially, Grace's own desire is latent and undirected, and, on her first visit to Felice Charmond, she is described as 'a vessel of emotion, going to empty itself on she knew not what' (53).[20] It is Felice Charmond who is her first object of desire or, as Fitzpiers would term it, 'the tree' upon which her 'rainbow iris is projected' (106). Grace dreams of being 'irradiated by love' but, as a result of her refined schooling, her desires are primarily orientated towards social recognition and material gain. Consequently it is not her anticipated wedding day but her meeting with Felice that leaves her, in Giles's words, with a face 'like th[at] [...] of Moses when he came down from the Mount' (61). For Grace, Felice represents an opportunity to become intimate with the rules of power – the power of social superiority and sexual knowledge – and the comparison between Grace's return from an audience with Felice and Moses's descent from Mount Sinai with God's Ten Commandments is an ironic comment on the strategic imperatives that govern women's desires.

However, as with Lucetta and Elizabeth-Jane, the terrain of same-sex companionship into which Felice invites Grace is far from untouched by modern constructions of sexual knowledge (Herring, 2007: 16). On the contrary, it is a space dedicated to, and shaped by, prevailing notions of predatory female sexuality, into which Felice seeks to initiate her young protégé. The walls of Little Hintock House are ornamented with mantraps, and Felice points out to Grace their metaphorical significance in the battle of the sexes:

> 'Man-traps are of rather ominous significance where a person of our sex lives are they not?' Grace was bound to smile; but that side of womanliness was one which her inexperience felt no great zest in contemplating. (54)

Where Lucetta appeared to Elizabeth-Jane as a 'dubious painting', Felice represents an altogether more accomplished work: her almond eyes resemble, ironically, those found in 'the angelic legions of early Italian art'. As a former play-actress she is a 'well-practised' woman, and her performance of femininity, which is knowingly critiqued by the narrator, is studied and proficient:

> She showed that oblique-mannered softness which is perhaps seen oftenest in women of darker complexion and more lymphatic temperament

than Mrs Charmond's; women who lingeringly smile their meanings to men rather than speak them, who inveigle rather than prompt, and take advantage of currents rather than steer. (55)

It is sexual jealousy that prompts Felice to abandon, somewhat precipitately, this project of female companionship. In a scene which echoes the confrontation between Cytherea Aldclyffe and her inexperienced maid Cytherea Graye, and Lucetta's solicitation of Elizabeth-Jane's views on her looks, the two women are juxtaposed in a mirror which 'faithfully' reflects the unmerciful 'killing or damaging' effect of Grace's youthful complexion on Mrs Charmond's own (57). This scene is repeated later, in a variant form, when Grace visits Fitzpiers for the first time to secure Grammer Oliver's release from the old woman's contract with the doctor who has paid her for her skull after death.[21] Both incidents suggest the extent to which Grace and her incipient desires are subject to the constraints of sexual knowledge which operate most forcefully within the confines of the domestic space. It is significant that it is Grace who is later caught in the mantrap and prevailed upon to return to her marriage with the philandering and inconstant Fitzpiers.

Felice derives her satisfaction from the self-legitimisation that comes with successful sexual conquest and consequent financial gain. She was, as Giles unknowingly puns, 'a bit of charmer in her time [...] a body who has smiled where she has not loved, and loved where she has not married' (205). She epitomises the concentration of desire in materialism and the body and as such appears antagonistic to the values of the local community nurtured by the forest.

However, *The Woodlanders* eschews an easy antithesis between Culture and Nature, Hintock and the world outside it. The forest can be seen to represent the signifying potential of the Other in relation to the Real: a space that is neither wholly outside nor wholly within the control or navigation of those who plant, manage and inhabit it. As such it represents potentiality within certain constraints rather than an innocent, unmediated 'natural' space. The walls and boundaries of Felice's Little Hintock House, rather like the childhood home in Hardy's 'Domicilium', are threatened by the encroachment of nature:

The ashlar of the walls, where not overgrown with ivy and other creepers, was coated with lichen of every shade, intensifying its luxuriance with its nearness to the ground till, below the plinth, it merged in moss [...]

The situation of the house, prejudicial to humanity, was a stimulus to vegetation, on which account an endless shearing of the heavy-armed ivy went on, and a continual lopping of trees and shrubs [...].

It was vegetable nature's own home. (53)

In her attempt to establish and defend her space of being against these threatened incursions, Felice expresses herself through the recognisable feminine identity of the powerful femme fatale. The mantraps symbolise the trammelling of female desire by prevailing discourses of heterosexual femininity that emphasise competition, acquisitiveness and entrapment. As such, Little Hintock House, in common with Grace's other potential 'homes', represents a deceptive and wholly unsatisfactory alternative to the patriarchal space of her family home.

Grace's aspiration to become Felice's companion indicates how far 'cultivation [...] had advanced in the soil of Miss Melbury's mind' in that her project of 'self-development' is directed towards a close association with, and assimilation of, Felice's feminine values (40). The prime indicator of a 'cultivated' woman is that she becomes, as Grace does, 'the wife of a cultivated man' (156); but the novel suggests that such aspirations, for a woman at least, constrain and ensnare. Grace becomes the victim of Felice's jealousy, duplicity and competitive sexuality and of Fitzpiers's inconstancy. The theatrical tropes employed in the novel suggest the contingent and performative aspects of conventional heterosexual feminine desire, which include Grace's 'anticipative satisfaction' when contemplating her wedding day: her 'cool pride' at being 'the heroine of an hour'. In her case it is a short-lived and somewhat pyrrhic victory.

In the preface to the novel, Hardy claimed that the question of marital infidelity and 'the immortal puzzle – given the man and woman, how to find a basis for their sexual relation' is 'left where it stood' (3), but at the very least the novel calls for a re-evaluation of the prevailing gender discourses that *actually* 'give' the man and woman. Its brief examination of the potential of female companionship is oriented towards the psychic evolution of the heroine; however, contrary to Sharon Marcus's formulation, this does not lead to the development of 'the emotional disposition necessary for companionate marriage' (Marcus, 2007: 82), but to a radical reconfiguration of conventional competitive bonds between women.

Significantly, Felice's guilty conscience at being Fitzpiers's mistress is stirred by Melbury's allusion to Grace's former love for her, which is contrasted with the threat to her moral integrity posed by her unconstrained erotic desire for Fitzpiers. Hintock Forest offers the chance to escape the constraining gaze of the patriarchal Melbury, her erotic involvement with Fitzpiers and an interview with the 'Continental follower', who will later take her life.[22] Grace accompanies Felice into the woods to avoid the potential agitation of a possible meeting between her intemperate father and her errant husband. The two women, along with Giles and Marty, meet briefly in a clearing that Giles and his men are creating in the forest. The clearing becomes a space in which Giles, and more especially Grace and Felice, experience what the narrator refers to as a 'troubling [of] each other's souls', in which old assumptions, aspirations and self-awarenesses are displaced by new cravings, mutual embarrassments, estrangements and 'inner turmoil'. Here 'Grace's formidable rival' is prompted still further in the 'generous resolves' initiated by Melbury's reminder of the younger woman's earlier affection for her (212–13).

The mirror scene between the two women at their first meeting in Little Hintock House is re-enacted here but, as in the relationship between Elizabeth-Jane and Lucetta, the desires and aspirations that the older woman once signified now appear foreign to the younger woman's self-conception, newly stimulated by her unhappy marital experience into a reconsideration of 'that homely sylvan life' she had formerly rejected:

> [Felice] held out her hand tentatively, while Grace stood like a wild animal on first confronting a mirror or other puzzling product of civilization. Was it really Mrs Charmond speaking to her thus? If it was she could no longer form any guess as to what life signified. (214)

Where previously both women stood side by side in the mirror, here each confronts the other; but what is reflected back, to Grace at least, is not her ego-morphic desire but her profound difference from Felice. Rather than seeing herself in the same glass as her older, would-be self, Grace sees only Felice for what she is. Both women experience a breaking down of previous self conceits, leading them to plunge deeper into the woods where they become, literally and figuratively, 'lost' to themselves. Grace's abandonment of the available roles of submissive companion, dutiful daughter and loyal wife, and her questioning of the social direction forced upon her by her father's aspirations, leave her temporarily 'dis-located' in terms of the local habitation of body and subjectivity. In Hintock Forest, which signifies the interplay between Real and Other, 'she soon found that her ideas as to direction were vague – that she had, indeed, no ideas as to direction at all' (216).

The deepening darkness and moaning wind in the wood effect a kind of sensory disorientation, and in this state Grace is impelled towards a similarly disorientated Felice. The two women cling together in a temporary 'nest' of dead fern, roofed by 'a clump of bushy hollies', whose primitiveness contrasts strongly with the stagey artificiality of Felice's boudoir in Little Hintock House (218) and Grace's homely little chamber in the keeper's cottage. Cold, lost and wretched, Grace and Felice temporarily overcome the barriers of competition and sexual rivalry between women, moving towards a new, more open, honest connection:

> They consequently crept up to one another, and, being in the dark, lonely, and weary, did what neither had dreamed of doing beforehand, clasped each other closely. Mrs Charmond's furs consoled Grace's cold face, and each one's body as she breathed alternatively heaved against

that of her companion, while the funereal trees rocked and chanted dirges unceasingly.

(*TW*: 218)

Gaston Bachelard writes of the nest as a provisional habitation for the self: 'a precarious thing, and yet it sets us to *daydreaming of security*' (Bachelard, 1958; 1994: 102). A nest is a sign of 'confidence in the world' and returns us, in our imagination, to the sources of the 'oneiric house' (103). In Hardy's novel the nest represents not a primitive return to the security of our childhood, but a provisional shelter, or intermediate space, for the self unhoused by choice or force from the more solid structures or accommodations of prevailing self-conceits.[23] Grace's sympathy for Felice's 'weakness' and 'misplaced affection' (216) dissipates when Felice confesses her sexual intimacy with Fitzpiers, but in leaving the shelter of the nest Grace is threatened by the immensity of the forest: 'deep darkness circled her about, the cold lips of the wind kissed her where Mrs Charmond's warm fur had been, and she did not know which way to go' (219). Consequently, she returns to Felice so that they may find a path out of the wood together.

This reconfigured relationship between the rival women is subsequently re-enacted in the most intimate area of Grace's own domestic space: the marital bedroom which, like the graveyard in *The Mayor of Casterbridge*, becomes the meeting place for female characters intimately connected to each other by a man. Grace's barbed invitation into the room: 'Wives all, let's enter together!' is softened into sympathetic tenderness for her rivals:

> It was well enough, conventionally, to address either one of them in the wife's regulation terms of virtuous sarcasm, as woman, creature, or thing. But life, what was it after all? She had, like the singer of the Psalm of Asaph, been plagued and chastened all the day long; but could she, by retributive words, in order to please herself the individual, 'offend against the generation,' as that singer would not? (234)[24]

As the narrator's reference to the 73rd Psalm of Asaph suggests, the very system in which Grace is entrapped will protect her in ways that are denied to her husband's mistresses. This active renewal of female relationships is instigated not by a rebellion against the sexual competitiveness inculcated by and within patriarchal formations but by a common sympathy with its victims. The amative bond developed between Grace and Felice in their precarious nest in Hintock Forest cannot be sustained in the rigid confines of the domestic and social space of her father's house. In Grace's case, the unsettling freedom that accompanies being 'lost to oneself' can only be resolved by lapsing to her preliminal state through a relationship with her childhood sweetheart, Giles Winterbourne. All possible directions out of the wood lead back to the paternal or marital home and the confines of femininity as constituted within patriarchy.

Grace's capitulation to Fitzpiers's desire to resume their marital relationship is attributed, as it is in *Jude the Obscure*, to woman's misguided and slavish obedience to form and, in addition, to the obvious meaning of accepted custom and social ordinance, 'form' here suggests, among other meanings, the particular mode in which subjectivity, especially female subjectivity, manifests itself, or by which it is recognised. Felice Charmond belatedly recognises the threat posed to her integrity by indiscriminate indulgence in her proscribed desire for Fitzpiers. Grace, schooled into an understanding of the importance of 'form', has a similar moment of revelation following the mantrap incident which shocks her, ironically, into turning back to the security of her marriage. The psychic development Grace undergoes in the precarious shelter of the nest in the wood leads only to a renewed embrace of existing forms of subjectivity. Trembling and encircled by the arm of the opportunistic Fitzpiers, Grace becomes, once again, 'oblivious of the direction of their desultory ramble' and wanders into another 'encircled glade'. Although it constitutes another clearing in the 'densest part of the wood', illuminated by the almost vertical rays of the moon, the suggestion here is one of confinement and exposure:

> Boughs bearing such leaves hung low around and completely enclosed them, so that it was as if they were in a great green vase, which had moss for its bottom and leaf sides [...]'I must go back!' she said, and without further delay they set their faces towards Hintock. (323)

Grace's journey from clearing to nest to 'great green vase' – from the mantrap festooned walls of Little Hintock House to the mantrap of a reconciliation with her philandering husband – suggests there is no space in which reconfigured female desire may be permanently recognised, sheltered or maintained outside of the patriarchal dwelling.

For John Schad *A Laodicean*, more than any other of Hardy's novels, 'draws upon the author's own professional experience of architecture' and, in the character of Paula Power, 'point[s] up architecture's capacity to depart from conventional ways of knowing'. Paula Power suggests it is 'an art which makes one [...] independent of written history' (Schad, 1997: xx). Here architecture functions as a metaphor for the re-imagining of space – in particular, the space of being. Paula Power's desire is to adapt the ancient castle of the de Stancys to create a home for herself: a physical and emotional space within which she can function with a degree of independence denied to women in marital, and indeed sexual, relationships in late Victorian England. Her restored castle is envisaged as a felicitous, 'sapphic' space in which she can enjoy a 'sweet communion' with her companion Charlotte de Stancy, and evade the coercive demands of male heterosexual

presumption, against which her wealth and property offer little or no protection. The novel is the record of her gradual disillusionment with her
own 'power' to shape her self, and the forms in which it is manifested,
in a new and radical integration of the ancient and the modern. In the
relationship between Paula Power and Charlotte de Stancy, described by
one character as 'more like lovers than girl and girl' (42), Hardy offers a
positive and sympathetic depiction of female amity and its potential to
construct alternative ways of being. On first hearing of their companionship, George Somerset raises a glass to 'the two generous-minded young
women who, in this lonely country district, had found sweet communion
a necessity of life, and by pure and instinctive good sense had broken
down a barrier which men thrice their age and repute would probably
have felt it imperative to maintain' (33). This 'sweet communion', in which
Paula's aunt is initially included, is threatened and eventually destroyed
by the romantic and sexual demands of Somerset and de Stancy, and the
social ambition of Will Dare, whose aim is to conscript the laodicean Paula
and his self-emasculated father back into the service of normative heterosexuality and to profit financially from their marriage. Paula's 'sweet
communion' also allows her to maintain her 'clandestine, stealthy inner
life' (12) and her laodicean prevarication. In addition it shields her from the
necessity to define herself according to the coercive demands of patriarchal
heterosexuality.[25]

Stancy Castle resembles Elaine Marks's gynaecium or 'women's house',
where 'in general men play secondary roles as fathers, spiritual advisers or
intrusive suitors' (Marks, 1979: 357). Indeed before the advent of Somerset,
Dare, de Stancy and Abner Power, men are wholly absent from the castle in
any role other than as retainers or domestic servants. Paula's boudoir, filled
with periodicals and popular papers – British and foreign; satirical prints;
books 'from a London circulating library'; 'light literature in French and
choice Italian'; the 'latest monthly reviews'; and the 'photographic portraits
of the artistic, scientific and literary celebrities of the day', represents a cultured milieu shared by her companion Charlotte (31). Paula's 'modernity'
is further emphasised by the newly-invented telegraph, which she operates
with skill and which the narrator cites as indicative of 'cosmopolitan views
and the intellectual and moral kinship of all mankind' as well as the 'fever
and fret' of modern life (31). Significantly, only the women know how to
operate this ultra-modern device and they use it to communicate with one
another 'in a language unintelligible to [Somerset]' (35). Somerset is not at
home here, and his masculine authority is imperilled in the sapphic space of
Paula's castle.[26]

The telegraph wire that enters the arrow-slit like a 'worm uneasy at
being unearthed', and her contemporary and choice reading matter – which
suggests the butterfly wandering of 'a stray hour from 1881' into her
thirteenth-century bedroom – demonstrate the enlivening of this 'fossil of

feudalism' by Paula's modern spirit. It strongly indicates Paula's iconoclasm and her desire to breach 'the hoary memorial of a solid antagonism to the interchange of ideas, the monument of hard distinctions in blood and race' (18). Here again the text suggests that sapphic communion, for Paula at least, signifies not the construction of an alternative, same-sex erotic space but the sublimation and re-orientation of desire towards human, moral and intellectual progress. The eclectic nature of Paula's desire is symbolised by her plans to erect a Greek peristyle around the inner court of the Norman castle (70–1), and her general evasiveness when asked by Somerset to specify her aesthetic and architectural preferences.[27] She has also installed a gymnasium 'according to the latest lights on athletics, and in imitation of those at the new colleges for women' (150).[28] Here she trains not quite naked, as the word 'gymnasium' suggests, but in a costume that suggests the more fugitive possibilities offered by cross-dressing [29] or androgyny: a 'pretty boy's costume' in pink flannel, in which she resembles 'a lovely youth and not a girl at all' (149).[30]

John Schad reads Paula's 'high-flying gymnastics' as representing her 'groundlessness', which he defines as 'not [...] just an absence of ground but also, in part, a release from it' (xvii). The sapphic space that Paula creates within the stout walls of Stancy castle extends Scott Herring's notion of a terrain 'indifferent' to modern constructions of sexual knowledge, Sharon Marcus's 'psychic space' and also Marjorie Garber's third 'space of possibility', into a larger, more encompassing and potentially radical alternative site of being.[31] It is significant that Paula's future plans include not just a redesigned castle but a complete new town dedicated to the utopian manufacture of Greek pottery 'of the best period' (30).

Paula's 'laodiceanism' or 'indifference' signifies not paralysed indecision but a fertile syncretism that the narrator equates with the empyrean realm of 'the dreamer': a realm that Somerset has 'contritely' abandoned in the interests of professional and financial advancement. The narrator reminds us that

> as has often been said, the light and the truth may be on the side of the dreamer: a far wider view than the wise ones have may be his [...] and his reduction to common measure be nothing less than a tragic event. (6)

At this point in the novel the narrator digresses to equate the disciplining of the maverick or independent mind to the operation of lunging a colt, [32] and it is precisely to avoid 'reduction to the common measure' of a wife, and to preserve her self-reflexive resistance to the social ideal (*AL*, 302), that Paula has contrived her sapphic space. Far from developing the 'the emotional disposition necessary for companionate marriage' (Marcus: 82), Paula strongly resists becoming an object of a man's desire in order to privilege her own.

Paula Power is 'emphatically a modern type of maidenhood'(11) and a prototype New Woman, whose character is more fully developed in the figure of Sue Bridehead. In the case of both heroines, contesting 'the social moulds' means seeking alternatives to the prevailing and legitimate modes of feminine self-expression and the forced accommodation of desire to the heterosexual and reproductive imperative which the marriage contract implies. Resisting or refusing the role of 'wife' means resisting the compulsion to place themselves entirely under the economic and physical power of a man, even a man with whom they appear to be in love. This refusal or resistance lies at the very heart of Paula Power's 'laodiceanism': her lukewarm, non-committal attitude to romance and marriage, which is enhanced by her ideological and architectural eclecticism. Indeed, Paula's loving companionship with Charlotte De Stancy is presented as an alternative to the confining embrace of a lover or a husband, allowing not only 'sweet communion' but a degree of freedom usually denied to a married woman:

> In a moment she arose and went across to Miss de Stancy. 'Don't *you* go falling down and becoming a skeleton,' she said – Somerset overheard the words, though Paula was unaware of it – after which she clasped her fingers behind Charlotte's neck, and smiled tenderly in her face. It seemed to be quite unconsciously done, and Somerset thought it a very beautiful action. Presently Paula returned to him and said, 'Mr. Somerset, I think we have had enough architecture for to-day'. (71–2)[33]

The role of Charlotte de Stancy in this relationship is deeply ambiguous. Like Elizabeth-Jane Newson and Grace Melbury, her function appears primarily to assist the more socially powerful woman in the achievement of her aims. However, where Lucetta and Felice's aims are directed towards securing a man, Paula's are orientated towards maintaining a space within which to exercise her reflexive resistance.

Scott Herring identifies a movement within queer theory away from 'the ongoing imperative to identify sexually, to affiliate sexually, and to band together sexually under the aegis of reverse discourse' and towards a 'suspicion of sexual hermeneutics' (Herring, 2007: 13). Herring's chosen texts and characters demonstrate a distancing from sexual visibility, sexual knowledge and social control that accompanied sexual classification:

> each revolves around mysterious individuals who refuse to self-identify as homosexual or to self-affiliate with a homosexual milieu. And each seeks out terrain perceived as indifferent to modern constructions of sexual knowledge. (16)

Charlotte de Stancy and, more particularly, the mysterious and illegitimate Will Dare illustrate this resistance to sexual classification that Herring describes. The romantic, perhaps even erotic, charge that short-circuits the relationships between Hardy's earlier female companions is expended in the figure of Charlotte, whose intriguing attachment to Paula is finally reconfigured into a conventional, if equally unreciprocated romantic desire for Somerset. In many respects Charlotte de Stancy resembles Terry Castle's 'apparitional lesbian': 'never with us [...] but always somewhere else: in the shadows, in the margins, hidden from history, out of sight, out of mind' (Castle, 1993: 2). Feeble, enervated and delicate she lacks sensual or moral authority and the right to articulate her desires in any direction, and is eventually 'expelled from the "real" world of the fiction – as if vaporized by the forces of heterosexual propriety' (Castle, 1993: 7), into the closed confines of a conventional sapphic space: an Anglican convent.

In contrast to the vapid Charlotte de Stancy, the effeminate Machiavellian dandy – the 'unrecognisable' Will Dare – whom Somerset describes as 'of no age, no nationality and no behaviour' (63), and whose sexual orientation is never fully ascertained, is the architect to the plot and presents the greatest threat to all of Paula's projects. Where Charlotte is 'vaporized', Dare initiates a conflagration that destroys Paula's sapphic space. Consequently, Paula's eclectic plans for her castle and her life are forced to give way to 'domestic politics' and 'the social idea' (302). Her abandonment of her castle, and her female companion, to pursue Somerset across Europe signals the conventional re-orientation of her desires along heterosexual lines. While she is preoccupied with her marriage to Somerset, Dare delivers the coup de grace to her castle before apparently disappearing in the same cloud of smoke that signals the end of Paula's own laodicean resistance.

The destructive incursion of patriarchy and masculine heterosexual desire into the alternative space of female companionship and solidarity is more poignantly illustrated in *Tess of the d'Urbervilles*, where potentially supportive female relationships between women of the labouring class are repeatedly undermined by the advent of a covetous or coveted male from outside. The novel begins with the 'club-revel or "club-walking" as it was called there', which Tess takes part in along with village women of all ages from puberty upwards. Originally a centuries-old, pagan celebration in honour of Ceres, the Roman goddess of agriculture, the Marlott club evolved into a money-raising society or 'benefit-club' to support the elderly, ailing or impoverished. The narrator of the 1892 edition of *Tess* comments: 'It had walked for hundreds of years, if not as benefit-club, as a votive sisterhood of some sort' (19). An early meaning of the word 'votive' is 'consisting in, or expressive of a vow, desire, or wish' (*OED*), and each woman is described as 'banded' together by their desires: the possession of 'a private little sun for her soul to bask in; some dream, some affection, some hobby, at least some remote and distant hope which, though perhaps starving to nothing, still lived on, as hopes will' (20). This broad arena of hope and female solidarity is first breached by the appearance of Tess's father returning home in his 'triumphal chariot' from The Pure Drop Inn, fresh from celebrating his newly-discovered aristocratic pedigree. Jack Durbeyfield's subsequent inability to take the beehives to market due to his inebriation sets in motion the betrayal, debasement and tragic fulfilment of Tess's youthful and as yet barely disciplined desire by patriarchal and heterosexual conscription.

Tess's distinct beauty and her red ribbon, however, have already marked her out as different from her other female companions: a difference that is exacerbated by her 'trained National teachings and Standard knowledge under an infinitely Revised Code' (29), which has provided all her information of 'what lay beyond her judgement' (42) and renders her, as Alec will rather crudely put it, 'mighty sensitive for a cottage girl' (61). The narrator tells us that

> In those early days she had been much loved by others of her own sex and age, and had used to be seen about the village as one of three – all nearly of the same year – walking home from school side by side, Tess, the middle one [...] marching on upon long stalky legs [...] the arms of the two outside girls resting round the waist of Tess; her arms on the shoulders of the two supporters. (43)

Tess's sixth standard education, and her ensuing self-awareness in relation to codes of morality and respectability, distances her from the other 'cottage girls'. It manifests itself in her threat to withdraw from the club-walking if 'any more jokes' are made about the spectacle of her father; but by the time they reach the green 'she had recovered her equanimity, and tapped her neighbour with her wand and talked as usual' (21).

The arrival of the women at the green indicates that the club-walking is, in reality, a prelude to the May-Day dance – itself an ancient fertility rite. The girls dance with each other but only until the end of the working day when the village men 'together with other idlers and pedestrians, gathered round the spot and appeared inclined to negotiate for a partner' (22). The appearance of the men signals a change in the emotional constitution of the 'votive sisterhood' from community and companionship to separation and competition. The process is initiated by the advent of Angel and his brothers who are not only strangers but also evidently of a 'superior class' to the locals. Angel's diversion by 'the spectacle of a bevy of girls dancing without male partners' (22), and his impulse to remedy the situation, focuses the diffuse and unspecified hopes and desires of the women on sexual rivalry and social advancement, in which the advantage would seem to belong to the most 'for'ard' (23) who distinguishes and distances herself from her companions in an open invitation to him. She is eclipsed by another and, 'although the name of the eclipsing girl, whatever it was, has not been handed down, [...] she was envied by all as the first who enjoyed the luxury of a masculine partner that evening'. Angel stimulates not only envy and desire among the

women but also competition and rivalry among the hitherto indifferent village men, 'who had not hastened to enter the gate while no intruder was in
the way' and now

> dropped in quickly, and soon the couples became leavened with rustic
> youth to a marked extent, till at length the plainest woman in the club
> was no longer compelled to foot it on the masculine side of the figure. (23)

At this point the narrator emphasises that Tess's sensitivity militates against
her survival in the race for life, as 'owing to her backwardness' she misses
out on the chance to dance with the attractive stranger. At the same time she
becomes galvanised by desire which articulates itself in the form of sexual
and social aspiration and is intensified by loss. This new desire completes
the process of Tess's separation and segregation from female companionship. As Angel looks back at the mass of whirling girls, who seem to have
forgotten him already, he notices 'a white shape [standing] apart by the
hedge alone. From her position he knew it to be the pretty maiden with
whom he had not danced' (24). Where Angel dismisses Tess from his mind
in his haste to catch up with his brothers, she becomes newly constituted
by desire for him and what he represents, which results in her dissatisfaction with her home and community and incites within her new and
compelling impulses, which, in the absence of their primary object – Angel
himself – will seek fulfilment in the available but unsatisfactory form of Alec
Durberville.

This new orientation of Tess's desire militates against the establishment
of an ideal 'sapphic space' constituted outside of the prevailing structures
of gender, sexuality and patriarchal exchange. The May-Day dance instils in
her a consciousness of 'the unspeakable dreariness' of her home and this,
combined with her sense of responsibility for the death of Prince and loss
of her family's main form of income, leads her to conspire, reluctantly, with
her mother's desire for her to 'claim kin' with 'the great rich lady out by
Trantridge, on the edge o' The Chase, of the name of d'Urberville' (32).
Like Grace Melbury before her, Tess sets out initially in pursuit of a position as a lady's companion, but Joan Durbeyfield's motivations are more
pragmatic and practical than even George Melbury's. Joan cuts to the chase,
in more ways than one, by seeing Tess's employment by the imagined Mrs
Durberville as primarily the means to her daughter's marriage with 'a noble
gentlemen' (33). The conversation in Rolliver's, which revolves around a
more realistic appreciation of Tess's 'fine prospects' – seduction and preg-
nancy – leads Joan to betray the closest bond between women – that of
mother and daughter – by literally pimping Tess out in return for financial
and practical assistance from Alec. Joan's refusal to pass on to Tess the wisdom of female experience of the 'danger in men-folk' constitutes yet another
betrayal of the maternal–filial bond arising, as it does, from a misplaced

belief that aristocratic codes of honour mirror those of the rural community: and that 'if he don't marry her afore he will after' (58).

Tess's 'difference', in terms of comportment and aspiration, from her female compeers also results in a competitive alienation from the Darch sisters, each of whom has preceded Tess as Alec's mistress, and her dismissal of their company as 'a whorage' leads the remaining women to unite with the Darch sisters 'against the common enemy': 'the husbands and lovers tried to make peace by defending her; but the result of that attempt was directly to increase the war' (76). In an echo of the May-Day dance, Tess once again stands 'apart from the rest, near the gate' isolated from her sex and class and vulnerable to the predatory Alec. Her departure with the agent of her personal tragedy elicits not compassion but satiric laughter from the rural sisterhood.

Tess's violation by Alec also places her in a new relationship to her former schoolfellows and female companions in Marlott who visit her, not as equals, but 'dressed in their best starched and ironed, as became visitors to a person who had made a transcendent conquest (as they supposed)' (95). Her revival in their company is stimulated by their envy and her sense of superiority in terms of her sexual knowledge and experience. However, it represents only a temporary re-admittance into the sapphic space, based as it is on a lie and a further betrayal of her own sense of self and the desires that characterised it: 'the illusion was transient as lightening; cold reason came back to mock her spasmodic weakness; the ghastliness of her momentary pride would convict her, and recall her to reserve and listlessness again' (96).

Tess's arrival at Talbothay's Dairy after the death of Sorrow, full of the energy of revived and renewed energy, signals not only her 'rally' to a new stage in her life, but also places her back in time on that May morning some three years earlier, when she walked with 'the votive sisterhood' of the Marlott club and danced on the green with them. The superb pathetic fallacy of the 'thyme-scented, bird-hatching morning in May', which elicits from her what the narrator prophetically refers to as 'a Fetichistic utterance in a Monotheistic setting', reflects the renewed energy of the libido purged, it seems, of sexual and social ambition: she now has no admiration for the tombs of her ancestors. The narrator comments tellingly that 'she almost hated them for the dance they had led her' (118). Moreover, her arrival at the dairy initiates her into the touchingly generous sapphic space of the bedchamber of Marian, Retty and Izz.

However, far from being a space outside the regulatory discourses of sex and gender, the milkmaid's bedchamber is supercharged with erotic desire for the unwitting Angel Clare. Even before Tess can enter this space she is distracted by the voice and then the sight of Angel milking in the field where she has just sat down to work. The 'flood of memories brought back by the revival of an incident anterior to her troubles' (128), not only rekindles her desire for him, but also emphasises the substitutive role played by

Alec d'Urberville. It also stimulates a self-conscious dismay at her difference from the girl she was then. On her first night in the milkmaid's bedchamber the very atmosphere in which Tess sleeps is permeated with desire for Angel, the milkmaid's whispered words about him seeming to be 'generated by the darkness' in which they floated (129).

Although the milkmaids offer Tess a companionate and supportive female space, it is one already constituted and defined by a desire for a man which will never be assuaged. Indeed, their love for Tess, though generous and without rivalry, is vicarious in that through her they live their desire for Angel. The only time they join together is to watch him through the bed-chamber window, 'their three faces still close together as before, and the triple hues of their hair mingling' (138), or to embrace Tess in lieu of him:

> And by a sort of fascination the three girls, one after another, crept out of their beds, and came and stood barefooted round Tess. Retty put her hands upon Tess's shoulders, as if to realise her friend's corporeality after such a miracle, and the other two laid their arms round her waist, all looking into her face.
>
> 'How it do seem! Almost more than I can think of!' said Izz Heutt.
>
> Marian kissed Tess. 'Yes,' she murmured as she withdrew her lips.
>
> 'Was that because of love for her, or because other lips have touched there by now?' continued Izz drily to Marian. (198)

This tableau, reminiscent as it is of Antonio Canova's neoclassical sculpture of *The Three Graces*, recalls a similar grouping of the younger, prelapsarian Tess and her schoolgirl companions at Marlott 'walking home from school side by side, Tess, the middle one [...] marching on upon long stalky legs [...] the arms of the two outside girls resting round the waist of Tess; her arms on the shoulders of the two supporters' (43).

However, although each of Tess's working companions is forced to reassess her love for her in the light of Tess's forthcoming marriage to the object of their desires, like Grace Melbury, they rise above the conventional response to a successful rival and almost the last words Tess hears from them are from Marian, entreating her to remember them, and how they could not hate her 'because you were his choice, and we never hoped to be chose by him' (199).

The centrality of Angel Clare to the constitution of this sapphic space means that it is his symbolic departure (on his engagement to Tess), and his actual removal on their wedding day, rather than Tess's, that brings about the near collapse of the companionate relationship between the milkmaids and the destruction of their sense of self, which centred on their desire for him. Marian takes to drink: 'a girl who hev never been known to touch anything before except shilling ale' (241); Retty tries to drown herself and becomes 'so thin and hollow-cheeked that "a do seem in a decline. Nobody will ever fall in love with wi" her any more' and Izz succumbs to depression (222). Retty disappears almost wholly from the text at this point, and Izz is later tempted to elope with Clare, but the 'fascination' Tess has exercised over her gives her 'grace' and she praises Tess's love for Angel over her own, despite the damage it will do to her suit (289). Marian, whose own life has been all but destroyed by drink, helps Tess to employment and defends her against the depredations of Farmer Groby at Flintcombe Ash even though she has grown so coarse that Tess would not have wished to renew their acquaintance had all been well. In the reed-drawing barn of Flintcombe Ash, Tess also experiences a grotesque re-enactment of the night of her seduction, featuring the Darch sisters, who do not recognise their former victim, and Farmer Groby, who does. Caught between the farmer and the 'Amazons' like 'a bird [...] in a clap net' Tess is rescued this time by the loyal Izz and Marian, who stay to help her finish her work but through whom she learns of Angel's near betrayal of her.

The relationship between Izz, Marian and Tess, and the influence Tess exercises upon those more feeling members of her own sex which is 'of a warmth and strength quite unusual, curiously overpowering the less worthy feminine feelings of spite and rivalry' (315), constitutes another positive presentation of the potential strength and companionship of women in the face of men's abuse of sexual and economic power. This is in stark contrast to the curiosity of Tess's Marlott friends, and the shrewish *schadenfreude* of the Darch sisters. Rejecting all feelings of rivalry or ill-will, Izz and Marian eventually unite in their letter to Angel to try and protect Tess against both Groby and Alec: the masculine agents of sexual and economic exploitation. Their failure is a tragic indictment of the prevailing economic, sexual and gender structures through which desire is incited and articulated.

For Richard Dellamora, Hardy's deliberate isolation of Sue Bridehead from any kind of intimacy with other women 'has a valence within the male homosocial economy of the book since Hardy was aware that her wish to retain control of her own body was liable to be construed in contemporary sexology as a sign of sexual inversion' (Dellamora, 1990: 461–2). In a letter to his friend Edmund Gosse in 1895, shortly after the publication of *Jude* in volume form, Hardy knowingly uses the language of sexology as developed by Symonds and Havelock Ellis to protest that

> there is nothing perverted or depraved in Sue's nature. The abnormalism consists in disproportion: not in inversion, her sexual instinct being healthy so far as it goes, but unusually weak & fastidious; her sensibilities remain painfully alert notwithstanding, (as they do in nature with such women).
>
> (CL, 2: 99)

Although Sue displays the ideological radicalism often associated with what Ellis refers to as 'the modern movement of emancipation', Hardy is anxious to distinguish her from the 'true' invert who is sexually drawn to other women.

Earlier he had described Jude and Sue to Florence Henniker as 'two persons who, by a hereditary curse of temperament, peculiar to their family, are rendered unfit for marriage, or think they are' (*CL*, 2: 94). He uses similar terms to Gosse and Edward Clodd, referring in his letter to Clodd to a 'temperamental unfitness for the contract, peculiar to the family of the parties' (*CL*, 2: 93). Whilst there is little evidence of Jude's temperamental unfitness for marriage, the disproportionate 'fastidiousness' that appears to lie at the heart of Sue's resistance opens her up to sexological specification. Sue uses terms such as 'a physical objection – a fastidiousness [...] pruderies' (221) in describing her marital relations with Phillotson. Living with him 'as a husband' is 'a torture' to her. However, if the Widow Edlin is to be believed, the unfortunate Phillotson might inspire such 'fastidiousness' in any woman, or at least any woman from her family:

> I can mind the man very well. A very civil, honourable liver; but Lord! –
> I don't want to wownd your feelings, but; there be certain men here and
> there than no woman of niceness can stomach. I should have said that
> he was one. I don't say so *now*, since you must ha' known better than I;
> But that's what I *should* have said. (198)

As discussed in Chapter 2, Sue may be fastidious but she is not frigid. As she herself admits, her 'unaccountable antipathies' are matched by her 'aberrant passions' (216), which she is unable to justify or enjoy in the moral and sexual climate of late nineteenth-century England.

The issue for Sue seems to be one of choice, and sovereignty of the self, rather than a general distaste for heterosexual or indeed any other form of sex. Her aim is to create a physical and emotional space within which she can function with a degree of independence denied to women in marital and sexual relationships at that time, and Hardy suggested retrospectively to Edmund Gosse that Sue controls her sexual intimacy even with the man she loves (*CL*, 2: 99). Sovereignty over the self could not be exercised within marriage due to the law of coverture and the concept of conjugal rights. In refusing sexual intercourse with her husband, Sue is actually breaking the law and it is this perhaps that lies behind her castigation of herself as 'wicked' (223). The knowledge that Phillotson is legally entitled to demand sex with her, even by force if necessary, partly or even wholly explains her action of jumping out of the window when he accidentally enters her room, as it explains Grace's 'Daphnean' flight to Hintock Forest on Fitzpiers's return to the marital home. As Sue tells Jude, an unaccountable antipathy towards one's husband was insufficient grounds for refusing physical intimacy, and marriage at that time carried with it 'the necessity of being responsive to this man whenever he wishes [...] the dreadful contract to feel in a particular way in a matter whose essence is its voluntariness!' (223). Sue's only hope of sovereignty over her self, and her body, is to remain 'uncontracted'.[34]

Hardy's sensitivity to the specifying language of sexology is significant and it seems to echo Sue's rejection of 'the moulds civilization fits us into' (215). As Martha Vicinus has pointed out, women's sexual attitudes and behaviour have 'never been isolated from or independent of the dominant male discourses of the age' (Vicinus, 1992: 485).[35] Indeed, in July 1895, less than four months before *Jude the Obscure* was published in volume form, Havelock Ellis had sent Hardy his pamphlet on 'Sexual Inversion in Women', which Hardy promised to 'read with interest' (*CL*, II: 83).[36] This awareness on Hardy's part of the new interpretations that might be brought to bear on Sue's desire for sexual autonomy may be behind her isolating herself from other members of her own sex and her vulnerability to the coercive pressures that are brought to bear on her conception of herself. Where Grace Melbury, Tess Durbeyfield, Izz, Retty and Marian consciously rise above what the narrator of *Tess* refers to as 'the less worthy feminine feelings of spite and rivalry' (315), Sue is driven to renege on her radical assertions of a woman's right to sexual autonomy by the reappearance of the 'low passioned' (277) Arabella and the sexual trap she feels Jude's former wife will set for him: 'he *might* enter the inn with Arabella, as they would reach it before closing time; she might get him to drink with her; and Heaven only knew what disasters would befall him then' (278). Jude also plays his part in entrapping Sue by using Arabella's appearance and the fact that, despite their divorce, Arabella is 'rather more' his wife than the celibate Sue, to blackmail her into a sexual relationship with him.

The all-female spaces of the ecclesiastical designers, and the Women's Teacher Training School at Melchester, are presented as repressive, coercive environments dedicated to the restraint and reconfiguration of aberrant female desires. Throughout the novel, Hardy constantly draws parallels between these enclosed and confined Christian establishments and the pagan desires of Sue which find their outlet and expression out of doors. Her spontaneous purchase of the pagan images – 'reduced copies of ancient marbles [...] divinities of a very different character from those the girl was accustomed to see portrayed' – incite desires that are anathematic to the environment in which she works and lodges:

> Though the figures were many yards away from her, the south-west sun brought them out so brilliantly against the green herbage that she could discern their contours with luminous distinctness; and being almost in a line between herself and the church towers of the city they awoke in her an oddly foreign and contrasting set of ideas by comparison. (94)[37]

The destruction of her images by the figure of repressive Christian feminine discourse, Miss Fontover, forces Sue to leave her employment and lodgings and take up Phillotson's offer of a position as his live-in pupil teacher – an offer that exposes her to his sexually-coercive patronage. It is fitting that Miss Fontover is a worshipper at St Silas Church in Beersheba (95), where the scourged and broken Sue finally prostrates herself after the deaths of her children.[38]

Sue regards the women's Teacher Training College at Melchester as 'worse than the ecclesiastical designer's; worse than anywhere. She felt utterly friendless' (135). Far from offering a space outside repressive patriarchal discourses, the ancient training-school gives Sue 'the air of a woman clipped and pruned by severe discipline' (136). The narrator refers to it as 'a species of nunnery', containing 71 young women mainly aged between 19 and 21, from a variety of backgrounds. Lying in their beds at night they bear on their faces 'the legend The Weaker [...] as the penalty of the sex wherein they were moulded, which by no possible exertion of their willing hearts and abilities could be made strong while the inexorable laws of nature remain what they are'. Later in their lives, we are told, they will recall 'the pathos and beauty' of their situation:

> amid the storms and strains of after-years, with their injustice, loneliness, child-bearing, and bereavement, their minds would revert to this experience as to something which had been allowed to slip past them insufficiently regarded (146).

Here, the sapphic space is presented as a potential sanctuary from the forces which will mould the women as 'the Weaker'. These forces are named as 'the inexorable laws of nature', but the training-school imposes strict and relentless laws of its own that mould them in ways that, far from mitigating nature's laws, combine with them to discipline their desire right down to its source.

On a visit to Whitelands Training School for schoolmistresses in May 1891, Hardy felt a similar protective tenderness for its community of young women, commenting: 'Their belief in circumstances, in convention, in the rightness of things which you know to be not only wrong but damnably wrong makes the heart ache, even when they are waspish and hard' (*LW*: 246). Neither the real nor the fictive training-school offers any respite or refuge from the 'storms and strains' of after-years and, as with the ecclesiastical establishment, Sue flees this distinctly unsapphic-space of Christian discipline and asceticism to attempt a mode of comradely relationship with a new, if obscure, man which has its origins in a more pagan configuration of desire.

It would seem that for Hardy's resistant or dissenting female characters there are no viable or permanent sapphic alternatives to the constricting accommodation of the domestic or marital home. The female-only spaces that exist in the built environment of mid- to late Victorian England – cottages, manor houses, town houses, boudoirs, castles, commercial premises, training institutions – are always already subject to the rules and regulations of a patriarchal, heterosexual 'architectural' practice. The alternatives are provisional, fragile shelters for the unhoused female self – nests, woods, temporary sleeping quarters – and subject to incursion by men. Constituting merely a brief interlude between single independence and marital subjection, the female companionate relationship initially admits the heroine into a liminal, in-between zone characterised by the relative free-play of desire in which she is temporarily liberated from patriarchal control by the death or disempowerment of a father or father-figure. Cytherea's employment as Miss Aldclyffe's maid, and then companion, is precipitated by her own father's fatal plunge from the tower: Miss Aldclyffe's father represents the patriarchal constraint upon the desires of a 'fallen woman', which find their belated and passionate outlet in the maid's bed as he dies in the room below. Elizabeth-Jane's formative relationship with the manipulative Lucetta Templeman is initiated by Henchard's unkindness and her virtual eviction from his home, and Grace takes refuge from George Melbury's patriarchal impetuousness and her husband's infidelity in Hintock Forest, where she is forced into the company, and the arms, of her arch rival Felice Charmond. The death of Paula Power's father leads her to invite Charlotte de Stancy into the ancient castle of her forebears as her companion and, after the obligatory period of mourning, permits Paula's embrace of repressed desires and her active involvement in conventionally masculine activities including architectural design, the employment of suitable professionals and labourers, a deeply personal struggle with religious belief and, eventually, the engineering of her own marriage, all of which directly contradict acceptable forms of feminine behaviour.[39] However, the novel's conclusion lends a note of uncertainty to the conventional marital 'happy ending' in Paula's final comment: 'I wish my castle wasn't burnt; and I wish you were a De Stancy!' (*Laodicean*, 1997: 379). Her lack of enthusiasm for Somerset's proposed 'new house beside the ruin' and her nostalgia for traditional, even feudal, habitations for the modern female self signify an uncertain response to the challenges and potentiality of new configurations of desire.[40]

In the case of Elizabeth-Jane and Lucetta, and Grace and Felice Charmond, an emulative, desirous relationship between the younger and the older woman is threatened and eventually destroyed by sexual jealousy and competition for masculine favour. In both cases, however, far from benefitting from the lessons in sexual strategy dispensed by her older, more experienced companion, the younger woman rejects the proffered model, or image, of feminine subjectivity in favour of a renewed address to the world of normative heterosexuality which, in Elizabeth-Jane's case, involves the displacement of Lucetta from Farfrae's residence and in Grace's, the mantrap of marriage to an unfaithful husband. In *A Laodicean* a similar but more passive and gently expressed rivalry for George Somerset contradicts Charlotte's deeply romantic love for Paula but results in the decampment of the socially disempowered companion to a conventional 'secluded home' beyond the boundaries of the text, where she can indulge and augment her affection for Paula 'by [...] retirement and meditation' (*AL*: 375). Where Tess is unable, finally, to benefit from the sapphic support of her companions, the absence of any viable alternative drives Sue Bridehead back to the repressive, coercive accommodation of the Church to the marital home and the marital bed. Hardy's 'sapphic' women briefly venture outside of the constraints of patriarchal discourse in search of a new accommodation for reconfigured female desire. They experience themselves as autonomous desiring subjects before being coerced into the full appropriation of conventional femininity. To be recognised, the female subject must take up a sexualised position shaped by a socially arbitrated definition of what is appropriately feminine. Any position outside of this threatens her with the undifferentiated realm of the Real, where her, as yet, inchoate desires are yet to be articulated. As Judith Butler proposes, 'without some recognisability I cannot live. But I may feel that the terms by which I am recognized make life unliveable'. At the same time, it is possible to see the potentiality of the indifferent terrain or liminal zone of the sapphic space of female desire in Hardy's texts as an example of what Judith Butler regards as 'the juncture from which critique emerges' (Butler, 2004: 4).

3
Sexual Desire and the Lure of the Erotic

> It is the libido, *qua* pure life instinct, that is to say, immortal life, or irrepressible life, life that has need of no organ, simplified, inde-structible life. It is precisely what is subtracted from the living being by virtue of the fact that it is subject to the cycle of sexed reproduc-tion. And it is of this that all the forms of the *objet a* that can be enumerated are the representatives, the equivalents [...] its figures.
>
> (Lacan, 1977: 198)

> 'We should mortify the flesh – the terrible flesh – the curse of Adam'.
>
> (*JO*: 363)

As J. Hillis Miller has so persuasively demonstrated, the emotion and expe-rience of human love in relation to a larger concept of desire 'is the urgent theme of [Hardy's] fiction and of his poetry':

> The experience of an 'emotional void' within, a distance of oneself from oneself, drives his characters to seek possession of another person. To pos-sess the beloved would be to replace separation by presence, emptiness by a substantial self.
>
> (1970: xii)

Desire itself, however, cannot be subsumed within any rational project of the subject. It is that which cannot be wholly represented in symbolic form: what remains unexpressed in and by its romantic or sexual expression. In 'From Love to the Libido', Lacan uses the term libido or 'lamella' to sig-nify what he calls an immortal self-subsisting life that persists beyond and in excess of sexuality. Indeed, he claims that this what the sexed being 'loses by having to pass, for his reproduction, through the sexual cycle' (1977: 196–9). Maire Jaanus explains it thus:

> From the perspective of the immortal libido, sexual realization is a decep-tion, urging us to an imaginary wholeness with another and tempting us

to reproduce another unsatisfied being who will, like us, suffer from a lack of immortal fulfilment.

(Jaanus, 1994: 131)

In Lacan's schema, sex is 'a false lure'; it is a 'gift of pleasure' which, like language, offers the subject the possibility of transference, which is the fundamental condition of its existence, and the expression of selfhood. The myth of Aristophanes, the drive to seek wholeness by uniting sexually with another, is merely the means through which we repress the ever-present death drive: the fundamentally negative immortality that the lamella/libido (the lost Other before signification) represents. However, despite and perhaps because of this, sexual desire is the driving force behind the subject's attempt at self-conceit:

From the perspective of the myth of the lamella, the myth of Aristophanes is a false lure or a merely partial pleasure. But from the perspective of the singular, mortal being love, sexuality and sublimation are all that we have. Because we are de-immortalized, we cannot afford also to be de-sexualized.

(Jaanus: 131–2)

At the same time, the subject is forced to confront the extent to which sexual desire is subject to the rules of gender, which 'explains' it at every level from the reproductive to the erotic.

Hardy's lovers, male and female, become fascinated by the beloved other, driven by the prospect of pleasurable possession to assuage the yearning at the heart of their being. Their desire is intensified in exact proportion to the unavailability of the beloved object, whilst possession (a rare phenomenon in Hardy) results not in fulfilment but, at best, indifference and, at worst, bitter disappointment and the troubling resurgence of desire for someone or something else. Desire is made conscious and palpable to Hardy's lovers through the erotic, which drives them to locate what they lack or aspire to in the material form of another, who is mis-recognised as the embodiment of what will make them complete. The beloved, and what they call forth in the lover, becomes another signifier of desire – Lacan's *'objet a'* – something that both stimulates and substitutes for desire but which only partially or metonymically represents it. The *objet a* makes unconscious desire conscious – sets it in motion so to speak – but can never wholly signify or assuage it.

For Lacan, the *objets a*, or pseudo-objects, which desire is sublimated to and distracted by, are the means through which the subject strives towards the illusion of self-presence. Lured by the sexual signifiers of desire, the subject moves along an endless chain of libidinally charged images, but never achieves ontological fulfilment. This is the condition manifested by so many of Hardy's lovers, most blatantly perhaps by Edred Fitzpiers, Eustacia Vye, Jocelyn Pierston and Ann Avice Caro, and which exercises Hardy's imagination at the tragic level. Fitzpiers recruits Spinoza to support his apparently arbitrary and successive attractions to women as disparate as the hoydenish Suke Damson, the refined and educated Grace Melbury and the histrionic Felice Charmond, while Pierston's aspiration to realise the unrealisable realm of pure desire in both his erotic and his professional life is constantly undermined by the recognition that ordinary, libidinal loves are what Henry Staten terms 'degraded version[s] of the real thing' (Staten, 1995: 184). Pierston witnesses the migration of his 'Well-Beloved' from 'human shell to human shell an indefinite number of times' until his desire, his appreciation of and search for Beauty in the ideal – his creative, libidinal impulse – burns itself out.

Terry Wright has demonstrated the extent to which the erotic, as it is revealed by Hardy, is 'a "fiction" ', 'a cultural phenomenon, a product of human perception and distortion of the biological "facts" of sex' (Wright, 1989: ix). This is what Lacan means when he says that 'the sexual relation is handed over to explanations that are given of it' (Lacan, 1977: 199). Although subjects experience their libidinal investments as authentic and autonomous, Hardy's novels suggest that such desires are already, and of necessity, mediated by language, culture and other signifying systems beyond their knowledge or control. The object that is desired must be presented and recognised as, in itself, desirable and necessary to the subject's sense of self-completion. This isn't just a simple case of sexual rivalry, although this is a strong motivating force behind erotic desire in a number of cases, but of something less tangible, more suggestive, that the desiring subject may not even be aware of but which is revealed at the level of the text.

Henry Staten critiques Lacan's downgrading of the libidinal investment of 'those ordinary loves in which humanity dissipates and has always dissipated its being, and which there seems little prospect of its ever ceasing to do' (Staten, 1995: 184), citing in his defence the extraordinary power of this lure: for 'the ineluctable character of the libidinal relation to an object [. . .], whatever it may be in itself, has only too exigent a reality for the desiring subject' (185). This chapter will explore the irresistible and compelling lure of sexual desire which lies at the heart of Hardy's fiction, its cultural expression in the erotic and its role in the subject's aspiration towards self-conceit and self-expression. It will also touch upon the fruitful, productive aspect of the energy of desire as it strives with and against the material circumstances and signifying systems that represent it.

Hardy's range of metaphors for the experience of erotic desire captures both its exigency and its fearful pleasure. For Geraldine Allenville in *An Indiscretion in the Life of an Heiress* (1878) a 'passionate liking for [Egbert Mayne's] society' creeps over her 'slowly, insidiously, and surely, like ripeness over fruit' (56). In *The Woodlanders* (1887), Felice Charmond is betrayed by her feelings into making an ill-advised confession to Grace of her sexual relationship with Fitzpiers. At the same time, she recognises, with some surprise, that the 'fiction' of erotic desire has created its own reality: 'somehow, in declaring to Grace and to herself the unseemliness of her infatuation, she had grown a convert to its irresistibility' (*TW*: 218). This infatuation, born out of boredom and depression, has led in turn to something that 'she dare not name' – not a Wildean desire perhaps, but a full and adulterous sexual liaison with another woman's husband.[1] She is distracted and arrested at the level of the powerful forces of the ego and libido, which converge to override conscience, morality and fair dealing to others of her sex. At the turning point of the novel, Felice experiences a brief moment of vision, as if she realises for the first time the extent of her subjection to the deceptive lure of the erotic:

> Felice had never so clearly perceived till now that her soul was being invaded by a delirium which had brought about all this; that she was losing judgement and dignity under it, becoming an animated impulse only, a passion incarnate. A fascination had led her on: it was as if she had been seized by a hand of velvet; and this was where she found herself – overshadowed with sudden night, as if a tornado had passed.
>
> (*TW*: 21)

Her name, Felice Charmond – with its French overtones – suggests the extent to which she seeks the felicity of self-expression through the 'pleasurable gifts' of the flesh (*chair*) and the world (*monde*), and identifies her with the self-seeking delirium of what the narrator of *Two on a Tower* calls 'mere [i.e. sexual] desire'.[2] Her fate, shot by one enraged and rejected lover while pregnant by another woman's husband, is overstated perhaps, but peculiarly apt.

The compelling power of erotic desire affects even those who find themselves living far outside the gates of the world; indeed, such a situation seems to concentrate and intensify the erotic expression of desire because it offer so few other outlets for its discharge. Fitzpiers describes how people who live 'insulated' by the solitude of Little Hintock 'get charged with emotive fluid like a Leyden jar with electric, for want of some conductor at hand to disperse it' (106). Felice uses a similar electrical metaphor to describe how the loneliness of her situation has left her supercharged with erotic energy. Hintock, she tells him, 'has the curious effect of bottling up the emotions till one can no longer hold them; I am often obliged to fly away and discharge my sentiments somewhere, or I should die outright' (*TW*: 158). Each of these appears to anticipate Lacan's contention in 'Of the Subject Who is Supposed to Know' that 'the object of desire is the cause of the desire, and this object that is the cause of desire is the object of the drive – that is to say, the object around which the drive turns' (Lacan, 1977: 243). All three cases suggest that erotic desire is generated and subsequently discharged by a culturally attractive, or adventitious, object or receptor. Grace Melbury is described, somewhat less dynamically, as 'a vessel of emotion, going to empty itself on she knew not what' (53) but the implication is the same: desire is made manifest by and in the objects that attract it. Felice Charmond's attraction to Fitzpiers is partly the result of boredom and frustration but it is also the delayed fulfilment of a previous, youthful romantic liaison that was thwarted by her parents' social scruples. Indeed, their affair is perhaps the most blatant example of the performative nature of the erotic; of how its fictions become real for those who define themselves by its terms:

> [...] the two or three days that they had spent in tender acquaintance on the romantic slopes above the Neckar were stretched out in retro-spect to the length and importance of years; made to form a canvas for infinite fancies, idle dreams, luxurious melancholies, and pretty alluring assertions which could neither be proved nor disproved. (175)

Terry Wright describes how in Lacanian theory, sexual attraction occurs through the ' "mediation of masks", visible images of the other that are filled with "meaning" by desire' (Wright, 1989: 16). However, the visual image is only a small aspect of the lure of the erotic for Hardy's lovers. Erotic desire engages all of the subject's sensory organs. Indeed it is its capac-ity to do this that so overwhelms, exhausts and dissipates those who fall under its influence. One of Hardy's most erotically suggestive episodes is when the scrupulously cerebral Henry Knight first experiences the erotic attraction of an imperceptive Elfride. At first she engages his vision, but immediately following the gaze comes the slow, sensual quickening that so threatens his project of mastery over himself and others. Elfride has already startled him with the intensity of *her* gaze: a gaze which the nar-rator recommends as a perfect subject for a painter. Her 'misty, shady' eyes that 'are a sublimation of all of her' – the blue of which 'had no beginning or surface, and was looked *into* rather than *at*' [Hardy's empha-sis] – draw the gazer in, threatening him with total absorption into their depths.[3]

Elfride's blue eyes, we learn, 'seemed to look at you, and past you, as you were then, into your future; and past your future into your eternity – not reading it, but gazing in an unused, unconscious way – her mind still clinging to its original thought' (150). Knight declares himself immune to her gaze, later declaring his preference for hazel eyes over blue ones (166), but nevertheless, it threatens his composure. Where Elfride seems able to look through and beyond his body, Knight finds himself, on the contrary, suddenly arrested by hers:

Knight could not help looking at her. The sun was within ten degrees of the horizon, and its warm light flooded her face and heightened the bright rose colour of her cheeks to a vermillion red, their moderate pink hue being only seen in its natural tone where the cheek curved round into shadow. The ends of her hanging hair softly dragged themselves backwards and forwards upon her shoulder as each faint breeze thrust against or relinquished it. Fringes and ribbons of her dress, moved by the same breeze, licked like tongues upon the parts around them, and fluttering forward from shady folds caught likewise their share of the lustrous orange glow. (151)

Hardy communicates the growing heat of Knight's erotic desire in which visual appreciation triggers a total, if imaginary, sensual engagement with the bodily surface of what is gazed at in both Knight and by extension the reader. We follow Knight's gaze from the 'bright rose' of her irradiated cheeks, down to the shadow of their curve and thence to her shoulders gently stroked by the dragging of her hair back and forth across them by the breeze. We not only witness, through his eyes, the erotic 'tongues' of the fringes and ribbons of her bodice 'licking' the parts of Elfride's body, but are encouraged to imagine those 'parts' for ourselves.[4] This marvellous evocation of erotic desire combines sight, heat, touch and taste in its suggestive affect. It is little wonder that when Knight does eventually touch Elfride, to thread the delicate gold wire of his earring through the highly erogenous zone of her pierced earlobe, we almost experience the young girl's palpitations ourselves.

It is precisely this exigent, dangerous dissipation of 'being' in 'ordinary human loves', the apparently self-annulling lure of the object of erotic desire, that so fascinates Hardy. What his language makes us feel as readers is the lover's passionate commitment to the drive: his or her sensual engagement with the object of desire and the irresistible, if essentially futile, urge to invest that object with significant meaning for the self. As the object of Knight's desire, Elfride is construed in impossibly contradictory terms. Like Tess for Angel Clare, she embodies Knight's virgin self in female form. While her gaze which seems to pass through and beyond the body signifies to Knight that the body, and all its complex urges, does not exist for her, she also represents the source of the sexual experience and bodily knowledge he desires.

Hardy's 'The Fiddler of the Reels' (1893) is a richly suggestive examination of the lure of the erotic for 'a young woman of fragile and responsive organisation' ('*FoR*', 1996: 139) which operates again not just at the level of the gaze but also at the level of touch and, most powerfully perhaps, at the level of sound. Its operation is vividly suggested by the metaphor of the violin whose feminine shape Mop Ollamoor plays, just as he 'plays' Car'line Aspent. It is important to distinguish here between 'erotic desire' and 'love', as does the elderly narrator of the tale. Love, such as the dependable Ned Hipcroft feels for the fallen Car'line, is a solid, domestic kind of emotion distinguished by 'warm feeling' and pleasant gratification: tenderness tempered by sound reasoning. This homely affection – the sort one may have for 'a cheap teapot which often brews better tea than a dear one' (141) – is not desire. Desire is embodied in Mop Ollamoor, and expressed by his strange unearthly music. It is an altogether different, more compelling emotion: beyond reason, diagnosis or cure. It can supplicate, fascinate, overpower, seduce. It makes the heart ache for something which it cannot name, it can even bring a child to spontaneous tears.[5] It is music with no notes, sound 'with a lingual character' (138) but neither the 'music' nor the 'lingual' sound signify in any meaningful sense. This is the desire that is beyond signification, but which is opened up by the sexual drive. It subjects the nerves to 'excruciating spasms' and 'blissful torture' (151). It can 'draw your soul out of your body like a spider's thread [...] till you felt as limp as withywind and yearned for something to cling to' (141). What Car'line clings too, in the extremity of her desire, is the body of the aberrant Mop Ollamoor, who embodies her deep-seated resistance to culture, domesticity and the regulation of the sexual instinct through marriage. Although this 'musician, dandy, and company man in practice; veterinary surgeon in theory' appears to be what Car'line yearns for, he is merely the player of the instrument: the 'fiddler of the reels' or the manifestation of desire itself. Mop represents the libidinal object around which Car'line's desires will cohere as a result of the giddying discomposure of her sense of self under the influence of his music.[6]

The sexual manifestation of desire in Hardy's work is transgressive. It draws its subjects into patterns of behaviour and modes of operation that override their will and distort their moral sense. It seduces Car'line out of the straight and narrow path of domestic security into the 'mazes of an infinite dance' (140). Although Mop is the beneficiary of Car'line's entrancement by desire, it isn't he who entices the 'London wife' back to her primitive Wessex ways, but 'the notes of [his] old violin' (150). They are not even 'notes', we learn, but 'crowds of little chromatic subtleties' which issue from the ancient fiddle 'as if it were dying of the emotion which had been pent up within it ever since its banishment from some Italian or German city where it first took shape and sound'. (152) The relationship of these 'chromatic subtleties' to the rhythms, tunes and steps of the dance – and to the fiddle itself – mirrors the relationship of desire to its signifiers. Beyond the tunes, the figures of the dance, the fiddle and even the fiddler himself lies the realm of the Real, the inexpressible excess or surplus that threatens the subject with utter negation.

J. Hillis Miller describes Hardy's dance of desire as a 'circulation of mutually fascinated characters around one another, in a graceful dance of crossings and exchanges' (Miller, 1970: 145).[7] Couples meet and part in figures of attraction, consummation, detachment and disdain. Where there is distance, accident or obstacle desire is intensified and prolonged; where there is satisfaction desire re-orientates itself towards a different object. The call of the dance is irresistible: Car'line, we read, 'did not want to dance; she entreated by signs to be left where she was, but she was entreating of the tune and its player rather than of the dancing man'. The intoxication and discomposition of the self under the influence of the dance of desire is dramatised in Car'line's body. No longer 'mistress of herself' she is reduced to paroxysms, hysterics, convulsions and finally an unconsciousness from which she awakes with no care or concern for her behaviour, her husband or the fate of her child.

'The Fiddler of the Reels' offers a set of opposing binaries: the metropolitan and the rural; the known and the foreign; the insistently modern and the persistently ancient; imperialism and the dark atavism which seems to threaten it at its heart. It is set in 1851 in 'an era of great hope and activity among the nations and industries', and the solidly practical Ned Hipcroft is employed in the construction of Joseph Paxton's Crystal Palace: a spectacular monument to national pride and imperialism built to house the first Great Exhibition (142). Car'line is taken there by Ned on their wedding day and, amidst the props and trappings of stylish domesticity, in 'one of the courts dedicated to furniture', she catches sight of what appears to be Mop's reflection in a mirror. Mop's presence in the capital is never verified and it is as if she sees not him but the manifestation of her own wayward aberrant desire – the energy that exceeds the forms that seek to contain and direct it. In giving birth to Mop's child, Car'line gives birth to this desire and also to its supplement. 'Little Carry' disappears with her foreign father Mop into 'the mass of dark heathland' to be heard of only in rumour, while her mother remains as the chastened but curiously indifferent wife of the respectable Ned Hipcroft.

In 'The Fiddler of the Reels', desire is likened to an 'unholy musical charm' that reaches back to some deep, sublimated, almost primitive or pagan energy ('FoR': 150). This is the true desire that the enthralled Car'line seeks to realise through her sexual liaison with Mop but which can never be satisfied or even expressed at this level. Although Mop has an independent, verifiable existence his music is the embodiment, the 'lingual sound' or 'chromatic subtlety', of the libido, the aberrant primitive desire that strives to be recognised and heard but which belongs in the realm of the Real. 'Weird', 'wizardly' and un-English, with his 'rich olive complexion and oiled, black locks', he arrives in Mellstock village from 'nobody knew where', to exercise his enviable, seductive power over 'unsophisticated maidenhood', and the 'unsophisticated' Car'line is constantly drawn back towards the threatening dissolution of self opened up by his music.

Eustacia Vye is likewise caught up in the dance of desire and in its continual displacement by unsatisfactory libidinal objects. The country dance, with its constant exchange of partners and its potentially endless figures that eventually return the dancers to their original position (but not quite their original position, for they have danced with others in the meantime) is the perfect metaphor for the subject's entrancement and distraction by the metonymic sexual objects of desire. The country dance exercises an irresistible fascination over Eustacia, drawing her into its charmed circle with her discarded lover Damon Wildeve, with whom she 'treads one measure'. Lost in its figures, the narrator tells us, 'a clear line of difference divided like a tangible fence, her experience within this maze of motion from her experience without it'. The dance offers her 'tropical sensations': a sweet compound of Wildeve, the moonlight and the secrecy, as opposed to the 'arctic frigidity' of a loveless marriage to the man who once seemed to embody what she yearned for herself (264).[8] Wildeve is the grip of the first law of desire which decrees that what you have lost to another will always eclipse what you have drawn to yourself. In 'a delirium of exquisite misery' he and Eustacia ride the 'whirlwind' of desire in a dance that 'had come like an irresistible attack upon whatever sense of social order there was in their minds, to drive them back into old paths which were now no longer regular' (264). The dance revives in them 'paganism', and 'the pride of life', offering the illusion of hope and happiness to all the dancers, but particularly to the two errant lovers (262). Reason and the sense are hypnotised in the repeated figures of the dance; the soul takes flight, we read, and the features become 'empty and quiescent, as they always are when feeling goes beyond their register' (263). Caught up in the motion of the dance, Eustacia is impelled by desire, but she is wise nevertheless to the distracting lure of the erotic. Wildeve, like Jocelyn Pierston's 'Well-Beloveds', is now just an empty cipher to her, not least because his desire turns back only to her rather than out towards the wider world which she longs for. For Eustacia, to be the victor in such a contest is to experience what René Girard calls 'that disappointment which is called possession' (Girard, 1965: 39):

> She could not admit at once that she might have overestimated Wildeve, for to perceive his mediocrity now was to admit her own great folly heretofore [...]

> Her lover was no longer to her an exciting man whom many women strove for, and herself could only win by striving with them. He was a superfluity. (101)

Budmouth, Wildeve (in an earlier manifestation) and Clym are revealed to Eustacia as desirable and so the 'perfervid' Eustacia desires them, but her desire is essentially narcissistic or, more accurately, ego-morphic. All the metonymic signifiers of erotic desire that we find in Hardy are the means through which the subject strives towards a sense of its own self-presence.

Eustacia becomes erotically fixated on Clym before she has even seen him and she is induced to see him as her masculine other, and thus the means by which she might effect her departure from Egdon into 'the centre and vortex of the fashionable world' (109). It is the mental rather than the visual image of Clym and his glamorous workplace, conjured by the gossip of Sam and Humphrey, which penetrates the walls of her grandfather's house and entrances her:

> Tis a blazing great shop that he belongs to, so I've heard his mother say. Like a king's palace as far as diments go. Ear-drops and rings by hat-fulls: gold platters: chains enough to hold an ox, all washed in gold. (106)

She is linked to this gilded vision by Humphrey, who regards the couple as 'Both of one mind', concluding: 'there couldn't be a better couple if they were made o'purpose' (107). Like Grace Melbury, Eustacia's self-entrancement by her vision induces her to leave her own home to speculate on the home of the new object of erotic interest: 'the old irregular thatched house' to which he is about to return. It is here that she meets, but does not clearly see, 'the soul of the house she had gone to inspect' (115). Clym appears to offer a new 'dwelling' for Eustacia's alienated self, but it is not the modest cottage at Bloom's End that she wants but the glittering Midas palace of her imagination, its contents all 'washed in gold'.

Hardy titles this chapter: 'How a Little Sound Produced a Great Dream' (115) and Eustacia's ego-morphic desire for Clym is induced not by what she sees but by what she hears, and what she hears is not the words he utters 'but the [...] voice that gave out about one-tenth of them'. According to Lacan in 'The Partial Drive and its Circuit', what the erotically entranced subject (or 'voyeur') is looking for and finds is 'the object as absence [...] merely a shadow, a shadow behind the curtain. There he will phantasize any magic of presence' (Lacan, 1977: 182). It is not the object that is 'the support of desire' but the 'phantasy' (185). The narrator describes the synaesthetic moment in which Eustacia falls in love with her ego-morphic image of Clym. So intent is she on picking out his shape in the gloom that her eyes become her ears and her ears the means by which she 'sees' in her imagination the fascinating 'man come direct from beautiful Paris laden with its atmosphere, familiar with its charms'. This self-induced image of Clym is superimposed upon the man who greets her, suggesting that Eustacia is, in effect, greeted by herself, translated by the imagined glory of Paris: 'all emotional things were possible to the speaker of that good-night. Eustacia's imagination supplied the rest – except the solution to one riddle. What could the tastes of that man be who saw friendliness and geniality in these shaggy hills?' (115). The answer to the riddle is that her speaker is not 'that man' but herself in his image.[9]

With her 'pagan eyes, full of nocturnal mysteries', their under lids much fuller than those of 'English women', Eustacia – like Mop Ollamoor – is herself a signifier of desire – an erotic object for the narrator as well as for young Charlie, Damon Wildeve and Clym, all of whom she distracts with the promise of physical as well as ontological satisfaction (*RoN*: 63). We learn that the flexible bend of the *cima-recta* of her mouth suggests the lip-curves of the fragments of 'foreign marbles lurking underground in the south' (65) and not, the narrator insists, the mouths 'that came over from Sleswig with a band of Saxon pirates whose lips met like the two halves of a muffin' (67).[10] The daughter of a Corfiote bandmaster and a Wessex girl, Eustacia combines the brooding instinctiveness of ancient Egdon with the sensual passion of the Southern Mediterranean – more precisely the Southern Mediterranean in its ancient, classical pagan phase.[11] She aspires, however, to the modern delights of glittering Budmouth, whose charms, like those of Jude Fawley's chimerical Christminster, exist mainly in her imagination. These influences and instincts combine to produce her as a 'random intertwining' of old and new, whose combustibility is intensified, as it is for Fitzpiers and Felice, by the constraints of her rural environment which she is condemned to pace with her telescope and hourglass: objects which suggest, respectively, distance and transience.

Eustacia's erotic desire is incited by, and orientated towards, objects that are beyond her reach, and intensified by the gradual erosion of its means of satisfaction: youth, beauty and the ever-decreasing span of her life. As well as Time, the hourglass symbolises what she calls Destiny: the law of desire that decrees that love alights 'only on gliding youth' and, like youth, 'any love she might win would sink simultaneously with the sand in the glass' (69). Her melancholy entrapment within the confines of primitive Egdon, bearing these icons, suggests the circumscribed, intensely solipsistic and in-turned nature of her desire, which manifests itself in an endless series of unsatisfactory signifiers: Budmouth, which is rapidly displaced by her dreams of Paris; Wildeve, who is now merely 'a superfluity' (101) and soon to be replaced by Clym; Clym himself, who could never match up to the 'romantic and sweet vision, scarcely incarnate' in which she first beholds him; and her 'great desire' which is 'to be loved to madness' (69): to be the continual object of the desire of the other – *any* other. It is this 'great desire' for desire itself that will lead her to her own annihilation. Just as Car'line Aspent is played by the 'chromatic subtlety' of the notes of Mop's violin, Eustacia is played by the pagan 'lingual music' of the heath; the treble, tenor and bass notes raised by the wind from the various trees on the heath, and a 'shrivelled and intermittent recitative' from the mummied heath-bells of the previous summer. This 'worn whisper' finds its echo in her spasmodic, abandoned, 'lengthened sighing': evidence, the narrator suggests, that 'she had been existing in a suppressed state, and not in one of languor or stagnation' (52). Having recognised the inadequacy of her libidinal objects to annul the vacancy at the centre of her being, Eustacia is finally lured to her own annihilation in the vortex of Ten Hatches Weir.

The dance of desire also features in *Tess of the d'Urbervilles* (1891), in which the lure of the erotic is a central motif. As with Egdon Heath, a close correlation is made between the lush, fertile, managed landscape of the Valley of Great Dairies and the erotically charged subject of desire – Tess herself. The libidinal drive that masters Tess, the 'irresistible, universal, automatic tendency to find sweet pleasure somewhere, which pervades all life' (119), is given meaning and direction – perverted we might say – by the pragmatic, aspirational, rural culture to which she belongs, and of which her father 'Sir' Jack Durbeyfield and her mother Joan are the tragi-comic representatives, and by the discourse of gender. It is embodied for Tess in Angel Clare and, in a more debased form, in Alec d'Urberville.

As I have suggested, Tess's desire for Angel is initiated at the May Day dance on the green at Marlott, not because they dance together but because they don't. The dance follows the 'women's club-walking' in which the women, young and old, walk in procession each holding a peeled willow wand and a bunch of white flowers. The origins of the walk lie in the pagan worship of Ceres, the Roman goddess of agriculture, but, as we have seen, this 'votive sisterhood' or sapphic space is invaded by the regulatory practices of patriarchal heterosexuality. Angel does not select Tess Durbeyfield, whose pedigree and lineaments fail to help her in 'life's battle' which is driven, among other things, by sexual selection and biological need. The narrator's somewhat cynical comment of 'So much for Norman blood unaided by Victorian lucre' helps to establish the underlying pecuniary aspect of this first meeting (23).

While Angel is able to dismiss the incident from his mind as he runs to catch up with his brothers, Tess cannot. In *The Woodlanders*, Grace Melbury is described as 'a vessel of emotion, going to empty itself on she knew not what' (*TW*, 2005: 53). The same phrase is used to describe the less sophisticated Tess who is presented to the reader as 'a mere vessel of emotion untinctured by experience' (*TdU*, 2005: 21). The result of this dance of desire, from which Tess is excluded, is to begin her education in this respect: to fix her emotion, her erotic investment, on the figure of the negligent, tantalising stranger:

> she did not so easily dislodge the incident from her consideration. She had no spirit to dance again for a long time, though she might have had plenty of partners; but ah! They did not speak so nicely as the strange young man had done. It was not till the rays of the sun had absorbed the young stranger's retreating figure on the hill that she shook off her temporary sadness and answered her would-be partner in the affirmative. (25)

Tess's erotic attraction to the refined Angel, and what he represents, finds its debased reflection in her liaison with Alec d'Urberville, which follows this event. This is initiated by Tess's mother Joan, who intensifies Tess's sense that, because she was responsible for the death of Prince, she is now the family's most valuable commodity. Joan's opportunistic manipulation of her daughter blatantly demonstrates the economic determinants of sexuality in a rural community. Following her violation in The Chase, Tess spends some weeks as Alec's mistress at Trantridge. After her sudden departure, he questions her motives for coming to him and her ensuing regret, and Tess admits that her 'eyes were dazed by you for a little, and that was all'. We are left to speculate about what it is that is so dazzling about Alec. As he is quick to remind her 'You didn't come for love of me, that I'll swear'. Tess assents adding 'If I had gone for love o' you, if I had ever sincerely loved you, if I loved you still, I should not be so loathe and hate myself for my weakness as I do now!' (89). The 'weakness' that Alec incites in Tess, which is the effect of her bedazzlement, suggests that her erotic response to him (such as it is) is closely linked to, if not the sole result of, his impressive wealth and the gifts he bestows on herself and her family.[12] Tess's desire for Angel, however, is stimulated by absence rather than presence and, unlike her response to Alec, by sound rather than sight and by something other than mere material considerations. Ironically, Angel offers Tess a vision of herself enhanced by culture, education and refinement.

As with Eustacia, the ear stimulates Tess's inner eye to imaginatively create the object of desire, which her eye then strives to match to the body of the man. The text makes clear that the 'Angel' that Tess falls in love with is as much a figment of her imagination as she is of his. At Talbothays she is immediately attracted by his voice and his clearly educated opinions on the 'faith of the past'. At first she does not recognise him as the negligent stranger of the May Day dance, but she discerns almost immediately that there is 'something educated, reserved, subtle, sad, differing' beneath the white pinafore, leather leggings and farm-yard mulch of this ersatz dairy farmer (127). The erotic lure of Angel Clare owes more than a little to Tess's identification with him as refined, educated and in touch with a wider world than the Valley of the Great Dairies. It is also stimulated by his desirability to others, including her female companions at Talbothays:

> There was no concealing from herself the fact that she loved Angel Clare, perhaps all the more passionately from knowing that the others had also lost their hearts to him. There is contagion in this sentiment, especially among women. And yet that same hungry heart of hers compassionated her friends. (161)

The primary effect of the narrator's essentialist and somewhat misogynistic aside is to locate the origin of Tess's desire for Angel in the realm of female biology and sexual competition. This is countermanded by her tendency, at other times, to try and move beyond the physical in her preference for a more transcendental form of communion.[13] It is here that Hardy begins seriously to examine the interrelation between desire and the erotic, and between the erotic and the ideal. This is strikingly suggested in her response to the lure of Angel's music, the notes of which lose their particularity of tune and sound and merge with the hazy, 'transmissive' atmosphere of that 'typical summer evening in June' in the overgrown garden. The notes of his harp, though poor in quality, have a startling effect on Tess when she hears them outside, separated at it were from the man who produces them: 'they had never appealed to her as now, when they wandered in the still air with a stark quality like that of nudity' (138). The atmosphere and the music draw her, as if fascinated, through the rank uncultivated garden where her body threatens to dissolve in the juices, mists, offensive smells, spittle, stains, milk and slime of untended Nature. Entranced by the pull of desire, this 'exaltation' becomes for Tess, as it is for Car'line, instant and unwitting:

> Tess was conscious of neither time not space [...] she undulated upon the thin notes of the second-hand harp, and their harmonies passed like breezes through her, bringing tears into her eyes. The floating pollen seemed to be his notes made visible, and the dampness of the garden the weeping of the garden's sensibility. Though near nightfall, the rank-smelling weed-flowers glowed as if they would not close, for intentness, and the waves of colour mixed with the waves of sound. (138–9)

The 'exaltation' or elevation that the narrator describes here is sublime, implying as it does the distillation of the sensibilities out of the body of Tess into inanimate nature, and a synaesthetic mixing of sight and sound so that each loses its particularity in the other. However, this disassociation of sensibility from the body is linked throughout the novel to Tess's eventual physical extinction, signifying as it does her yearning to return to the realm of pure desire before individuation which for Lacan is the realm of death. She describes to the assembled dairy workers at breakfast this ability to separate her soul from her body 'at will by gazing at a star' (135) until 'you are hundreds and hundreds o' miles away from your body, which you don't seem to want at all' (136). Dairyman Crick listens with 'his great knife and fork [...] planted erect on the table like the beginning of a gallows' (135) in a grim, if unwitting, anticipation of Tess's eventual execution for the quite literal separation of the body and soul of Alec d'Urberville. It is, however, Angel's denial of the body, his refusal to allow her even the sexual realisation of herself, that effectively ends her existence. Following her confession of her past to him on their wedding night, Tess accepts his rejection of her sense of self as a 'grotesque prestidigitation' (228). She was one person, now she is another and that 'other' is not the woman validated by his own desire but 'another woman in [her] shape'. Eventually, Tess submits to Angel's pronouncement of her death and his symbolic, and almost actual, burial of her body (247).

Another of Hardy's richly suggestive evocations of erotic desire is the description of the dairymaids, Marion, Izz and Retty, who are more blatant than Tess in their fascination with and by Angel Clare. Along with Tess, they exist in a tantalising, almost excruciating proximity to him but their looking can be done only from a distance, and their touching only through layers of clothing – however diaphanous, airy and studded with trapped butterflies that clothing might be. This heightened state of continuous, and unconsummated, arousal makes Clare the object of desire *par excellence*. They are indeed arrested at the level of unfulfilled biological need, the 'mechanical throwing into gear of the sexual impulse' as Lacan terms it (Staten, 1995: 23) but with no ensuing motion:

> They writhed feverishly under the oppressiveness of an emotion thrust upon them by cruel Nature's law – an emotion which they had neither expected nor desired. The incidents of the day had fanned the flame that was burning the inside of their hearts out, and the torture was almost more than they could endure. The differences which distinguished them as individuals were abstracted by this passion, and each was but a portion of one organism called sex. (162)[14]

As we have seen in the previous chapter, the dairymaids' unfulfilled erotic investment in Angel also undermines their integrity as subjects, as it does with Tess. On Tess and Angel's wedding day, Retty Priddle attempts suicide, Marian is found 'dead drunk by the withy bed' and Izz is 'very low in mind' (240–1).

Angel claims to be in retreat from the world, from culture and from God. His erotic investment in Tess is stimulated by his association of her with 'something that was familiar, something which carried him back into a joyous and unforeseeing past, before the necessity of taking thought had made the heavens gray' (120). She represents his personal portal back to a state of 'nescience', to the Real that exists before signification, which he mistakenly associates with a pastoral, pre-lapsarian Eden: what Lacan might regard as the lost feminine maternal space of *jouissance*.[15] In a complete reversal of Eustacia Vye's conception of Clym Yeobright, Tess becomes the embodiment of Angel's lost innocence, not least his own virginity forfeited, we presume, in the 'eight-and-forty hours' dissipation with a stranger' in London (243).[16] Communion with Tess seems to promise not only a pure, unmediated communion with 'the great passionate pulse of existence, unwarped, uncontorted, untrammelled by those creeds which futilely attempt to check what wisdom would be content to regulate' (158) – access to a Hardyian version of Lacan's 'lamella' – but also a seamless reunion with his lost, virgin self. However, his perceptions of Talbothays and Tess are mediated by the Old Testament, classical mythology, philosophy, art and literature: in particular, the exaltation of the rural environment and its inhabitants by nineteenth-century cultural arbiters, including Wordsworth, the Pre-Raphaelites and Walt Whitman, whose star was high in England from the 1880s onwards. Indeed, with more than a touch of irony perhaps, Hardy added some lines from Whitman's 'Crossing Brooklyn Ferry' to the 1891 edition of *Tess* (2003:153) to describe Angel's experience at Talbothays.[17]

Tess of the d'Urbervilles demonstrates how even our most basic biological drives are invested with meaning by interpretive frameworks that pre-exist us. However, the text suggests that the libidinal investment in Tess that Angel experiences is more than the simple subjection to biological need, more even than the seduction by the erotic fiction he weaves around her. It is an attempt to deny the body in favour of a 'purer' communion with the spirit which is itself shaped by a late nineteenth-century dichotomy of femininity. As such it constitutes a gross betrayal of the human and a denial of the productive, affirmative dimension of desire that expresses itself – however imperfectly – in sexual self-realisation.The narrator comments that Angel's love 'was ethereal to a fault, imaginative to impracticability'. What is under discussion here is not, specifically Angel's love of Tess but the nature of his *loving* in general. 'With these natures' (i.e. natures such as Clare's), the narrator informs us:

> Corporeal presence is sometimes less appealing than corporeal absence; the latter creating an ideal presence that conveniently drops the defects of the real. She found that her personality did not plead her cause so forcibly as she had anticipated. The figurative phrase was true: she was another woman than the one he had desired. (244)

This is one of Hardy's strongest critiques of the denial of the body, surpassed only by his excruciating portrayal of the repression of the sexual and erotic impulse practised by Sue Bridehead and Jude Fawley. Alec's debasing of Tess's body and Angel's rejection of it amount to a similar failure of respect, not just for Tess, but for 'a woman living her precious life'. As Angel himself realises, but quickly forgets, the consciousness 'upon which he had intruded was the single opportunity of existence ever vouchsafed to Tess by an unsympathetic first cause; her all; her every and only chance' (172).

Marion and Tess mitigate the harshness of Flintcombe Ash with nostalgic memories of Talbothays Dairy, 'that happy green tract of land where summer had been liberal in her gifts; in substance to all, emotionally to these' (305), whose 'gleam' Marion claims to be able to see from the 'starve-acre place' when the weather is fine (286).[18] This example of the 'sublimation' of the real to the ideal is, we learn, evidence of 'the two forces [...] at work here, the inherent will to enjoy, and the circumstantial will against enjoyment' (305). What is unclear, however, is the precise nature of the circumstantial will that thwarts 'the inherent will to enjoy', the latter seeming closely linked to the plastic power of the imagination to refashion the material world. Tess is Hardy's most poignant representation of the subject of desire. Alienated from her own body[19] and prevented from realising herself through the erotic expression of desire for Angel, until it is too late, Tess is also unable to express herself within a signifying system that has yet to understand the concept of purity in any other than a purely literal, moral sense (as Hardy himself was to discover), that explains women to themselves in contradictory terms as both the portal to a lost innocence and the debasement of sex, and that allows Alec to recast himself as on the 'side of the spirit while she remained unregenerate' (326).[20] Ventriloquising through Tess herself, the narrator, pushes against the limits of the discourse of sexuality and the 'explanations that are given of it' (Lacan, 1977: 199):

> Was once lost always lost really true of chastity? She would ask herself. She might prove it false if she could veil bygones. The recuperative power which pervaded organic nature was surely not denied to maidenhood alone (112).

Tess's later recognition that 'Bygones would never be complete bygones till she was a bygone herself' is a bitter indictment of a seemingly 'implacable' signifying system that 'explains' her to herself and to others as exempt from the recuperative power of nature.

Lacan claims that in investing one's desire at the level of the libidinal object, the human subject becomes 'a captive of the type', trapped in the endless deferment of meaning that is the signifier. Tess seems at once a victim of biology, a debased class system, historical determinism, myth and superstition and a moral double standard.[21] Tess is doubly alienated from desire in that the signifying system through which she strives to articulate it is itself biased against her as a woman. Judith Butler summarises it thus:

> To desire at all means to participate in the right to desire, a right that the male still retains; although he cannot desire the original object, he can nevertheless still desire, if only a substitute object. The particular fate of the female, however, is to deflect from satisfaction twice, and in the course of the second deflection [...] she is obliged to become a sign or a token of the forbidden maternal, an ideal or fantasy which can never be fully appropriated, but only believed in.
>
> (Butler, 1987; 1999: 203)

Perhaps Hardy's valedictory recourse to the 'President of the Immortals' is not so out of place here after all – especially if we bring Lacan's concept of the big Other into play, which Slavoj Žižek explains as 'the inexorable logic of an automatism that runs the show, so that when the subject speaks, he [sic] is, unbeknownst to himself, merely "spoken", not master in his own house' (Žižek, 2006: 40). Tess is thwarted at a deeply fundamental level. In her case 'the irremediable ills' do triumph over the remediable ones. However passionate and well-meaning her desires and aspirations might be, there is no sense that they will help to mitigate the consequences of pitching on a 'blighted' star.

Jude the Obscure states more clearly the conviction that that 'the circumstantial will against enjoyment' is as much (perhaps more) the result of social and moral signifying systems than any supernatural or even theological prohibition. In its very negativity and bleakness it suggests ways in which we might at least mitigate what Hardy referred to as 'man's inhumanity to man – to woman – and to the lower animals' (Ray, 2007: 35) and insists that such mitigation lies not in the denial of the flesh and the desexualisation of the subject, but in finding new productive and generative erotic expressions that escape the rigid prescriptions of the patriarchal order. In the Preface to the first edition of the novel, Hardy claimed that his novel

> attempts to deal unaffectedly with the fret and fever, derision and disaster, that may press in the wake of the strongest passion known to humanity; to tell without a mincing of words, of a deadly war waged between flesh and spirit; and to point the tragedy of unfulfilled aims.
>
> (*Jude*, 1998: xxxv)

This is strong language, and in this novel Hardy gives us his most negative and traumatic presentation of the sex drive, coupled with an impassioned critique of impractical idealism – especially where that idealism is centred on an unreal conception of the feminine. Fret and fever, derision and disaster are all consequences of Jude's subjection to both the biological drive of sex and his urge to transcend the material conditions of his existence, as is evidenced by his erotic obsession with a feminised, maternal Christminster and Sue Bridehead, which act as foils to his enslavement to the baser instincts embodied in the figure of Arabella. *Jude the Obscure* reverses the patterns of desire that structure *Tess of the d'Urbervilles* in that Jude's erotic investment in Sue is a more clearly articulated version of Tess's aspirational identification with Angel Clare, while Sue, in her early libidinal investment in Jude, seeks to evade the material constraints of her sex and her assigned gender role. As their tragedy unfolds, however, Jude's self-annihilation is contrasted with Sue's growing mental and physical enslavement to signs: particularly the sign of marriage and that of God. In both cases each is caught up in a life-denying mortification of the flesh.

As many critics have demonstrated, Sue embodies the life of scholarship and culture, the life of the mind that is symbolised for Jude by Christminster.[22] Arabella, however, represents the powerful pull of biological need that Jude associates with distraction from his 'dream of the humaner letters' (36) and the deferral of his higher, if delusional, desires for

Christminster and later Sue. Jude's struggle between the flesh and the spirit is embodied in his movement between Arabella, who continually draws him back into the 'mire', and Sue, to whom he looks to save him from his baser instincts. But the dichotomy is not as clear as Jude would have it. As Marjorie Garson has demonstrated, one of the many disabling conditions that Hardy inflicts upon Jude is what she terms 'logocentric wistfulness'. This manifests itself in his stubborn insistence on 'a transcendent reality behind words and signs' (Garson, 1991:153) and even that most blatantly physical of signs: the 'pig's pizzle'. More than any other of Hardy's novels *Jude the Obscure* expresses a traumatic idea not of the erotic but of the pull of sex divested of its cultural clothing: the 'grossness' (as Sue puts it) of the visceral power of this particular biological drive. This is especially true of the relationship between Jude and Arabella.

Jude's first meeting with Arabella shows him not 'lured by the erotic' but, quite literally, assaulted by sex: a force that for him, if not for Arabella, is unmediated and unconnected to any material determinant. Its blatancy and violence is strikingly conveyed by the means through which Arabella attracts his attention: the detached 'pig's pizzle' that so unceremoniously smacks him 'sharply on the ear' (*JO: 35*). For Eustacia and Tess, the ear is the primary sense through which the 'fiction of the erotic' is created: the 'inner eye' through which reality is misperceived and misconstrued. Jude's ear catches not the suggestive, inspiring tones of the beloved's voice but 'a piece of flesh, the characteristic part of a barrow-pig', useless, when separated from its original owner, for any purpose other than greasing a countryman's boots (35). The generative part of the pig functions as a metonymic device here to isolate the reproductive instinct from erotic desire.[23] The erotic is the result of the investment of sexual desire with cultural significance; it is the expression of how 'men and women read each other as signs' (Wright, 1989: 2), signs that ultimately fail to express or fulfil their desire but which lead them out of the loop of biology and into the realm of culture. Jude does not 'read' Arabella in any meaningful way at all at this point, certainly not as he reads Sue Bridehead as the incarnation of his aspirational and spiritual desire, and when he does the impulse is revealed as wholly misguided, if not fatuous. Arabella is fully aware of this, as the narrator explains:

> She saw that he had singled her out from the three as a woman is singled out in such cases, for no reasoned purpose of further acquaintance, but in commonplace obedience to conjunctive orders from headquarters, unconsciously received by unfortunate men when the last intention of their lives is to be occupied with the feminine. (36)

Jude fleetingly recognises Arabella's blatant sexual manipulation of him but only 'as by the light of a falling lamp one might momentarily see an inscription on a wall before being enshrouded in darkness' (39). The imagery strongly suggests the overwhelming of Jude's reason by his basic instinct: the effacement of the cultural sign by the primitive drive.[24]

Unlike Angel Clare, Jude is a virgin in mind and body, existing in blissful ignorance of this particular 'something glaring, garish, rattling' that 'hit upon the little cell called your life, and shook it, and warped it' (13). Up to this point he 'had never looked at a woman to consider her as such, but had vaguely regarded the sex as being outside his life and purpose' (38). Consequently, exposure to sex – to what is 'simmering in the minds around him' (36) – results in a near fatal contagion: 'He had just inhaled a single breath from a new atmosphere, which had evidently been hanging round him everywhere he went, for he knew not how long, but had somehow been divided from his actual breathing as by a sheet of glass' (38). Jude is unceremoniously hailed by what the narrator calls 'the unvoiced call of woman to man [...] uttered very distinctly by Arabella's personality' and by her body:

> He gazed from her eyes to her mouth, thence to her bosom, and to her full round naked arms, wet, mottled with the chill of the water, and firm as marble. 'What a nice-looking girl you are!' he murmured. (38)

Unlike the furtive Henry Knight, Jude's appreciation of Arabella is open and unabashed. Where Knight allows only his eyes to be drawn to what Elfride's frills and flounces are 'licking', Jude's mind and body are totally engaged in the contemplation of Arabella's eyes, mouth, breasts and arms as if he mentally undresses her. He is held to the spot 'against his intention – almost against his will, and in a way new to his experience' (37). His movement along the chain of signifiers of desire – from Phillotson to Christminster to Arabella – is the result of the sudden, intractable engagement of the gears of sexuality that will drive him, again and again, into her arms and into her bed. So powerful is this force that it briefly annuls the erotic desire that offers to raise him from the harrowed mud of Marygreen's concave, circumscribing fields: he is 'lost to all conditions of things in the advent of a fresh and wild pleasure, that of having found a new channel for emotional interest hitherto unsuspected though it had lain close beside him' (39).[25] The imagery used to describe Jude's submission to the urgency of sexual desire is surprisingly violent. He is seized, 'as if materially' by 'a compelling arm of extraordinary muscular power':

> This seemed to care little for his reason and his will, nothing for his so-called elevated intentions, and moved him along, as a violent schoolmaster a schoolboy he has seized by the collar, in a direction which tended towards the embrace of a woman for whom he had no respect and whose life had nothing in common with his own except locality. (41)

The trauma of sexual desire, for Jude at least, is registered in the text at the level of the masculine and the authoritarian – 'orders from headquarters'; 'a violent schoolmaster' – whilst the image of a boy seized by the collar suggests Jude's assault by Farmer Troutham before being beaten (symbolically perhaps) by his own 'clacker'.

However, even at this early stage in his life Jude attempts to recast his most blatant manifestation of sexual desire as a deeper transcendent longing. Gazing at the imprint of his and Arabella's feet in the dust, where they had stood locked in an embrace the previous night, Jude focuses on the absence of her body at that moment rather than its all too obvious availability at any other time: 'She was not there now, and "the embroidery of imagination upon the stuff of nature" so depicted her past presence that a void was in his heart which nothing could fill' (46). This quotation from Voltaire's *Philosophical Dictionary* ironically points up Jude's hyperbolic romanticism. In a plainer version of Lacan's theory of the fantasy of human desire, Voltaire praises man's ability to 'perfect the gift of love' through the exercise of the imagination, as a tendency that raises him above animals, who merely copulate.[26] It is clear here, however, that Jude's idealisation of Arabella is an act of deliberate self-deception: 'For his own soothing' we are told, Jude 'kept up a factitious belief in her. His idea of her was the thing of most consequence, not Arabella herself, he sometimes said laconically' (56). The text is at pains to emphasise that the thing of most consequence, as far as Jude is concerned, is Arabella's intimate connection with that most blatant symbol of Jude's violent subjection to the biological drive – a subjection that will lead to his own emasculation and eventually his death – his subjection at the level of the species. Contemplating the seeming inevitability of his shotgun marriage to Arabella, Jude muses:

> There seemed to him, vaguely and dimly, something wrong in a social ritual which made necessary a cancelling of well-formed schemes involving years of thought and labour, or forgoing a man's one opportunity of showing himself superior to the lower animals, and of contributing his units of work to the general progress of his generation, because of a momentary surprise by a new and transitory instinct which had nothing in it of the nature of vice, and could be only at the most called weakness. (61)

It is the combination of Jude's inability, in this instance, to desire beyond the biological, coupled with the impracticality of his spiritual aspirations towards Christminster, that destroys him. This dichotomy is forcefully expressed in the character and opinions of Sue Bridehead.

Prior to their meeting, Jude regards Sue as 'a more or less ideal character, about whose form he began to weave curious and fantastic daydreams' (90). Following the failure of his marriage to Arabella, he is lured to Christminster by emotion rather than intellect, 'as is often the case with young men', the narrator informs us. The warring impulses of flesh and spirit are suggested even as Jude first gazes on the photograph of 'a pretty girlish face in a broad hat with radiating folds under the brim like the rays of the halo' (78). In retreat from sex, following his brutal initiation into it, Jude weaves his own erotic fictions around the image of Sue until she takes on the role of as a social and spiritual 'anchorage' for his thoughts, but the atmosphere of ecstasy that sustains him blows, we are told, 'as distinctly from Cyprus as from Galilee' (93). Jude's misprision of Sue is closely linked to his misprision of Christminster. Despite his conviction that acceptance by Christminster University will allow him to contribute to 'the general progress of his generation', the text suggests otherwise. It is Sue who puts her finger on this, telling Jude that it is 'the artisans, drunkards and paupers' who see life as it is 'but few of the people in the colleges do' as is proved by their dismissal of men such as himself (156). Following his rejection by T. Tetuphenay of Biblioll College, Jude stands on the actual and metaphorical Fourways at the centre of the city and realises that 'The town life was a book of humanity infinitely more palpitating, varied, and compendious, than the gown life. These struggling men and women before him were the reality of Christminster, though they knew little of Christ or Minster' (121). The goal of the life of the mind should be to improve the life of the body and this is what Jude forgets, most ironically perhaps on that fateful Remembrance Day when he and his family return to the city. By aspiring to what the narrator calls the 'carcase' of Christminster and neglecting the living, breathing bodies of a heavily pregnant Sue and their children, Jude is strongly implicated in the tragedy that, in one way or another, destroys them all.

But if Jude's desires are thwarted by a childlike, impractical spiritual aspiration, they are also betrayed by his all too human and masculine desire for the body, not only the body of Arabella but also the body of Sue, which seems more amenable to erotic transference than her predecessor's. Sue, however, more than any other of Hardy's characters, aspires beyond the entrapping biology of her sex and the deceptions of the erotic towards a life of free intellectual comradeship, and in doing so she expresses, in theory at least, a sentiment even more revolutionary than Jude's aspiration to breach the stolid class barriers of Christminster University. Judith Butler draws attention to the specific gender bias of Lacan's schema of desire: 'Desire is still in search of the Absolute, but this desire has become specified as a male desire, and this Absolute is understood to be the fantasy of maternal fulfilment that women are obliged to represent'(1987; 1999: 203).[27] For Lacan, 'female desire is resolved through the full appropriation of femininity: that is, in becoming a pure reflector for male desire, the imaginary site of an absolute satisfaction' (Butler, 1987; 1999: 202–3). Unlike Tess, Sue negotiates and attempts to resist Jude's appropriation of her as a 'reflector' for his desire, but this results in her eventual wholesale rejection of the body and the potential for sexual realisation that it offers her.

Where Arabella uses her sexuality to overcome Jude's 'higher' aspirations, Sue resists his, or any man's, call on her body – in both physical and imaginative terms – in her own aspiration to better and higher things and her own pursuit of 'self-delight' (363). Hardy seems to have confused himself regarding the nature of Sue's sexual instinct, informing Edmund Gosse that her nature was neither 'perverted' nor 'depraved'. The 'abnormalism', if any, he claims, consists in 'disproportion: not in inversion'; Sue's sexual instinct is 'healthy as far as it goes, but unusually weak & fastidious; her sensibilities remaining painfully alert notwithstanding, (as they do in nature with such women)'. Hardy implies that Sue is drawn from his personal experience of 'such women', but at the same time he seems hardly to know them or his own creation.[28] Sue stoutly denies that she is 'cold-natured' or 'sexless', likening herself to 'the most passionately erotic poets [who] have been the most self-contained in their daily lives' (154). Later Hardy gives Gosse specific, and extra-textual, details of her sex life with Jude, claiming that though they have children 'her intimacies with Jude have never been more than occasional, even while they were living together' (*CL*, 2, 20 November 1995: 99). This contradicts Jude's agonised response to Sue's ejection of him from their bedroom and from their bed following the deaths of the children: 'I mustn't stay? – Not just once more? And it has been so many times – O Sue, my wife, why not!' (273). We may add to this the fact that they live together as man and wife for at least four years and during that time Sue not only conceives three children but also purchases a tastefully embroidered nightgown to please Jude, whom she admits to still loving 'grossly' even after her remarriage to Phillotson. This is a case of trusting the tale rather than the teller and Sue's own term – 'self-contained' – seems nearer to the truth than Hardy's post-publication implications of frigidity.

Sue recognises the need for advanced women of her time to pursue a new kind of transference if they are not to be entirely ruled by their biology and the laws of reproduction. She aspires to a new relationship between men and women, one that recognises 'the wide field of strong attachment where desire plays, at least, only a secondary part [...] the part of [...] Venus Urania' (174), and by desire, here, Sue specifically refers to sexual desire and its manifestation in the erotic.[29] It is the combination of Jude's insistence and his manipulation of her insecurity regarding Arabella that breaks down her hard-won resistance to him. After the deaths of their children and Sue's near death from the miscarriage induced by the tragedy, Jude recognises that he 'was the unhappy cause of the change' (372): 'I seduced you [...]. You were a distinct type – a refined creature, intended by Nature to be left intact. But I couldn't leave you alone!' (362).

As I have suggested earlier, Sue's main objection to marriage, at a time when conjugal rights were enshrined in law and marital rape was not a criminal offence, is that it licenses her 'to be loved on the premises', and obliges her to be 'responsive to this man whenever he wishes [...] the dreadful contract to feel in a particular way in a matter whose essence is its voluntariness!' (223).[30] Marriage, even with Jude, would remove her choice in this matter. In this respect, the civil law conspires with the law of Nature to constrain women at the biological level. Jude blames 'human nature' but Sue, almost in fulfilment of Jude's earlier predictions, and forgetting the example of Arabella, blames men: 'An average woman is in this superior to an average man – that she never instigates, only responds. We ought to have lived in mental communion, and no more' (372).[31] Sue is no more frigid than Jude is an erotoleptic, but the brutal killing of her children intensifies her previous wariness of the free enjoyment of sexual desire into a masochistic conviction that the flesh should not only be mastered but mortified, that 'vain' 'self-delight' should make way for 'self-abnegation' (363).

Marjorie Garson concludes that Jude's desire for a quasi-spiritual wholeness, 'a wholeness which completely transcends the body, does not depend upon the body – is intrinsically unrealizable' (Garson, 1991: 157). For Sue the denial of the body merely grants it a new, more powerful significance which results in her enslavement to both the form and the legalised sexual requirements of marriage. In mortifying the flesh, Sue succeeds in subsuming her aspirational desires even more firmly within it. Likewise, Jude finds himself newly enslaved by Arabella and 'bound in honour to marry her' yet again (403).

Jude speculates that it will be at least another 50 years before a productive balance is achieved between the urges of the flesh and the aspirations of the spirit. Lacan suggests, however, that there can be no appeal to tomorrow to assuage the yearning for a harmonious union between subject and signifier or between signifier and any signified. As Judith Butler concludes, 'There is no "appeal to tomorrow" precisely because this disjunction [the alienation of the subject from the sign that signifies it as such] is constitutive of human experience and human culture universally and cannot be resolved through any kind of progressive journey. An appeal to "tomorrow" would be an appeal beyond culture itself; hence an impossibility' (Butler, 1987; 1999: 190). The implication is that if Jude was living 'fifty years hence' and was more able to realise the full and frank expression of his sexual instinct and indeed his spiritual aspirations, his true desire would still remain 'obscure' or, as Lacan has it, 'opaque'.[32] In Garson's words, Jude would still 'be wanting [...] constituted in lack' (Garson, 1991: 154). Nevertheless, here, as in *Tess of the d'Urbervilles*, Hardy begins to ponder the productive, positive nature of the energy of desire as it pushes the subject towards a more positive realisation of the self within the constraints of the symbolic order. This conception of desire, particularly as it operates in the realm of art and creative endeavour, will be more fully explored in the final chapter of this study.

4
Poor Men and Ladies: Aspirational Desire

> Man's desire is the desire of the Other [...] it is in seeing a whole chain come into play at the level of the desire of the Other that the subject's desire is constituted.
>
> (Lacan, 1977: 235)[1]

> It has become a normal thing that millionaires commence by going up to London with their tools at their back, and half a crown in their pockets. That sort of origin is getting so respected [...] that it is acquiring some of the odour of Norman ancestry.
>
> (*BE*, 2005: 70–1)

In *The Theory of Moral Sentiments* (1759), the economist Adam Smith describes the poor man – in particular the poor man's son – as a classic subject of desire, constituted as such by a force outside of himself: the coercive drive of industrial capitalism. Inspired by an admiration of the condition of the rich, the poor man's son 'finds the cottage of his father too small for his accommodation, and fancies he should be lodged more at his ease in a palace'. He is thus 'enchanted with the distant idea' of a felicity, which he may never attain, that 'appears in his fancy like the life of some superior rank of beings'. Urged on by this fancy he devotes himself 'for ever to the pursuit of wealth and greatness' at great cost to his youth, health and peace of mind.[2] If he does succeed, reduced by 'spleen', disease or old age, he finds it no compensation for the 'real tranquility' which he has sacrificed in its pursuit. The poor man's son does not believe the rich to be happier than himself or anyone else, but he imagines that wealth offers them greater means and more opportunities to achieve this enviable state. What he principally admires is their ability to direct their energies, ingeniously and artfully 'to the end for which they were intended'. Only when he has achieved his aims does the poor man's son realise that, while 'those great objects of human desire' may protect him from the 'summer shower', they leave him as exposed as ever to the 'winter storm': to 'anxiety, to fear, and to sorrow; to diseases, to danger, and to death', and represent a lamentable misdirection of his energies (Smith, 1759: 71).

Smith's poor man's son does not choose to desire in this way. The condition is visited upon him by what he calls 'heaven in its anger' and, as Regenia Gagnier indicates, this 'deceptive' desire is part of what Smith considers to be the driving force of economic progress: 'In his wrong-headed pursuit of the wealth he covets in others, the poor man's son will make the world more comfortable for us all'. He is 'led by an invisible hand [...] without intending it, without knowing it [...] [to] advance the interest of the society, and afford means to the multiplication of species' (Gagnier, 2000: 22).

Gilles Deleuze cites advanced industrial capitalism as instrumental in the constitution of desire as 'lack' (or scarcity) and need rather than as 'a productive and generative activity'. As Judith Butler notes, in *Anti-Oedipus* (1972), Deleuze claims that:

> Lack (*manque*) is created, planned and organized through social production. The ontological condition of a 'lack' is revealed as the reification of the economic concept of scarcity, appearing as a necessary condition of material life, impervious to social transformation. Deleuze thus subjects the entire discourse on desire and negativity to an ideology-critique which exposes the ostensibly private character of desire as the effects of concrete material deprivation.
>
> (Butler, 1987; 1999: 205)

Smith's 'invisible hand' is not supernatural in origin, but merely the self-justifying practices of the dominant economic system of the Western world that later Social Darwinists regarded as fundamental to the evolutionary 'progress' of that world. Capitalism constructs the subject as a consumer who is never satisfied and who strives endlessly to assimilate to him or herself those objects that are presented as desirable in a futile attempt to banish the emptiness at the heart of his/her being. The subject of capitalism is always wanting. Aspirational desire is thus revealed as another *vanitas*: a deceptive lure that falsely promises to satisfy the ontological yearning of the subject.

Smith's social and political conservatism is reflected in the frequent interrogation, by both narrator and character, of Jude Fawley's cultural, intellectual and economic aspirations.[3] At times, Jude recognises that his desire for an education is neither authentic nor original to himself but simply part of an increasing dissatisfaction and restlessness endemic to his class: 'he sometimes felt that by caring for books he was not escaping commonplace nor gaining rare ideas, every working-man being of that taste now' (66). His old fancy of entering Christminster and becoming a bishop was not driven by ethical or theological considerations but was 'a mundane ambition masquerading in a surplice':

He feared that his whole scheme had degenerated to, even though it might not have originated in, a social unrest which had no foundation in the nobler instincts; which was purely an artificial product of civilization. (133)

Jude's aspirations are presented as the product of a socially inspired need. They exist in a dialectical relationship with the perceived desires of others that are generated by a system which pushes on, inexorably, towards its own larger ends. This is not, however, to deny the exigent reality of such aspirations for Jude and for all of Hardy's previous 'Poor Men'.[4] Constituted in a system in which wealth and social success are presented as desirable objects, the subject reacts by attempting to efface the difference between himself and those whom he perceives as better off than him. Social aspiration is one of the powerful imperatives that transform biological need into erotic desire: Jude's desire for a Christminster fellowship, to make it and all that it signifies part of his identity, becomes inextricably linked to his desire to possess Sue, in every sense of that word. Like Christminster, Sue becomes 'a signifier in which Jude signifies himself', an object in which he recognises and loves himself (Borch-Jacobsen, 1991: 208).

Jude the Obscure is the culmination of Hardy's 'Poor Man and Lady' novels, which include *Under the Greenwood Tree* (1872), *A Pair of Blue Eyes* (1873) and *Far from the Madding Crowd* (1874), as well as the shorter *An Indiscretion in the Life of an Heiress* (1878). These texts demonstrate how, for the Poor Man, aspirational desire coheres around and in the body of a Lady. In desiring the Lady, the Poor Man desires to assimilate to himself the social and cultural advantages that she signifies.[5] However, the Lady in these earlier novels is not always condemned to play the role of 'pure reflector for male desire' (Butler, 1987; 1999: 203). *The Hand of Ethelberta* (1876) actually reverses this pattern by focussing on the Poor Lady, Ethelberta Petherwin, who is portrayed as a desiring subject in her own right rather than 'the imaginary site of an absolute satisfaction' for her poor, or even her wealthy, lover (Butler, 1999: 203). Ethelberta resists the desire of Christopher Julian to entice her back to his lowlier social sphere in order to validate his lack of social ambition, and Lord Mountclere's desire to make her solely an ornamental emblem of his wealth. She achieves this through the creative and productive medium of language. Through the exercise of her literary aspirations, Ethelberta projects herself into being beyond the constraints of her gender and of the text itself. Viviette Constantine, however, can only realise herself and her own desires by luring her Poor Man's gaze away from astral bodies and towards her own. Hardy's 'Poor Man and Lady' novels demonstrate how the discourse of gender constitutes the male and female subject of desire in different ways. This chapter will examine the ego-morphic desire of the Poor Man for the Lady and the extent to which her erotic appeal is a product of his aspirational desire. Aspirational desire is a potent combination of libidinal energy, idealised object and distance caused by the apparently insurmountable barriers of class, wealth and social position. It is granted recognition by bourgeois notions of ambition and 'getting on'.[6]

Although Hardy's first novel, *The Poor Man and the Lady*, failed to find a publisher and was eventually destroyed, the basic plotline and some of the material was recycled in his later novels and shorter fiction, including *Under the Greenwood Tree* (1872), *A Pair of Blue Eyes* (1873), *Far from the Madding Crowd* (1874), *The Hand of Ethelberta* (1876), *An Indiscretion in the Life of an Heiress* (1878) and *Two on a Tower* (1882).[7] In *Under the Greenwood Tree*, Hardy's treatment of the Poor Man's idealisation of his Lady appears light-hearted. However, this early novel anticipates the more complex treatment of the theme in *Far from the Madding Crowd* (1874) and *The Woodlanders* (1887). In *Under the Greenwood Tree* Hardy also draws attention to the textual precedence for this particular manifestation of desire, anticipating the productive potential of future literary endeavours dimly glimpsed in *The Hand of Ethelberta*.

Fancy Day may not be a Lady in the aristocratic sense, but she does stand to inherit Geoffrey Day's accumulated wealth and she has been educated far above the level of the other inhabitants of Melstock. In this respect she demonstrates how Dick can consolidate his social ambitions through a romantic and erotic connection legitimised by marriage. Unusually, in this early novel, the difference in social status proves to be only a short-lived obstacle to the consummation of Dick's desire. Dick's father describes Fancy's first appearance as 'as near a thing to a spiritual vision as ever I wish to see!' (34). However, the text demonstrates that, for Dick, this vision comes to embody a particularly 'earthly' ambition. In Rossetti's 'Blessed Damozel', the lover and his Lady inhabit the disparate spheres of the earthly and the spiritual separated by the golden bar of heaven.[8] Fancy and Dick are separated by the sill and the architrave of her bedroom window, through which Fancy gazes 'into the grey world outside with an uncertain expression – oscillating between courage and shyness' (34). Rossetti's ghastly depth of Space, the flood of ether and the flames and darkness of day and night are echoed bathetically in the social gulf between the schoolteacher and tranter's son.[9]

As Simon Gatrell suggests, Hardy's original inspiration for Fancy was Wordsworth's 'She was a Phantom of Delight', in which the beloved is described as 'a lovely Apparition, sent / to be a moment's ornament' but who nevertheless possesses sufficient earthly virtues to make her a perfect wife: 'a creature not too bright or good / for human nature's earthly food' (Gatrell, 1999: xviii). The suggestive effect of Wordsworth's intertext is to emphasise the very earthly, human failings of Dick's ideal, and idealised, beloved. Wordsworth's distinction between the properties of 'Fancy' and 'Imagination' is also useful here, especially when applied literally to the plastic power of Dick's imagination to shape and reshape the 'reality' of Fancy Day, and ironically to Fancy's desire to 'improve' Dick socially and materially. In the Preface to the 1815 edition of the poems, Wordsworth writes concerning Fancy:

If she can win you over to her purpose, and impart to you her feelings, she cares not how unstable or transitory may be her influence, knowing that it will not be out of her power to resume it upon an apt occasion. But the Imagination is conscious of an indestructible domain [...] if once felt and acknowledged by no act of any other faculty of the mind can it be relaxed, impaired or diminished.

(Preface, 1815, 3: 36–7)

Where 'Fancy' attracts and seduces with what *is*, the 'Imagination' applies itself to what could be: 'Fancy is given to quicken and to beguile the temporal part of our nature. Imagination to incite and support the eternal' (36–7).[10] However, the 'eternal' – even 'essential' – nature of Dick's desire for Fancy is revealed as surprisingly temporal and material in origin. Dick's 'Fancy' is the site of an imaginary (and imagined) satisfaction of his social aspirations: the mirror of his own desire.

Fancy's name has additional connotations of delusion, mental image and inclination as well as something fine and decorative.[11] As Dick's 'fancy', she is the signifier and focus of his aspirational and his erotic desire. Her appearance at the window on Christmas Eve leaves him a 'lost man', his eyes fixed on the tantalising illuminated lattice of her bedroom window in an image that nicely combines the dual nature of his desire (38). Fancy's position is one of elevation and power. She represents an educated and ambitious apprehension of and engagement with the grey world of the future that she gazes into. At the same time, this gaze is framed by her perceptions, shaped as they are by bourgeois notions of gender and social elevation. By focussing on her, Dick is able vicariously to deflect and extend his own gaze into the realm of possibility beyond the restrictions of his immediate environment that her gaze seems to represent. Fancy's gaze however is, we are told, 'uncertain', 'oscillating between courage and shyness' (34). The illuminated window represents a virtual barrier between two worlds – the present reality and future possibilities – as well as between the male desiring subject and the object of his desire. Fancy's appearance in her night-time *déshabillé*, illuminated 'to a vivid brightness' by the candle, and her tempting gesture of briefly opening the widow to suggest the removal of this barrier, combines the spiritual, the material and the erotic in a powerful visual image that provides a vivid focus for Dick's libidinal energies. Tranter Dewy's reference to Fancy as a 'spiritual vision' is deeply ironic then, in that what she really represents is the fusing together of the aspirational and the erotic into a material symbol of Dick's own desire. Dick anticipates Fancy's attendance at church the next day:

> 'Perhaps the new young wom –sch–Miss Fancy Day will sing in church with us this morning,' he said. The tranter looked a long time before he replied, 'I fancy she will; and yet I fancy she won't.'[12]

The tranter's pun on Fancy's name, which is not lost on Dick, unwittingly draws attention to her dual identity as a physical woman and a conceit: something which can be grasped and enjoyed and yet remains elusive, chimerical and deceptive.[13] As Tranter Dewy tells his neighbours: ' "God bless thee Dicky my sonny," I said to myself, "There's a delusion for thee" ' (75). For Dick, Fancy combines the spiritual and physical, the real and the ideal. She is a visual sign of his desire for upward mobility, but, as the final line of the novel implies, she can never satisfy his deeper ontological longings.

At the Dewys' Christmas meal, Dick's urge to fuse with the object of his desire is presented fetishisitically – he takes pleasure in using Fancy's discarded glass; touching the lower verge of her dress with his boot sole; eating vegetables that had briefly alighted on her plate; and receiving into his own lap the cat that had lain unobserved in hers, 'touching him with fur that had touched her hand a moment before' (58) – and, of course, in the physical closeness engendered by the dance and the mistletoe. The emphasis on touch and proximity suggests the potential merging of subject with object: a brief dissolution of the barrier that separates them and the possibility of an actual assimilation of Fancy's person into Dick's own body. This barrier is reconstituted, however – both actually and symbolically – when Fancy puts on her outdoor clothes, which are symbols of her elevated status, to leave the party.[14] Dick laments:

> 'Look at this lovely Fancy – through the whole past evening touchable – squeezable – even kissable. For whole half-hours I held her so close to me that not a sheet of paper could have been slipped between us; and I could feel her heart only just outside my own, her life beating on so close to mine that I was aware of every breath in it. A flit is made upstairs – a hat and a cloak put on – and I no more dare to touch her than – ' Thought failed him, and he returned to realities. (60)

Despite his chagrin at Fancy's sudden distancing of herself, Dick continues to fetishise the remaining evidence of her dainty femininity which, to him, symbolises a level of acquired gentility that contrasts greatly with his own rusticity: her glass with 'the romantic teaspoon of elder wine at the bottom that she couldn't drink by trying ever so hard in obedience to the mighty arguments of the tranter, (his hand coming down upon her shoulder the while like a Nasmyth hammer)' and the 'nine or ten pretty little crumbs she had left on her plate'. Her empty chair now looks 'like a setting from which the gem has been torn', and Dick is vexed by a sense of the 'disagreeable closeness of relationship between himself and the members of his family now that they were left alone again' (61). Finally, Dick's class sensitivities are emphatically voiced by the shrewish chorus of his socially conscious mother 'leaving off the adorned tones she had been bound to use throughout the evening and returning to the natural marriage voice' (61).

Significantly, Dick informs a startled Parson Maybold of his impending marriage to Fancy at the same time as he describes the growing success of his father's tranter's business, presenting the news of his engagement along with a business card 'prented' 'to kip pace with the times' (175).[15] The talk at Dick and Fancy's wedding party is as much about money as it is about romance and reproduction, and Thomas Leaf's apparently inconsequential story of the man 'who lived in a house' and made his ten pounds into 'A THOUSAND [sic]' using nothing but a simple act of mathematical prestidigitation gives the occasion a decidedly fiscal air (197). By the end of the novel, Dick appears to have attained the object of his desire and all she symbolises, in addition to the prospect of a position as manager of a branch of his father's ever expanding haulage business, at least one of the extra couple of horses they intended to buy, 'brown as a berry – neck like a rainbow – fifteen hands and not a grey hair in her', an excellent new spring cart and a new cottage at Melbury. However, the delusion at the heart of Dick's belief that Fancy can be fully appropriated is maintained right to the end. Her secret 'that she would never tell' (198) signifies something fundamentally unattainable and unassimilable to Dick's project of self completion. It is also evidence, however slight, of her appropriation of the male's prerogative to desire as a woman in her own right.

A similar exploration of ego-morphic desire can be discerned in *A Pair of Blue Eyes*. Although Hardy claimed to have taken the surname of his hero from the architect Professor Thomas Roger Smith, we may infer that Adam Smith was in his mind during its composition from the comparison of Stephen's father to the rural 'pin maker' despised by the economist in *The Wealth of Nations* as an 'inefficient' worker but respected by Macaulay as an 'artist' (*BE*, 2005: 84).[16] Stephen describes himself as a 'possible maker of' his own fortune: the son of a mason and dairywoman, who left his father's cottage to 'push [...] on in the world' with the help of his friend and mentor Henry Knight. Stephen's architectural training has been purchased from his father's savings. In this respect, both he and his father epitomise the social aspirations of their class. As Stephen's mother opines: 'Every man you meet is more the dand than his father' (86).

On his journey to Endelstow Rectory, Stephen is first attracted by Endelstow House, the mansion of Lord Luxellian, which he discerns through the trees and which he 'keenly scrutinized [...] with an interest which the indistinct picture itself seemed far from adequate to create' (10–11). Stephen repeats the name and owner of the mansion 'mechanically' and stares at it so intently that Robert Lickpan, the driver of the dog-cart, enquires whether he has changed his mind as to their final destination. Stephen's confessed interest in 'the house' is significant and not just because, unbeknown to Leaf and the more significant inhabitants of Endelstow, his mother is a servant there. The incident is prophetic in that this will be the final dwelling of his Lady – Elfride Swancourt – who will eventually become the wife of the manor's incumbent: Baron Spenser Hugo Luxellian. Lickpan's possibly apocryphal description of the meteoric rise of Lord Luxellian's ancestor from common hedger and ditcher to the aristocracy, after saving the saving the life of the fugitive King Charles the Second, also sets a precedent for Stephen's social advancement.

> 'Well, as the story is, the King came to the throne; and some years after that, away went Hedger Luxellian, knocked at the King's door, and asked if King Charles the Second was in. "No, he isn't," they said. "Then is Charles the Third?" said Hedger Luxellian. "Yes," said a young feller standing by like a common man, only he had a crown on, "my name is Charles the Third, and – " '

> 'I really fancy that must be a mistake. I don't recollect anything in English history about Charles the Third,' said the other in a tone of mild remonstrance.

> 'O that's right history enough, only 'twasn't prented'. (11)

Endelstow House is transformed by the deepening darkness into a set of 'squares of light' representing the newly illuminated windows, and takes on an almost visionary appearance for Stephen. As in *Under the Greenwood Tree*, the window is a liminal sign, signifying a virtual barrier between poverty and social advancement for the Poor Man, and Stephen is drawn to the bright possibilities that they symbolise.

Stephen is more obviously suspended between social spheres than the tranter's son, Dick Dewy. A 'youth in appearance and not yet a man in years', possessing a fresh face bearing few traces of the 'smoke and mud and fog and dust' of London, he has already been 'unhoused' from his previous humble existence by his education and training and by the influence of his mentor Henry Knight, who, Stephen explains to Elfride, 'came originally from the same place as I, and taught me things'. Stephen's desire, as he expresses it to her, is to emulate Knight: to 'get richer and better known, and hob and nob with him' (60). On his arrival at Endelstow Rectory, Stephen learns, again from the well-informed Lickpan, that Parson Swancourt officiates at his own church and that of Lord Luxellian. In this respect the Rectory comes to represent a space of possibility between the two social extremes of Stephen's father's cottage and Lord Luxellian's mansion. Here Stephen is able to rehearse and perform both the gentlemanly role and the role of a lover. By the end of the novel, not only is he on equal terms with Knight and his kind but also, according to Mr Trewen, the bank manager, with 'deputy governors and Parsee princes and nobody-knows-who in India' (322).

It is at Endelstow Rectory that Stephen's social aspirations are recognised and given an erotic and spiritual valence. Elfride appears before him, like Fancy before Dick, in a state of tantalising *déshabillé*: 'in the prettiest of all

feminine guises [...] in demi-toilette, with plenty of loose curly hair tum-
bling down about her shoulders' and 'an expression of uneasiness' (14) and,
shortly after their meeting, Parson Swancourt gifts him a spurious blue-
blooded pedigree. Elfride subjects him to the role of a lover through her
knowing manipulation of him at the piano where she sings romantic songs,
including Shelley's poignant (and prophetic) lament for the frailty of love
and desire: 'The Flight of Love', 'in a pretty contralto voice'. With her 'aure-
ola' of hair, accidentally frizzled by the light from a nearby candle into a
'nebulous haze of light surrounding her crown', and her mischievous 'positive smile of flirtation', Elfride combines the aspirational, the spiritual and
the erotic in an image of desire that is forever engraved 'on the table of her
true love's fancy' like 'a patron Saint [...] in a medieval illumination' (21).
Once he learns the truth about Stephen's origins, however, the parson with-
draws any recognition of the Poor Man's desires, simultaneously stripping
him of his pretensions to the professional class and to Elfride's hand and, in
a damning statement that anticipates Angel Clare's rejection of Tess, accuses
him of dissembling: 'He appeared a young man with well-to-do friends, and
a little property; but having neither, he is another man' (78). As 'the son of
one of my village peasants', Stephen can no longer claim recognition by his
superiors and is summarily dismissed as a counterfeit: 'anybody can be what
you call graceful, if he lives a little time in a city, and keeps his eyes open.
And he might have picked up his gentlemanliness by going to the galleries
of theatres, and watching stage drawing-room manners' (78). Swancourt's
suggestion is that Stephen has learnt to ape the manners of his betters not
by studying the real thing but by copying actors in a play. Stephen appears
doubly dissembling: an imitator of an imitation.

Up to this point, like Phillotson for the young Jude Fawley, Henry Knight
has been Stephen's main object of desire.[17] Stephen has adored him, we are
told 'as a man is very rarely adored by another in modern times' (226). It is at
this point that, metaphorically speaking, Stephen lets Henry Knight 'drown',
abandoning him and what he represents in favour of an object of desire in
which the aspirational, the erotic and the spiritual can more legitimately
cohere. When Elfride commits herself to him by the ill-judged, failed elopement, Stephen becomes, quite literally, performed by desire: reconstituted as
a subject through his aspiration to eventually appear before her father and
claim her as the wife of 'a man of established name' (90).

That Elfride retains her spiritual significance in his imagination, despite
her desertion of him for Henry Knight, is proved by his continued idealisation of her face in his drawings of the feminine saints and the Virgin
(331) long after he has prospered in his profession and has been celebrated
by the mayor in a speech at the dinner of aptly named 'the Every-Man-his-
own-Maker Club' (322). Contrary to Adam Smith's example, Stephen Smith's
desire is both productive and generative rather than, as in Jude's case, self-
negating. Stephen's desire for his Lady has transformed him into a rich man,

nullifying the old distinctions of class and locale. He actually becomes what Parson Swancourt mistook him for: 'illustrious, even *sanguine clarus* judging from the tone of the worthy Mayor of St. Launce's' (338). As Elfride unwittingly predicted, Stephen is almost literally 'ennobled' by social and material success (19).

When Gabriel Oak first meets Bathsheba Everdene in *Far from the Madding Crowd*, she is even less of a Lady than Fancy Day. Nevertheless, she appears to him as a tangible correlative for his own desire to better himself. From its outset, as Bathsheba herself discerns, their relationship is determined more by economic than romantic considerations. In a far clearer anticipation of Lacan's notion of the 'phantasy', the narrator notes how the most rational and clear appreciation of an object is coloured and moulded by the subjectivity of the observer, 'according to the wants within us' (*FMC*: 20). Gabriel, we learn, has 'for some time known the want of a satisfactory form to fill an increasing void within him', and the erotic transformation of that ontological 'want' or lack into a material and aspirational one is underlined by his first meeting with Bathsheba, where he sees her 'household goods and window plants marginally earlier than he sees the young and attractive woman throned on top of them'. It is fitting that their first exchange (if indeed it can be called one) is monetary in nature. Gabriel overhears her haggling, through her waggoner, at the turnpike gate and, by providing the disputed twopence, he effects her passage through the tollgate. In the process he not only loses her her point, he also places her, quite literally, in his debt. Subsequent encounters are also tinged with monetary considerations. Later he overhears her wish that she and her aunt were 'rich enough to pay a man' to tend the sick cow and recognises her 'as the heroine of the yellow wagon, myrtles and looking-glass: prosily as the woman who owed him twopence' (20). When they eventually speak, he is aware of her interest in the size of his farm, and his growing desire for her is described in terms that appear more influenced by economics than by romantic or sexual desire. Just as Bathsheba calculates the exact amount she is willing to pay to pass through the tollgate (twopence less than the tollgate man's own estimate), the narrator views Gabriel's matrimonial prospects with the eyes of a shrewd investor:

> Love, being an extremely exacting usurer (a sense of exorbitant profit spiritually, by an exchange of hearts, being at the bottom of pure passions, as that of exorbitant profit bodily or materially is at the bottom of those of a lower atmosphere) every morning Oak's feelings were as sensitive as the Money Market in calculations upon his chances. (29)

Although the narrator is careful here to distinguish between higher (pure) and lower (mercenary) forms of desire, the metaphor of usury implies that both are driven by an enhanced appreciation of material profit and loss.

Gabriel has lived a frugal life and borrowed money to stock his 'snug little farm', and his proposal to Bathsheba is formulated in relation to the trappings of the middle-class life of an independent farmer's wife – a piano, musical duets in the evening, ten-pound-gigs, 'nice flowers and [...] cocks and hens [...]. And a frame for cucumbers – like a gentleman and lady' (34). Bathsheba recognises, and resents, Gabriel's prosaic and materialistic approach, suggesting that as a farmer just beginning he should 'in common prudence' marry a richer woman than herself who could assist him materially with his aspirations and, to the detriment of his suit, Oak is forced to agree (36). It is ironic that the eventual breaking and humbling of Bathsheba by Troy allows Oak to do both.

Bathsheba's refusal of Oak's marriage proposal, and her departure from the neighbourhood, provides the distance necessary to the elevation of desire from the purely material and erotic to the ideal in Gabriel, who 'felt the secret fusion of himself in Bathsheba to be burning with a finer flame now that she was gone' (38). The phrase 'secret fusion of himself' suggests not only his ego-morphic identification with her but also the division in his self-conceit between who he is (a recently rejected and newly impoverished man) and how he envisages himself (Bathsheba's prosperous husband). This division can only be healed through a union with, and assimilation of, the now wealthy Bathsheba, and this union can only be achieved once he has made his fortune. Their eventual marriage also fuses together two adjacent properties – Bathsheba's and Boldwood's, which Gabriel leases as his own and acquires through his marriage, making him the master of the far larger farm that he originally aspired to.

Feminist critics of the novel have expressed reservations concerning the implications of this marriage for Bathsheba.[18] In his initial proposal to her, Gabriel described a scenario in which each would become the reflection of the other: 'And at home by the fire, whenever you look up there I shall be – and whenever I look up there will be you' (34). For a woman more used to gazing at her own reflection in a mirror this seems an unconscionable appropriation of Bathsheba's individuality. By the end of the novel, however, Gabriel's prediction has come true and Bathsheba, at his request, dresses to appear 'in his eyes remarkably like the girl of that fascinating dream' years ago on Norcombe Hill (388). Bathsheba relinquishes her own desire to become the mirror of his and their marriage signifies Gabriel's attainment of his sexual and aspirational desires in the fusion of her body with his. As in *Under the Greenwood Tree*, it is the rural characters whose vision is perhaps the most penetrating: the final line of the novel is Joseph Poorgrass's confused quotation from Hosea 4: 17 – 'Ephraim is joined to idols: let him alone' (389).

In *An Indiscretion in the Life of an Heiress*, the narrator describes the schoolteacher Egbert Maine's 'unreasoning and wilder worship' of the heiress Geraldine Allenville thus:

> The great condition of idealisation in love was present here, that of an association in which, through difference in rank, the petty human elements that enter so largely into life are kept entirely out of sight, and there is hardly awakened in the man's mind a thought that they appertain to her at all.
>
> (*ILH*: 55)

Geraldine Allenville's rank and wealth place her so far out of the Poor Man's reach that she becomes, for him, a figure apparently removed from all worldly considerations. However, although Egbert's desire is given shape and focus by the physical raw material of the beloved woman, it is incited precisely by those 'petty human elements' that seem to form no part of her conception. His desire for Geraldine is essentially narcissistic. To deny this, as Hardy's idealising lovers are wont to do, is to be doubly self-deceived.

Geraldine Allenville becomes the embodiment of Egbert Maine's as yet inchoate desire for social advancement. He literally 'invests' his desire in her. We learn that his father was a painter 'of good family, but unfortunate and improvident' (45), and Geraldine represents a social sphere close to that once inhabited by Egbert's family and which he now aspires to rejoin. His prompt intervention to save her body from becoming 'a mangled carcase' in the new steam threshing machine – itself a symbol of the progress that will threaten the status and even the survival of the feudal system that the Allenvilles represent – initiates a bond between them and stimulates 'an emotion, which became this man's sole motive power through many following years' (45).

Later in church, Maine's eyes become fixed on 'some object before him': 'a square pew, containing one solitary sitter. But that sitter was a young lady, and a very sweet lady was she' (43). Egbert's focus becomes more intense as his view of Geraldine's figure is refined by the diminishing light in the church. The aisle, the pew and her body clothed with a bonnet and dark dress become 'by degrees invisible, and at last only her upturned face could be discerned, a solitary white spot against the black surface of the wainscot' (44). This slow synecdochic transformation of Geraldine's dark body to the white spot of her face, illuminated by the candles, is a visible sign of her transformation in Egbert's eyes from sexual to aspirational object. Geraldine is transmuted from a physical body that he has already 'seized hold of and swung round by the arm to a distance of several feet' (45), firstly to a dark shape and finally to a solitary white spot. Against the black surface of the wainscot her illuminated face takes on the appearance of the moon – the classic symbol of unattainable desire. Egbert's worldly ambition is thus eroticised and idealised in the unattainable symbol of Geraldine's face. As he gazes at her in the encroaching gloom we see her face, through his eyes, continue its prophetic metamorphosis: crowned by the material record of her noble ancestry and social position, it changes to the symbol of that most poignant – and thus most potent – of all compelling distances: death.

Over her head rose a vast marble monument, erected to the memory of her ancestors, male and female; for she was one of high standing in that parish. The design consisted of a winged skull and two cherubim, supporting a pair of tall Corinthian columns, between which spread a broad slab, containing the roll of ancient names, lineages, and deeds, and surmounted by a pediment, with the crest of the family at its apex.

As the youthful schoolmaster gazed, and all these details became dimmer, her face was modified in his fancy, till it seemed almost to resemble the carved marble skull immediately above her head. (44)

The sublimation of Geraldine's desires in those of her impoverished lover and her wealthy family will lead, inevitably it seems, to her actual demise. As was the case with the window in *Under the Greenwood Tree*, the social and economic barrier to Egbert's desire for his 'Lady' is manifested by her segregation from him, and the rest of the congregation, in the large 'square pew', in whose corner she reclines. Egbert meditates on the troublesome nature of a world where such inequalities exist and 'how painful was the evil' when a man of his keen susceptibility and 'unequal history' aspires to cross that vast gulf (44). What is curious here is the nature of his desire for Geraldine, which seems at once subservient and avaricious:

He even wished that he might own her not exactly as a wife, but as a being superior to himself – in the sense that a servant might be said to own a master. He would have cared to possess her in order to exhibit her glories to the world, and he scarcely ever thought of her ever loving him. (46)

This is a purely narcissistic desire and wholly independent of any reciprocal feeling in its object. Egbert's desires are more materialistic than matrimonial: he wants his Lady as a symbol of his own social and financial success. Hardy's curious use of the word 'own' is striking here in that it signifies possession, recognition and an acknowledgement of subjection. In subjecting himself to her, as a servant is subjected to a master, Egbert seeks to arrogate to himself her wealth and superior social status. The desire to possess what the Lady embodies is transmuted into a desire to possess the Lady. Erotic and material desire cohere in a fierce romantic attachment, or susceptibility, to a woman far beyond the Poor Man's social sphere, to provide him with the direction and 'the stimulus which such a constitution as his required' (80). She becomes, in one of Hardy's favourite quotations from Shelley's 'Epipsychidion', 'the loadstar of [his] one desire'.[19] Even when physically before him in the schoolroom later, Geraldine assumes a visionary quality, seeming 'like something he had dreamed of and was not actually seeing' (48).

In the discussion that ensues between them, Geraldine quizzes him, half-teasingly, on his lack of ambition in accepting a position that came to him more by chance than aim. Egbert claims to have his own ambitions, to which she responds with the social conservatism that marks Adam Smith's analysis of the poor man's son: 'Everyone has nowadays. But it is a better thing not to be too ambitious'. Egbert answers in a similar vein agreeing that 'If we value ease of mind, and take an economist's view of our term of life, it may be a better thing' (48). He may be reiterating a purely practical assessment of the possibly inverse ratio of effort to achievement that often marks ambition. He may also be alluding, somewhat prophetically, to Adam Smith's conviction that the ambitious Poor Man necessarily sacrifices his tranquillity and peace of mind in his desperate and unequal struggle to be wealthy.

The relationship between Egbert and Geraldine, then, is couched in terms of ownership and obligation. His rescue of her from the threshing machine is repaid by her objection to his grandfather's dispossession – 'such casually performed solicitous deeds' encouraging in the doer 'a sense of proprietorship in the recipient, and a wish still further to establish that proprietorship by other deeds of the same' (55). The death of Egbert's grandfather however, which is inadvertently caused by Geraldine's need to remind Egbert of his place following his impulsive and ill-advised embrace, cannot be compensated for and places her so completely in his debt that it overrides all other considerations. From this point on they appear equal in one another's eyes: their affection shifting briefly from antagonism to truce, from a battle to a 'settlement' (68), and Egbert is able to deceive himself, when looking back over this period in their attachment, that 'the love that worked within him' was 'instinctive and uncalculating' (69).

Events now conspire to further widen the gulf between them reminding each of 'their differing habits and of those contrasting positions which could not be reconciled' (71). This increasing distance only intensifies Egbert's desire to advance himself and, like Adam Smith's poor man's son, he devotes himself to a 'visionary scheme' to 'rise to her level by years of sheer exertion' (75). Once again, Egbert's remedy for his situation is a curious one. His aim is not simply to make enough money to support an aristocratic wife, but, like Stephen Smith, quite literally to work his way up and into her social sphere – the one to which his own unfortunate father once belonged. As Geraldine advises him, in order to establish himself in her father's ambit: 'You must get to talk authoritatively about vintages and their dates, and to know all about Epicureanism, idleness, and fashion' (78–9). Egbert conflates Geraldine with the lifestyle that she represents, convincing himself that the same 'luminousness of nature' that had attracted him to her will also attract fame and success to him. As Parson Swancourt suspected was the case with Stephen Smith, spurious literary, cultural and scientific knowledge now becomes valuable currency in his bid for social solvency. Egbert adopts the previously condemned habits of 'the ambitious classes' using his studies as 'factors in a game of sink or swim': 'Bonozzi Gozzoli was better worth study than Rafaelle, since the former's name was a learned sound to utter, and all knowledge got up about him would tell' (81).[20]

The narrator questions whether love for Geraldine, or indeed any woman, is sufficient justification for this 'desire to shine' (81). In some of the more cynical observations that pepper Hardy's fiction, educated or 'refined' women, such as Fancy Day, Grace Melbury and particularly Felice Charmond and Ethelberta Petherwin, signify to excess the shaping, performative force of cultural and ambitious desires on female subjectivity. Geraldine laments to her lover that 'to be woven and tied in with the world by blood acquaintance, tradition, and external habit, is to a woman to be utterly at the beck of that world's customs' (88). To be a 'Lady' is to be incorporated into the very fabric of this 'troublesome world', to be 'complicated, exclusive and practised': a '*finished* creature' in every sense of the term (89; 91). Geraldine is induced to see herself as merely an emblem or motif of wealth and privilege. While Egbert is working 'like a slave' to become a practiced and finished gentleman, Geraldine also grows in sophistication, becoming, in her own words, 'a woman who can speak, or laugh, or dance, or sing before any number of men with perfect composure' (89). In their journey from the humble schoolroom to the drawing rooms of high society both Egbert and Geraldine prostitute their desire, metaphorically speaking, in return for wealth and status.

Egbert's pursuit of his Lady is so inextricably entwined with the pursuit of fame and wealth that in losing her he loses all impetus to continue the game. Yet, as with Adam Smith's poor man's son, Egbert's deceptive desire for Geraldine has contributed to his social and economic advancement, and in this respect he is both cause and effect of the upward social mobility that benefitted Hardy and his class. However, in a reversal of Smith's paradigm, Egbert seeks to regain his lost contentment by returning not to his grandfather's village but to the 'old home of his mother's family' in order to escape what the narrator describes as 'that intricate web of effort in which he had been bound these five years' (93). He exchanges the desires of a wealthy celebrity for those of a hermit and, in order for the lovers to consummate their desire for one another, Geraldine must also detach herself from the network of 'blood, acquaintance, tradition and external habit' in which she has her being, to join him at 'Monk's Hut': their 'hermitage' in the woods. However, like Tennyson's Lady of Shalott, Geraldine's attempt to extricate herself from the social fabric is at the cost of her own unravelling. The strain of her love affair and marriage to Egbert, and her father's disapproval, bring about a series of haemorrhages, and this 'fair and unfortunate lady [...] sighed twice or three times; then her heart stood still; and this strange family alliance was at an end for ever' (113). Egbert's history remains unknown.

The Hand of Ethelberta (1876) and *Two on a Tower* (1882) resist the Lacanian proposition that the privilege of desiring belongs ultimately to men and that the desire of woman must be to mirror that desire rather than experience it in her own right. In *The Hand of Ethelberta* the focus shifts away from the Poor Man to an oxymoronic subject – the Poor Lady – and, in Ethelberta's case, the energy of desire is revealed as transformative rather than self-negating, if only in the meta-fictional world of the novel itself. *The Hand of Ethelberta* is probably the least-liked and most undervalued of Hardy's novels. However, as Peter Widdowson insists, it is a 'self-reflexive novel of a highly complex order' (Widdowson, 1989: 157). In his introduction to the Penguin Classics edition, Tim Dolin suggests that

> *Ethelberta* is so superficial and synthetic a fiction that it raises important questions about the artificiality of other kinds of fictions – class fictions, fictions of gender, and especially that most compelling of all Hardy's fictions, the mythology of Wessex.
>
> (Dolin, 1997: xx)

The novel also exposes the equally compelling fiction of desire as it manifests itself in the interaction between erotics and economics in a patriarchal capitalist society. Because Ethelberta recognises it as a fiction, she also recognises how it might be re-written. She maintains and consolidates her position in the aristocracy through telling stories, her 'reserved' one being the story of her own precarious social rise. She achieves the role of a Lady though her marriage to the elderly roué Lord Mountclere, which allows her the financial freedom to pursue her more personal literary desires. More than any other of his novels, *The Hand of Ethelberta* demonstrates how life might be lived as 'a scientific game' rather than as an 'emotion' (*LW*: 89) and, as such, it constitutes Hardy's most cynical critique of marriage and the fictions of love and romantic desire in its almost clinical exposition of their economic basis. While Hardy's Poor Men take an active place in the wider professional world, his Ladies, such as Ethelberta and Viviette, have their 'greatness' thrust upon them – either through birth, inheritance or accident – and must consolidate and secure it through an advantageous marriage.

Ethelberta's position as a Lady is a fascinating one in that it is revealed from the start as a clever performance or contrivance.[21] However, far from masking an alternative *reality* – which is her lowly origin as the daughter of the servant class – her performance is the means through which she achieves or brings into being her fictional self.[22] *The Hand of Ethelberta* exposes, with ruthless clarity, the mechanisms of enticement that aspiring members of the working classes – male and female – are subject to, as well as the complicated contrivances they become enmeshed in.[23] Judith Butler asserts that 'desire is always a desire for recognition' as a 'socially viable person', and the terms by which we measure that viability are 'socially articulated and changeable' (Butler, 2004: 2). In this way, Ethelberta's apparently cynical social ambition is driven by the desire to escape not only the perceived anonymity but also the perceived *abhumaness* of the rural and urban working class of that time, particularly the 'tribe of thralls' that is the servant class (*HoE*, 259). According to Ethelberta's personal maid 'Mrs' Menlove, rural servants are 'considered to be of different blood and bone from their employers, and to have no eyes for anything but their work' (22). This notion of the servant classes as genetically and *racially* different from their employers is challenged, through irony, by the narrator's cynical reference to *arrivisme* at the start of the novel and those who 'for reasons of heredity discover[...] graces only in those whose vestibules are lined with ancestral mail, forgetting that a bear may be taught to dance' (12).

Ethelberta endeavours to maintain a critical and transformative relationship to a set of norms which will withhold 'recognition' from the daughter of a servant, whilst at the same time appearing estranged from those which will define her as a Lady. Once relieved of the 'rubbish of her necessities', she is free as Lady Mountclere to aspire to a new identity made possible through her authorship of an epic poem. Tim Dolin demonstrates how 'as something of a pastiche' herself, Ethelberta 'writes and performs her own multiple identities in an effortless orchestration of contradictory narrative possibilities' (Dolin, 1997: xxii). Just as Ethelberta reads her way into becoming a Lady, she will write her way into becoming the poetess she aspired to be at the start of the novel. Her eventual disappearance from the novel, following her marriage to Lord Mountclere, into 'my lady's office' and the library of Lychworth manor, neatly symbolises how, through careful housekeeping, studious application and the moral management of her elderly husband, she will seek, in Butler's words, to 'shelter and maintain [a] life that resists models of assimilation' (Butler, 2004: 4). Although that life remains a *textual* construction, Ethelberta's new identity as the author of epic poetry is a potentiality. Unlike Jude Fawley's, her existence is imaginatively projected into a future beyond the boundaries of the novel.

Ethelberta's textuality, in turn, points up the fictional nature of Christopher Julian's desire. Indeed their renewed courtship, such as it is, is conducted through mainly literary channels: Ethelberta stimulates Christopher's erotic and romantic interest by sending him her newly published volume of poems *Metres by Me*. Julian presumes that its provocatively placed 'whimsical and rather affecting love-lament' – 'Cancelled Words' – is addressed to him, prompting the speculation that 'thinking me no longer as a practical chance, she would make me ornamental as a poetical regret' (76). The only possible marriage between Christopher and Ethelberta is 'a marriage of [her] verse and [his] tune' (78). By the end of the novel Ethelberta has moved so far beyond his reach as to be 'the brilliant book he cannot afford to buy' (312).

Hardy's symbolic use of houses and other buildings to suggest sites of being is neatly reflected in the 'The Old Fox', where Julian and Ethelberta first meet after their long estrangement. The inn is itself a curiously liminal place: originally situated at the heart of Anglebury it has been pushed to its border due to the reconfiguration of the town in relation to the newly-built railway. As such it symbolises the reversed fortunes of the two main characters, who also 'stand on the border [...] without being built there' (15): in their case the border between classes. Julian, once 'a gentleman at ease, who had not the least notion that I should have to work for a living' (28) has been much reduced. Ethelberta, on the contrary, through education and a good marriage has risen from the working class to 'that gentle order of society which has no worldly sorrow except when its jewellery gets stolen' (11). We learn that they were nearly affianced but, as a result of frequent tiffs and (Christopher surmises) out of pique, Ethelberta married the son of her wealthy employer. Convincing himself that he is attracted to her purely in her own right, Christopher's apparent sympathy with Ethelberta's position, suggests another, less laudable motive for attempting to renew their relationship:

> I think I may say without presumption that I recognise a lady by birth when I see her, even under reverses of an extreme kind. And certainly [...] the fact of having been bred in a wealthy home does slightly redeem an attempt to attain to such a one again. (19)

Though his address is to Ethelberta here, his observation fits his own situation rather better than hers, especially as his assessment of her is mistaken. Ethelberta, with her 'diadem and sceptre bearing' (11), reminds Christopher of his own elevated social position before the demise of his family's fortunes. His pilgrimage to her residence, and his vigil beneath her windows as he tries to ascertain which room is hers, suggests the aspirational as much as the romantic and sexual nature of his desire. Like Dick Dewy and, to some extent, Stephen Smith, the tantalising barrier of his Lady's bedroom window draws the Poor Man to imagine what lies behind it and, in doing so, to envisage himself there. The gradual illumination of each window in the upper story of Rookington Park symbolises the revival of his love (69) and also of his ambition for professional success and social advancement: one that is weaker and more short-lived than either Dick's or Stephen's. Christopher is, we are told, 'a thinker by instinct' but 'a worker by effort' and, as such, like many a potential genius before him, seems doomed to pass into obscurity (67). In the end his Lady's ambition eclipses his.

Christopher's future – romantic and professional – is literally in Ethelberta's hands, depending as it does on the receipt of one of the two letters she composes to thank him for his musical setting of her poem 'When Tapers Tall'.[24] The first, in which she is moved to disclose the secret of her humble birth, founders on the significant line 'When the well-born poetess of good report melts into [...]' (83). The metaphor of melting here suggests her possible dissolution back into the obscurity of her lowly origins in 'a peculiarly stigmatised and ridiculed multitude' (83) should she marry him. Unable to countenance this, she destroys the letter and composes another that seems designed to stimulate in her would-be-lover the kind of ambition that might lead him on to fame and fortune. Julian is twice gratified: first, by an apparent indication of her romantic interest in him and, second, by her encouragement to mix the power of his genius 'with [...] the ingredient of ambition – a quality in which I fear you are very deficient' (84). It is ironic that Ethelberta's destruction of the letter that might have secured her as the wife of a humble music teacher is closely followed by Lady Petherwin's burning of the will which will make a more politic marriage essential if she is to maintain her social position as a Lady.

Before her marriage to Lord Mountclere, Ethelberta is described as being of 'that curious undefined character which interprets itself to each admirer as whatever he would like to have it' (79). Ethelberta assumes an idealised, almost visionary, status in Christopher's imagination, and he is stimulated to a renewed effort in his career and a move to London by 'a belief in a far more improbable proposition, impetuously expressed, [which] warmed him with the idea that he might become famous there' (89). However, his choice of music as a means towards that fame is indicative of his lack of ambition and probable failure in both enterprises. Christopher's lack of ambition will cost him his Lady, as is suggested by the omen of the now unilluminated fan light over the door of Ethelberta's London house, and the 'white and sightless' aspects of its windows, whose shutters and blinds are 'shut tight from top to bottom' (93).

Christopher's role as the Poor Man is very different from that of his predecessors in that his aim appears to be to lure his Lady back to his own (and her original) social sphere in order to validate his humble position as an impoverished music teacher and composer. On his visit to Arrowthorne Lodge – Ethelberta's rural retreat – he sees her and her sisters illuminated by 'ecclesiastical lancet light' in the apsidal-shaped room, and imagines them as 'a delightful set of pretty saints, exhibiting themselves in a lady-chapel' (108). At this point it becomes clear that Christopher desires Ethelberta as an idealised female complement to himself as he *is* rather than what he could be. The narrator informs us that what 'might have grated on the senses of a man wedded to conventionality was a positive pleasure to one whose faith in society had departed with his own social ruin' (111). However, Ethelberta resists Christopher's appropriation of her as the mirror of his own desire. In her contrasting self-presentations as 'Rural Madonna' and 'Lady', she appears to represent the opposing sides of the social border that Julian's family misfortunes have placed him on. She is in a similarly precarious liminal zone herself and, presented with the option of 'a little shop of fiddles and flutes, a couple of pianos, a few sheets of stale music pinned to a string, and a narrow back parlour where she would wait for the phenomenon of a customer', as opposed to the fairytale staircase of Lychworth

Court, Ethelberta moves decisively to the other side from that of the humble music teacher. Julian's acceptance of the disappointment of his romantic and erotic desires is matched by the further waning of his ambition. He was, we learn, 'So well accustomed to the spectacle of a world passing him by and splashing him with its wheels that he wondered why he had ever minded it'(318). A dreamer rather than a doer, he is forced to content himself with a 'sublimated' (319) Ethelberta rather than the 'vigorous', 'plump-armed' (43) version that is now the property of another, much wealthier, man.

The novel ends almost where it began, with Christopher's return visit to the curiously liminal 'Old Fox' Inn at Angelbury. However, though the inn and the landscape are the same as they were almost three years earlier, he is a changed man. The improvements in his prospects have been achieved not through his own application but through his sister's 'provoking' legacy: 'a tantalising sum: not enough to enable us to change our condition, and enough to make us dissatisfied with going on as we are' (398). Two and a half years in Italy appear to have resigned him to his position and he is now unmoved by the sight of the object of his previous desire, who 'lessened in his gaze, and was soon out of sight. He stood a long time thinking; but he did not wish her his' (401). In exchanging the unreadable and tergiversating Ethelberta for the timid, malleable and constant Picotee, Julian appears to have resisted the pull towards Adam Smith's 'deceptive desire' in that, even with his sister's modest legacy, he is unlikely to contribute much towards the collective enrichment of his kind. Picotee's striking likeness to Ethelberta, and her dowry from Lord Mountclere, allows him to consolidate his position in the genteel middle class with a substitute Ethelberta. By marrying a 'gentleman', however, Ethelberta gains a freedom of spirit and imagination that Sue Bridehead can only dream of. The right to desire, it seems, belongs not just to men but to those who are 'rare hand(s) at contrivances' and who are willing to engage in the patriarchal laws of exchange. Ethelberta maintains a critical distance between her self-conceit and the way she is conceived by the men who desire her, and in doing so asserts her own right to the masculine province of desire.

Where Ethelberta Petherwin crosses Christopher Julian's field of vision 'like a returned comet whose characteristics were becoming purely historical' (43), in the early sections of *Two on a Tower*, Viviette Constantine appears as little more than a variable star that has yet to attract the attention of her Poor Man astronomer Swithin St Cleeve. *Two on a Tower* is concerned less with the Poor Man's aspirational desire for a Lady than it is with the Lady's appropriation of the Poor Man – more specifically of the Poor Man's right to desire. In the 1895 preface to the novel, Hardy wrote of his intention to 'set the emotional history of two infinitesimal lives against the stupendous background of the stellar universe, and to impart to readers the sentiment that of these contrasting magnitudes the smaller might be the greater to them as men' (*ToT*, 1999: 289). Judith Butler argues that desire is the fundamental energy of the human subject 'and the mode through which that subject rediscovers or constitutes its necessary metaphysical place'. As we have seen in 'The Fiddler of the Reels', if desire was to escape the structures of the known and meaningful, 'if it were to follow its own laws or not to follow any laws at all, the human subject, as a desiring being, would constantly risk metaphysical homelessness and internal fragmentation' (Butler, 1984: 5).

The 'stupendous background of the stellar universe' of *Two on a Tower* can be read not just as a symbol of the vast class and social difference that separate the 'Poor Man' and his 'Lady' but as the undifferentiated realm of the Real: 'a vast formless something that only reveals a very little of itself' (*ToT*, 57), and which constantly threatens both Swithin and Viviette with this sense of metaphysical homelessness and subjective fragmentation. This is perhaps even more the case with the uncharted depths of the southern hemisphere, which is, the narrator informs us, 'less the historic haunt of human thought' (250). As a man, Swithin is able to negotiate his subjective relationship to this vast formlessness through the translation into human meaning of one infinitesimally tiny aspect of it: initially, the study of a perceived periodicity in the so-called irregularity of one particular variable star, and later translating what to the unpractised eye might seem like 'a new arrangement of ordinary points of light' in the southern hemisphere into 'a treatise which should possess some scientific utility' (249). Swithin's 'discovery' represents the metonymic object of desire that will sustain him in the face of the abyss of the Real. The discovery that his theory had been published some six weeks earlier strikes at the very heart of his integrity, resulting in an immediate 'wild wish for annihilation' in the young man, who attempts suicide by exposure to the pitiless March rain. The 'strenuous wish to live' is re-stimulated in him by the advent of a comet that serves as a new focus for his desire, leading him away from the 'the bottomless abyss of death' to re-orient himself in relation to the 'unfathomable blue ocean' of space (67). It is here that the perceptible effects of the shaping force of gender on the articulation of desire are most clearly felt.

In *A Pair of Blue Eyes*, Elfride Swancourt muses on what she sees as the fundamental difference between men and women and in the process makes a virtue out of a necessity: 'I am content to build happiness on any accidental basis that may lie near at hand' she tells her lover Stephen Smith, 'You are for making a world to suit your happiness' (1912: 64). Geraldine Allencourt informs Egbert Maine that to be a Lady is to be woven and tied into the fabric of the world to an extent that a man – even a poor man – can only imagine. Doubly constrained by her gender, her class and her subjection to her husband's wishes, Viviette is immured at Welland House, languishing for the want of 'something to do, cherish or suffer for' (22). At the same time, like Felice Charmond, her rural isolation leaves her with frustratingly few outlets for this pent-up energy. Such a state of 'suspended pathos' the narrator informs us, in a passage that was cut from the 1895 and later editions of the novel, 'finds its remedy in settling on the first intrusive shape that happens to be reasonably well organized for the purpose, disregarding social and other minor accessories' (84). Swithin appears to Viviette as a legitimate object for her surreptitious desires, providing her with something to do – in the vicarious pursuit of astronomy – as well as something to cherish, and eventually suffer for in the form of his young and sexually attractive person. Through the appropriation of his body, which she does bit by bit, beginning with the purloined golden curl, Viviette also appropriates the phallic tools of desire: the tower (which is already hers in name) and Swithin's telescope, using her wealth to purchase a better lens for it. However, simply by virtue of his gender, the Poor Man is able to escape and evade 'the trammelling body', in every sense of the word, and sets his sights on the more ambitious prospect of astronomical fame. Through his equatorial (another enabling love-gift from his Lady), Swithin is able to 'decompose' the 'hybrid suns, fire-fogs, floating nuclei, globes that flew in groups like swarms of bees', revealing them as beginnings of new phenomena rather than the ends of old ones (250). However, while Swithin's desire is incited by the distance of the stars, Viviette's is stimulated by the distance created by his 'mental' (and initially physical) 'inaccessibility'. To her, the bright insistence of the planet Jupiter suggests only the immediate earthly joys of love and youth; for him, it exists as a preliminary to the exploration of vaster universes beyond the immediate solar system.

As a woman of her time, Viviette's subjectivity depends upon being recognised as an object of desire by Swithin. Her task is to refocus his gaze away from the stars in the heavens and into the stars of her eyes. Swithin's sudden romantic and erotic recognition of Viviette is a classic example of how the object of desire must be revealed as desirable in order for the human subject to recognise it as such. At the same time his deluded 'fancy' for Viviette is ruthlessly exposed as an example of the illusory inherent affinity between desire and its object. Overhearing the labourers gossip at the base of the tower about himself and Viviette, the scales fall from his eyes and, in anticipation of Jude Fawley, the virgin Swithin is assailed by the 'new and [...] indescribable idea' of sexual desire, which leads him, temporarily, to abandon his astronomical aspirations for 'the better heaven beneath' (81). As Felice Charmond discovered, the specification of sexual desire in language sets in motion a process in which subjects are forced to reiterate that desire in terms whose meanings pre-date them and which make up (quite literally) the fiction of romantic and erotic love. Viviette also finds herself impelled by the momentum of the language of sexual desire: 'As the words in which a thought is expressed develop a further thought, so did the fact of her having got so far influence her to go further', and she finds herself drawn to the tower where Swithin is seemingly against her will (26). Caught up in this discourse, she is astonished to discover how it forces her to articulate herself. Having penned and delivered an impassioned and wistful note to Swithin, she declares: 'What could have possessed me to write in that way!' (43). Later, in another passage that was deleted from the 1895 and subsequent editions, Swithin participates in a comparable moment of self-interrogation during which his desire is similarly formulated: 'The first word of self-communing about her in this aspect begot a second, and the second a third, and so on to the end of the chapter of development which makes up the growth of a love' (84). Swithin is aware of the inadequacy of the terms available to him:

'What's the use of saying, for instance, as I have just said, that I give myself entirely to you, and shall be yours always, – that you have my devotion, my highest homage? Those words have been used so frequently in a flippant manner that honest use of them is not distinguishable from the unreal.' He turned to her, and added, smiling, 'Your eyes are to be my stars for the future.'

'Yes, I know it, – I know it, and all you would say!' [...] she replied. (88)

Viviette, however, becomes literally undone by her desire which seeks to assert itself outside of the conventional marital formulation. Unable to give a name to her sexual and emotional relationship with him, she is unable to give a name to herself: 'Viviette what? She exclaimed to herself hopelessly, as she flung down the pen' (191).[25]

In common with *The Hand of Ethelberta, Two on a Tower* offers an interesting variant on Hardy's 'Poor Man and Lady' plot in relation to the compulsion of desire and its manifestation in its objects. Impoverished by her first husband's fecklessness, and morally compromised by false reports of his death, Viviette is no longer able to provide Swithin with a spiritual image upon which to graft the potent combination of libidinal and aspirational energy that will advance him personally and professionally. Had she retained her fortune she might have retained this role, as she unwittingly prophesies early in their relationship when she teases him that having lost her 'glory [...] and [being] poorer than my tenants, and can no longer buy telescopes [...] I fear I have lost the little hold I once had over you' (76). Rather than symbolising what Swithin aspires to, in terms of wealth and social advancement, Viviette becomes merely a tantalising distraction from his larger and wider ambitions. It is Swithin himself who debunks the 'great fallacy' that 'an ardent love serves as a stimulus to win the loved one by patient toil' (96). The satisfaction of his bodily and emotional needs leads him to assert another ego-morphic object of desire, quite literally over her dead body: the chance to study the transit of Venus aided and abetted by Tabitha Lark, who skirts the phallic tower and whose education will potentially alter relationships between men and women irrevocably. Desire is experienced vicariously by Viviette. Sublimated into financial assistance, sexual need and maternal instinct, desire results in her 'giving birth' to Swithin, metaphorically – in terms of his astronomical career – and almost literally in the form of his golden-haired son. Although the boy's father may not have literally 'gone to heaven' (256), as he has been told, he is certainly well-acquainted with the astronomical 'heavens' thanks to Viviette's emotional, sexual and financial support. Tabitha Lark also approaches the tower to support Swithin, but with a trained intellect rather than inherited wealth. However, despite the narrator's arch description of her as having 'joined the phalanx of Wonderful Women who have sternly resolved to eclipse masculine genius altogether and humiliate the brutal sex to the dust' (256), it is clear that Tabitha's role, for now at least, will be confined to that of assistant and amanuensis.

Interestingly, the limitations placed on Viviette's and Tabitha's desires by the proscriptions of gender are challenged by the futuristic vision of a Comtean new Humanism, in which sexual and aspirational desire might be redirected towards 'benevolence' as an alternative to what the narrator calls 'mere desire' between man and woman (215).[26] This offers an intriguing vision of desire as a creative and productive force, as opposed to its negative self-denial as constituted by the self-justifying practices of an economic system that is built on scarcity, want, consumption and envy. The next chapter will explore how Hardy's female characters seek ways of articulating their desires by 'inhabiting' – literally taking up their abode – in the dress and bodily gestures of those for whom desire is not so proscribed: men.

5
As You Like It: Cross-Dressing and the Gendered Expression of Desire

> Fantasy is what establishes the possible in excess of the real; it points [...] elsewhere, and when it is embodied, it brings the elsewhere home.
>
> (Butler, 2004: 217)

In *Thomas Hardy Writing Dress* (2011), Simon Gatrell notes Ethelberta's melodramatic and sensational tale of cross-dressing: one that she tells so well that her would-be lover Christopher Julian is convinced that it must have actually happened. Gatrell comments:

> This is not quite so unintelligent a conclusion as it appears out of context; Hardy has one of the newspaper reviewers of her first public performance make the point that its chief interest lay in the success of 'the method whereby the teller identifies herself with the leading character in the story'.
>
> (Gatrell, 2011: 143)

He concludes that Ethelberta's narrative may be regarded as 'as a kind of wish-fulfilment; throughout the novel Hardy emphasizes that she has to forge a path for herself and her family in a society structured and ruled by men' (144).[1] In taking on her father's role in providing for her family, and managing to outmanoeuvre her suitors in the marriage game by skilfully playing the trump cards in her 'hand', Ethelberta's desire to live 'in excess of the real', in Butler's terms, leads her to engage in various forms of 'transgression', or 'going beyond the limits' in which she crosses classes, genders and, most strikingly perhaps, the line between what is real and what is possible. Her fantastical 'self-fashioning' in her life and in her art is the means by which Ethelberta 'brings the elsewhere home' (Butler, 2004: 217).

Lacan barely engages with the issue of gendered desire except to comment on the difficulty of the feminine position as an object of exchange in a patriarchal system, and a sign or object of masculine desire. His statement that 'a woman is a symptom'[2] is helpfully clarified by Dylan Evans: 'a woman is a symptom *of a man*, in the sense that a woman can only ever enter the psychic economy of men as a fantasy object (a), the cause of their desire' (Evans, 1996; 2005: 221). Jacqueline Rose is more specific: 'As the place onto which lack is projected, and through which it is simultaneously disavowed, woman is a "symptom" for the man'. As such, 'the woman' does not exist except as a signifier of the 'fantastic place' of both difference and loss: of what man (and woman) has renounced in their entry into the symbolic order. Lacan does not argue that woman has some privileged access to a primal libidinal *jouissance* of her own, for all subjects function only through individuation in language and there is no femininity outside it. However, while all speaking subjects are induced to position themselves on one side or other of the gender division 'anyone can cross over and inscribe themselves on the opposite side from that to which they are anatomically destined'. As Jacqueline Rose suggests, this shifts the concept of bisexuality away from Freud's notion of an undifferentiated sexuality prior to individuation in the symbolic order 'to the availability to all subjects of both positions in relation to that difference itself' (Mitchell and Rose, 1985: 49).[3]

If the subject is a conceit in language, and language a signifying system within a patriarchal order, according to Lacan's schema of desire, women who invest in the signifier 'I' will find themselves doubly displaced by the very system that brings them into being. Judith Butler notes that for Lacan 'The "double-alienation" of the woman is thus a double alienation from desire itself; the woman learns to embody the promise of a return to a pre-oedipal pleasure, and to limit her own desire to those gestures that effectively mirror [man's] desire as absolute.' For Lacan, the differentiation of genders must be understood as a difference between those with the privilege to desire and those who are denied it (Butler, 1987; 1999: 203). As I suggest in Chapter 4, Angel Clare's conception of Tess as the embodiment of and the means of access to 'the great passionate pulse of existence, unwarped, uncontorted, untrammelled' may be read in these terms (*Td'U*: 158).

Slavoj Žižek insists that, for Lacan, psychoanalysis

> does not show an individual the ways to accommodate him- or herself to the demands of social reality; instead it explains how something like 'reality' constitutes itself in the first place. It does not merely enable a human being to accept the repressed truth about him- or herself; it explains how the dimension of truth emerges in human reality.
>
> (Žižek, 2006: 3)

If, as Michel Foucault explains it, truth is a function of discourses which work through the operation of language, then it is at the level of language that changes in 'human reality' may be effected. For Elizabeth Grosz,

Lacan demonstrates how women are constructed by negative, phallocentric definitions by and in a culture whose fictions and narratives are neither definitive nor incorrigible. This is because language itself 'is inherently open to new meanings, reinterpretations, recontextualisations that are capable, by deferred action, of giving it meaning other than that intended' (Grosz, 1990: 189). This chapter will focus on how, through various forms of 'crossing over', or self-embodiment through and against the available signs of class, gender and race, the creative potential of language – in its broadest sense – is harnessed in the service of new and radical articulations of women's desire. Using Marjorie Garber's concept of the 'third space', I argue that Hardy's cross-dressed characters strive to inhabit a new form of human reality in which they might become symptoms of their own desire.

Dress is one of the ways through which the female subject expresses herself and seeks recognition. It is also a means of subverting or evading recognition, provoking misrecognition or a refusal to recognise: a *méconnaissance*. The subject 'invests' herself in, or 'inhabits', assigned subject positions and these very terms contain within them the vocabulary of dress. 'Inhabit', meaning 'to dwell in', is formed from 'habit' among whose meanings are 'to attire' and 'habited' (from 1807), signifying 'clothed or dressed'. To 'inhabit' is to 'take up one's abode in', to be signified by, one's outer appearance. 'Invest' – 'to clothe' or 'to cover as a garment does' – has a supplementary meaning of 'to endow with power, authority or privilege' (*SOED*). Clothing, particularly in the period in which Hardy was writing, is a mode through which the body speaks itself masculine or feminine, upper or working-class, empowered or disempowered. Gatrell goes further in surmising: 'do some clothes not shape or reshape the body, make the body in their own image, so that the connection [between them] is stronger than the separation?' (Gatrell, 2011: 3). If clothes are inseparable from the self and 'give a visible aspect to consciousness itself' then investing in the clothing of the sex (and in Ethelberta's case the class) which is the more privileged subject of desire offers a woman the opportunity to inhabit that subject position herself.[4] This chapter will focus specifically on the articulation of proscribed female desire by the crossed-dressed female characters of Eustacia Vye in *The Return of the Native* (1878), Lizzy Newberry in 'The Distracted Preacher' (*Wessex Tales*, 1879/88), Ella Marchmill in 'An Imaginative Woman' (*Life's Little Ironies*, 1894) and Sue Bridehead in *Jude the Obscure* (1895).

As recent theorists on transvestism have suggested (Garber, 1992; Suthrell, 2004), clothing is one of the many forms through which identity and self-image are articulated. The choices individuals make regarding their dress can fix them securely into an assigned gender space or, conversely, can provide the means through which gender identity can be experimented with: 'slipped on and off', but also *inhabited* in a deeper, more meaningful sense (Suthrell, 2004: 3). Charlotte Suthrell indicates how clothing can function as an 'objectification' of the problematic questions of sex, gender and sexuality as well as of the limits to and constraints on the expression of desire in the abstract sense. The impulse to cross-dress is regarded as arising, primarily, from the need to articulate desires deemed inappropriate or inapplicable to an individual's assigned gender role. Cross-dressing allows the construction of an alternative identity and also, more radically, it offers a passport into an otherwise interdicted realm of emotional, psychological and sometimes sexual self-expression: 'to enter into the clothing of the opposite sex is as close as one can become [without surgical intervention] to *being* one of that sex; to participate in activities which would otherwise be proscribed'. 'What we wear on our bodies becomes part of the transactional relationship we have with the world' and can indicate not only how we wish to present ourselves but also the group with which we wish to associate (Suthrell, 2004: 8).

The term *cross*-dressing (*trans*-vestism) implies a movement from one realm to another.[5] It also suggests a transitional, liminal space somewhere between the opposite ends of the gender continuum, a space within which the dictates of birth-sex and assigned gender may be, if only temporarily, evaded: what Marjorie Garber defines as a 'mode of articulation, a way of describing a space of possibility': a 'third space'. Transvestism challenges and deconstructs the apparently stable and harmonious 'binary symmetry' of gender, which is itself a 'fiction of complementarity' (Garber, 1992; 1997: 11–12). It reflects 'shades of difference and similarity' (Lacquer, 1990: 21). In each of the cases from Hardy's fiction discussed here, 'drag' offers the potential for a female character to take up and deploy a different set of received interpretations of the body, temporarily freeing her from the constraints of femininity without fully inscribing her in those of masculinity. It also allows her to inhabit, experience and express desires that are deemed inappropriate to her assigned gender role; to become the subject rather than the object of desire. Like Madeline de Maupin in Théophile Gautier's iconic transvestite novel *Mademoiselle de Maupin*, the cross-dressed character is 'no longer a woman but not yet a man' (Gautier, 1835; 2005: 268) and thus inhabits a new liminal subject position *between* the sexes – a performative hermaphroditism – from which she experiences, articulates and sometimes elicits desires which threaten and undermine the acceptable sexual codes.[6]

Hardy's novels also expose and critique the means by which the woman is re-inscribed into her 'proper' role and, in the case of Eustacia, Ella and Sue, the devastating effect the re-gendering of desire has on her self-conception. Intertextual references to Ovid's *Metamorphoses* in *The Return of the Native* and *Jude the Obscure* reinforce the notion of the power of myth and fantasy to transform reality. In *Jude the Obscure*, references to the figure of Ganymede from classical mythology echo Hardy's fascination with the character of Rosalind/Ganymede from Shakespeare's *As You Like It*, further complicating the relationship of sex to desire. In each case the discourse of the heterosexual erotic is revealed as instrumental in re-inscribing women more firmly in their prescribed gender role. At the same time, gender is revealed as a fictional or textual construct that is open to resistance and revision. The creative and productive liminality of the cross-dressed woman, as well as the ontological challenge of being outside recognised gender forms, is suggested in these novels though the trope of water. In addition to its fluid, life-giving potential, water is a dangerous medium symbolising the threat to the subjective investment of those whose desires extend beyond the security of their assigned gender role.

Ovid's tale of Hermaphroditus and Salmacis recounts the creation of the first hermaphrodite. The metamorphosis takes place in the pool of the nymph Salmacis, whose fountain was believed to have the power to make men effeminate.[7] Although the myth of Ovid is concerned with the feminisation of the 15-year-old Hermaphroditus (Atlantiades), his transformation is brought about by Salmacis's desire for his body – her desire to possess him erotically and also to arrogate his masculinity for her own purposes. Both are transformed by the 'fast embrace': 'their limbs were knit, they two were two no more, nor man, nor woman – one body then that neither seemed and both' (Ovid, 1977: 4: 104). Grace Tiffany has drawn attention to how, in classical myth, water is the symbolic medium associated with androgyny in that it suggests the fluid, liminal position from which the androgyne can both connect with and separate him/herself from his/her beloved (Tiffany, 1995). In *The Return of the Native*, 'The Distracted Preacher', *Jude the Obscure* and 'An Imaginative Woman', water is closely associated with the 'space of possibility' opened up when women assume the androgynous role by adopting the dress of the opposite sex. However, these texts also register the danger as well as the possibility inherent in this more fluid concept of gendered desire.

As I suggested in Chapter 3, Eustacia Vye's extravagant dream of dancing 'to wondrous music' with a silver knight is the result of her fantastic passion for a man she has never met, but who appeals to her as the means by which she may effect an escape from Egdon Heath, which is denied to her as a woman. The dual plunge of Eustacia and her dream knight into 'one of the pools of the heath' echoes that of Hermaphroditus and Salmacis into the nymph's pool, and the erotically charged moment of the embrace between Eustacia and the mystery knight the conjugal embrace of the mythical pair: ' "It must be here," said the voice by her side, and blushingly looking up she saw him removing his casque to kiss her' (117).

However, before this embrace is accomplished, Eustacia's dream is rudely broken by the maidservant opening the window shutter downstairs: 'there was a cracking noise and his figure fell into fragments like a pack of cards'. This noise demonstrates the dream-shattering incursion into Eustacia's imaginative life of the domestic and the practical systems that regulate class and gender identity, and sets the pattern for her re-inscription into the feminine realm of suppressed and vicarious desire. Convinced that her mysterious knight in shining armour 'was meant for Mr Yeobright', Eustacia develops what the narrator calls 'a fancy' for the unknown man and ponders how she might meet him without compromising her 'maidenly' pride and dignity. As I have suggested, the knight/Clym Yeobright with whom Eustacia fancies herself in love is a self-projection; a masculinised image of herself which enjoys the freedom, glamour and material comforts that she is denied. Entranced by the sound of Clym's voice, and frustrated by the conventional 'tender schemes' (118) developed for meeting members of the opposite sex: frequent walks upon the hills and a probably profitless attendance at the Christmas Day church service, Eustacia adopts a more daring expedient by taking the role of the Turkish knight in the Christmas Eve Mummer's performance of *St George*.

The mumming play can be read as a hypodiegetic narrative, a text within the text that draws attention in a more schematic form to the first text's dominant theme or themes. The play literally dramatises the performativity of gender and women's double alienation from desire in the power play that is the patriarchal system within which Eustacia has her being. The narrator informs us that women were traditionally excluded from taking part in mumming. Female parts, where they existed, were performed by young men or omitted altogether.[8] Ironically then, even were a female part available to Eustacia she would be forced to play it parodically: imitating a boy imitating a stereotype of femininity. To play a female part as a woman would be to risk discovery and embarrassment through being too authentic. However, while Eustacia's masculine costume gives her access to Clym on a temporarily equal footing without compromising her feminine modesty, she finds herself engaged in a complex double performance in which she must not only present a convincing Turkish Knight but also a convincing young man in order to be recognised as a 'genuine' or authentic member of the troop. The mumming play is an example of what Judith Butler describes as 'a parodic inhabiting of conformity' (1993: 122), which draws attention to the way in which subjection to prevailing gender roles both enables and violates the subject.

The narrator distinguishes between the 'survival' and 'revival' of a 'traditional pastime':

> while in the revival all is excitement and fervour, the survival is carried on with a stolidity and absence of stir which sets one wondering why a thing that is done so perfunctorily should be kept up at all. Like Balaam and other unwilling prophets, the agents seem moved by an inner compulsion to say and do their allotted parts whether they will or no. (120)

Eustacia's cross-dressed performance is a reproduction of an ossified role that only marginally challenges the stability of meaning of the original. On the surface, the mumming play appears immune to even the minor mutations that are implicit in all iterative practices in that mummers perform their parts 'unweetingly' (120). In arrogating to herself the knight's role, Eustacia fuses masculine and feminine into one parodic body whose agency is severely compromised by the limited recognition which attends it.

Traditionally, we are told women were restricted to assisting behind the scenes, especially with the making of the costumes: 'without the assistance of sisters and sweethearts the dresses were likely to be a failure' (120). Interestingly, while the personalising of individual costumes with 'loops and bows of silk and velvet in any situation pleasing to their taste' (120) signal their collusion in the heterosexual desire codes of ownership and sexual competitiveness, this active intervention in the production has the effect of undermining the signifying effect of the costumes themselves. These additional bows, brilliant silk scallops, ribbon tufts and rosettes on the costumes of the Valiant Soldier, Saint George, the Turkish Knight and The Saracen blur the necessary distinctions between masculine and feminine as well as between Christian and Moslem: 'In the end The Valiant Soldier, of the Christian army, was distinguished by no peculiarity of accoutrement from the Turkish Knight; and what was worse, on a casual view Saint George himself might be mistaken for his deadly enemy The Saracen' (120).

On one level, Eustacia's intervention loses its subversive potential because it is both neutralised by the context in which it occurs and undermined by the narrative power of the traditional mumming plot and its inevitable dénouement, becoming what Judith Butler calls 'high het entertainment' which merely confirms existing power structures (Butler, 1993: 126). On another level, however, her surreptitious participation in the play – like that of the female costume-makers – undermines the narrator's definition of this 'fossilized survival' as 'a spurious reproduction': the product of a 'refurbishing age' (120). As a result of women's stealthy intervention, this performance of *St George* becomes a re-iteration in which the stability of the roles is challenged and potentially undermined.

Eustacia does succeed in moving briefly from the spectatorial role, to which she has previously been confined, to a more active part in the proceedings under cover of the anonymity the costume confers.[9] However in this androgynous position, she is able initially to establish an unconventional connection with the object of her desire only at the expense of her own embodied power as a woman. She becomes not herself but 'some imaginary person' (139) whose agency is severely compromised. In her performance as the Turkish Knight, Eustacia does not intervene in the production of her own cultural history as a woman. On the contrary, she becomes more deeply compromised by her illicit engagement in the patriarchal practices from which women are traditionally excluded. This serves to defuse the subversive potential of her actions, as does her insistent subscription to romantic heterosexual modes of desire, which Hardy's novels suggest always work to the disadvantage of those who espouse them unthinkingly. In the context of the play, Eustacia's disguise silences and restricts her, threatening embarrassment and shame rather than the freedom of speech that Sue Bridehead will later enjoy in Jude's 'Sunday suit', the smuggler Lizzy Newberry in her dead husband's overcoat or Ethelberta in her projected career in the masculine world of letters.

Eustacia becomes 'nettled by her own contrivances' (141) and the imperative that she is not recognised makes her 'unrecognisable' in Judith Butler's sense of the socially articulated and changeable terms which confer or withhold agency (Butler, 2004: 2). Her frustration at having to compete in a masculine theatrical costume with the excessively feminine and conventional Thomasin echoes Rosalind's dilemma in Shakespeare's *As You Like It* when hearing that Orlando is in the Forest of Arden: 'Alas the day, what shall I do with my doublet and hose?' (*AYLI*, III.2: ll.212–13).

> The power of her face all lost, the charm of her motions all disguised, the fascinations of her coquetry denied existence, nothing but a voice left to her: she had a sense of the doom of Echo. (*RoN*: 141)

The linking of Eustacia with another of Ovid's nymphs, one who 'has not learned to speak first herself [...] and gives back the sounds she has heard', suggests the nature of her iterative performance of gender, and of her alienated desire (Ovid, 1977, III: 83–4), and even as she speaks the lines set down for her by custom and tradition she adopts the disabling expediency of putting a pebble in her mouth to disguise her voice (123).[10] As the mumming play implies, Eustacia's rebelliousness is founded on an over-identification with, rather than a challenge to, the prevailing myths (in her case the myths of romantic heterosexuality) in response to the culturally and morally restricted environment of haggard Egdon. The rigidly prescribed role of the Turkish Knight, who despite his braggadocio is eventually killed by St George, the agent of order and control, is bound by a traditional and ancient script and therefore offers limited and even more rigidly prescribed opportunities for the re-enactment of the self than conventional drag. It also demonstrates that, despite her smouldering Promethean rebelliousness, Eustacia is perhaps the most conservative and ideologically constrained of all Hardy's heroines, committed as she is to the articulation of her desires solely through 'congealed', 'reified' – even fossilised – gender roles. Unable to emerge from her 'space of possibility' in a newly reconfigured form, it is fitting, dramatically at least, that she drowns in the raging waters of Shadwater Weir (355): a death that is foreshadowed in the watery conclusion of her extravagant dream. Her body is pulled from the water, along with the entwined bodies of both of her putative 'knights': Clym and Wildeve. Eustacia's attempt to arrogate masculine privileges to herself, leads not to her metamorphosis but to her solitary demise in treacherous waters.

However, along with the female costume makers, the cross-dressed Eustacia presents a dangerous and potentially destabilising alternative to normative heterosexual desire, beyond what even the guardian of such norms, Mrs Yeobright, anticipates. Clym's response to Eustacia in boy's costume is interesting, though less so than Jude's to the androgynised Sue, or Richard Stockdale's to the image of Lizzie Newberry dressed as a young man. The narrator observes how Eustacia's performance as the Turkish Knight both mimics and *modulates* the traditional role: it is 'the same thing, yet how different'. In adding the 'softness and finish of a Rafaello after Perugino' she 'faithfully reproduce[es] the original subject' while 'entirely distanc[ing] the original art' (123). In using such a metaphor drawn from the visual arts, Hardy suggests the potential of iteration which, depending on the circumstances and contexts of the repetition, can produce different, and potentially transformative, meanings especially in the realm of gendered desire. Whether or not Clym discerns her sex beneath the fluttering ribbons of her visor is left to conjecture. The narrator tells us that Clym 'looked at her wistfully, then seemed to fall into a reverie, as if he were forgetting what he observed' (139). He is intrigued by and drawn to the figure of the Turkish Knight, but the narrator does not confirm whether he is attracted by the boyishness of Eustacia's costumed figure or to the femaleness, which, despite her appearance, might emanate from her like the 'preternatural perfume' that betrayed the presence of the disguised Venus to her son Aeneas (139). This lends a certain piquancy to his question 'Are you a woman – or am I wrong?' (142) and demonstrates the subversive erotic potential of this 'space of possibility' that is more fully explored in later texts such as 'The Distracted Preacher' and *Jude the Obscure*.

'The Distracted Preacher' (1879) is the earliest of the *Wessex Tales*, Hardy's first collection of short stories published in 1888. It recounts the story of Richard Stockdale, a 'provisionally selected' young Methodist preacher who has been sent to the village of Nether-Moynton pending the arrival of its permanent incumbent. Here he meets, and takes lodgings with, Lizzy Newberry – a young widow, a 'trimmer' and a cross-dressing smuggler – who distracts him from his professed allegiance to one side of the many binaries that are under interrogation in this story. She also initiates him into theft, the consumption of illicit alcohol, smuggling, Episcopalianism and 'tub-broaching' – an activity that is curiously suggestive of pre-marital oral sexual activity – in the base of the neighbouring church tower. Lizzy tells Stockwell to take the broached barrel ' "between your knees, and squeeze the heads; and I'll hold the cup". Stockdale obeyed; and the pressure taking effect upon the tub [. . .] the spirit spirted out in a stream' (173). The process of watering down the barrel is similarly intriguing:

By her direction he held the tub with the hole upwards, and, while he went through the process of alternately pressing and ceasing to press, she produced a bottle of water, from which she took mouthfuls, conveying each to the keg by putting her pretty lips to the hole, where it was sucked in at each recovery of the cask from pressure. When it was full again he plugged the hole, knocked the hoop down to its place, and buried the tub in the lumber as before. (174)

These transgressive, indeed sacrilegious, activities culminate in a tableau of cross-dressed queer desire.[11] In this story, a complementary set of binaries serves as a corollary to that of gender, and various liminal 'spaces of possibility' exist as controversial alternatives to the rigid separations insisted upon by the Methodist minister Richard Stockdale and the customs officer Will Latimer, who represent the normalising and disciplining forces of early to mid-nineteenth-century England.[12] These two are pitted against the cross-dressing Lizzy Newberry and her cousin Owlett, whose own transvestism and surname with its echo of 'owl-light' – dusk or twilight – suggests his liminal potential also.[13]

The village of Nether-Moynton itself represents a matrix or locus of subversive possibilities, a 'third space' in its own right. The narrator distinguishes between Nether-Moynton's chapel and church-goers, using a metaphor that reflects the fascination with matters of race and racial purity that were particularly current in the final decades of the nineteenth century. The 'hundred-and-forty Methodists of pure blood' are supplemented by a 'mixed race which went to church in the morning and chapel in the evening, or when there was a tea', which includes even the vicar among its number.[14] Hardy's arch use of what was then perceived as a biological metaphor of race to describe a cultural and secular choice has the effect of challenging the basis of biological determinism itself. The 'mixed race' of those who frequent both church and chapel vary their allegiance not because of an act of divine interpellation but for reasons of contingency – namely the availability or otherwise of superior refreshments. This opportunistic 'crossing over', or 'trimming' as it is referred to in the text, even confounds the taxonomic power of the census: the official mechanism for collecting and registering population data, deployed by what the narrator refers to as 'the denser gentry of the district around Nether-Moynton', who cannot account for the fact that 'a parish containing fifteen score of strong, full-grown Episcopalians, and nearly thirteen score of well-matured Dissenters, numbered barely two-and-twenty score of adults in all' (167).[15]

From the outset the indigenous population of Nether-Moynton is presented as existing in defiance of the discourses of religion, the law and other mechanisms which delimit, determine and assign identity. This linking together of religious calling, racial and gender difference as assumed cultural positions, rather than biologically or divinely ordained identities, challenges binary positions and simultaneously suggests the radical potential of 'trimming'. The distracting Lizzy Newbury not only 'trims' between religious faiths and places of worship but also between marital states (being neither married nor single but a young widow), opposing sides of the law and opposing nations. However, as Gilmartin and Mengham suggest, here the French and English meet at sea not as enemies but 'according to a different configuration by which they are partners and allies against the official central authorities of both France and England' (Gilmartin and Mengham, 2007: 46–7). The metaphor of the watery channel that separates the two countries is an image of a fluid, liminal position of possibility between opposing extremes. In addition to smuggling contraband brandy, Lizzy also smuggles her own illicit desires for adventure and excitement under the overcoat, hat and breeches of her deceased husband, and in this respect she 'trims' between opposing genders too.

At the end of the story, Latimer and his officers are hilariously stalled, outwitted, robbed, fettered and confused by a group of cross-dressed Nether-Moynton men:

> six or eight huge female figures whom, from their wide strides, Stockdale guessed to be men in disguise [. . .]

> '[. . .] There is no walking up this way for the present,' said one of the gaunt women, who wore curls a foot long, dangling down the sides of her face, in the fashion of the time. Stockdale recognised this lady's voice as Owlett's. (215)

The fact that these cross-dressed men also have 'blackened faces' strengthens the race/gender connection and leaves the customs officers uncertain as to the identity, sex and origin of their assailants, leading Latimer not only to give up all pursuit of the smugglers but, controversially, to express envy of their success in evading the circumscribing power of the law:

> For my part, I'd sooner be them than we. The clitches of my arm are burning like fire from the cords those two strapping women tied round 'em. My opinion is, now I have had time to think o't, that you may serve your Gover'ment at too high a price. (217)

The cross-dressed men of the village are able to go about their illegal activities protected by the innocence and timidity conventionally ascribed to women, although this is comically undermined by Latimer's bemusement at the strength of the 'strapping women' who tie him to a tree (217). Latimer's change of heart stands as a sharp contrast to the persistence of Richard Stockdale, the Methodist preacher who pursues his mission to discipline the prevaricating villagers, and more especially Lizzy Newberry, right to the end of the story – at least as it appeared in print.

Although it is clear that Lizzy has serious designs on Stockdale as a second husband, her satisfaction at the positive effect of her flirtatious manipulation of the handsome young preacher savours, we are told, 'more of pride than vanity' (218). Indeed, at the fateful moment of Stockwell's proposal she appears strangely distracted herself. Gilmartin and Mengham note that, despite the fact that she has fallen in love with him, Lizzy's response to Stockwell 'is comically removed from the conventional response to a marriage proposal in the literature of the period' (Gilmartin and Mengham, 2007: 46). This is because Lizzy is no conventional heroine. The masculine domain of smuggling, which she must quit if she is to take up the role of a conventional minister's wife, offers her the satisfaction and stimulation that is missing from the traditionally feminine domestic sphere:

> It stirs up one's dull life [...] and gives excitement, which I have got so used to now that I should hardly know how to do 'ithout it. At nights when the wind blows, instead of being dull and stupid, and not noticing whether it do blow or not, your mind is afield, even if you are not afield yourself; and you are wondering how the chaps are getting on. (218)

Both Stockwell and the reader are initially led into the trap of making assumptions about Lizzy's behaviour based on assumed codes of femininity and morality, which are systematically exposed by the minister's conventional response to her motives and activities. His wilful misreading of her conversation with Owlett as 'the only talk between a young woman and man that is likely to amuse an eavesdropper' (180) leads to a series of farcical assumptions on Stockwell's part that she is sexually compromised not only by her cousin but possibly by several of her 'old neighbours' also. Discovering newly brushed masculine attire in her room, he assumes that she is receiving a male visitor in her own bedchamber. Although Stockwell is both relieved and intrigued to discover that the 'intruder' is none other than Lizzy herself in 'her late husband's coat and hat' (189), his belief that her activities 'will be the ruin of her' (191) conflates sexual with legal and financial consequences. His declaration 'You are in man's clothes and I am ashamed of you' leaves the reader unsure as to what, precisely, the source of shame is: her lack of decorum, her illegal activities (192) or both. Lizzy assumes that his concern is with her attire and is quick to reassure him that it is purely a matter of sartorial convenience: a superficial solution to a practical difficulty that has no bearing whatever on her gender identity:

> 'I am only partly in man's clothes,' she faltered, shrinking back to the wall. 'It is only his great-coat and hat and breeches that I've got on, which is no harm, as he was my own husband; and I do it only because a cloak blows about so, and you can't use your arms. I have got my dress under just the same – it is only tucked in.' (192)[16]

In donning her husband's outer garments, Lizzy is not concerned to 'pass' as a man or to exchange her feminine privileges for masculine ones. Her cross-dressed figure is a compound of both genders: her outline and gait betray her female shape and identity to Stockdale just as her dress, which she wears under the overcoat in lieu of a shirt and under-linen, 'protects' her from full-identification with a masculine subjectivity. Lizzy's justification of her cross-dressing as morally acceptable, as the clothes belonged to her own husband, comically inverts the legal notion of the *femme couvert* (literally 'covered woman') in which a woman's rights and existence were subsumed under those of her husband. In her combined feminine and masculine attire, like the cross-dressed Nether-Moynton men, she is an excellent example of Garber's 'third' space: not itself 'a third one' but a mode of self-articulation that 'challenges the possibility of harmonious and stable binary symmetry' (Garber, 1997: 11).

What is striking here, as is the case with both Eustacia and Sue Bridehead, is the effect her cross-dressing has upon her 'straight' admirer, which is to challenge and undermine the binary symmetry of heterosexual desire itself. Stockwell has already found the combination of her feminine 'warming' eyes and striking mouth, offset by a 'wide, sensible, beautiful forehead' (169) quite irresistible. As he witnesses the successful landing of the smuggled tubs, he is sufficiently stirred by Lizzy's 'experienced manner and bold indifference' to offer her his arm (which she refuses) despite her masculine attire, and his subsequent passionate declaration of feeling, coupled with the pose they subsequently adopt – cheek by cheek and framed at the window as they watch the customs men search for the contraband brandy – presents an image of two young 'men' in an unconventionally intimate relationship (202). The various 'distractions' embodied in the cross-dressed figure of Lizzy serve to unsettle the 'provisionally selected' young minister so completely that he finds himself irrevocably placed in the spaces of possibility between 'conscience and love', waking and sleeping (203), the smugglers and the Preventatives, his love for Lizzy and his ministerial 'calling' and even, by implication, hetero- and homosexual desire. It is significant that these distractions take place in the period between 'moon and moon': Nether-Moyton's term for the brief darkness between the waning of the old moon and the appearance of the new (193).

Stockdale's own innocent, 'fair and downy' appearance and his religious dress place him above suspicion, as far as the customs officers are concerned, and are the means by which he smuggles his own illicit desires for the unconventional Lizzy, and the excitement her activities generate within him, past the agents of normalisation and moral control. At the climax of the story, Latimer unwittingly re-inscribes Stockdale even more firmly in his provisional identity, including him in his disdain for the slippery Nether-Moynton villagers by declaiming: 'There's not a man about the place but the Methodist parson; and he's an old woman' (206), and to his surprise and consternation Stockdale briefly becomes a 'trimmer' himself. Accompanying Lizzy to warn the men hiding in the church tower, he finds himself going

against the nonconformity that has 'been in the Stockdale blood for generations' and 'among consecrated bells for the first time in his life'. The idea
of a religious calling – a 'natural' tendency or divine guidance – stands as a
corollary to all other apparently 'inherent' binary positions and is revealed
to be a simple matter of choice and as subject to contingency as any other.

> 'What, be you really one of us?' said the miller.
> 'It seems so,' said Stockdale, sadly.
> 'He's not,' said Lizzy, who overheard. 'He's neither for nor against us. He'll
> do us no harm.' (207)

In fact Stockdale does do harm through his determination to re-assign himself and Lizzy along conventional lines: at least this is what is suggested
by the conclusion Hardy gave to the published version of the story. Lizzy
compares Stockdale's dissent from the Church with her own from the State,
suggesting that in this they are 'well matched'. However, she is unclear
regarding the reasons behind her illicit desires. Is her desire to smuggle 'second nature' or merely a practical solution to financial difficulty. The effect
of her apparent contradictoriness is to draw attention to the possibility of
resistance and evasion of the 'duties' levied upon conventional subjects of
gender, and the subversive measures adopted by those resistant subjects
who seek to smuggle the contraband of their proscribed desires past the
'preventatives' of normalisation. At the same time, she is unable to register
the profanity of her suggestion that if marriage to a smuggler is a violation of
Stockwell's calling as a man of God, then *he* should be the one to renounce
his profession not her. Lizzie's declaration: 'I have got this large house; why
can't you marry me, and live with us, and not be a Methodist preacher
anymore?' (218) violates not only his calling but also the 'natural' order of
things that dictates that a woman annexes herself to her husband and not
the other way round. This implies that 'inviolate' gender roles and religious
vocations can be taken up and put off as easily as a gown and false curls or
an overcoat and breeches. However, Stockwell is unable to avail himself of
the radical opportunities for a thorough reconfiguration of his own identity
offered by the fluid medium of Nether-Moynton. In order to avoid becoming 'weak and faltering in my course', he leaves the attractive indeterminacy
of Lizzy and her village in the suggestively grey light of early morning for an
unnamed Midland town.

'The Distracted Preacher' should have ended here and indeed, Hardy
claimed that it was his original intention to conclude the story on this
sad, yet highly appropriate note of irresolution and unassuaged desire.[17]
However, the published ending has Owlett badly wounded and captured
by Latimer's officers, and tried and acquitted at the local assizes before emi-
grating to America, leaving behind a much chastened and repentant Lizzy,
whose hand bears the indelible scar of her brush with the king's customs

officers. Stockwell marries Lizzy in a chapel in a neutral neighbouring town, and takes her away from Nether-Moynton to 'a home he had made for himself in his native country, where she studied her duties as a minister's wife with praiseworthy assiduity' (222). Disciplined into a highly conventional feminine role, Lizzy changes from rebel to purveyor of gender, moral and religious conservatism, contributing 'an excellent tract called *Render unto Caesar; or, the Repentant Villagers*' based on her own experience, which is corrected, expanded and printed by her husband, 'and many hundreds of copies were distributed by the couple in the course of their married life' (223).

In 'An Imaginative Woman' (1894), as the title suggests, Hardy moves beyond the realm of material reality to the realm of art and the potential role of the imagination in the fulfilment of proscribed desires. Robert Trewe is the quintessential object of desire in that Ella's longing for him intensifies in proportion to his unavailability, while Trewe's own suicide is a direct result of his unassuaged – indeed unassuagable – desire for the 'unattainable [...] undiscoverable [...] elusive [...] imaginary woman', conceived of as his 'trewe' complement (27). 'An Imaginative Woman' is a perfect fable of desire, suggesting as it does that, for both sexes, desire is incited and defined by the impossibility of its fulfilment within the existing symbolic order. In its refusal to even countenance the possibility that Ella and Robert might find fulfilment and wholeness in each other, the story enacts its own thesis. For both, satisfaction lies outside the realm of the real, in the potentiality of the Other, which can only be accessed through the imagination. Hardy explored this theme more positively in the metafictional *The Hand of Ethelberta* and, as I shall demonstrate in the following chapter, pursues it more fully in his last published novel *The Well-Beloved* (1897).

Ella Marchmill, the wife of a thriving professional arms manufacturer in another 'midland town', is described as 'life-leased' to her 'proprietor' (*LLI*, 1996: 8). Her husband, an arms manufacturer aptly named Will, is presented as 'supremely satisfied', expressing himself in 'squarely shaped sentences' and 'with a condition of sublunary things which made weapons a necessity' (8). His wife, however, professes herself 'a votary of the muse' (7) who 'shrink[s] humanely' not only against the conditions of existence that make her husband's trade a necessity, but also against the productive constraints of gender that seek to limit her desires to the realm of femininity, wifedom and motherhood. Unable to find an outlet for her romanticism, eroticism and creativity she increasingly inhabits the world of the imagination, in which all things, in theory, are possible. This involves her in a complex act of transference in which her desire is signified by the melancholy poet Robert Trewe, whose thoughts and feelings she imagines as 'the selfsame thoughts and feelings as hers' (19). As with Eustacia's identification with an imaginary Clym Yeobright, Ella's 'magnetic attraction' to a man she has never met can be read as an attempt to unite with an imaginary masculine self-projection. The fact that Trewe is a published poet adds a further dimension to this exposition of desire. The process is initiated by her adoption of the male pseudonym 'John Ivy' to publish her poetic 'effusions' – a move which she notes, with some irony, was never contemplated by her idol, who 'with a man's unsusceptibility to the question of sex, had never once thought of passing himself off as a woman' (11).[18] Here Hardy demonstrates his sensitivity to the prohibitions that operated on women poets at the time, and the constraints that worked against their full and free access to literary expression and to desire in their own right.[19] Ella's decision is motivated by the realisation that the prosaic realities of her actual life militate against her credibility as an artist in the class- and gender-conscious age in which she lives, a realisation she shares with her creator.[20]

In its fascination with the relation of the imaginary to the real 'An Imaginative Woman' is a variant on the theme of Hardy's last novel *The Well-Beloved*, which was published in serial form as *The Pursuit of the Well-Beloved* in the previous year. Like so many of his characters, Ella's desire exists in tacit form, and she is driven by what the narrator calls 'the instinct to specialize a waiting emotion on the first fit thing that came to hand' (14). As 'fitness', in Ella's terms, exists only in the realms of her imagination, her desire coheres around the nebulous image of Robert Trewe: an image that she distils from his poetry to fill the vacancy at the heart of herself. As such Trewe remains a 'circumambient, unapproachable master [...]. To be sure, she was surrounded noon and night by his customary environment, which literally whispered of him to her at every moment; but he was a man she had never seen' (14). The imagination exists here as a powerful source of resistance to prevailing gender and sexual norms and the instrument through which desire may potentially be brought into the realm of signification and knowledge. As in the case of the sculptor Jocelyn Pierston, the sexual, emotional and creative frustration experienced by Ella Marchmill is the result of a desire that drives her beyond the limited forms of self-articulation available to her in reality The power of the imagination to make and remake the world by, as Judith Butler states, 'establish[ing] the possible in excess of the real' (Butler, 1993: 217) through the medium of art will be discussed in relation to Hardy the poet in the final chapter of this study. In both cases, the 'elsewhere' that art has the power to 'bring home' exists, as yet, only in fragmented, inchoate form like the 'half-obliterated pencillings' on the wallpaper above Trewe's bed: 'phrases, couplets, *bouts-rimés*, beginnings and middles of lines, ideas in the rough like Shelley's scraps [...] inscribed shapes of the poet's world, "Forms more real than living man, / Nurslings of immortality" ' (19).

Ella's idealised and perfervid desire for self-expression results only in the abortive publication of an unremarked and derivative volume of verse, the unwanted birth of another of her husband's children, and her own demise. However, in an imaginative move that links biological with artistic creativity, Ella's last child, with his uncanny resemblance to the dead poet, persists as a symbol of his mother's illegitimate desires, a material or 'Trewe/true' embodiment of 'a transmitted idea' (32).[21] The father rejects the toddler in the mistaken belief that Trewe is his biological father, but while the reader castigates Marchmill for his crass literalism we are left with the conclusion that, in her imagination at least, Ella has indeed played her husband false.

Unlike Ella, Robert Trewe – who is aided by 'a little income of his own' (11) – appears free to attempt self-expression in defiance of 'the excellencies of form and rhythm'. His espousal of radical verse forms (in contrast to William Marchmill's deployment of 'squarely shaped sentences'), his pessimistic philosophy and his tendency to let 'feeling out[run] his artistic speed', suggest his challenge to existing forms, whilst also functioning as Hardy's defence of his own poetic practice. Ella, however, must write her poems in the guise of a man

> in an endeavour to find a congenial channel in which to let flow her painfully embayed emotions, whose former limpidity and sparkle seemed departing in the stagnation caused by the routine of bearing children to a commonplace father. (11)

More than 'a mere multiplier of her kind' but 'less than a poet of her century', Ella's attempt to take speech for herself becomes an act of linguistic 'cross-dressing', the unsatisfactory, because merely imitative, nature of which sends her 'into fits of despondency' (12). In the end her stillborn poems, and her attempt at self-articulation, are totally eclipsed by her re-inscription into the feminine role of wife and mother.

Watery metaphors are used, once again, in relation to Ella's desire. Her emotions are 'painfully embayed' within her 'in the natural way of passion under the too practical conditions which civilization has devised for its fruition' (14). By adopting a male pseudonym, imitating Trewe's poems, taking possession of his rooms at Solentsea (an amalgamation of 'solen' or channel and 'sea' again suggesting the liminal but constrained possibilities of water) and subsequently dressing herself in the poet's mackintosh and cap – 'The mantle of Elijah' (15) – Ella attempts a more fluid reconstruction of herself within the existing structures of signification.[22]

> 'The mantle of Elijah,' she said. 'Would it might inspire me to rival him, glorious genius that he is!'

> Her eyes always grew wet when she thought like that, and she turned to look at herself in the glass. *His* heart had beat inside that coat, and *his* brain had worked under that hat at levels of thought she would never reach. The consciousness of her weakness beside him made her feel quite sick. (15)

Ella's desires are expressed in an erotic fantasy not just of transference but of metamorphosis. Denied Trewe's actual physical presence, Ella makes a fetish not only of his clothes but also of his poetry, his vacated bed and his photograph, uncovering the latter at night alone when 'a more romantic tinge [might] be imparted to the occasion by silence, candles, solemn sea and stars outside' and 'getting rid of [her] superfluous garments' (18). As with Eustacia's identification with the knight of her dream, Ella's identification with Trewe becomes an attempt to realise those vital, erotic aspects of herself that have been denied in the interests of the achievement of a stable 'feminine' subject position as faithful wife and devoted mother:

> And now her hair was dragging where his arm had lain when he secured the fugitive fancies: she was sleeping on a poet's lips, immersed in the very essence of him, permeated by his spirit as by an ether. (20)

She likewise takes part in a complex 'drag' fantasy, which echoes the erotic fusion of Hermaphroditus and Salmacis, only to find herself more firmly re-inscribed within her gender role by the realities of her sex and her biology. Just as her husband interrupts her cross-dressing 'freak' (15), so his actual body displaces the photograph of Trewe, with which Ella is communing in the marital bed. Her idealised romantic and imaginary connection with the poet is forced to give way to the erotic and reproduction compulsions of the Victorian marriage bed, and her introjection of the imagined Trewe results only in the conception of another of her husband's children.

Ella's failure to write after the abortive publication of her first volume of verse becomes a failure to live after the birth of her fourth child. Found by her husband at the grave of the newly dead Trewe, it is as if her own re-gendered, newly animated self has been buried just as her body will shortly afterwards be. Hardy chooses Dante Gabriel Rossetti's sonnet 'Stillborn Love' to illustrate Ella's thoughts on hearing of Trewe's death.[23] This is interesting in the context of the repeated tropes of water and androgyny noted in this chapter, and Marjorie Garber's theory of the 'space of possibility'.

> The hour which might have been yet might not be,
> Which man's and woman's heart conceived and bore
> Yet whereof life was barren,—on what shore
> Bides it the breaking of Time's weary sea?
> Bondchild of all consummate joys set free,
> It somewhere sighs and serves, and mute before
> The house of Love, hears through the echoing door
> His hours elect in choral consonancy [...]
>
> (from *House of Life* 1881)

The conclusion of this story, as with so much of Hardy's writing, suggests that as yet this radical 'third position' exists only in the realm of the imagination and of art. The stillborn 'little outcast', conceived of man and woman's hearts could be read here as an imagined reconfiguration or rebirth of the desiring self: 'The hour which might have been yet might not be'. It is stranded away from the fluid medium of androgyny and cannot survive or articulate itself within or outside the existing confines of discourse.

Jude the Obscure offers a more detailed challenge to the ways in which, as Judith Butler describes it, bodies *'come into being* in and through the mark(s) of gender' (Butler, 1990: 8). For Butler, the physiological, anatomical differences between male and female are not ' "prediscursive", prior to culture' but 'the effect of the apparatus of cultural construction designated by *gender'* (Butler, 1990: 7). Such constructions have the effect of calling erotic desire into being and channelling it along strictly heterosexual lines. In addition, the novel examines the potential for evading and reconstituting conventionally gendered transactional relationships with the world, and with others, through the adoption of the 'third' position in the space of possibility opened by the temporary androgyny of cross-dressing. Again, water functions as a metaphor for a potentially more fluid state of being, and being in relation to others. Contemplating Sue, dressed in his Sunday suit while her own clothes dry before the fire, Jude muses: 'If he could only get over the sense of her sex, as she seemed to be able to do so easily of his, what a comrade she would make' (*JO*: 159). Jude's understanding of the 'sense of sex' here refers primarily to biological difference and the gender differentiation, which, according to Judith Butler, both determines and is determined by it. During the course of the novel, Jude and Sue's 'sense of sex' – their awareness of gender difference and its constraining or enabling effect on the articulation of desire – undergoes a process of development leading to an interrogation, by the narrator and the principal characters, of the ways in which desire is eroticised and the limited potential for dissention from that norm.

The precarious relationship to prevailing codes of masculinity exhibited by the distracted preacher Richard Stockdale and the poet Robert Trewe is examined here in earnest in Jude's anguished attempt to articulate his desires in the context of conflicting and class-related discourses of gender. At the point of puberty Jude negotiates between two competing models of masculinity in the forms of the aspiring schoolteacher Richard Phillotson and the farmer Mr Troutham, who represent middle-class intellectualism and masculine rural labouring codes respectively. Both Jude and Phillotson aspire to radical reconfigurations of masculinity which have implications for the erotic expression of their desire. Phillotson's views on a woman's right to divorce a man she does not love, and to be a unit with her children 'without the man' are, as Gillingham's reaction attests, quite radical for the time (*JO*: 247). Jude's aspirations are imitative, however, and his identification with Phillotson, like Eustacia's with her imaginary knight and Ella's with her idealised poet, takes on a strongly erotic dimension.[24]

Phillotson's middle-class aspirations 'to be a university graduate, and then to be ordained' offer a more 'feminised' model of masculine subjectivity than that offered to the impressionable and emotionally deracinated Jude by the rural community of Marygreen. Jude pauses in his domestic chores, which have been interrupted by the schoolteacher's departure, to mimic Phillotson's actions of peering down at 'the shining disk of quivering water' in the depths of the ancient draw-well which is described in 'feminine' terms with its 'lining of green moss near the top, and, nearer still the hart's tongue fern', whose Latin name, *'Phyllitis scolopendrium'* echoes the schoolteacher's surname (5). Jude's wistful action is rudely interrupted by Drusilla's inter-pellatory address that re-inscribes him into his role as a dependent male orphan of the labouring classes: 'Bring on that water, will ye, you idle young harlican' (5). Drusilla's admonition of the young Jude draws attention not only to his disempowerment but also the performative nature of the mas-culinity into which he is to be inscribed, and which will help to constitute one of the devilish and crippling gins that he seeks unsuccessfully to avoid for the remainder of his short life.[25] His choice between rural and bour-geois codes of masculinity is suggested through the metaphor of clothing. The 'harrowed field' where the young Jude is employed as a human scare-crow threatens, almost literally, to trap him in his class, his gender and his heredity: 'the brown surface of the field went right up towards the sky all round, where it was lost by degrees in the mist that shut out the actual verge, and accentuated the solitude' (8). The 'fresh harrow-lines' that 'channel' the field, reducing its gradations and history to 'a meanly utilitarian level' are 'like [...] a piece of new corduroy', a simile that gives a specifically sartorial class connotation to Jude's situation, in that corduroy is the traditional cloth from which the rural labourer's clothes were made. Opposed to this is Jude's 'Sunday suit' probably made from worsted or some other form of woollen fabric.

Jude's 'escape' from the harrowed field which had witnessed his punish-ment, and from the fog of Marygreen to the 'bluer, moister atmosphere' of the strange landscape beyond it, is symbolic of his quest for an alternative mode of being, less circumscribed by the expectations incumbent upon his physical and social body. From the vantage point of the barn onto which he climbs in order to see the distant city roof, the air increases 'in trans-parency' to reveal Christminster in the image of 'The Heavenly Jerusalem', the literal or figurative reconstructed city that represents the earthly site of paradise in Christian thought, where the spirit is freed from the con-straints of its material form and where Jude believes he can realise his aspirations 'without fear of farmers, or hindrance or ridicule' (21).[26] The contrast between the Heavenly Jerusalem and the purgatorial, if not hellish, reality of Christminster is central to Hardy's project of contrasting the real with the ideal, the 'model' with the visionary, and recurs as a leitmotif throughout the novel. This is echoed in the metaphor of water and its fluid potential.

In the *Book of Revelations* the Heavenly Jerusalem is bisected by the pure river of the water of life, echoing the one that flowed from the Garden of Eden in Genesis, from which the newly eroticised and self-consciously gendered Adam and Eve are expelled. An ironic and more 'earthly' version of this river is the stream in Marygreen in which Arabella and her friends wash the intestines of the pigs from her father's smallholding. Arabella's crude distraction of Jude from his intellectual musings with 'the characteristic part of a barrow-pig, which the countrymen used for greasing their boots' (*JO*: 35) mirrors Aunt Drusilla's hailing of him at the well and likewise serves to re-inscribe him in his 'legitimate', heterosexual masculine role. In obeying her order to bring the pig's severed penis back to her, Jude signifies his abandonment of the alternative possibilities offered by Christminster and a life of the mind, to embrace the life of the body, in particular the body of Arabella, and to identify himself with the symbolic sign of heterosexualised, if castrated, masculinity. At this point, the novel suggests that the libidinal energy that urges him on to new forms of being and becoming is redirected into the same restrictive channels as it was for his predecessors: the lovers under the hedges and in the ancient cornfields of Marygreen who enact and re-enact the age-old traditions of copulation, birth and bitterness that determine the lives of the rural labouring class. The possibilities of change and renewal offered by the well and the stream are foreclosed by Aunt Drusilla and Arabella, who literally call him back to the material realities of his class and his 'sense of sex'.[27]

If Aunt Drusilla and Arabella undermine the liminal aspect and transformative possibilities of the water by insisting it be put to a crudely utilitarian use, Sue Bridehead emphasises the potential for the reconstitution of the gendered self and eroticised desire that is symbolised by the androgynous role. In Jude's lodging, Sue is forced to change into his Sunday suit because she has waded through 'the largest river in the county' (149). Her transvestite garb suggests a fluid relation to prevailing class and gender roles and concomitant forms of sexual expression and connection in that it temporarily places her outside the heterosexual, and indeed the sexual, imperative that drives her relationship with Jude, allowing her the space to describe her experimental, sexless and comradely liaison with the Christminster undergraduate (153–4).[28] Jude turns from the image of Sue 'masquerading as himself on a Sunday' (150) to 'turning' her feminine outer and under clothes before the fire in order to dry them. As he engages in a conversation on the theological misappropriation of 'ecstatic, natural, human love' with Sue, whom his landlady has already mistaken for a young man, his own desires are confused and disrupted by her contradictory manifestations of herself. After she is driven to a conventionally feminine response of petulant tears by Jude's recalcitrance over the falsification of Solomon's Song by 'four-and-twenty-elders or bishops, or whatever', and exhibiting 'soft severity' at his endearments, Sue's eyes meet his 'and they shook hands, like cronies in a tavern' (158). Sue appears here as frankly conciliatory in a 'manly' and artless way and yet simultaneously adept in the art of feminine sexual strategy. Jude is forced to look away from her 'for that epicene tenderness of hers was too harrowing' (159).[29] Sue's 'epicene' quality is 'harrowing' for Jude in that it unsettles him, forcing him to re-examine the erotic orientation of his own desire and to speculate on the possibility of its reconfiguration:

> If he could only get over the sense of her sex, as she seemed to be able to do so easily of his, what a comrade she would make; for their difference of opinion on conjectural subjects only drew them closer together on matters of daily human experience. She was nearer to him than any other woman he had ever met, and he could scarcely believe that time, creed, or absence, would ever divide him from her. (159)

Sue's aim, as she frames it to Jude, is 'to ennoble some man to high aims; and when I saw you, and knew you wanted to be my comrade, I [...] thought that man might be you' (158). As a woman debarred from recognised intellectual and academic pursuits at this time, Sue's project of 'ennobling' Jude suggests a desire to live vicariously through him and his intellectual achievements: in donning his clothes Sue appears as Jude's 'slim and fragile' bourgeois double (150). It also involves the sublimation or redirection of the erotic desires initiated in him by Arabella, whose assault on him with the pig's pizzle enkindles 'a new channel for emotional interest hitherto unsuspected though it had lain close beside him' (39). Jude enjoys some success in displacing his response to Arabella, and to the 'frolicsome girls who made advances', with the idealised image of Sue, 'the sweetest and most disinterested comrade that he had ever had [...] so uncarnate as to seem at times impossible as a human wife to any average man' (279) and tells her:

> All that's best and noblest in me loves you, and your freedom from everything that's gross has elevated me, and enabled me to do what I should never have dreamt myself capable of, or any man, a year ago. (279)

However, as Richard Dellamora has persuasively indicated, Sue's desire for a platonic relationship with Jude derives from the 'manipulation of conventional ignorance, including her own, concerning the erotic investments involved in male friendships' (Dellamora, 1990: 462). As far as the relationship between Jude and Sue is concerned, the novel appears sceptical on the possibility or advisability of maintaining celibacy in such circumstances but sympathetic to the problematic aspects of active sexuality, in particular its biological implications for women and its legal implications for men in same sex relationships.

Despite the failure of her experiments in 'Ouranian' or 'celestial' love with the Christminster undergraduate and later with Jude (174), Sue's 'epicene' performance in Jude's lodgings implies the fluidity of gender identity and the inherently undifferentiated origin of desire, or as Stephen Orgel puts it, 'the radical instability of our essence' (Orgel, 1996: 27). In her metamorphosis from male tavern crony to emotionally vulnerable and manipulative young woman, Sue teases Jude by appearing to offer an erotic connection that is then withdrawn, and also disconcerts him in that her 'performances' also 'tease' out of him desirous responses that are both unconventionally erotic, directed as they are to one who appears to be of the same sex as himself, and asexual. The narrator describes the sleeping Sue through Jude's eyes as 'boyish as a Ganymedes' (*JO*: 36) and Hardy's substitution of 'Ganymedes' in the 1895 volume edition for the manuscript's 'Cupid' is significant.[30] Hardy would have read John Addington Symonds's discussion of Homer's legend in 'The Dantesque and Platonic Ideas of Love' which centres on this conflicting interpretation of pedagogic eros in ancient Greece (Thomas, 2007: 6). In her combined and persuasive demonstration of conflicting gender characteristics and correspondingly diverse desirous responses, Sue embodies, however briefly and parodically, the contingent and performative aspects of gender identity as well as the 'space of possibility' within which the fabric of identity – constituted through gendered, heterosexualised and eroticised desire – might be undone or refashioned.

Jude's distinction between 'conjectural' subjects and 'matters of daily human experiences' in formulating his sense of his closeness to Sue echoes her scepticism concerning the accuracy of the model of Jerusalem built according to 'conjectural maps' (108). It suggests a degree of incompatibility between, for example, how the experience of desire is structured and made manifest by the social formations which shape the lives of Sue and Jude, and the complex potential of human interaction, which cannot be wholly subsumed within or effaced by a reductive and over-simplifying gender binary. As Sue declares to Jude:

> the social moulds civilization fits us into have no more relation to our actual shapes than the conventional shapes of the constellations have to the real star-patterns [...]. I am not really Mrs Richard Phillotson, but a woman tossed about, all alone, with aberrant passions, and unaccountable antipathies. (215–16)

Sue's eloquent distinction between 'social roles' and 'actual shapes' in relation to the 'conventional shapes of the constellations' and the 'real star patterns' is an interesting and complex metaphor for a desire that cannot, as yet, be articulated. Sue's belief in an essential self – 'our actual shapes' – is revealed to be yet another 'social mould', that of 'a woman tossed about, all alone, with aberrant passions, and unaccountable antipathies'. These passions and antipathies could not exist outside a patriarchal signifying system of gender that recognises them as 'aberrant' and 'unaccountable' for a married woman of a certain class and historical moment.[31]

The 'real star patterns' that Sue identifies with are themselves a form of signification in that they are variously composed of the 'light signals' from stars that no longer exist. As revealed in *Two on a Tower*, the constellations suggest another way of 'reading' the vast formless potential of space: the undifferentiated realm (which Lacan calls the 'R/real') where all that is beyond signification inheres. Lacan claims that 'it is in relation to the real that the level of phantasy functions. The real supports the phantasy, the phantasy protects the real' (Lacan, 1977: 41). In 'inhabiting' Jude's Sunday suit, Sue inhabits the fantasy of what she perceives to be male gender privilege – a privilege that Jude discerns as the result of 'the common enemy, coercion': a structure of gender signification, and gender relations that makes a man like him 'only the helpless transmitter of the pressure put upon him' (301). Though she cannot step outside the constraints of prevailing discourses of gender, sexuality and the erotic, cross-dressing allows her temporarily to access other forms of self-articulation denied to her as a woman. Judith Butler argues that cross-dressing or 'drag' is related to a melancholic heterosexual gender identification; it is a *re-enactment* of gender that signals desires that have been rejected in the interests of becoming a 'stable' subject: 'the melancholy of gender identification [...] must be understood [...] as the internalization of an interior moral directive which gains its structure and energy from an externally enforced taboo' (Butler, 1990: 64). As is the case with all the texts under discussion here, such a re-enactment has significance for the production and enactment of sexual or erotic desire. In a gesture that acknowledges the potential of a provisional hermaphroditism for the expression of desire, whilst also anticipating Sue's agonised conclusion that 'We must conform' (361), Jude places her dry female garments beside her sleeping form and, symbolically 'touching her on the shoulder, he went downstairs and washed himself by starlight in the yard' (159). Sue and Jude's separate symbolic immersion of themselves in water suggests the possibility of reconfigured gendered and desiring selves, but the tragedy of the novel, as in the case of Eustacia Vye and the published ending of 'The Distracted Preacher', is that this possibility remains unrealised. Jude's last suicidal walk to Sue in the driving rain signals the death and annihilation of a desiring self, unable to find recognition outside the rigid structure of class, gender, sexuality and creed. It is fittingly ironic that this fatal sleep in the rain occurs near to the very field that witnessed his childhood emasculation at the hands of Farmer Troutham.

As You Like It was one of Hardy's favourite Shakespeare plays.[32] The wooing of the cross-dressed Rosalind under the name of Ganymede establishes a teasing sexual ambiguity throughout the play, which also provides the dénouement to Théophile Gautier's iconic transvestite novel of sexual experimentation, *Mademoiselle du Maupin* (1835) – which Hardy owned, read and quoted from (*LN*, 1842: 2). The role of Rosalind challenges recognised gender identities by revealing how they are constructed and performed and how they excite erotic desire within a social matrix constructed in relation to an ideology of separate spheres. In *Jude the Obscure*, the confluence of Shakespeare's Rosalind and Ovid's Ganymede in the figure of the cross-dressed Sue presents a radical challenge to gender individuation and the structuring of erotic desire according to a heterosexual imperative by demonstrating that gender is a 'corporeal style' rather than the essence of an individual. As is the case with Lizzy Newberry and Richard Stockdale in 'The Distracted Preacher', Jude is under no illusion that the 'slim and fragile being masquerading as himself on a Sunday' is anyone other than the female Sue, but Lizzy's and Sue's corporeal style, reinforced by their sartorial disguise, elicits and defines the varying desirous responses that they and their male lovers experience, which temporarily overrides any assumptions about their sex. Sue becomes temporarily uncategorisable and her nonconformity to a recognised gender binary unsettles the course and nature of Jude's desire for her. As is the case with all of the texts under discussion here, cross-dressing is revealed as a parodic performance that emphasises the imitative nature of recognised gender identities. At the same time, it indicates how, if only for now in the realm of fantasy and the imagination, desire may be liberated from the circumscription of gender, how the 'elsewhere' that is beyond the current signifying system may, in Butler's words 'be brought home' (Butler, 2004: 217).

6
Art, Aesthetics and Masculine Desire: *The Well-Beloved* (1897)

> Nobody would ever know the truth about him; *what* it was he had sought that had so eluded, tantalized, and escaped him; what it was that had led him such a dance, and had at last, as he believed just now in the freshness of his loss, been discovered in the girl who had left him.
>
> (*The Well-Beloved*: 191)

> Recollection is not Platonic reminiscence – it is not the return of a form, an imprint, a *eidos*, of beauty and good, a supreme truth, coming to us from the beyond. It is something that comes to us from the structural necessities, something humble, born at the level of the lowest encounters and of all the talking crowd that precedes us, at the level of the structure of the signifier, of the languages spoken in a stuttering, stumbling, way but which cannot elude constraints.
>
> (Lacan, 'Of the Network of Signifiers', 1973, 1977: 47)

Hardy's last novel *The Well-Beloved* (1897) focuses more precisely on the relationship between women and woman as symptom of man's desire. It is Hardy's most concentrated interrogation of a gendered model of desire in which woman is constituted as 'a sign or a token of the forbidden maternal, an ideal or fantasy which can never be fully appropriated, [but] only "believed in"' (Butler, 1987; 1999: 203). Its protagonist Jocelyn Pierston is a sculptor and a 'fantast' driven in his emotional and his creative life by his restless and compelling pursuit of the 'Eternal Feminine'.

Covering a period of 40 years in the life of an individual man, lover and artist, the novel examines indepth the complex relationship between the evolving masculine subject and his experience of desire inscribed in and mediated by a patriarchal language and culture, and by the depredations of time as measured by the human lifespan. *The Well-Beloved* demonstrates how desire is incited and defined by the impossibility of its fulfilment: by the surplus or excess that persists in the face of every attempt to contain it within, or satisfy it with, a signifier, object (or as Lacan terms it *objet petit a*) or situation. At the same time, it offers a compelling critique of the male artist's confusion between the woman as constituted by the reality system, and the 'Real' which, for Lacan, designates the realm beyond articulation: that 'essential part' that is left 'a prisoner in the toils of the pleasure principle' (Lacan, 1977b: 55). Pierston nicely illustrates Lacan's model of transference in his attempts to satisfy his desire to touch the Real through his emotional and sexual relationships with women who appear to embody his conception of the Eternal Feminine. As Edward Neill suggests, in his portrayal of a man 'perennially caught "between repetitions"', Hardy 'seems to be playing with a Lacanian idea avant la lettre' (Neill, 2004: 115). Pierston's personal life is mirrored in his attempts at creative self-expression through his sculptural renditions of this Eternal Feminine in the form of the 'well-beloved', which, by definition, represents his ultimate *objet a,* or the object that incites his desire.[1] Desire is manifest here at the level of biological need, ontological fulfilment and aesthetic expression. In every case, Pierston looks to a fantasy of woman for satisfaction: a fantasy with which the three main women in his life (the three Avices) cannot, or will not, identify. As J. Hillis Miller suggests, *The Well-Beloved* is a novel about art – in particular about the literary arts – and the theme 'surfaces in the form of an interrogation of the relation between erotic fascination, creativity, and Platonic metaphysics' (Miller, 1982b: 149).[2]

At the heart of the novel is an understanding of the defining problematic of gender and of the tension between desire and signifying forms, which include language and Pierston's chosen media as an artist: plaster and marble. All of this is set against the massive limestone outcrop of the Isle of Slingers, 'a peninsular carved by Time out of a single stone', a 'rocky coign of England [...] standing out so far into mid-sea that touches of the Gulf Stream soften the air till February' (*WB*: 'Preface' 1912: 4). For Pierston, and to some extent for the narrator also, the island is a signifier of permanence, stability and 'home', in the domestic as well as in the broader ontological sense. The novel explores the ego-morphic desire of its central protagonist in relation to a man's desire to possess and assimilate to himself his 'feminine' other, and an artist's urge to express this other – which is also himself – through his creative activity. In this respect, *The Well-Beloved* is an intensely personal novel, dealing as it does with the artist's struggle to create, out of the raw material of life, an art that will exceed or transcend the limits of its form, and give access to what Lacan calls a transgressive jouissance. Pierston is driven by the impossible desire for self-expression or self-actualisation in the realm of the Real, the urge to push beyond the limits of the signifier into an imagined seamless unity of self with other, signifier with signified, inspiration with execution. However, he is barred from access to the unattainable realm of ontological plenitude by his investment in the symbolic order: in particular, his insistent identification of the ultimate object of desire with the patriarchal myth of the Eternal Feminine. The trauma of his personal and aesthetic failure leaves him bereft of all desire except the desire to be free of any yearning to realise himself other than at the level of material satisfaction: what Lacan defines in 'The Deconstruction of the Drive' as 'a subjectifying homeostasis' (1977: 167). In 'Alienation' Lacan describes how the signifier makes the subject manifest only by reducing 'the subject in question to being no more than a signifier, to petrify the subject in the same movement in which it calls the subject to function, to speak as a subject' (1977: 207). In *The Well-Beloved*, Hardy claimed to have attempted to introduce what he called 'the subjective theory of love into modern fiction' (*LW*: 304) resulting on one of his most experimental and least realistic novels. In a letter to Swinburne he referred to it as a 'fanciful exhibition of the artistic nature [with] [...] some little foundation in fact' (*LW*: 305). In this respect *The Well-Beloved* is a transitional work; standing on the border between Hardy's career as a major nineteenth-century novelist, and his re-invention of himself as one of the greatest twentieth-century poets. The final chapter of this study will explore this creative struggle in relation to Hardy's elegiac poems.

Written as he approached his sixth decade, *The Well-Beloved* also develops Hardy's acute perception of the relationship of time and ageing to desire, previously glimpsed in the figure of Eustacia Vye, wandering the heath with her telescope and hourglass. The progressive degradation of Pierston's mental and physical resources renders the prospect of fulfilment and satisfaction ever more remote and chimerical. The ageing Hardyian male artist is thus revealed as the paradigmatic subject of desire: in desiring to be free of desire, he desires, in fact, his own dissolution, but achieves instead only the stagnation of the self that results from the death of the creative impulse. Driven to despair and mental and physical breakdown as he grows older by the intensification of desire incited by the increasing elusiveness of its object, the diminution of his aesthetic powers and the ageing of his face and body, Pierston finally renounces his 'Well-Beloved', and all that she signifies, losing in the process not only his libido and his affective capacity but also his aesthetic appreciation and creative ability. In terms of the trope of water previously discussed, Jocelyn's renunciation of the potentiality and motivational energy of desire is neatly symbolised by his involvement in a scheme to close up the natural fountains in the Street of Wells because of their possible contamination. Pierston deliberately caps 'the ever-bubbling spring of emotion' which, without its 'conduit into space', will 'ruin all but the greatest of men' (50). In an oddly ironic *fin de siècle* reversal, he 'degenerates' from the resistant subject of polymorphous desire to the compliant object of bourgeois conformity. His desire is attenuated to the appreciation of stability and a calmness that amounts to extreme homeostasis. Rounding out the whole in a marriage of convenience with his elderly ex-lover Marcia, he abandons the nebulous possibilities of future *becoming* for the satisfaction of simple needs and social require-ments in the present, and is attenuated, as a result, to a 'gray shadow' of a man.

Pierston's early conversation with his friend, the painter Somers, centres on erotic and romantic desire and on the sculptor's apparent inability to remain in love with any one woman who, as flesh, 'dies daily, like the Apostle's corporeal self; because when I grapple with the reality she's no longer in it, so that I cannot stick to one incarnation if I would' (52). At this level, Pierston's 'Well-Beloved' appears as the personification of the fugitive attraction that certain women hold for him, which evaporates on contact or possession. Pierston is another casualty of 'the disappointment that is pos-session' (Girard, 1965: 39). None of these women is the ultimate expression of the 'Well-Beloved', they are merely its 'transient condition': the forms through which Pierston attempts to express and apprehend her. Indeed, Pierston's fundamental error lies in assuming that the 'Well-Beloved' – the ultimate object of desire – is indeed his feminine other. The novel demon-strates, better than Lacan does, that the feminisation of the Other simply subjects desire to the constraints of the signifier, arresting it at the level of a masculine, heterosexual pleasure principle. The 'Well-Beloved' – as gender-neutral ultimate object of desire – constantly slips out from under the forms in which Pierston attempts to contain it: flesh, plaster, marble, language and a patriarchal concept of the feminine:

> Essentially she was perhaps of no tangible substance: a spirit, a dream, a frenzy, a conception, an aroma, an epitomized sex, a light of the eye, a parting of the lips. God only knew what she really was; Pierston did not.
>
> She was indescribable. (16)

For Pierston, the 'Well-Beloved' is caught up in the endless chain of signifiers or partial objects through which he attempts to specify his desire: woman, youth, innocence, art, 'home' – all of which signify what can never be grasped and yet tantalise with the promise of fulfilment, permanence and the end of all yearning. His 'Well-Beloved' is a compound of Victorian myths of the feminine which promise to offer meaning and fulfilment to the masculine subject. Indeed, the signifiers of his success – profes-sional advancement, election to the Royal Academy – are meaningless without their feminine counterpart: 'a domestic centre round which hon-ours might crystallize'. Without this 'soul-anchorage' or personal 'shrine', his achievements evaporate, along with his sense of integrity: 'they dis-persed impalpably without accumulating and adding weight to his material wellbeing' (50). In seeking to add substance to his nebulous self-conceit: Pierston defines his 'material wellbeing' as dependent upon his immaterial

'Well-Beloved': a feminine other that will validate the masculine self through its very difference.

Pierston's realisation, after the death of Avice Caro, that the Isle of Slingers represents 'the terminal spot of [the Well-Beloved's] migration' – the 'end' of his desire – indicates that his 'other' is primarily something missing or lacking in himself. Like the self-alienated, nostalgic speakers of Hardy's 'home' poems, which formed the focus of Chapter 1, Pierston is engaged on a quest for a sense of home that eventually brings him back to his natal isle, back indeed to the very house of his birth, and to the belated realisation that his Well-Beloved is 'a subjective phenomenon vivified by the weird influences of his descent and birthplace' (16). Like Hardy's Matthäus Tina, Giles Winterbourne, Grace Melbury and Jude Fawley, Jocelyn Pierston is afflicted with a profound nostalgia for an earlier, younger, more integrated self, as he imagines himself to have been before the 'fashionable person' displaced the simple 'island man', and before the nescience of the child was displaced by the self-consciousness of adulthood (12). He equates the possession of the 'Well-Beloved', and the re-possession of his natal isle, with the satisfaction of his nostalgia for that 'being-at-home' that eludes so many of Hardy's characters, riven as they are with a profound sense of alienation that defines them, among other things, as Victorian subjects possessed of a modern sensibility. After meeting the 'Second Avice' – Ann Avice Caro – 'there came to [Pierston] a wild wish – that, instead of having an artist's reputation, he could be living here an illiterate and unknown man, wooing, and in a fair way winning, the pretty laundress in the cottage hard by' (81).[3] As Edward Neill has indicated, Ann Avice, and her mother Avice Caro, represent for the society artist the genius loci of his birthplace (Neill, 2004: 118-19). They also embody the home of his youth and 'the rejuvenated Spirit of the Past' – above all, his own past.

In Part II–viii 'His Own Soul Confronts Him', Pierston meets his match in the restless, fickle desires of Ann Avice Caro, daughter to the first Avice, whom he reads as a female version of himself.[4] He explains the idiosyncratic similarities between them as the result of 'some remote ancestor common to both families, from whom the trait had latently descended and recrudesced' and is prepared to accept her coolness and lack of sophistication for 'the pleasure of possessing one in whom seemed to linger as an aroma all the charm of his youth and his early home' (105).[5] The link between the phantom of the first Avice and that of Pierston's lost youth, both represented for him in Avice's daughter Ann, is strengthened in a typical Hardyesque irony in which Ann Avice actually moves into Pierston's old childhood home (143) and her daughter, the third Avice, sleeps in his former bedroom (149).[6] The fact that the third Avice already bears Pierston's surname reflects her role as his perceived feminine counterpart even before their proposed marriage. The almost incestuous identification between Jocelyn and his 'Well-Beloved' in the form of the three Avices is emphasised by the curious relationship he would have to each of them as a result of his marriage to the youngest. Concerned by the severe illness of Ann Avice, Pierston enquires of his betrothed: 'How is mother? – our mother, as I shall call her soon' (175). If marriage with the third Avice would make the second Avice his mother-in-law, the first Avice, who was Pierston's peer in terms of age, would be his grandmother. Pierston's marriage to Avice Caro's granddaughter was to bring him 'home' in every sense; back, it would seem, to the 'maternal' place of his earliest origin. It is significant that at the end of the novel he abandons his fashionable style of dress and appears 'always in a homely suit of local make, and of the fashion of thirty years before, the achievement of a tailoress at East Quarriers' (202). Although this 'homely' suit serves to identify him still further with the island of his birth, it is little more than a visible sign of his new contentment with 'the defiles of the signifier', the 'definition of the sign' (Lacan, 1973: 157).

Jocelyn Pierston insists on translating an 'abstraction' of femininity into a 'real personage', and an idea into an endlessly reiterated form. Eventually the 'form' overwrites the idea and threatens to constrain the real women who inspire it:

> He had watched the marble images of her which stood in his working-room, under all changes of light and shade – in the brightening of morning, in the blackening of eve, in moonlight, in lamplight. Every line and curve of her body none, naturally, knew better than he; and, though not a belief, it was, as has been stated, a formula, a superstition, that the three Avices were interpenetrated with her essence. (148)

Pierston's urge to express the mutable essence, or idea, of beauty in material form is a symptom of his quest for self-actualisation: for that fugitive sense of *chez-soi* that will assuage his ontological homesickness. As an intellectual product of his time, he has been 'unhomed' by the undermining of God as the guarantor of human subjectivity and, like so many of his contemporaries towards the end of the nineteenth-century, embraces an alternative 'truth system' of neo-paganism. Hardy puts into play here two major and closely interconnected signifiers of Pierston's desire: the ancient Isle of Slingers (which signifies permanence, unity and 'home' to the deracinated native and self-alienated subject) and the 'Well-Beloved': 'the migratory, elusive idealization he called his Love' (13) and the inspiration for his art. Both are closely connected with paganism in that the 'Well-Beloved' appears to Pierston in the figure of the implacable goddess Aphrodite, whose shrine is said to have existed on the island in pagan times.[7] Avice is so closely identified with the Isle of Slingers as to seem to Pierston part of its geologic structure, as does her daughter Ann Avice, of whom Pierston declares to Somers, 'I know the perfect and pure quarry she was dug from: and that gives a man confidence' (108).

In his preface to the 1912 edition of the novel, Hardy describes the model for Jocelyn's birthplace – Portland Island – as 'for centuries immemorial the home of a curious and well-nigh distinct people, cherishing strange beliefs and singular customs, now for the most part obsolescent' ('Preface', 1986: 3). The 'ancient Vindilia Island, and the Home of the Slingers' (9) is not only the location of a long-vanished temple to Venus/Aphrodite but also 'possibly one to the love-goddess of the Slingers' before the Roman colonisation of the island. Pierston imagines Avice Caro (whose surname Hardy chose because it suggests the Italian for 'dear' or 'cherished') as the product of 'a Roman lineage, more or less grafted on the stock of the Slingers' (*LW*: 304). The Caro heritage, combining as it does Ancient Britain with Ancient Rome, seems to have been untouched at base by the Christian conversion of Britain, as does the Isle of Slingers itself. Pierston's second sojourn on the island follows a visit to the museums and galleries of Rome, where he had dimly fancied 'in the Roman atmosphere, in its lights and shades, and particularly in its reflected or secondary lights, something resembling the atmosphere of his native promontory' (140). The old, and ironically named, Hope Church on the Isle of Slingers, which was destroyed by a landslide some time before, 'seemed to say that in this last local stronghold of the Pagan divinities, where Pagan customs lingered yet, Christianity had established itself precariously at best' (18). Like the narrator of Henry James's 'The Last of the Valerii' (1874), Pierston's 'spiritual ear' is sensitive to echoes of the old pagan religion that still reverberate within his island home (31) and are reflected in the ancient island custom through which engagement is ratified by sexual intercourse and marriage follows only when a couple has 'proved' themselves to be fertile. In the tight-knit community of Slingers, where property and business was passed from father to son or possibly daughter, fertility was of more account than social standing or reputation.[8]

The reluctance of the 'modern' educated Avice Caro to take part in this formal ratification of a betrothal signals the beginning of a shift in values towards a more bourgeois, metropolitan view of marriage and separation centred in a Christian moral structure, which results in Pierston's abandonment of her for the less scrupulous Marcia. Ironically, this also helps to establish Avice, who it is implied died of a broken heart, as the focus of his longing. In his imagination, she remains forever young and forever virgin, her lily-white corpse in its winding sheet irradiated by the fitting symbol of a new moon, whose 'divinity [...] was not more excellently pure than she, the lost, had been' (73). His imaginary Avice is entombed at the heart of her island house, which is 'framed from mullions to chimney-top like the isle itself, of stone', and reached 'only by the faint noises inherent in the isle; the tink-tink of the chisels in the quarries, the surging of the tides in the Bay, and the muffled grumbling of the currents in the never-pacified Race' (73). Pierston's yearning to unite with the dead Avice Caro is also a yearning to fuse with the island on which she has died and on which he was born. In this respect, the Ancient Isle of Slingers has a maternal significance for Pierston: his desire to return there can be read as the expression of a desire for a pre-oedipal fusion with the maternal body. If so, then once again Pierston's desire is constrained at the level of, in this case, an insistently material signifier, in which houses and gardens are subsumed into 'the unity of the whole island as a solid and single block of limestone four miles long', sedimented with meaning like the 'infinitely stratified walls of oolite, "The melancholy ruins/Of cancelled cycles" ' which compose it (9).[9] It is significant then that after his breakdown, and 'the extinction of the Well-Beloved and other ideals', Pierston abandons his pursuit of beauty in favour of a wholesale modernisation of the rock, 'acquiring some old moss-grown, mullioned Elizabethan cottages, for the purposes of pulling them down because they were damp; which he afterwards did, and built new ones with hollow walls, and full of ventilators' (205).[10]

During his final illness, the poet Heinrich Heine, whose work Hardy admired, wrote 'The Gods in Exile', an essay that profoundly influenced Walter Pater, who quoted from it in the preface to his study of Mirandola. Pater was fascinated by Heine's description of how the iconoclastic frenzy of the early Christian monks deprived the ancient pagan gods of their temples and sustenance, forcing them into exile on earth in the humble guise of woodcutters, day labourers, shepherds, soldiers and even, in the case of Bacchus, the Superior of a Franciscan monastery.[11] Hardy alludes to this idea in his description of Eustacia Vye, who is 'the raw material of a divinity', having 'the passions and instincts which make a model goddess' rather than those that make 'a model woman' (63).[12] It is more fully developed in the portrayal of the three Avices, especially Ann Avice (the second). Pierston dreams one night that 'he saw dimly masking behind that young countenance "the Weaver of Wiles" herself, "with all her subtle face laughing aloud" ' (92). The first of these quotations is from line two of Moreton John Walhouse's rendering of a fragment by Sappho, placed as number I in Wharton's *Sappho, Memoir, Text, Selected Renderings, and a Literal Translation* (1895), while the second – and indeed Pierston's situation – is borrowed, once again, from Swinburne's *Anactoria*, an extract from which is also included by Wharton as a 'paraphrase' or rendering of the fragment.[13] Here Sappho dreams that Aphrodite answers her complaint of unrequited love for Anactoria (62).[14] Pierston's experience of desire is deliberately mediated through Sappho's as presented in Wharton's edition, which Hardy bought for himself in August 1895 between the publication of the serial version of *The Pursuit of the Well-Beloved* in the *Illustrated London News* in 1892 and the revised novel *The Well-Beloved* in 1897. In a passage that directly refers to Sappho, which does not appear in the earlier serial version, Pierston tells Somers that he is 'posed, puzzled and perplexed by the legerdemain of a creature – a deity rather; by Aphrodite, as a poet would put it, as I should put it myself in marble' (35).

The classically educated reader of *The Well-Beloved* is encouraged to see (through Pierston's eyes) Aphrodite – the goddess of love and sexuality – masquerading in the shape of the three Avices, particularly Ann Avice, whom Pierston recognises as 'the phantom of Avice, now grown to be warm flesh and blood', imbibing 'the haunted atmosphere of Roman Venus about and around the site of her perished temple there' (83). For Pierston, Ann Avice is no semi-illiterate washerwoman: 'In front of her, on the surface of her, was shining out that more real, more inter-penetrating being whom he knew so well' (89). Ann Avice is merely 'the subserving minion', the 'temporary creature' who embodies 'the indispensable one' – Aphrodite herself – in human form. The destruction of the ancient temple of Aphrodite by the Christianised Romans has its modern counterpart in Pierston's demolition of the island's Elizabethan cottages. At the same time, Pierston, and perhaps the narrator also, is confused as to the origin of the punishment or curse he feels himself to be under. Is his frustration the curse of Aphrodite for his sins against her in his art, or a Christian emanation from her ruined temple 'wrathfully torturing him through the very false gods to whom he had devoted himself both in his craft, like Demetrius of Ephesus, and in his heart' (112). Like Eustacia Vye, Sue Bridehead and Michael Henchard before him, Jocelyn Pierston externalises the virtual yet palpable forces that constrain and frustrate him. For Lacan, those frustrations are part of the language from which subjectivity is constituted.

In Wharton's *Sappho*, fragment 90, the speaker laments her inability to weave, 'broken as I am by longing for a boy, at soft Aphrodite's will' (Wharton, 1895: 129). It is this utter subjection to a force beyond the control of reason – 'soft Aphrodite's will' – that Pierston experiences in his 'sudden Sapphic terror of love', when he is forced to consider the absurdity of his infatuation with Ann Avice: a pretty, uneducated laundress who lacks even the culture and refinement of her mother. In this respect, Pierston's desire for the dead Avice Caro reincarnated, as it were, in her daughter and grand-daughter is not to be confused with his more prosaic sexual attraction to Marcia Bencombe.[15] This rather sudden and short-lived infatuation with the Junoesque Marcia is presented as a bathetic substitute for his 'true' desire for Aphrodite (Avice). The intertextual references to Shakespeare's *Romeo and Juliet* in relation to these offspring of rival stone merchants, fail to convince the reader that the flitting of the Well-Beloved 'from the remoter figure' of Avice to the far more forthcoming 'near one in the chamber above' is anything more than the satisfaction of frustrated sexual desire. The curiosity aroused by Marcia's peculiar situation and her striking independence, is stimulated to interest by her handsome, commanding, imperious face and fanned to arousal by the sensation of warmth emanating from the lady in furs, whom he is forced to clasp close to his side against the wind (29). The 'migration' is completed as he 'overhaul[s]' and dries her underclothes before the fire. After ten minutes of this peculiarly intimate activity, which mirrors Jude's drying of Sue's saturated garments after her flight through the river from the teacher training college, Pierston 'adored her' (31).[16] However, three days of 'ardour' and 'passion' is sufficient to satisfy them sexually (39) and Pierston faces the fact that his desire far exceeds his physical needs and biological drives: 'the exact moment of [the 'Well-Beloved's'] complete withdrawal Pierston knew not [...]. Their acquaintance, though so fervid, had been too brief for such lingering' (48).

After Marcia leaves him, Pierston 'sighs' for her but only as 'a friend of sterling common sense in practical difficulties' (56). Their marriage at the end of the novel is one of simple convenience and signals Pierston's abandonment of the ideality for the real, the potentiality of the future for the satisfaction of immediate needs. As he informs his elderly lover, the malignant fever that accompanied his breakdown 'has killed a faculty which has, after all, brought me my greatest sorrows, if a few little pleasures' (201). He has, he claims, 'no love to give [...]. But such friendship as I am capable of is yours till the end' (204).

Pierston's temporary attraction for Nichola Pine-Avon is another case in point. He meets her at his first entry into society for several years following his father's death, when he is in such a heightened state of sexual anticipation that it seems that any female form would do to embody the 'Well-Beloved', even – for a brief moment – that of his hostess Lady Channelcliffe (57). He puts this down to 'the highly-charged electric condition in which he had arrived by reason of his recent isolation' (58). The electrical metaphor recalls the state of Felice Charmond and Edred Fitzpiers, supercharged with desire and in search of a suitable object through which to discharge it. On this occasion, Pierston does not consider, as he seems to have done before, that this 'presentiment' that he is about to meet 'the Well-Beloved' 'was, of all presentiments, just the sort of one to work out its own fulfillment' (58). As with Marcia, it is Nichola's physical charms that capture his attention, the 'exceeding fairness' and 'unblemished' quality of her neck and shoulders, her 'luminous' grey eyes and shining chestnut hair (64). This fleshly desire fades, quite literally, into insignificance at the news of the death of Avice Caro, the only woman he never desired but who is now so poignantly placed beyond his possession as to become his ultimate object. The news from the present transports Jocelyn to the unreachable past, from experience to memory, from the flesh to the spirit. Hardy gives us a fine 'slow dissolve' as Lady Channelcliffe's crowded fashionable dinner table recedes before Pierston's and the reader's eyes behind 'the vivid presentiment of [the virgin] Avice Caro' as he last saw her 20 years earlier 'and the old, old scenes on Isle Vindilia which were inseparable from her personality'. Mrs Pine-Avon, by contrast 'seemed to grow material, a superficies of flesh and bone, a person of lines and surfaces; she was a language in living cipher no more' (70). The palpable, sexually attractive Nichola no longer signifies as desire's object, and Pierston moves beyond her, beyond the lingual and the material into the realm of recollection and dream. By contrast with his desire for her, and Marcia before her, his desire for the dead young Avice Caro of his past has an 'intrinsic, almost radiant, purity', the flesh is 'absent altogether; it was love rarefied and refined to its highest attar' (72–3).

Pierston's desire for Avice's daughter Ann is intriguing. Where his attraction to Nichola is sexual, Ann Avice is clearly an erotic object. His conception of Ann as the phantom of Avice now grown to be warm flesh and blood indicates how the sexed body of the woman is inscribed with cultural meaning. Throughout Pierston's disingenuous interrogation of his new washerwoman, he is 'thinking of the girl'

> or as the scientific might say, Nature was working her plans for the next generation under the cloak of a dialogue on linen. He could not read her individual character, owing to the confusing effect of her likeness to a woman whom he had valued too late. He could not help seeing in her all that he knew of another, and veiling in her all that did not harmonize with his sense of metempsychosis. (90)

For Pierston, Ann Avice signifies something beyond the reach of biology and the simple Darwinian urge to reproduce. He is drawn to the illiterate washerwoman because she is pretty but also because she bears a startling resemblance to the signifier of his ultimate desire: her dead mother Avice Caro. As J. Hillis Miller surmises, Pierston

> now loves by mediation as he never could love directly. He desires the first Avice by way of the second. This is quite different from his loves so far. These have been an attempt to find the ideal permanently incarnated, without equivocation and without distance, in a living person [...]. The first Avice lives in the present with an intense combination of presence and absence which guarantees that Jocelyn's love will never change [...] because he is separated from the object of his desire by an impenetrable barrier and so can never consummate his love.

Ann represents her mother Avice 'in an irresistibly fascinating combination of tangible flesh and intangible spirit' (Miller, 1970: 173). Pierston turns his desire away from the body of Ann Avice and towards what that body signifies for him: the incorporeal, enigmatic feminine symbolised by the image of her dead, virgin mother. His scrupulous avoidance of physical contact with Ann Avice, and his regard for appearances when she goes to live with him as his housekeeper in his London flat, contrasts strongly with his previous liaison with Marcia. However, in an ironic replay of the situation between Pierston and her mother at their last meeting, Ann Avice has already followed 'island custom' and now belongs to the man whose child she carries: her cousin Ike Pierston.

The Well-Beloved demonstrates how desire is not simply a lack of having. Jocelyn Pierston's subjectivity is constituted in relation to a lack of being: his desire is driven by a fundamental absence at the heart of his sense of self which he strives to fill, or satisfy, through the pursuit of those metonymic objects which entice desire, offering themselves in its place but failing, ultimately, to capture it. Pierston's attempts to grasp, or recognise, himself in relation to these objects only reveals this absence, and the revelation becomes clearer and more inescapable as the narrative progresses through 40 years of his life. Pierston, like Narcissus, seeks himself in what is outside, beyond or other to himself (see Laycock, 1999: 397), and the absence at the heart of this desire is nowhere clearer than in his ultimate confrontation of/with himself – quite literally in his own reflection. However, where the beautiful youth Narcissus famously desired his own image so passionately that his bodily self faded away, the ageing Pierston regards *his* reflection as an insubstantial spectre compared with his conception of the vibrant, younger man he feels himself to be. His desire to shake off his 'withering carcass' (166), as his 'Well-Beloved' has done so often, finds expression in his compulsion to unite with increasingly younger versions of the first Avice.

Besotted at the age of 60 with what he regards as the third reincarnation of Avice Caro in her 19-year-old granddaughter Avice Pierston, Jocelyn is forced to face up to the realisation that, while his sweetheart is 'secondly renewed', he is not (158). Like the memory of his past love, for the narrator of 'Thoughts of Phena: At News of her Death' (dated March, 1890), Avice Caro is 'fined (or refined) in [his] brain' as she appeared 40 years earlier, and this mental image becomes conflated with and inseparable from Pierston's youthful conception of himself. His desire for the young Avice Caro is his displaced desire for his own lost youth. At news of Avice's death, which he receives in Lady Channelcliffe's fashionable dining room, Pierston's sight is usurped by his 'unsight' (Hynes, I: 81): perceivable reality is slowly displaced by memory and imagination as he muses on her (70).[17] Back in his room he gazes on an old-fashioned photograph of Avice, 'taken on glass in the primitive days of photography, and framed in tinsel in the commonest way':

> It was Avice Caro, as she had appeared during the summer month or two which he had spent with her on the island twenty years before this time, her young lips pursed up, her hands meekly folded. The effect of the glass was to lend to the picture much of the softness characteristic of the original. (72)

For Pierston, memory and imagination have more valence than reality, and there is no 'real' Avice – the betrayed, broken woman: widowed, bereaved of one son, abandoned by another and prematurely dead at the age of 40 – to contradict him. The old-fashioned 'collodion' glass photograph clarifies and gives substance to this conception of Avice: re-fining it, as it were, in his brain. The photograph on glass becomes a substitute for Pierston's own reflection in the glass, and as he engages in a 'long contemplation of the likeness [which] completed in his emotions what the letter had begun', what he sees is the image of his own nostalgic desire for himself 20 years younger (72). From this point on, he associates this 'fined' image of Avice – whether existing in his memory or radiating through the figures of her daughter and granddaughter – with this self-conceit, which increasingly contrasts with the reality of his ageing body. Pierston struggles to locate himself in the space between the intangible memory of his youth and the all too pressing reality of his physical decline. He finds that the 'rejuvenating power' of Ann Avice – 'Avice the Second' – 'had ineffable charm. He felt as he had felt when standing beside her predecessor; but, alas! he was twenty years further on towards the shade' (93). It is Ann who forces Pierston to begin to confront and accept his own corporeal decline. Quizzing her on her fickleness, Pierston asks, with a pomposity that is quickly deflated by her honest reply:

> 'What made the being of your fancy forsake my form and go elsewhere?'
> 'Well – though you seemed handsome and gentlemanly at first –'
> 'Yes?'
> 'I found you too old soon after.' (103)

It is she who most clearly reveals to him the discrepancy between the ideal and reality. Facing his actual image in the mirror, he experiences a radical disjunction between his mental conception of himself and the reflection that gazes back at him:

> he looked considerably younger than he was. But there was history in his face – distinct chapters of it; his brow was not that blank page it once had been. He knew the origin of that line in his forehead; it had been traced in the course of a month or two by past troubles. He remembered the coming of this pale wiry hair; it had been brought on by the illness in Rome, when he had wished each night that he might never wake again. This wrinkled corner, that drawn bit of skin, they had resulted from those months of despondency when all seemed going against his art, his strength, his happiness. (124)

Pierston's confrontation with his reflected self prompts self-reflection as he reads and, in the process, writes the history of his past on the face that confronts him in the mirror.

In his essay 'Consciousness It/self', S. W. Laycock suggests that reflection

> feeds only upon the past, upon the husks of experience that have elapsed, lapsed, rendered up their vitality and become hollow form. The 'self'

thematised in reflection, the agency thus recaptured, is lifeless. It has no voice. And reflection can only inscribe the site of a once-living experience [...]. As Trinh thi Minh-ha remarks, '[t]o see one's double is to see oneself dead'.

(Laycock, 1999: 400)

Reflection, in both senses of the word, exposes the disunity and dis-integration of the self. Laycock cites David Levin's contention that 'to be "possessed by" the visible is to be *a cogito* dispossessed: an ego not in total possession of itself; an ego not totally present to (for) itself':

> Reflection thematizes exactly what is *not* consciousness, and cannot bring to presence that which *is*. And since reflection disrupts the immediate life of pre-reflective consciousness, and recaptures it only subsequent to this disruption, we must credit Derrida's remark that '[a] more or less argot translation of the *cogito*' would be: 'I am therefore dead'. (400)

Pierston continually loses himself in the aporia between the idea (his chimerical younger self, around which his desires cohere) and its hollow form (its physical representation in the 'dead' reflection). This prompts a soliloquy – a dialogue between his self-conceit and his self-reflection – which articulates their incompatibility: 'You cannot live your life and keep it, Jocelyn,' he said (160).[18]

In the second of these mirror incidents, self-reflection *precedes* the disclo-sure of the reflected self, which appears to him as a spectre which haunts him with what he has tried to repress: the physical evidence of his ageing body:

> As he sat thus thinking, and the daylight increased, he discerned, a short distance before him, a movement of something ghostly. His position was facing the window, and he found that by chance the looking-glass had swung itself vertical, so that what he saw was his own shape. The recognition startled him. The person he appeared was too grievously far, chronologically, in advance of the person he felt himself to be.
>
> Pierston did not care to regard the figure confronting him so mockingly.

But the figure begins to assert its hold over him as he is forced to confront, and own, his ageing form: 'the question of age being pertinent he could not give the spectre up, and ultimately got out of bed under the weird fascination of the reflection' (166). It is his gradual self-investment in this hollow form that signals the waning of his desire: the end of his 'becoming' and the beginning of his end. It is fitting that this confrontation takes place at dawn: in the liminal, unspecifiable space between night and day. In this ironic 'aubade', the 'lover' Pierson addresses is not the third Avice but his own impending death.[19]

In 'their first meeting under the solar rays' the third Avice is shocked by Pierston's appearance, and this prompts him to confess not only his previous relationships with her mother and grandmother, but also the chronological evidence that belies his youthful appearance:

> 'Mother has never told me that. Yet, of course, you might have been [her lover].
> I mean, you are old enough.'
> He took the remark as a satire she had not intended, 'O yes – quite old enough,' he said grimly. 'Almost too old.'
> 'Too old for mother? How's that?'
> 'Because I belonged to your grandmother.'
> 'No? How can that be?'
> 'I was her lover likewise [...].'
> 'But you couldn't have been, Mr. Pierston! You are not old enough? Why, how old are you? – you have never told me.'
> 'I am very old.'
> 'My mother's, and my grandmother's,' said she, looking at him no longer as at a possible husband, but as a strange fossilized relic in human form.
> Pierston saw it, but meaning to give up the game he did not spare himself.
> 'Your mother's and your grandmother's young man,' he repeated.
> 'And were you my great-grandmother's too?' she asked. (167)

As age and experience inscribe themselves upon, overwrite, the body of this desiring subject, Pierston finds his desires likewise delineated in ways he cannot control. The tables are turned and he now sees himself reflected through the eyes, and the address, of the youngest Avice: not as the immortal youth but 'a strange fossilized relic in human form', not as the object of her desire but of everything she repudiates. After the breakdown brought on by her elopement with her youthful lover – Marcia's son Henri Leverre – Pierston exists only as a relic; 'a gray shadow' of his former self. Unable finally to close the gap between his real and ideal selves, between the real and the ideal woman, between himself and his elusive 'Well-Beloved', he relinquishes his ideal for a more prosaic and quiescent reality. As he muses on the elopement of the third Avice beside the corpse of the second, the 'ghostly outlines' of his previous 'Well-Beloveds' gather round her bed:

> Many of them he had idealized in bust and in figure from time to time, but it was not as such that he remembered and reanimated them now; rather was it in all their natural circumstances, weaknesses, and stains. And then as he came to himself their voices grew fainter; they had all gone off on their different careers, and he was left here alone. (191)

It is at this point that Pierston rejects 'Woman' in the abstract in favour of one particular woman. His *'marriage de covenance'* with the elderly Marcia is not the fulfilment of desire, for by this point Pierston has lost even the desire to desire: 'he was no longer the same man that he had hitherto been. The malignant fever, or his experiences, or both, had taken away something from him, and put something else in its place' (197). It is 'a round[ing] off' of their histories 'in the best machine-made conventional manner' (203). It is fitting, then, that in abandoning the youthful mask of make-up, Marcia makes a similar investment in the reality of *her* ageing face and body.

Among the many texts with which *The Well-Beloved* can be read in creative dialogue are Hardy's poem 'I Look into my Glass'[20] and Tennyson's 'Tithonus' – a mispunctuated quotation from which provides the epigraph to the final chapter of Hardy's final novel.[21] Each of these offers a different perspective on the 'end' of desire. In 'I Look into my Glass', the ungendered speaker laments how age wastes the body but does not mitigate the seemingly ceaseless urging which 'shakes this fragile frame at eve with throbbings of noontide' (Hynes, I: 106).[22] The oxymoron linking 'noontide' and 'eve' in the single frame of the body yokes physical decay with spiritual rejuvenation and locates the speaker in the liminal 'twilight' zone. Like Pierston, the ageing speaker finds himself irrevocably defined by his ageing form or 'frame', while seeking to express an unspeakable desire – which is unrecognised by 'hearts grown cold to me' – and whose 'throbbings' are liable to be mistaken for the palsy of old age.

The eponymous narrator of Tennyson's 'Tithonus' laments, in another striking oxymoron, how he is 'consumed' by 'cruel immortality'. A mortal enamoured of the goddess Aurora, granted eternal life but not eternal youth, each daybreak he 'withers slowly' in the arms of his beloved whose 'strong Hours'

> [...] beat me down and marr'd and wasted me
> And tho' they could not end me, left me maim'd
> To dwell in presence of immortal youth,
> Immortal age beside immortal youth,
> And all I was, in ashes.

> (Poetical Works 1950: 97)

Tithonus is consumed by desire, which is itself continually renewed in the form of Aurora, the goddess of the dawn. He begs to be 'let go' so he may rejoin the ranks 'of happy men that have the power to die' (97). But even this ardent wish for release is itself a desire – to be free of desire. Its object is no longer the goddess, whose youth and beauty is renewed each day, but 'that dark world where I was born' – the night – which he glimpses only briefly in the tantalising, ungraspable moment before the dawn beats the twilight into 'flakes of fire'. In the classical myth on which the poem is based, Tithonus is transformed into a grasshopper, condemned endlessly to reiterate the frica-tive of unassuaged desire. Jocelyn Pierston persists beyond the diminution of desire, beyond its end and its ending, but as a mere 'gray shadow'. The aesthetic sense, sexual desire and romantic yearning, the creative urge, nos-talgia for his youth and the denial of prohibition, have all been replaced by what the narrator refers to as the appreciation of 'utilitarian matters' (198) – what is useful to the present rather than what draws one on into the future.

At the conclusion of his *'apologia pro vitâ meâ'* (35), Pierston's friend Somers neatly surmises: 'You are like other men, only rather worse. Essen-tially, all men are fickle, like you; but not with such perceptiveness' (40). Hardy made a more considered connection between Pierston the artist and other men in a letter to *The Academy* on 3 April 1897 in which he stated: 'there is, of course, underlying the fantasy followed by the visionary artist the truth that all men are pursuing a shadow, the Unattainable' (*LW*: 286). The 'perceptive' artist figures here as *ne plus ultra* of the desiring subject, driven to push beyond the conventional forms in the search for new, more satisfying modes of being and doing. Without the energy of desire, we learn, he 'would not have stood where he did stand in the ranks of an imaginative profession' (98). But desire, in its very restlessness and refusal to submit itself to the constraints of forms designed to regulate it, militates in every sense against a settled existence as 'a citizen and a national unit' (98). 'You ought not to marry' Somers advises the younger Pierston, and the text supports this view. The artist in Pierston is incompatible with the wooer and anathema to the domestic: 'how useless he was likely to be for practical steps towards householding though he was all the while pining for domestic life' (65).

However, though Pierston may be unconventional in terms of his lifestyle, his art is presented as fundamentally conservative, reassuring and populist. His repeated attempts to capture the essence of beauty in female form hit 'a public taste he had never deliberately aimed at, and mostly despised' to the detriment of his artistic reputation (52). The very popularity of his work testifies to its conventionality and also to his. His desire to capture the essence of Aphrodite – a lifelike and vital female beauty – in his sculpture, is matched by the belated desire to secure, as his own, her human representa-tive – Avice Caro or her direct female descendents, the 'phantom[s] of Avice, now grown to be warm flesh and blood' (83). Pierston gazes on his sculptures with despair at his failure to capture 'the Dea's form' (63): 'How futilely he had labored to express the character of that face in clay, and, while catch-ing it in substance, had yet lost something that was essential' (122). Like all artists, he is attempting the impossible: the direct translation of fugi-tive inspiration into permanent form whilst retaining the immediacy and vitality of his original conception. While they please and reassure the undis-cerning public and help him achieve membership of the Royal Academy, his sculptures are merely 'seedlings, grafts, and scions of beauty, waiting for a mind to grow to perfection in' (201). Neither the artist nor the man can get beyond prevailing conceptions and representations of woman as domestic angel, goddess, masculine romantic fantasy or feminine complement to the masculine self.

In the preface to the novel Hardy describes Pierston as 'one that gave objective continuity and a name to a delicate dream which in a vaguer form is more or less common to all men, and is by no means new to Platonic philosophers' (3). The similarities between Plato's concept of the 'Ideal' and Lacan's Real – 'the not yet symbolised or imaged; that which is impossible as such since it has not yet been articulated' (Grange, 1989: 164) – have been noted by critics including Richard Hunter (2004: 115–20) and Joseph Grange. However, in Pierston's case, the 'delicate dream' is continually displaced by the reiterated process of objectification. Pierston exemplifies Lacan's contention in 'The Partial Drive and its Circuit' that it is

> the phantasy [...] not the object that is the support of desire. The subject sustains himself as desiring in relation to an ever more complex signifying ensemble. This is apparent enough in the form of the scenario it assumes, in which the subject, more or less recognizable, is somewhere, split, divided, generally double, in his relation to the object, which usually does not show its true face either.
>
> (Lacan, 1977: 185)

The sculptured images of Pierston's Well-Beloved that fill his studio, the long list of 'relics' or 'mournful emptied shape[s]' (40) of the women he has loved and left testify to 'the compulsion [...] to repeat' that drives Pierston towards the impossible realisation of his desire (Miller, 1982b: 147). Patriarchal myths of femininity constantly interpose themselves between him and the realisation of his desire, regulating it at the level of the sign.

The radical potential of art, for Hardy, lay in its transformative relationship to reality: the just aim of art was, he felt, to be 'more truthful than truth' (Orel, 1966: 134). Hardy's word-play is interesting here in relation to his struggle against the constraints of Realism, the form of the novel itself and his concentration on poetry following the publication of *The Well-Beloved* in 1897. In 'The Science of Fiction' he opposes 'creativeness in its full and ancient sense – the making a thing or situation out of nothing that ever was before' to realism which he glosses as 'an artificiality distilled from the fruits of closest observation' (Hardy, 1967: 136).[23] Certainly, in his appreciation of the visual arts, Hardy was more interested in the attempt to render 'abstract imaginings' than in 'the "simply natural"' and was drawn to the later works of Turner, Whistler and the Impressionists (*LW*, 1989: 192). Hardy believed that the artist should be a visionary and a radical: a visionary in that 'he' sought to reach beyond material realities, beyond the pleasure principle, as it were, to the as yet unrepresented and unrepresentable realm; and a radical in that this could only be done through the invention of new experimental forms of expression and the wresting of new meanings out of those that already existed.

For René Girard, aesthetic desire is not a desire of possession but of expression: it is 'the ending of all desire, a return to calm and joy' (Girard, 1965: 34); but for most artists and writers, and Jocelyn Pierston is no exception, the discrepancy between the idea and the 'mark' or form through which it is expressed is rarely, if ever, effaced. In his essay on 'The School of Giorgione', Pater addresses the pursuit of beauty through art, and reasons why all the arts address neither 'pure sense' not 'pure intellect' but 'the "imaginative reason"' and why they do so through 'the senses', through pure affect. In painting, it is this direct and sensuous 'delight of the senses' that is 'the vehicle of whatever poetry or science may lie beyond them in the intention of the composer' (Pater, 1877: 49).[24] However, each of the arts of painting, architecture, sculpture and poetry is subject to 'a partial alienation from its own limitations'. This results in an '*Anders-Streben*' or 'other-striving' which expresses and seeks to resolve itself through synaesthesia, a reciprocal lending of forces from one to the other. Pater isolates music as the one art for which this alienation from its limitations is less overt. If it is the constant aim of all art to 'obliterate' the distinction between matter and form, then music is the art that comes closest to achieving this, leading to his proclamation that '*all art constantly aspires to the condition of music*' (51).

Overhearing Ann Avice's conversation one day, Pierston is attracted by the 'cadences of her voice':

The charm lay in the intervals, using that word in its musical sense. She would say a few syllables in one note, and end her sentence in a soft modulation upwards, then downwards, then into her own note again. The curve of sound was as artistic as any line of beauty ever struck by his pencil – as satisfying as the curves of her who was the World's Desire. (95)

The reference to *Analysis of Beauty* (1793) – in which William Hogarth defines the double-curved line as the signifier of vitality and kinetic energy in a static artwork or object – in relation to the accents and modulations of Ann Avice's voice, adds to Pierston's conviction that she is the embodiment of the abstract qualities of beauty. In taking care not to hear her words but merely to catch and enjoy the musicality of her voice, Pierston enjoys a Pateresque ecstatic communion with beauty, but in doing so must forgo not only her meaning but also her presence. In this respect, Ann Avice's singing recalls Mop Ollamoor's music with no notes, sound 'with a lingual character' ('FoR': 138) and the pagan 'lingual music' of Egdon Heath.[25]

Every art, declares Pater, has 'its incommunicable element, its untranslatable order of impressions, its unique mode of reaching "the imaginative reason"', but it is in music, rather than in poetry, where we find 'the true type or measure of perfected art' (53).[26] However, it was to poetry that Hardy returned, wondering if it might offer a means of expressing 'more fully [...] ideas and emotions which run counter to the inert crystallized opinion [...] which the vast body of men have vested interests in supporting' (*LW*, 1989: 302). Hardy seems to be referring specifically to his ideas on the 'Prime Force or Forces', or the energy behind the universe and human existence, but the idea and emotion of desire in relation to art and the conception of the self are also explored here. His first volume of verse – *Wessex Poems* – published fewer than 18 months after *The Well-Beloved*, contains poetic treatments of some of the themes and ideas that form the central concerns of his novel, such as 'Thoughts of Phena' (written in 1890) and 'I Look into my Glass'.[27] His next book, *Poems of the Past and Present* (1901) includes the Pateresque 'Rome, The Vatican: Sala delle Muse' (1887), 'The Dream-Follower' and the poem 'The Well-Beloved', in which the spirit of the 'Well-Beloved' emanates from where 'the Pagan temple stood / In the world's earliest day' and informs the lover of the Kingsbere woman: 'Thou lovest what thou dreamest her; / I am thy very dream!' (Hynes, I: 168).

In March, 1897 – the month of the publication of *The Well-Beloved* – Hardy explained the theory behind 'this fantastic tale of a subjective idea [...] exemplified in a poem bearing the same name, written about this time [...]: the theory of the transmigration of the ideal beloved one, who only exists in the lover, from material woman to material woman – as exemplified also by Proust many years later' as well as the antagonistic response of the reviewers to what some regarded as his 'sex-mania' (*LW*, 1989: 303–4). 'Such were the odd effects of Hardy's introduction of the subjective theory of love into modern fiction' we are told in the *Life*, 'and so ended his prose contributions to literature ... his experiences of the few preceding years having killed all his interest in this form of imaginative work, which had ever been secondary to his interest in verse' (*LW*, 1989: 303–4). In *The Well-Beloved*, this 'fanciful exhibition of the artistic nature', landscape, Pagan goddess, woman and Platonic Ideal[28] are sublimated into what was to become Hardy's most poignant, and powerful, signifier of the ultimate object of desire: the dead beloved woman, who symbolises for the sculptor not only 'the darling little figure' of Avice as she was at the time of their early courtship, but also the essence of himself, 'independent of physical laws and failings'. However, it was in the sublime 'Poems of 1912–13', inspired by the death of a woman he had ceased to love, that Hardy was to reach his purest expression of the phantom of desire, the 'special spectre, situated between perception and consciousness', between the signifier and the signified and between the idea and its creative realisation (Lacan, 1977b: 45).

7
'Scanned Across the Dark Space': Poetry, Desire and Aesthetic Fulfilment

> That the subject should come to recognise and to name his desire;
> that is the efficacious action of analysis. But it isn't a question of
> recognising something which would be entirely given [...]. In nam-
> ing it, the subject creates, brings forth, a new presence in the world.
>
> (Lacan, 1977: 275)

> There is no new poetry; but the new poet – if he carry the flame
> on further (and if not he is no new poet) – comes with a new note.
> And that new note it is that troubles the critical waters. Poetry is
> emotion put into measure. The emotion must come by nature, but
> the measure can be acquired by art.
>
> (*LW*: 322)

> Forms more real than living man,
> Nurslings of immortality
>
> (Shelley, 'The Poet's Dream', '*IW*': 19)

This study began by exploring the ways in which the alienated Hardyian subject strives to create a 'vital space' – a sense of harmony or an imagined integrity and security within the self – and how the trope of homes and homelessness, in particular the lost or the oneiric childhood home, functions as a powerful metaphor of this desire, what Lacan terms the 'want-to-be', for the adult self. In 'He Wonders About Himself', for example, the narrator strives to realise himself in moments that he can only apprehend in retrospect and which are now irretrievable. He is thus condemned endlessly to 'wonder [/wander] about himself': about and around the hollowed out space at the heart of his being, the space of unassuageable desire (Hynes, II: 256).

In 'The Function and Field of Speech and Language in Psychoanalysis', Lacan insists that the subject comes to consciousness of itself through the process of individuation initiated by its entry into the symbolic order: the 'I' is the first mark of the subject but 'I identify myself in language [...] only by losing myself in it like an object' (2006: 247). Subjectivity is defined by two opposing forces: a yearning to recover what has been lost through our entry into the symbolic order and the urge to push beyond its constraints into new realms of meaning, through which we may more fully articulate our desire. These forces unite in the Lacanian concept of desire: 'the function of desire is a last residuum of the effect of the signifier in the subject' ('Sexuality', 1977: 154). The 'before' of the subject is a kind of nothingness: unconstituted, inarticulate. It is symbolised for Lacan as the undifferentiated realm of the pre-oedipal, the libidinal, before the entry into the 'Other' of language. The 'beyond' of the subject is conceived as an impossible desire for individuation beyond the existing structures of signification, and is expressed in 'the invocatory drive', which is 'the closest to the experience of the unconscious' ('Of the Gaze', 1977: 104). The course of the various (partial) drives constitutes for Lacan 'the only form of transgression that is permitted to the subject in relation to the pleasure principle' ('The Partial Drive', 1977: 183). It is here that we may locate the positive, productive aspect of desire.

Lacan himself recognised the potentiality of language as first indicated by Freud in his examination of the dream, parapraxis, 'the flash of wit', which is where Freud sought the unconscious: 'In a spoken or written sentence something stumbles [...]. There, something other demands to be realized – which appears as intentional, of course, but of a strange temporality' ('Freudian Unconscious', 1977: 25). It is in this 'stumbling', 'impediment', 'failure' or 'split' (as he defines it) in the spoken or written sentence that Lacan, following Freud, locates *'the discovery'*: the peculiar affective quality of what we might call 'fine' or, to use a Hardyian term, 'fined' 'language' ('Thoughts of Phena', Hynes, I: 81). Lacan describes it thus:

> This discovery is, at the same time, a solution – not necessarily a complete one, but, however incomplete it may be, it has that indefinable something that touches us, that peculiar accent that Theodore Reik has brought out so admirably – only brought out, for Freud, certainly noted it before him – namely, *surprise*, that by which the subject feels himself overcome, by which he finds both more and less than he expected – but, in any case, it is, in relation to what he expected, of exceptional value.
>
> (1977b: 25)

This *'discovery'* or *'surprise'* [Lacan's emphasis] is fugitive, transitory: 'as soon as it is presented it becomes a rediscovery and, furthermore, it is always ready to steal away again, thus establishing the dimension of loss' (25). This 'solution' to desire, then, is a compound of surprise and rediscovery, discovery and loss. We may see it in the complex satisfaction that is achieved and continually discovered in the best poetry; not least in its devices of defamiliarisation and affect and in its experimentation with form. Lacan draws upon the myth of Orpheus and Eurydice to describe this moment of discovery achieved in 'the relation between Orpheus the analyst and the unconscious'

(25). However, as the history of Jocelyn Pierston demonstrates, the myth has a peculiar valence for the artist as an expression of the relationship between conception and execution, inspiration and expression in material form. The artist seeks to bring his or her desire into the material realm of recognition and knowledge but, in the process of realisation (looking, signifying), risks losing it forever.

In this respect, successful or, to use Martin Amis's term, 'achieved' art represents a means towards the satisfaction of desire and the resolution of the alienation of individuation. Admirers of Hardy's novels locate his uneasy relationship with realism, and the formulation of his aesthetic practice, as evidence of his bringing something new into the world. However, Hardy's 'newness', in terms of form and content is, I would argue, particularly apparent in his poetry, and it did indeed 'trouble [...] the critical waters' (*LW*: 322). His poetry was criticised by reviewers and admired by leading modernists, including Joyce and Pound, but reviled by T.S. Eliot.[1] Pound, in particular, praised it for its freshness, 'clarity', 'solidity' and 'compression'.[2] In his retrospective homage to Hardy in his 1938 *Guide to Kulchur*, Pound wrote:

> When a writer's matter is stated with such entirety and with such clarity there is no place left for the explaining critic [...] Poem after poem of Hardy's leaves one with no more to say [...]. No man can read Hardy's poems collected but that his own life, and forgotten moments of it, will come back to him, a flash here and an hour there. Have you a better test of poetry?
>
> (Peck, 1973: 6)[3]

As Peck suggests, in yoking Hardy with Joyce, Pound was 'gauging the undertow of *moeurs contemporaines* (to use Pound's phrase from Gourmont)' (6). For W.H. Auden, Hardy, with his unusual verse forms and ' "modern" rhetoric', was a necessary transitional figure between the literary character of England in 1907 ('Tennysonian in outlook') and that of 1925 ('The Waste Land in character'). He concludes 'I cannot imagine any other single writer could have carried me through from the one to the other' (1965: 141).[4]

Hardy's poems exemplify the artist/poet's aesthetic desire to push beyond the recognisable limits of language in order to 'bring forth a new presence in the world,' and in the word.[5] This concluding chapter will explore Hardy's elegiac poems in relation to loss but also, somewhat paradoxically perhaps, in relation to the possibilities of fulfilment: of grasping and perfecting the fleeting moment of plenitude through the stabilising medium of language. It is a critical commonplace to regard him as the quintessential poet of unfulfillment, lost chances, unassuaged desire; but this is to underestimate the potential of the imagination and the creative act itself as a means towards the attainment of satisfaction. The poems under discussion here can be seen to demonstrate how the subject might bring 'his' desire to recognition through its representation in language. Emma Hardy's sudden death, emotionally devastating as it was for her husband, was immensely stimulating to him creatively and artistically and resulted in an extraordinary series of poems, some of which are among the finest of the twentieth century. He reportedly told A.C. Benson that 'the verses came; it was quite natural. One looked back through the years and saw some pictures; a loss like that makes one's old brain vocal' (cited in Morgan, 1974: 503).[6] This most personal and irrevocable of losses moved Hardy to produce some of his most creatively satisfying, 'achieved' works of art.

In Lacan's schema, all subjects of desire are bereaved and in mourning for what they lack or have lost in the process of individuation through language. Peter Sacks suggests that every word 'is an elegy to what it signifies' and, if this is true, what can be made of 'an elegist's painful renegotiation with the substantive and artificial nature of his own words?' (Sacks, 1985: xiii). Can language be fined down in such a way as to address and express *mortal* loss satisfactorily? Jahan Ramazani goes further in suggesting that every elegy is 'an elegy for an elegy – a poem that mourns the diminished efficacy and legitimacy of poetic mourning' (Ramazani, 1994: 8). An elegy for a dead woman, therefore, offers the perfect paradigm for the examination of desire and the complex and painful negotiation with the substitutive nature of language. The beloved woman mourned by the bereaved (male) subject is triply alienated from him. She is constituted as a symptom of his lack, in words that mourn their separation from what they signify and in a poetical form that may not be able, ultimately, to console the bereaved subject for what he has lost.

In focussing on the elegiac sequence 'Poems of 1912–13', I want to explore how this triple alienation is negotiated, and eventually overcome in, and more importantly, by these creative acts. William Morgan has demonstrated that 'in the most important principles of form in the group – the patterns of time and the controlled use of the elegiac tradition' the 'Poems of 1912–13' is 'a carefully ordered work' in its own right, artfully arranged 'to provide a five-part linear structure' that depicts 'a movement from *recent past* to *present*, then from *distant past* to *recent past* to *present*' (Morgan, 1974: 496–7). Subsequent critics have likewise discussed the apparent coherence of these poems.[7] However, Dennis Taylor notes how Hardy breached the original boundaries of the group by transferring into it poems from elsewhere for the *Collected Poems* of 1919 (Taylor, 1993: 22), and Ramazani suggests that the 21 poems that constitute 'Poems of 1912–13' represent 'only about a fifth of his elegies for Emma' (Ramazani: 61). I register this as evidence of Hardy's artful manipulation of the sequence and, for the purposes of my argument, I will refer to poems placed before and after it in *Satires of Circumstance*, with particular focus on the textuality of these elegies: the frequent use of crafting and, in particular, scribal metaphors to express the mutually transformative relationship between life and art, and the importance of the symbol as a way of substantiating the fugitive moment through language.

In 1897, Hardy claimed to have abandoned writing novels, whose narratives 'he had mostly aimed, and mostly succeeded' in keeping 'as near to poetry in their subject as the conditions would allow, and had often regretted that those conditions would not let him keep them nearer still'. The novel, he claimed, was 'becoming a spasmodic inventory of items, which has nothing to do with art', and he concluded that poetry was the art form through which he could get nearer to the expression of 'abstract imaginings' (*LW*, 1984: 309–10). He was introduced to the expressive potential of the symbol by the work of Baudelaire and Mallarmé. Ten years before Arthur Symonds published his influential book *The Symbolist Movement in Literature* (1899), Hardy copied into his *Literary Notebook* an extract from an article by Ferdinand Brunetière on the 'Symbolistes et Décadens', published in the *Revue de Deux Mondes* on 1 November 1888, in which Brunetière cites the Symbolist movement as evidence of a new transformation of literature which 'wishes now to take possession of the means of music' (*LN*, I: 1640). A previous note declares:

> At a time when, under pretext of <u>naturalism</u>, art had been reduced to being no more than an imitation of the exterior contour of things, the Symbolists...appeared to teach that things have also a soul, of which the bodily eyes only seize the envelope, or the veil, or the mask [...] between ‹[external]› nature & ourselves there are 'correspondences,' ‹latent› 'affinities,' mysterious 'identities,' & that it is only so far as we seize them that, penetrating to the interior of things, we can truly approach the soul of them.
>
> (*LN*, I: 1639)[8]

Hardy copied several passages from John Addington Symonds's *Essays Speculative and Suggestive*, in particular from his essay on Pater's 'The School of Giorgione' in which Pater expatiates on music as 'the ideally consummate art' and concludes that lyrical poetry, 'just because in it you are least able to detach the [essential] matter from the form without a deduction of something from that matter itself, is artistically the highest form of poetry... [its] perfection seems to depend on *a certain suppression or vagueness of mere subject, so that the definite meaning almost expires*' (*LN*, II: 1864). Hardy also noted Symond's views on symbols:

> The range of human thoughts & emotions greatly transcends the range of such symbols as man has invented to express them; & it becomes therefore the business of Art to use these symbols in a double way. They must be used for the direct repres^{n} of thought & feeling; but they must also be combined by so subtle an imagination as to suggest much which there is no means of directly expressing.
>
> (*LN*, II: 1865)

Symonds's notion of art's 'double' use of symbols is useful in relation to Lacan's reverence for certain forms of poetry. In 'The Function and Field of Speech and Language in Psychoanalysis', Lacan declares that 'the symbol manifests itself first of all as the murder of the thing, and this death constitutes in the subject the externalization of his desire' (1977: 104). The poetic symbol, therefore, manifests itself as the murder of the symbol (or sign) or, at least, as Pater puts it, the 'expiration' of the sign's *'definite meaning'*, while preserving Lacan's 'discovery,' and is thus not only the 'externalisation' but also the eternalisation of the subject's desire. The poetic symbol occupies a place on the borderline between language and what cannot be signified, between desire and its object, between pleasure and the ecstasy that is *jouissance*. A poetic symbol reaches beyond itself towards something that cannot be stated or expressed precisely, bringing it into the realm of knowledge but retaining that sense of what is beyond articulation: the excess or surplus. Chief among the symbols featured in this chapter is the female ghost or phantom as a figure of the unattainable object of desire, and her role in the movement from shadow to substance, from the lost past moment of plenitude to the linguistic manifestation of that moment for the present and future. I discuss three symbols in particular as counterparts to the phantom woman: the 'spot' that is the imagined embodiment of the locus of desire in 'Ditty (E.L.G)'; the image of the spot's actual inscription on an imagined landscape, for example the burnt circle of 'Where the Picnic Was', which is the final poem in the sequence; and the 'chalice' of the lost picnic glass in 'Under the Waterfall'.[9]

For Lacan, desire inheres in the gap between the signifier and the signified; it is what cannot be represented in language, and yet language is the medium through which the subject constantly strives towards the illusion of self-presence through the materialisation of his or her desire. We constitute ourselves in language, and we are urged and exhorted to make our desires recognised in and through this medium that seems constantly to fail us. To be subjected to language is to be infinitely displaced from original meaning. As Judith Butler expresses it:

Desire is then, the expression of a longing for the return to the origin that, if recoverable, would necessitate the dissolution of the subject itself. Hence desire is destined for an imaginary life in which it remains haunted and governed by a libidinal memory it cannot possible recollect. For Lacan, this impossible longing affirms the subject as the limit to satisfaction.

And the ideal of satisfaction necessitates the imagined dissolution of the subject itself.

(Butler, 1987; 1999: 186–7)

The urge to substantiate ourselves in language would seem to represent the opposite to the death drive, which describes the urge to dissipation that is represented in the desire to return to the pre-lingual realm: the original libidinal bond with the maternal body. However, our desire to push beyond the pleasure principle into the realm of non-signification also carries this threat of dissolution with it: the threat of incoherence, non-recognition, the unravelling of being. The aim therefore must be to balance the necessary delusion of integrity – the 'fiction' of plenitude that Lacan regards as inherent in the pleasure principle – with the desire to reach towards a better, more satisfying fiction. Judith Butler suggests that "the desire to create a metaphysically pleasurable fictive world, fully present and devoid of negativity, reveals the human subject in its metaphysical aspirations as a maker of false pretences, constructed unities, merely imagined satisfactions' (Butler, 1987; 1999: 185).

However, as Hardy noted from John Addington Symonds's essay, 'Art is bound to introduce an equivalent for it cannot represent' (*LN*, II: 1833). The subject's desire to bring the elements of the Real that resist symbolisation into the realm of the symbolic is creative and is nowhere more so than in the act of artistic production: what in 'The Decay of Lying' (1891) Oscar Wilde called 'the telling of beautiful untrue things' that Life may eventually make its own (1989: 239).[10]

Hardy's views on art and aesthetics have been much rehearsed, but it is useful to remind ourselves of some of them here, for they apply to his career as a poet as well as a novelist, and reveal his affinities with some aspects of the aesthetic movement of the late nineteenth century. The publication of *The Well-Beloved* in 1897 was followed by eight books of verse, concluding with the posthumously published *Winter Words in Various Moods and Meters* in 1928. In January 1886 Hardy wrote: 'My art is to intensify the expression of things, as is done by Crivelli, Bellini, &c. so that the heart and inner meaning is made vividly visible' (*LW*: 183). Three years later he was struck by an exhibition of Turner's watercolours at the Royal Academy and by how Turner 'gives for that which cannot be reproduced a something else which shall have upon the spectator an approximate effect to that of the real'. He concluded, 'Art is the secret of how to produce by a false thing the effect of a true' (*LW*: 226). Later, he reminded himself that 'in getting at the truth, we get only at the true nature of the impression that an object, etc. produces on us, the true thing in itself being still, as Kant shows, beyond our knowledge' (*LW*: 261). Hardy's 'real' here refers to the visual perception of reality – in Turner's case 'all that is in a landscape' – and the impossibility of depicting it with minute fidelity. Instead, he argues, Turner concentrates on creating an 'impression' which will communicate a comparable, perhaps even more powerful effect. Nevertheless, Hardy's conclusion that through the 'false thing' of Art the artist is able to reach beyond material realities to communicate something that is more 'true', more meaningful and moving has a resonance for Lacan's understanding of the relationship between art, desire and language.

If language is 'the pleasurably fictive world' (Butler, 1987; 1999: 185) within which the subject attains the illusion of self-presence, then poetry – which seeks to sublimate the elements of that fictive world still further – refines or fines down language to bring it as close as possible to expressing the inexpressible. Hardy noted Symonds's conviction that

> In poetry of the first order, almost every word (to use a mathem! metaphor) is raised to a higher power. It continues to be an articulate sound & a logical step in the argument; but it becomes also a musical sound & a centre of emotional force.
>
> (*LN*, II: 1865)

Poetry also offered Hardy the chance to exploit the polysemic, neologistic potential of language. Lacan himself became increasingly interested in the ambiguity and creatively suggestive potential of literary language – its use of homophones, metaphors and neologisms as a means towards the expression of the non-communicable. These he regarded as examples of '*lalangue*': a raw unmediated form of language which can lead directly to *jouissance*. It exists as a 'primary chaotic substrate of polysemy out of which language is constructed, almost as if language is some ordered superstructure sitting on top of this substrate' (Evans, 1996: 97). Language, Lacan claimed, is 'an elucubration of knowledge [savoir] about *lalangue*' (S20, 127, cited Evans: 97).[11]

In the elegiac 'Poems of 1912–13' Hardy reintroduces with a deeper force and poignancy the figure of the ghost or phantom which is a recurring poetic device in earlier and later poems.[12] The phantom figure – in particular the phantom female figure – is produced out of the inexpressible space of loss. This space figures in metaphors such as 'your great going' and the 'yawning blankness' of the perspective at 'the end of the alley of bending boughs' in 'The Going' (Hynes, II: 47). It symbolises not only the narrator's confrontation with the beloved's absence from her usual walk, but also the hollowing out of someone who confronts 'his' own 'great going' in that sickening perspective ('The Going': 277). The 'cleft' in the rock at the bottom of the pool in 'Under the Waterfall' (Hynes, II: 45), the 'look' of the empty room that the bereaved walker confronts on 'his' return ('The Walk', Hynes, II: 49) are also manifestations of this space, as is the 'vanishing' of 'Without Ceremony' (Hynes, II: 53) and 'After a Journey' (Hynes, II: 59). 'After a Journey' is constructed around 'the dark space wherein I have lacked you'. This is the space between past and present, presence and absence, signifier and signified, the mourning subject and the lost beloved, between the living and the dead.[13] The figure of the phantom female beloved provides a means for Hardy to expatiate upon distinctly modern concerns with being, desire and language and, as John Addington Symonds expressed it, 'to suggest much which there is no means of directly expressing' through the potency of the symbol (*LN*, 2: 1865).[14]

The 'dark space' of desire is also figured by the poems themselves, which offer several examples of this painful struggle, of what Sappho called the 'broken tongue' (Wharton, 1895: 64) that struggles to express the agonising power of desire and loss: the fragmented line, the strong caesura, often following a series of spondees or insistent stresses, that renders on the page the gap between word and emotion or idea; the ellipsis and the emotional ejaculation – 'Ah' and 'Oh' – that both mirrors and transcends the expressive failure of language; or the antiphonal line that gives the poem a musical quality, bringing it close, perhaps, to Pater's 'perfected art' that offers an unmediated conduit to the 'imaginative reason' through the delight of the senses. For DeSales Harrison, Hardy's elegies demonstrate 'a very special form of incapacity' which is inherent in writing itself, in that what the poems strive to ' "record" is the mark of what they must perforce fail to record'. This incapacity 'deforms or disrupts the representational surface of the work, occluding its representational transparency' (Harrison, 2010: 422). However, 'representational transparency' is not the aim of these poems. Rather than seeking to re-create 'the voice of the beloved', the materiality of her landscape, or the minute detail of the events they describe, the poems strive to communicate the moment of recognition that this is, indeed, impossible. The lost beloved can never be brought back, her voice can never be heard again by the narrator.[15] While the medium of writing may not 'embody' the experience, it does embody and communicate the devastating moment of realisation. Hardy's poetic devices bear witness to the artist's attempt to push beyond the limits of language, beyond the pleasure principle, into the painful realm of pure affect. This, combined with the use of the symbol, becomes the vehicle through which the translation of the idea or emotion is achieved and communicated to the reader.[16] The dead beloved is beyond possession and, yet, also fully possessed, integrated into the mourner's subjectivity and bodied forth in poetic language.

Hardy's presentation of the lost female beloved as a phantom object of desire allows for an examination of the male subject of desire in relation to a specific disembodied notion of the female other. She has been read as a symbol of the original unity with the maternal body before individuation by language, haunting the texts and their narrators with libidinal memories they cannot apprehend. The mourning subject's longing for this spectral female symbolises the desire to return to this pre-lingual realm, which is the space of dissolution, the realm of death. Jahan Ramazani suggests that the 'red-veined rocks' of 'The Going', signify 'an encompassing "red-veined" [maternal] body', similar to the 'sympathetic and maternal landscape' to which the narrator imaginatively returns her in 'I Found Her Out There' (Hynes, II: 51), 'where she becomes the joyous child he never knew', and that 'the representation of her childhood self is an image of preoedipal harmony' (Ramazani, 1994: 54). Many of these poems take place within the narcissistic space or interior landscape of the mourning subject who, at times, is clearly gendered as male. They chart the initial movement towards the realm of dissolution, the realm of pre-lingual nescience, in the narrator's desire to unite with the lost female beloved. However, they also explore the mourning subject's gradual detachment from and abandonment of the phantom in order to bring his desires into the substantial realm of language, knowledge and recognition in the present and for the future. In certain of the poems that form the focus of this chapter the symbol of the phantom woman is replaced by images of materialisation, inscription and recording.

In July 1926 Hardy noted that the theory of desire demonstrated in *The Well-Beloved* in 1892 had been developed still further by Proust in *A La Recherche du Temps Perdu* (1913–27):

> Peu de personnes comprennent le caractère purement subjectif du phénomène qu'est l'amour, et la sorte de création que c'est d'une personne supplémentaire, distincte de celle qui porte le même nom dans le monde, et dont la plupart des élèments sont tirés de nous-mêmes. (Ombre, ii.158, 159).

> (*LW*: 467)[17]

Lacan suggests that for man/Man, woman/Woman exists only as a fantasy object, not a real subject but the cause of his desire. He suggests that 'object love', love or desire for the '*objet a*', is all that stands between 'man' and narcissistic love, but that this object is not a sexed partner or other but his own phantom or fantasy 'cut out, restricted and logically articulated' (Benvenuto and Kennedy, 1986: 187).

On one level, Hardy's elegiac poems present woman – the dead female beloved in particular – as the *objet a* par excellence: a metonymic manifestation of man's 'true' desire which is for de-individuation: dissolution back to the original libidinal bond with the maternal body. As explored in Chapter 5 above, if Woman is situated in the symbolic order only as a symptom of man's desire – an object fantasised as its cause – then she is doubly displaced from being a subject of desire in her own right. However, as in all of the texts discussed in this study, this conception of the feminine is under interrogation in Hardy's elegies, including those in the sequence 'Poems of 1912–13'. In the narcissistic space that is the narrator's consciousness, the female object of desire is not only 'phantomised' – voiceless, disembodied, mercurial – she is also revealed as a *figment* – an invention or projection of the mourning narrator's desire.[18] Many of them place the female phantom of desire at the very heart of their negotiation of the tension between object love and narcissistic love. She is apostrophised, interrogated, appraised and finally abandoned as the mourning subject finds new, more concrete symbols through which to express desire.

It is ironic, prophetic perhaps in respect of the 'Poems of 1912–13', or merely a powerful example of the aesthetic principle that Life imitates Art, that Jocelyn Pierston is also infatuated with 'the only woman whom I never rightly valued [...] and therefore the only one I shall ever regret' (71). Pierston loves the 'dead and inaccessible' Avice Caro 'as he had never loved her in life':

> now the times of youthful friendship with her, in which he had learnt every note of her innocent nature, flamed up into a yearning and passionate attachment, embittered by regret beyond words. (72)

Although the originating sense of loss for Hardy in the 'Poems of 1912–13' is indisputably the sudden death of his first wife Emma, I propose to read these poems not as biographical records of that loss but as artworks which test the expressive capacity of language.[19] David W. Shaw reminds us that 'all elegists are mourners, but not all mourners are elegists'. In making an elegy, a mourner performs and creates 'the work of mourning', which invites the critic to engage with 'how an elegist's language emerges from, and recreates, an originating sense of loss' (Shaw, 1994: 50). For Peter Sacks:

> each elegy is to be regarded, therefore, as a *work*, both in the commonly accepted meaning of a product and in the more dynamic sense of the working through of an impulse or experience – the sense that underlies Freud's phrase 'the work of mourning'.
>
> (Sacks, cited in Shaw, 1994: 50)

I offer my readings as a supplement to the biographicalism favoured by the majority of the commentators on these poems.[20] As the previous chapter has demonstrated, the trope of the lost phantom beloved predates the publication of the 'Poems of 1912–13' by almost 20 years. Over and above what we know (or what we think we know) about Hardy's life and, in particular, his first marriage and Emma's sudden death, in their constant references to other texts (including Hardy's own and classical myths); to crafting, weaving and writing; to language, painting and art, these poems can be seen to dramatise the condition of the artist poet who strives to bring what is lost or absent into the domain of language through the use of technical devices, and the creation and communication of affect.

Many of the narrating subjects of the '1912–13' poems have been read by critics biographically as male, despite the fact that they are often ungendered. Where I have chosen to gender the mourning narrators, or indeed the phantom beloved, in the absence of evidence in the poem itself, I have tried to remain mindful of their slipperiness in this respect and to register that an assumption that the speaker/narrator is male is not to negate the other, differently gendered readings that Hardy's poems so powerfully and generously permit.[21] I have adapted a simplified form of Derrida's use of '*sous rature*' to suggest a purely strategic use of the pronoun.[22] My focus will be on the textual construction of the mourning subject and the object of desire, and on the poems not as real life experiences in the lives of Hardy or Emma, but as artworks that develop, invent and produce those experiences in texts woven out of language and shaped by what Hardy himself referred to in his essay on 'The Science of Fiction' as 'the Daedalian faculty for selection and cunning manipulation [...] with an eye to being more truthful than truth (the just aim of Art)' (Orel, 1967: 134).

'After a Journey' is a pivotal poem in the 'Poems of 1912–13', coming just over half-way through the sequence (Hynes, 1987: 59–60).[23] Its title is ambiguous. The 'Hereto' that begins it seems to refer to the actual land-scape of the Pentargon Bay of the poem's addendum. However, close reading reveals it to be a landscape of the mind: an imaginary creation, or re-creation, of the place which the narrator may, or may not, have just visited.[24] The action of the poem takes place just before dawn and the imagery of 'the stars clos[ing] their shutters' gives it an interior feel.[25] The 'voiceless ghost' is a phantom of the narrator's imagination, and the poem describes a com-promised and problematic attempt to communicate with a spectral woman with 'nut-coloured hair, / And gray eyes, and rose-flush coming and going'. The line 'Scanned across the dark space wherein I have lacked you' suggests the desire to close up or efface the gap between mourner and mourned, seer and ghost, subject and lost object of desire. For Lacan, desire inheres in just such impossible spaces. 'Scanned' is one of Hardy's marvellously freighted words. Among the meanings listed for it in the *OED* are: 'close scrutiny; per-ception, discernment'; 'to analyse, the structure or "correctness" of verse by reciting it with an emphasis on metre and rhythm'; to 'criticise, judge or form an opinion on'; 'to interpret, assign a meaning to' and 'to perceive, dis-cern or examine with the eyes'. A later, but equally suggestive, meaning for our purposes is 'to resolve (a picture) into its elements of light and shade for purposes of transmission'.[26] Although anachronistic, this definition derives from the earlier poetic or interpretive associations of the word, adding to them the notion of 'transmission' from one medium to another.

> Yes: I have re-entered your olden haunts at last;
> Through the years, through the dead scenes I have tracked you
> What have you now found to say of our past —
> Scanned across the dark space wherein I have lacked you?
>
> (Hynes, II: 60)

'Scanned across' suggests the attempt to bridge the 'dark space' of 'lack' between subject and lost object, mourner and mourned, either with a per-ceiving glance or an act of interpretation or testing; and the use of 'lack', with its metrical pairing with 'track' (to follow marks or traces left in the wake of something), implies the possibilities of language or writing to provide this link or crossing between two separate or separated entities, transmitting not the presence of the lost beloved but the experience of that loss into the material realm of art.

This 'dark space' that is 'scanned' here is constituted by time and memory – 40 years and 'dead scenes' – that make up the distance through which the narrator has tracked the ghost woman in order to 're-enter [...] your olden haunts at last'. These are not new scenes haunted by a new ghost but 'olden haunts' saturated with the ghostly presence of a woman much younger than the narrator and her own embodied original. The narrator can only close up this space by crossing from the present to her side in the past, becoming a ghost in order to join her in 'the spots we knew when we haunted here together'. In the first stanza, the narrator 'comes to view' the ghost whose presence is everywhere in the remembered landscape; a fickle, whimsical, teasing ghost who cannot be coaxed or challenged into language. She remains 'voiceless' in contrast to the 'unseen waters' ejaculations' and the 'hollow voice' of the cave with its hint of mockery and deception. The narrator has to ventriloquise the phantom's response to the question posed to her – 'What have you now found to say of our past— ' in a way that both recognises and challenges the fact that the only articulate voice heard is the narrator's own. This is registered by the missing quotation marks, and the two interrogation marks at the end of each of the 'responses'. It is not the ghost who offers 'Summer gave us sweets, but autumn wrought division? / Things were not lastly as firstly well / With us twain [...]?' but the narrator. The phantom does not take up the challenge to say something different in her 'olden haunts' from what she said in her recent ones.[27] This is a one-sided conversation in the narcissistic space of the narrator's mind.

The narrator's attempt to raise the spirit of the young beloved of the past and bring her back to the other side of the 'dark space' – into the material realm – is fraught with compromise. This is a deceitful phantom who 'leads me on' as well as drawing the narrator back into their old haunts, and she metamorphoses from the blushing, bright-haired woman of the narrator's fantasy into a 'thin ghost'.[28] This is a curious variation on the Orphic quest noted by critics including Melissa Zeiger (1997) and Catherine Maxwell (2008). As dawn whitens, this Orpheus loses Eurydice to Hades but not before, as the narrator of 'The Going' puts it, gaining 'one glimpse' of her (Hynes, II: 47). This dynamic of an imaginary journey to the other side and the glimpsing, and subsequent vanishing, of Eurydice will be re-enacted in many of the 'Poems of 1912–13'. In every case, the lost woman will materialise not in the flesh but as text in the permanent record of the poem. It is language, rather than nostalgic desire, that offers the means through which the dark space may be scanned and spanned.

The 'journey' to the other side of the dark space of loss, time and memory leaves the narrator bewildered, 'lonely, lost' and in awe: threatened with disempowerment and loss of self. To be 'just the same as when / Our days were a joy, and our paths through flowers', the narrator must deny his own lived reality as frail and possibly elderly, and join the ghost; for the moment of quality desired – 'the then fair hour in the then fair weather' – can only be seen and grasped in the past.[29] The imminent dawn, the time when all ghosts and phantoms traditionally vanish, seems to bring the narrator back to consciousness of himself in the present but leaves him still identifying with his own phantom self in the past and with his own dissolution. The narrator claims not simply to *feel* but to *be* 'just the same'. Across the space of 40 years, the phantom woman and that particular time in the remembered place glow with the radiance of nostalgic idealisation, and the desire to live again in the spent moment, however briefly, threatens to strand him in a 'dead scene'. The poem beautifully captures the dilemma that besets the elegist, who must avoid entrapment in the 'then fair hour' by bringing it into the realm of the 'lour[ing]' present through the enabling medium of art. The sequence of 'Poems of 1912–13' reveals the Orphic poet striving continually to name, create and bring forth loss into the material world; to take possession of the incomprehensible 'voices' of the imagined natural world – the libidinal pre-lingual realm – and exploit the creative potential of the substrate of language. Ramazani reads the 'dark space' as 'a curious metaphor, ambiguously alluding to both the span of time since [Emma's] death and the span of time since the death of their love'. In either case 'Hardy begets his poetry in the dark space of his lack' (Ramazani, 1994: 58).

The role of the phantom is affectingly realised in 'The Haunter' (Hynes, II: 55), which is narrated in the phantom's ungendered voice: a voice that the haunted mourner in the text has no access to. Here the phantom narrator offers consolation and compensation for the missed opportunities of the past which the haunted man seeks to regain in his imagination.

> He does not think that I haunt here nightly:
> How shall I let him know
> That whither his fancy sets him wandering
> I, too, alertly go?—
> Hover and hover a few feet from him
> Just as I used to do,
> But cannot answer the words he lifts me—
> Only listen thereto!

This is the other side of the narcissistic dialogue of 'After a Journey'. If there the phantom is female and a passive Eurydice, repeatedly conjured and lost by the Orphic narrator, in 'The Haunter' she can only be a voiceless Echo 'who cannot answer the words he lifts me—/ Only listen thereto'. Again the title of the poem is richly suggestive in its ambiguity. Who exactly is the 'haunter': the phantom who speaks to the reader but not to the mourner, or the man whom the phantom 'companions' in 'the places only dreamers go': the 'old aisles where the past is all to him'? If the phantom cannot speak to the mourner, then to whom is its plea directed? One clue may lie in the scribal metaphor of the 'long paces' 'print[ed]' by the hares. The ghostly muse is speaking to the poem's reader, pleading for us to reassure the haunted man that it is striving to ensure 'that his path may be worth pursuing'. This poem describes the artist's fantasy that, unlike the experience of Jocelyn Pierston, this muse will cooperate in trying to bring about the calm and satisfaction that is achieved by the successful artwork, to 'bring peace thereto' through the printed paces of the poem.

'The Voice' (Hynes, II: 56) similarly, and stunningly, enacts the painful relationship between artist and muse, idea and expression. The 'woman much missed' is the dead or lost object of desire which the mourning narrator yearns to apprehend: to see and hear in the material realm. The dark space of desire between mourner and mourned, subject and object of desire, is expressed on the page in the strong caesura and fractured rhythm of the final stanza:

> Thus I; faltering forward,
> Leaves around me falling,
> Wind oozing thin through the thorn from norward,
> And the woman calling. (57)

Here grief and frustrated yearning are literally materialised in Sappho's 'broken tongue'. Again the title is richly ambiguous. Whose is the voice materialised on the page? Is it the 'woman calling' or the sound of the listless breeze which becomes the 'Wind oozing thin through the thorn'? In 'The Haunter', which immediately precedes it in *Satires of Circumstance*, the 'faithful phantom' 'cannot answer the words he lifts me—/ Only listen thereto!'. In 'After a Journey' the ghost is 'voiceless'. This suggests that the 'Voice' of the title is the bereaved narrator speaking aloud, or to an imagined ghost. The trajectory of the poem moves towards, and is halted by, the spondee of 'Thus I': its insistent stresses bringing the reader's attention to the narrator's predicament and situating the scene firmly in the narcissistic space of his imagination. Though she fails to appear in the flesh, her ghost materialises in the narrator's mind's eye, and on the page, as the waiting woman in 'the original air-blue gown'. If this is an Orpheus whose Eurydice stays firmly out of sight, it is, also, as DeSales Harrison registers, a Narcissus whose Echo not only hears but repeats 'the words he lifts' her ('The Haunter'): 'Woman much missed, how you call to me, call to me'.[30] In the final stanza of 'The Voice', the narrator 'falters forward': drawn onwards by the calling woman and accompanied by the imagined sound of her voice, or reluctantly drawing away from her and leaving her 'voice' behind. If the act of speaking is not the designation of a specifically localized subjectivity, but the designation of a dislocation inherent in all subjectivity', (Harrison: 2005: 57) this frail Narcissus falters on into this very dislocation accompanied by the voice of the woman and the voice of the thorn, and the acceptance – ('Thus I') of the impossibility of bringing either into the realm of the articulate. However indistinct and unverifiable one of the voices is within the poem, the narrator's voice – in its struggle to express the inexpressibility of loss – is richly evocative and its resonance for the reader is intense.

In addition to the quality of its affect, the superb image of the wind 'oozing thin through the thorn from norward' suggests two further intertexts: the myth of Pan and Syrinx and Hardy's own poem 'The Voice of the Thorn' (Hynes, I: 284), published earlier in *Time's Laughingstocks and Other Verses* (1909).[31] Peter Sacks has noted how from ancient Egyptian times the wind instrument is associated with mourning (Sacks, 1985: 3) and how the figure of the priapic Pan, together with the 'blend of plaintiveness and oblique sexuality' of his 'woeful reedlike instrument', is 'integral to the elegy' (7). Pan's flute, fashioned out of the reeds into which the nymph Syrinx was transformed, becomes 'a consoling sign that carries in itself the reminder of the loss on which it has been founded'.[32] In 'The Voice', the thorn is played by the wind and produces not recognisable music but the suggestion of the indistinct and untranslatable voice of the lost woman, and the lost libidinal bond. This sound is played by the poet through the poem itself, which becomes an equally 'consoling' sign that likewise retains the sense of that irrevocable loss. In 'The Voice of the Thorn', the indecipherable sound made by the wind is translated into language. The narrator hears 'the thorn on the down' quivering 'naked and cold' in the winter and 'fully tressed' in summer, and remarks on how the seasons alter its message for those that who hear it. For the narrator, however:

> But by day or by night,
> And in winter or summer,
> Should I be the comer
> Along that lone height,
> In its voicing to me
> Only one speech is spoken:
> 'Here once was nigh broken
> A heart, and by thee.' (186)

This poem intensifies and supplements the meaning of the complex line: 'When you had changed from the one who was all to me' in 'The Voice', which can be read as the woman's passive falling from favour or as the narrator's active dismissal of her as an object of affection. In the later poem, imagining her voice in the wind in the thorn, the narrator asks for visual corroboration that it is indeed she 'who was all to me, [...] as at first, when our day was fair'. As in 'After a Journey', the narrator of 'The Voice' yearns to join the woman again in the past, 'where you would wait for me', and the poem seems to open out into the prospect of the narrator's own death, as we imagine this ephemeral 'air-blue' gowned woman waiting still.

Critics who have commented on the role of the landscape in 'Poems of 1912–13' invariably specify it as either the Dorset of Hardy's failed marriage and sudden, shocking bereavement, or the Cornwall of his and Emma's romantic courtship.[33] What is missed is the self-conscious textual weaving of places into landscapes of the mind, sites of desire and sources of creative, poetic inspiration. This is especially true of another early poem 'Ditty (E.L.G.)' written in 1870, over 40 years before the death of its dedicatee, and published in Hardy's first volume, *Wessex Poems*, in 1898. 'Ditty (E.L.G.)' testifies to Hardy's early conviction that 'the poetry of a scene varies with the minds of the perceivers. Indeed, it does not lie in the scene at all' (*LW*: 52). This poem is an early example of a narrator's knowing reworking and representation of a scene and its dweller as the locus of ontological and aesthetic desire.

> Beneath a knap where flown
> Nestlings play,
> Within walls of weathered stone,
> Far away
> From the files of formal houses,
> By the bough the firstling browses,
> Lives a Sweet: no merchants meet,
> No man barters, no man sells
> Where she dwells. (21–2)

'Where she dwells' is imagined as the site of the narrator's ideal state of being: youthful (like the 'flown' nestlings that still play there or the 'firstling' browsing the bough) and secure 'within walls of weathered stone', and the favoured 'bond-servant' of Chance. Its fluid, uncharted but benign wilderness offers a pastoral alternative to the constraints and pressures of urban capitalism. The beloved and her 'spot' are imaginatively appropriated by the narrator:

> To feel I might have kissed—
> Loved as true—
> Otherwhere, nor Mine have missed
> My life through,
> Had I never wandered near her,
> Is a smart severe. (22)

The poetic contraction of 'nor Mine have missed' in stanza four suggests not just 'my beloved' but also that which belongs or pertains to me, and draws attention to the ego-morphic nature of this locus of desire. The 'thought that she is nought, / Even as I, beyond the dells / Where she dwells' testifies to the *textual* existence of subject and object in this imagined landscape, while simultaneously rehearsing the severe 'smart' occasioned by the thought of their obliteration.

The poem also contains images of writing and crafting, which specify the landscape as a metaphoric tapestry. 'Upon that fabric fair / "Here is she!" / Seems written everywhere / Unto me', and the proviso of that 'Seems' emphasises the subjective, artful or fabricated nature of the vision it describes. The 'lucid legend' of the beloved's dwelling place – that bright inscription – is 'descried' by the narrator alone, and its fictive status is emphasised by the word 'legend': an inscription or motto, an unauthentic story, especially that of the life of a saint (*SOED*). The inspirational potential of this landscape, already realised in its 'fabrication' in the poem, is recognised here in the metaphor of running water that recurs so often in Hardy's texts and features so suggestively in the novels discussed in Chapter Five above, in particular *The Well-Beloved*:

> Should I lapse to what I was
> Ere we met;
> (Such will not be, but because
> Some forget
> Let me feign it)—none would notice
> That where she I know by rote is
> Spread a strange and withering change,
> Like a drying of the wells
> Where she dwells. (22)

A mutually fertile relationship is imagined between the landscape and the narrator's inspiration which is stimulated by love for its dweller: 'she I know by rote'. The 'lapsing' of his love is imagined as effecting 'a strange and withering change, / Like a drying of the wells / Where she dwells'. To read the 'Poems of 1912–13' in conjunction with 'Ditty (E.L.G.)' is to register this early identification of the creative, poetic potential for the narrator of both the lost beloved and her 'spot'. She is *genius loci* of the landscape, and the inspiration for the art through which it is materialised. 'Ditty (E.L.G.)' is a suggestive, premonitory intertext for 'A Death Day Recalled', written over four decades later, in which the landscape of Beeny, Juliot, 'thin Vallency's river' and 'Targan mouth' are upbraided for *failing* to register the death of 'their former friend' (61).

The line 'Here is she' in 'Ditty (E.L.G.)' registers both the presence of the beloved in the landscape, and the presence of the landscape in her: each is an embodiment of the other and the combined 'spot' an embodiment of the narrator's desire. She is, quite literally, part of the fabric of the place: woven into and embroidered onto its imagined knaps and dells like a motto in a sampler. Like a sampler, the 'spot' is presented here as 'a model, pattern or archetype' for future poetic fabrications; a demonstration, or specimen of a beginner's skill that the narrator will improve upon in later textual embroideries. The last line of 'Ditty (E.L.G.)' contains what must be one of Hardy's most prophetic lines 'I but found her in that, going' which, isolated from the syntax and punctuation of the poem, offers a startlingly succinct resumé of the paradoxical poetic project of the 'Poems of 1912–13' with its echoes of 'I Found Her Out There' and 'The Going'. The 'Poems of 1912–13' both find (locate) and establish (found) the lost or inaccessible object of desire in the trope of the phantom woman and the imagined Cornish landscape. Out of the space of the 'great going', Hardy conjures the phantom woman and her imagined landscape: two of the most polysemic, suggestive and *jouissant* images of desire itself.

In 'A Dream or No', the narrator queries both the reason for and the value of revisiting, in whatever form, the landscape of desire that is Saint-Juliot and its hidden incumbent:

> Why go to Saint-Juliot? What's Juliot to me?
> Some strange necromancy
> But charmed me to fancy
> That much of my life claims the spot as its key.
> Yes. I have had dreams of that place in the West,
> And a maiden abiding
> Thereat as in hiding;
> Fair-eyed and white-shouldered, broad-browed and brown-tressed.

> (Hynes, II: 58–9)

In this poem we have Hardy's strongest manifesto of the necessary distinction between art and life, and the creative, fulfilling role of the imagination and the work of art it produces. The answer to the questions 'Why go to Saint-Juliot? What's Juliot to me?' is contained in the third stanza: 'There lonely I found her, / The sea-birds around her, / And other than nigh things uncaring to know'. This is not Emma but the phantom woman of 'After a Journey' written into and on the texture of the landscape, its *genius loci*, and the embodiment of the narrator's powerful muse. 'A Dream or No' demonstrates the necromancy of the imagination: the charm of art itself. This 'spot' that is both real and imagined, nebulous and solid, becomes 'the key' that will unlock the creative flow and, in the process, scan across the dark space between desire and its object, helping to fill the hollow at the heart of the mourning subject of desire. 'I Found Her Out There' charts the process through which the phantom of the beloved is located and established 'out there' in the landscape of the mind, and the tricky process of '[bringing] her here' to 'lay her to rest'. It is a wonderfully suggestive paradigm of the process of artistic creation that Hardy explored in such detail in *The Well-Beloved*. For art to be successful, it must retain its fluid, suggestive 'haunting' connection to the Real. Its signifiers must preserve their tenuous, slippery relation to what they seek to 'lay to rest' in the process of signification. Language is always haunted by what it cannot express: the spirit of desire that escapes from the 'loamy cell' of the word across 'the murmuring miles', the 'swells', 'sobs' and 'thobs' of its origins in the pre-linguistic realm.

Melissa Zeiger acknowledges Hardy's 'evaluative, reflective, revisionary' reading of the elegiac tradition in relation to his private experience but regards his persistent recalling of Emma 'often literally as a ghost', and 'the impassioned poetic sequence' in which he does this, as 'somewhat paradoxical in light of [his] notorious estrangement from Emma and his fatalistic "plotting" of his own marriage', as if the role of 'art', as opposed to biography, is always to faithfully reflect life. For her, both Hardy's anomalousness as an elegist and his revisionary power lie in 'his [...] focus on a specifically conceived historical woman' (Zeiger, 1997: 19). She insists that in those traditional elegies that follow the structural paradigm of the myth of Orpheus and Eurydice, Pan and Syrynx, Daphne and Apollo, men's losses are the only ones that count: the loss or 'suffering of women is doomed to remain speechless, incoherent, or excessive' (Zeiger, 1997: 6).

Insofar as the male melancholic gives words to women's grief, he thereby incorporates 'the feminine' into his own highly privileged cultural persona.

The male melancholic thus at once denies symbolic expression to woman's grief and loss and appropriates it as a symbol. The 'loss' is inevitably seen as the male's.

(Zeiger, 1997: 6)

Zeiger discusses how the phantom woman is an empowering force for the male subject (Hardy): 'a personal muse, specially and intimately bound to the poet, as he is to her, through a conjugal tie seemingly indissoluble even by death and subsequent remarriage'. This constitutes a major aspect of Hardy's innovative practice as an elegist 'to which subsequent poets would indeed be indebted' (45). And yet, there remains for her the threat of 'ghostly contagion' in Hardy's figure of the phantom female: the threat of 'catching death from the dead', which leads him eventually to exchange the dead female body for poetic empowerment (50). She reads 'The Shadow on the Stone' (*Moments of Vision*, 1917) as describing the fatal 'turn' of Orpheus to his wife, Eurydice, thereby condemning her to Hades forever. The narrator,

(Hardy), imagines he sees the 'shade' of Emma on the Druid stone in their garden and is torn by the urge to turn to see her and the desire to preserve the fantasy of her presence behind him by resisting this urge (51):

> I would not turn my head to discover
> That there was nothing in my belief.
> Yet I wanted to look and see
> That nobody stood at the back of me;
> But I thought once more: 'Nay, I'll not unvision
> A shape which, somehow, there may be.'
> So I went on softly from the glade,
> And left her behind me throwing her shade,
> As she were indeed an apparition –
> My head unturned lest my dream should fade.

> (Hynes: 280)

For Zeiger, it is not the loss or destruction of the Eurydicean female that 'Hardy finds most poetically generative' but the 'turn': 'that moment of losing which comprehends both contact and irreversible separation' (50). Thus, the poem 'remains irreconcilably divided between not wanting to look and wanting to, between believing in the ghost and not believing in her' (51).

What Zeiger misses here, perhaps, is the 'knowingness' of the poem in relation to the imagined shadow and the significance of that shadow as a disembodied symbol of the narrator's muse. The narrator knows that there is 'nothing in my belief' and that the shade of the dead woman is imagined or even 'dream[ed]' – but prefers to keep in play the fancy that she might indeed be there, not least because of her creative potential. He leaves the shadow behind, however, 'As she were indeed an apparition': the awkwardness of the line suggesting the suppression of 'if' ('as though', 'as the case would be if') between 'as' and 'she', possibly to retain the poem's dominant iambic and anapaestic tetrameter. Unlike Orpheus, who turns to reassure himself that Eurydice *is* there, the narrator preserves the *illusion* that she 'may be' behind ~~him~~ by not turning. It follows, then, that instead of losing her the narrator succeeds in bringing Eurydice out of Hades, not as 'a specifically conceived historical woman' (Zeiger: 19), but as 'a phantom of his own figuring' ('The Phantom Horsewoman', Hynes, II: 65) and a textual construct woven out of intertexts which include this recurring myth.[34] It is significant that in this poem the narrator walks away from the phantom instead of trying to join it, as in so many of the 'Poems of 1912–13'. The metaphors of shifting shadow, apparition, shade, dream – like those used by Pierston to describe his elusive 'Well-Beloved' – testify to the difficulty of stabilising or realising the exquisite moment in language even while they manage to do precisely that. This poem suggests that this mourning narrator is seeking more concrete manifestations of ~~his~~ desire, and the image of the shadow figured on the Druid stone is a prefiguring of the turn to the material record.[35]

'The Shadow on the Stone', whose addendum offers the information 'Begun 1913: finished 1916', has a suggestive intertextual relationship with the 'Poems of 1912–13', in particular perhaps 'At Castle Boterel' (Hynes, II; 63). Here the narrator is situated, significantly, at 'the junction of lane and highway'. Looking back through the drizzle he sees, on the sloping 'byway' behind, the spectres of 'Myself and a girlish form benighted / In dry March weather'. This is another Orphic turn in which the narrator sees not only the Eurydice figure of the phantom woman but also the phantom of Orpheus climbing the steep road that will return him to the place he has just left. As in 'After a Journey', the narrator can join the lost beloved only by also becoming a ghost. While the 'turn' condemns the phantom woman to return to the dark realm of death, it liberates the narrator to move away from the 'benighted' lane and forward onto the highway, back into the realm of life. This is a superb realisation of a lost moment of plenitude – 'a time of such quality' – which can never be revisited and whose 'substance' can never be grasped again, for, like the girlish form, it has been 'ruled from sight' by Time:

> What we did as we climbed, and what we talked of
> Matters nor much, not to what it led,—
> Something that life will not be balked of
> Without rude reason till hope is dead,
> And feeling fled.

Unlike the narrators of 'The Voice' and 'The Shadow on the Stone', this narrator moves forwards while still looking backwards, keeping the 'phantom figure' in view, seeming to wish neither to stay there with her in phantom form, nor bring her over to the other side. This is because, in ~~his~~ imagination, the moment has already been committed to the material realm. The shades of the ghosts are permanently inscribed on the rocky banks of the byway as they pass by:

> Primaeval rocks form the road's steep border,
> And much have they faced there, first and last,
> Of the transitory in Earth's long order;
> But what they record in colour and cast
> Is—that we two passed.

Out of the space of desire – again figured on the page in that strong, affective caesura in the last line – the narrator brings forth a material record that will last for posterity and is manifested on the 'primaeval rocks' in the poem, and on the page in the form of the poem itself.

It is worth noting, that the narrator describes this shrinking shape as 'one' rather than 'her' phantom figure, as we might expect. While on one level it seems that the remaining figure can only be that of the 'girlish form', there is some ambiguity as to its identity. This is increased by the line 'As when that night / saw us alight'. On 'that night', two alighted 'to ease the sturdy pony's load'. Where is the other, and who is the shrinking one that is left behind? If it is the 'girlish form' then where is her phantom companion? As in 'The Voice' it is possible to read this poem as a dramatisation of the split subject as it strives to realise itself in the moment – not the moment of the past but that of the present and future – stabilised and immortalised in the 'record'. It is this achievement that allows the narrator to continue forward, newly present to ~~himself~~ as the phantom self shrinks to nothing in the past: in 'old love's domain'. The line 'for my sand is shrinking' registers the narrator's acceptance of mortality, but the 'transitory' nature of the human is compensated for by the permanence of art.

'The Phantom Horsewoman', with its doubly displaced ungendered narrator whose vision encompasses the man who is said to see the 'ghost-girl-rider', completes the process of the artful distancing of the phantom woman into the realms of hearsay and story.

> I
> Queer are the ways of a man I know:
> He comes and stands
> In a careworn craze,
> And looks at the sands
> And the seaward haze,
> With moveless hands
> And face and gaze,
> Then turns to go...
> And what does he see when he gazes so?
>
> II
> They say he sees as an instant thing
> More clear than to-day,
> A sweet soft scene
> That was once in play
> By that briny green;
> Yes, notes alway
> Warm, real, and keen,
> What his back years bring—
> A phantom of his own figuring. (65)

This complex framing device turns the phantom woman into a picture or a series of moving pictures played out in the imagination of the 'man'. The narrator becomes the reader of both the 'man' and his vision, reading and, in the process, realising on the page, this 'phantom of [the man's] own figuring'. The intertextual reference to the myth of Tithonus, 'And though, / toil-tried, / He withers daily, / Time touches her not', brings in *The Well-Beloved* as a further intertext. The time-worn, toil-tried, careworn and crazed narrator suggests the figure of Jocelyn Pierston as he struggles to be free of the curse of the Well-Beloved by successfully and permanently capturing her in the body of a woman or a work of art, and thereby fulfilling the aesthetic desire of expression that will return him to 'calm and joy' (Girard, 1965: 34).

Once again the poem hinges on the 'broken tongue' of the ellipsis that marks the 'man's' turn away from 'What his back years bring' and the strong caesuras that fracture and energise the description of the 'ghost-girl-rider'. It is beautifully ironic that the man's inability permanently to separate himself from these images of the past results in this enduring image of the phantom woman, who rhythmically 'sings to the swing of the tide' on that 'shagged and shaly / Atlantic spot, / And as when first eyed'.[36]

Two poems will conclude this chapter, and this book: 'Under the Waterfall' and 'Where the Picnic Was'. Both of these focus on an event from the past the significance of which can only be grasped in the present. Both poems also 'bring forth' (to use Lacan's terminology) a symbol of permanence and plenitude out of the space of loss and desire. 'Under the Waterfall', placed immediately before 'Poems 1912–13', describes a picnic from the past and captures a fugitive epiphanic moment of a love affair in the potent, transformative symbol of the chalice. The suggestive symbol of the lost, 'opalized' picnic glass – misted and made more 'prized' by time – works as a metaphor for how the language of poetry might bring the realm beyond the material into the realm of knowledge in a kind of aesthetic communion.

> Whenever I plunge my arm, like this,
> In a basin of water, I never miss
> The sweet sharp sense of a fugitive day
> Fetched back from its thickening shroud of gray.
> Hence the only prime
> And real love-rhyme
> That I know by heart,
> And that leaves no smart,
> Is the purl of a little valley fall.

> (Hynes, II: 45)

The poem begins with two material things: a domestic object (a large china washing basin with a leafy pattern) and the act of washing (plunging an arm into a bowl of spring water), only to move beyond them to what they suggest to the imagination of the poem's narrator: the pool, the 'brook-side ledge' and 'the hanging plants that were bathing there', and thence to the refining down of all of these elements to the image of the lost, opalised picnic glass, which is a permanent symbol of love untouched by life or lip. The image of the patterned china basin filled with cold spring water is made to carry and express a surplus, which is given further imaginary form in the memory of the event and, finally, refined down to the symbol of the lost, yet ever present, glass.

The physical sensation of plunging an arm into a basin of cold spring water initiates in the narrator the 'sweet sharp sense of a fugitive day', which results in a 'throe / From the past': a memory 'thrown' back from the past that brings 'throbs' to the narrator's soul.[37] The use of 'throe' and 'throb' invoke that sense of violent or palpitating pain that Lacan associates with the movement beyond the pleasure principle into *jouissance*, and the poem has the effect of centring the reader's imagination on the exquisite image of the lost, intact, iridescent glass, 'jammed darkly' in 'a crease of the stone' at the bottom of pool. The lost glass is a perfect example of absent presence: the lost and inaccessible object of desire that is 'past recall' and yet is re-called into being by language. The lovers plunged their arms in vain into the pool to receive the glass. At a much later date, one of them plunges an arm into the basin and retrieves a memory of that glass and the romantic event of its loss, evoked by the sensation of cold spring water on warm flesh. This memory is given stability and substance by the narrator's 'paint[ing]' of the scene (l: 30) which allows repeated access to what is 'beyond recall' – the lost fugitive moment of love. The lost drinking-glass is imagined as whole and, as Catherine Maxwell notes, transmuted into a chalice, which, with the shared wine-drinking, suggests the Eucharist or Holy Communion (Maxwell, 2008: 203). China basin, pool and the lost glass mediate between the narrator and the inaccessible, lost moment of love. 'Under the Waterfall' offers another example of the trope of water in relation to desire. The cold spring water in the basin reminds the narrating lover of 'the purl of a little valley fall' that has flowed since time immemorial, and its remembered sound 'is the only prime / And real love-rhyme / That I know by heart, / And that leaves no smart'. Desire is eternal and far surpasses its metonymic manifestation for human beings as erotic or romantic love.

Two things are worth noting here: the unspecified gender of the narrator and also the suggestiveness of the phrase 'to paint the scene'. Maxwell notes the 'unsettling ripple across gender' in the poem and suggests that 'reading the poem for the first time (especially if one has no knowledge of Emma's memoir), the reader might well assume that the speaker is male till the very end of the piece where one meets the qualification "his and mine" ' (Maxwell, 2008: 204). However, as is the case here, this uncertainty can only be resolved by bringing into play the critic's own assumptions concerning gender and sexuality, or through recourse to Hardy's biography, although, as readers of Hardy's *Life* will know, it was Hardy himself who sketched (though did not paint) the scene.[38] Maxwell suggests that

> it would be more interesting, in this poem about hallucinatory preserva-
> tion, to preserve the hallucinatory marks of a reading where an apparently
> masculine voice transforms into a feminine one, as Hardy, plumbing the
> depths of consciousness, plunges through the more immediately evident
> upper strata of masculine identity in an attempt to reach and capture the
> elusive delicate vessel of the woman's fantasy; in such a reading the poem
> does, in fact, become something like the pool of Hermaphroditus, fusing
> male and female experience. (205)[39]

As I have tried to suggest, this 'unsettling ripple across gender' is a dominant feature of Hardy's poetry and fiction and testifies to the extent to which his work constantly challenges the myths of masculinity and femininity, partic-ularly in relation to desire. Nevertheless, if we accept Maxwell's conclusion that the narrator is female, then 'Under the Waterfall' offers an interesting variation on the mourning male subject of desire.[40] At the same time, the phrase 'to paint the scene' establishes this narrator as a self-conscious artist – possibly a painter but almost certainly engaged in fixing the moment in the medium of language: visual, spoken and finally recorded on the page.

Originally 'Poems of 1912–13' ended with the testament to the power of art dramatised by 'The Phantom Horsewoman'. Five years later, when Hardy published his *Collected Poems* (1919) he decided to alter the sequence by adding three more poems, including 'Where the Picnic Was', which now concludes it. This poem, with its echoes of the Virgilian epigraph '*Veteris vestigia flammae*', variously translated as 'traces' or 'embers' (Sacks, 1985), 'ashes', 'sparks' or 'cinders' (Armstrong, 2000: 134) of an old flame, rounds the sequence up beautifully.[41] Several critics have explored the complex rela-tion of this epigraph to Hardy's life, but it also has a significance for his art and particularly for his poetry.[42] '*Vestigia*' is etymologically related to '*ves-tigo*', 'to follow in the track of'; '*vestigium*', 'foot-track'; '*vestigio*', 'a trace, mark, track or vestige'. Tracks, marks, prints and traces are recurrent motifs in the poems under discussion here, especially in relation to the role of writ-ing in tracking down, recovering and retracing the events of life as art. 'After a Journey' dramatises various possible quests, including the narrator's quest to 'scan' the phantom woman of his memory: to see her and also to resolve her into literary, poetic form. In 'Where the Picnic Was', the narrator climbs 'through the winter mire' to 'the forsaken place' where, just a year ago, he and three companions picnicked together, one of whom 'has shut her eyes / For evermore' (Hynes, III: 69–70). Already we sense the relative immediacy of both the moment and the memory. This narrator scans across a dark space of just one year, as opposed to the 40 years of 'After a Journey'. The narrator of 'After a Journey' claims to be 'just the same' as he was 40 years earlier. The narrator of 'Where the Picnic Was' declares: 'Yes, I am here / Just as last year'. The difference is striking. The unresolved desire enacted in 'After a Journey' (which is, I suggest, resolved by the poem itself) is more clearly resolved in 'Where the Picnic Was'. The narrator is able to 'scan and trace' and apprehend the departed companions, the dead woman and the moment of plenitude when they picnicked there together, in the symbolic mark of the burnt circle. We might also note the specificity of the place which, unlike the sweeping, dramatic landscapes of 'After a Journey', 'Beeny Cliff', 'I Found Her Out There' and 'Ditty (E.L.G.)' resolves itself to this one 'spot': the circle of burnt grass that marks the location of last summer's picnic fire. The blackness of the mark and the charred 'stick-ends' are highly suggestive of the black mark on a page and the instruments of writing.

The poem features three strong caesuras. In the last stanza, two of them register as spaces of desire and grief marking the dispersal of the group:

> —But two have wandered far
> From this grassy rise
> Into urban roar
> Where no picnics are,
> And one—has shut her eyes
> For evermore.

> (Hynes, III: 70)

In the first stanza, however, the caesura signals the narrator's satisfaction at finding the spot: 'a burnt circle—aye' that signifies both the presence of the group there in the previous summer and their absence now: in particular, it registers the presence and absence of the dead woman. In this richly suggestive line, the space of desire separates, and is bridged by, the symbol of the burnt circle and the exclamation 'aye', which expresses both grief and satisfaction. This is now the spot 'where she dwells': a discernible, concentrated circle or mark indelibly burnt into the landscape, not fancifully embroidered onto it as in 'Ditty (E.L.G.)'. The 'burnt circle' displaces the phantom woman as a symbol of the permanence of art, as opposed to the transient, ephemeral nature of memory and nostalgic desire. In 'Her Immortality', published in *Wessex Poems* (1898), the ghost of the dead woman pleads with her lover not to end his life because 'In you resides my single power / Of sweet continuance here' (Hynes, I: 72). 'Where the Picnic Was' dramatises Hardy's belief in the power of art to far outlast those who produce it, as well as those by whom it was inspired. For this reason, it makes a fitting end to the moments of desire that are so artfully and satisfactorily realised in 'Poems of 1912–13'.

As Peter Sacks has suggested, absence or loss may be already inherent in language, but the elegist refines that language still further to make it *figure* loss in an attempt to close the gap between mourner and mourned, sign and signified, subject and object of desire: to bridge 'the spaces of absence or dislocation' (Sacks, 1985: xi). Hardy's contemporary, Walter Pater also noted the ability of art to give substance and stability to the moment. In the conclusion to *The Renaissance*, Pater describes all forms as 'but the concurrence, often renewed from moment to moment, of forces parting sooner or later on their ways' (1873: 44). Our apprehensions of experience are limited and infinitely divisible by time so that 'all that is actual in it [is] a single moment, gone while we try to apprehend it, of which it may ever be more truly said that it has ceased to be than that it is'. These 'tremulous wisps' or 'single sharp impressions' are the refined or 'fined' elements of 'what is real in our life', their constant gathering and dissolution contributing to 'that strange perpetual weaving and unweaving of ourselves'. Poetry is one means through which these moments might be invested with the solidity of language whilst still retaining what Pater calls 'a relic more or less fleeting, of such moments gone by'. It is an art that 'seeks to give nothing but the highest quality to your moments as they pass, and simply for those moments' sake' (1873: 45). In this way Art, at its very best, allows the subject not only to recognise and name his/her desire, but to bring it forth as a new and fulfilling 'presence in the world' (Lacan, 1977: 275). As Hardy noted from John Addington Symmond's *Essays Speculative and Suggestive* (London, 1890), 'It is the artist's duty to perpetuate [...]fugitive perfections' (*LN*, II: 1833), the 'discovery' and 'rediscovery' that 'is always ready to steal away again, thus establishing the dimension of loss' (Lacan 1977b), 'The Freudian Unconscious': 25).

Laurence Lerner specifies desire or longing as the energy that makes art possible. For Michael Mason loss is, paradoxically, a 'necessary inspirational "creative sorrow"' (both cited in Hutcheon, 1998: 4). Philip Larkin, whose admiration for Hardy is well known, claimed that 'deprivation is to me what daffodils were to Wordsworth' (Larkin, 1983: 47). The making of art is, therefore, an attempt to give substance to the insubstantial, to give immediacy and presence to what is absent, lost or lacking, and to secure it in the present and for the future. In the case of Hardy the poet, the work of art that is the elegy secures a sense of plenitude in the face of that most disruptive and challenging threat to the fiction of self-presence: the subjective 'undoing' ('The Going') or unravelling that is initiated by the death of someone in whose love (imagined or real) we locate our own reflection.

Evidence of this may indeed be found in Hardy's life. On Boxing Day, 1920, Florence Hardy wrote to Sydney Cockerell describing her husband's delight in performance and art:

At the party (of the Mummers etc) last night he was so gay – & one of them said to me that he had never seen him so young & happy & excited. He is now – this afternoon – writing a poem with great spirit: always a sign of well-being with him. Needless to say it is an intensely dismal poem.

(Millgate, 1996: 171)

Notes

Introduction

1. In 'The Ethics of Psychoanalysis', Lacan declares that 'from an analytical point of view the only thing of which one can be guilty of is of having given ground relative to one's desire' (1992: 319).
2. In 'Pleasure and Reality', Lacan notes: 'we only grasp the unconscious finally when it is explicated, in that part of it which is articulated by passing into words' (1992: 32).
3. Miller was, however, the first of Hardy's more contemporary critics to recognise the centrality of *The Well-Beloved* to an understanding of Hardy's conception of desire. He developed his insights over a decade later in *Fiction and Repetition* (1982).
4. See Widdowson (1989); Rimmer (2009) and Thomas (2009) for further discussion of Hardy's classification of his novels in the 'General Preface to the Wessex Edition'.
5. See Widdowson (2007) and Thomas (1999).
6. I aim to contest Judith Mitchell's assertion that Hardy's novels follow a model of erotic relationships 'characterized by the troubled and destructive nature of an interaction between an active, desiring subject (usually male) and a passive, desired object (usually female)' (1994: 3). Mitchell also claims that Hardy was unable to 'break free of patriarchal psychic configurations' (207). She does, however, 'applaud the attempt' on Hardy's part to 'push against this convention' whilst offering few examples to justify this somewhat condescending approbation (23).
7. Robert E. Lougy likewise notes the similarities between Foucault and Lacan, particularly in Foucault's recognition that by 'setting itself the task of making the discourse of the unconscious speak through consciousness', psychoanalysis 'advances "in the direction of that fundamental region in which the relations of representation and finitude come into play" ' (Lougy, 2004: 16).
8. See Rutland (1938); Wright (1967); Kelly (1982); Thomas (1999) and Mallett (2009).
9. See Thomas (1999), Chapter 1, for a fuller discussion of Hardy's ideas in this respect, and Miller (1970), for a discussion of the relationship of 'the texture' of a literary text to the evolving web of language (xviii–ix).
10. 'No doubt very few people understand the purely subjective character of the phenomenon that we call love, or how it creates, so to speak, a supplementary person, distinct from the person whom the world knows by the same name, a person most of whose constituent elements are derived from ourselves. Desire is excited, satisfies itself, disappears – and that is all. Thus the young girl who one marries is not the one with whom one has fallen in love' (Proust, 1913–1927; 1980: 505). The serial version of *The Well-Beloved* was published in the *Illustrated London News* from 1 October to 17 December 1892 under the title *The Pursuit of*

the Well-Beloved and was issued in revised volume form as *The Well-Beloved* in the middle of March 1897.

11. However, as Butler suggests, it is unclear whether this lost infantile *jouissance* can ever have existed, 'considering that our only access to this pleasure is through a language that is predicated on its denial', which leads one to ask 'whether Lacan has not rediscovered a religious dream of plenitude in a fantasy of lost pleasure that he himself has constructed'. Nevertheless it is the nostalgia for such a state that 'characterises all human desire' (1999: 204). See Mitchell' Juliet and Jacqueline Rose (1985) and Grosz (1990: 147–87) for a resumé of sympathetic feminist responses to Lacan's views on the nature of femininity.

12. Deleuze also regards the experience of desire as predicated on 'lack' as the product of industrial capitalism rather than something inherent in the subject (Deleuze,1972).

13. These lines form part of Sappho's rebuke to Anactoria in Swinburne's poem 'Anactoria' 1863–65 (McGann and Sligh, 2004: 98, lines: 189–95).

14. David Bromwich claims that writing poetry is an act of self-invention: 'Its end is to produce a text from life that counts as an exemplary case of the emergence of the individual' (Bromwich, 1987: 120). Faced with extinction, the poet regards the work as 'an almost material deposit'. As Sappho, Swinburne and Hardy have so poignantly registered, 'the catastrophe that interests them is never extinction as such, but rather the fate of namelessness which others have suffered before' (128).

15. For instance, Judith Mitchell's conflation of Hardy's various narrators with the author leads to the absurd conclusion that 'the authorial perspective we can sense in Hardy's novels, in fact, is simply the conventional perspective of a heavily defended, psychically isolated male towards the castrated, castrating female Other' (Mitchell, 1994: 159–60). She also insists on 'the glaring fact that both the narrator and the implied reader in all of Hardy's novels are invariably male, and sexist as well' (156) whilst seemingly oblivious to the problematic nature of each of these terms. Linda Ruth Williams rightly takes Rosemarie Morgan to task for 'falling into the psychobiographical trap of projecting onto characters past histories and unconscious lives which are never there in print' (Williams, 1995: 189, nt. 12). J. Hillis Miller reminded us almost a quarter of a century earlier than Mitchell's book that, in his fiction, Hardy speaks 'not in his own voice but in that of a narrator he has invented' (1970: 39). Any point of view, whether issuing from the narrator of a poem or a novel 'is only one moment of vision among many' (45).

16. Miller notes that that the narrators of Hardy's novels, like the speakers of his poems, 'are roles Hardy plays' and that he often insisted that that his poems are 'imaginary monologues, "dramatic or impersonative even where not explicitly so" ' (1970: xiii).

1   House and Home: Nostalgic Desire and the Locus of Being

1. In 'The Direction of the Treatment and the Principles of Its Power' Lacan declares 'while desire is the metonymy of the want-to-be, the ego is the metonymy of desire' (Lacan,2006: 534).

2. Uli Knoepflmacher notes how the separation of an inner circle of female domesticity from 'an outer sphere of male traffic' contributed to the feminisation of the home which became increasingly associated with childhood and nurturance (Knoepflmacher, 1990: 1055).

3. As opposed to 'the designation of "builder", denoting a manager of and contractor for all trades [which] was then unknown in the country districts' (*LW*, 1984: 12).
4. In his preface to *A Pair of Blue Eyes*, Hardy echoes William Morris's convictions as expressed in the 'Manifesto for the Society for the Protection of Ancient Buildings', concerning the inadvisability of restoring 'the grey carcases of a medievalism of whose spirit had fled' (*PW*, 1967: 7). In 1906 Hardy wrote a speech entitled 'Memories of Church Restoration' to be delivered at the General Meeting of the 'Society for the Protection of Ancient Buildings', in which he recounts his own 'brief experience as a church-restorer' and laments 'the drastic treatment' dealt out to such buildings in the hope of preventing further damage to those still left untouched by the craze (*PW*, 1967: 203–25: 205).
5. See Hardy's extracts from Symonds's comments on Pater in *Essays Speculative and Suggestive* (*LN*, 1: 1864; 1865).
6. Knoepflmacher associates the imagined childhood house with what he regards as Hardy's attempt to recover the feminine, or Bachelardian, ' "dream memory" of an original maternal envelope' (1990: 1056).
7. See Hardy's poem 'Before Life and After' (Hynes (1982, I: 333)).
8. We know from Aunt Drusilla that Jude was born in or near Marygreen but was taken as a baby to Mellstock, South Wessex, following his parents' parting and his mother's suicide. His father ' "was took wi" the shakings for death, and died in two days' (*JO*, 1998: 7) when Jude was ten, at which point he moved back to Marygreen to live with his aunt.
9. Jude's home echoes with Drusilla's oft repeated wish that 'Goddy-mighty had took thee too wi' thy mother and father, poor useless boy' (7) and the reminder that 'You didn't grow up hereabouts' (13).
10. Whilst aware of the biographical background to this, and others of Hardy poems, I have chosen to employ a text-centred approach.
11. I am indebted to David Bagchi for his observation, based on Charlton T. Lewis and Charles Short's 1879 edition of *A Latin Dictionary*, that, compared with other synonyms, 'domicilium' appears to give emphasis to the idea of living in a place rather than the bricks-and-mortar (or equivalent), although other synonyms such as 'habitatio', and 'mansio', whose root means 'staying' or 'remaining', might have conveyed the act of habitation or dwelling more obviously. 'Mansio', however, carried a resonance of grandiosity implicit in the English word 'mansion'.
12. For Wolfreys, the Latinate title of 'Domicilium' also signals 'a history of colonial possession and dispossession' (2009: 6).
13. Hardy made frequent visits to his own birthplace at Bockhampton. His last visit was on 1 November 1926 to see about 'tidying and secluding' the place with fences and trees. The comment in the *Life* is that 'It was always a matter of regret to him if he saw this abode in a state of neglect, or the garden uncherished' (*LW*: 468).
14. Peter Simpson notes the aptness of the title of Hardy's second collection – *Poems of the Past and Present* – in which 'The Self-Unseeing' first appeared, for 'it is a poem "of the past and present": of the past in the sense that it derives from a memory of Hardy's own childhood, of the present in the sense that the present moment of remembering is as important to the effect of the poem as the past experiences being recollected' (Simpson, 1979: 45).
15. See: Simpson (1979) and Knoepflmacher (1990).

16. Simpson registers how, to the reader who is unaware of the specific biographical detail of the repositioning of the front door of the cottage at Higher Bockhampton, the line 'Here was the former door' carries 'a doubleness of meaning'; however, I am unable to read it as 'Here is the same old door' (Simpson, 1979: 46). The use of 'was' and 'former' suggests: 'Here is where the door that used to be was'.

17. Hardy appears to be echoing Wordsworth, whose narrator in 'Elegaic Stanzas Suggested by a Painting of Peele Castle in a Storm, Painted by Sir George Beaumont' describes the painter's ability to add to a scene 'the gleam, / The light that never was, on sea or land, / The consecration, and the Poet's dream'. This was reiterated by Edward Burne Jones, who wrote: 'I mean by a picture a beautiful romantic dream of something that never was, never will be – in a light better than any light that ever shone – in a land no-one can define, or remember, only desire' (Latham, 2003: 5).

18. Marjorie Levinson notes how the word 'childlike' suggests 'the inauthenticity' of the nostalgically remembered innocence 'its status as impersonation rather than [...] immediate and unself-conscious being' (Levinson, 2006: 572).

19. Galia Benziman discerns 'a double resistance' in Hardy's nostalgic descriptions of childhood in which his adult narrators do not simply 'mourn the loss of their earlier innocence, but question its very existence in the first place' implying doubt on the narrator's part about the validity of that nostalgia (Benziman, 2012: 16).

20. Donald D. Stone notes 'Because of the considerable hold on their imaginations of homes past, homes forever lost, the satisfaction of a home regained or newly constructed was virtually impossible for Pater and Hardy; and each might be described (in Pater's words) as a "seeker after something in the world that is there in so satisfying measure, or not at all" ' (Stone, 1984: 304).

21. Tim Armstrong likewise maintains that Hardy's work 'teaches us above all about the entry into history, the trauma of *becoming-historical* which is central to nineteenth-century conceptions of the human' (Armstrong, 2000: 2).

22. In her 1892 essay 'In Praise of Old Houses' Vernon Lee also speaks of the need to encourage the 'historical habit of mind' in relation to buildings and other 'works of man' (3). Older dwellings, she claims, are 'rendered habitable for our soul by the previous dwelling therein of others, of other souls', which gives them a charm which is not to be found in newer dwellings, towns or cities. For Lee, the past is charming because it is 'the one free place for our imagination'. It is 'the unreal and the yet visible [...] the unreal whose unreality, unlike that of the unreal things with which we cram the present, can never be forced on us. There is more behind; there may be anything' (6). However, at the same time as we are drawn by the infinite re-imagining of the past, we realise its meretricious nature: 'for there is no end to the deceits of the past; we protest that we know it is cozening us, and it continues to cozen us just as much' (6). The past is not made by those who inhabited it, Lee claims. On the contrary, *they* are made by the past (7) in the refining crucible of the memory and the imagination. This 'fabrication' of the past is necessary to our sense of integrity and wholeness of being because it is the means by which we situate ourselves in a linear narrative which gives us a sense of continuity and contiguity with who and what has preceded us.

23. In the poem 'At a House in Hampstead', published in *Late Lyrics* (1922), the narrator draws comfort and reassurance from the conviction that the Hampstead home of John Keats 'where sang he' holds more of the poet's presence, even if only in

spectral form, than the grand pyramid in Rome that marks his grave (Hynes, II: 340).

24. The *Shorter Oxford English Dictionary* offers a definition of the word 'utter' as 'irregular marks made on a surface by the vibration or too great pressure of a tool'. In this respect the written or printed word offers itself as a particular form of 'utterance'.

25. See 'Old Furniture' for this sense of the living inhabitant crowded out of existence by the hands, fingers and faces of the dead (Hynes, II: 227).

26. Hardy copied into his notebook and underlined an extract from Matthew Arnold's essay on the poet Heinrich Heine concerning the relationship of the modern individual to the constraints of the systems in which he or she has their being:

> Modern times find themselves with an immense system of institutions established facts, accredited dogmas, customs, rules which have come to them from times not modern. In this system their life has to be carried forward; yet they have a sense that this system is not of their own creation, that it by no means corresponds exactly with the wants of their actual life, that, for them it is customary, not rational.

It is precisely the awakening of this sense of the necessary constraints of history that Arnold sees as the harbinger of 'the modern spirit' (*LN*, 2: 1017), and this trauma of alienation from the enabling structures of the past is at the heart of Hardy's exploraton of nostalgic desire.

27. The apostles were able not only to preach eloquently but simultaneously in the language of everyone around them: 'And at this sound the multitude came together, and they were bewildered, because each one was hearing them speak in his own language. And they were amazed and astonished, saying, "Are not all these who are speaking Galileans? And how is it that we hear, each of us in his own native language? Parthians and Medes and Elamites and residents of Mesopotamia, Judea and Cappadocia, Pontus and Asia, Phrygia and Pamphylia, Egypt and the parts of Libya belonging to Cyrene, and visitors from Rome, both Jews and proselytes, Cretans and Arabians—we hear them telling in our own tongues the mighty works of God." And all were amazed and perplexed, saying to one another, "What does this mean?" ' (*Acts*, 2: 1–44, v. 6–13).

28. See the migrations on Lady Day in *Tess of the d'Urbervilles* (2005: 379).

29. After the close of Giles's tenure in Hintock 'people said that a certain laxity had crept into his life; that he had never gone near a church latterly, and had been sometimes seen on Sundays with unblackened boots, lying on his elbow under a tree, with a cynical gaze at surrounding objects' (*TW*, 2005: 156).

30. Julian Wolfreys notes 'If the light that reaches us comes from a star already extinguished, in effect we are receiving that which only remains as a trace, and that which no longer exists as such. This being the case, we glimpse in the abyss our own-having-become-extinct' (2009: 4).

31. Hardy began 'The Melancholy Hussar' in July 1888, just over a year after the publication of the three volume edition of *The Woodlanders* in March 1887. He worked on the story in the interval between Tillotson's rejection of the early sections of *Tess of the d'Urbervilles* in September 1889 and the publication of the novel in censored form in the *Graphic* in October of the following year. 'The Melancholy Hussar' was completed in October 1889 and published in various provincial newspapers in 1890, before being finally collected in the 1912 edition of *Wessex Tales*.

32. We may detect here an anticipation of the central motif of Hardy's poem 'The Voice' which will be discussed in the final chapter.
33. Hutcheon notes the etymology of 'nostalgia': from the Greek *nostos* 'to return home' and *algos* meaning 'pain'. Originally a medical-pathological definition coined in 1688 by a Swiss medical student to describe the condition of Swiss mercenaries exiled from their mountain home (1998).
34. Hardy develops this idea in 'Drummer Hodge' who will forever be 'portion of that unknown plain' (Hynes, I: 122).

2   Desire, Female Amity and Sapphic Space

1. U. C. Knoepflmacher has discussed how many of Hardy's poems 'rely on an increasingly elaborate nexus of mother-feminine-house configurations to work out a gender configuration he would like to abolish' (Knoepflmacher, 1990: 1055–70).
2. Helena Michie notes how Tess's exhortation to Angel to marry her sister 'Liza-Lu 'establishes a relationship between women that cannot be shattered by competition for male attention'. However 'Liza-Lu and Tess are denied a meaningful adult relationship and the younger sister appears only as the prelapsarian 'ghost of the other' (Michie, 1989: 420).
3. Nemesvari notes the reader's 'uncertainty' concerning the 'resolutions' such marriages provide (2011: 177). Linda Shires offers an interesting reading of Bathsheba's retreat to 'what seems like a womb-like haven' in the damp ferny hollow following the scene with Fanny Robin's coffin. For Shires the space is intruded upon by masculinity in the form of the contrasting sounds of the ploughboy's whistle and the dunce's re-iteration of his lesson. These and the descriptions of the spot by daylight 'masculinise' it in terms of 'labour, sexuality, religion and education'. It is Liddy's appearance that allows Bathsheba to 'recognise her femininity and her power' which lies in 'independence, economic wealth and "standing your ground" ' (Shires, 1991: 174–5).
4. Elaine Marks defines what she calls the 'Sapphic Fairytale', which she regards as a common variation on romantic friendship 'in which an older women teaches a younger woman about sexual desire and life; in most cases the relationship is brief, as the younger woman outgrows her initial attraction' (cited Vicinus, 1992: 476). Marks also identifies two other instances of 'Sapphic intertextuality': 'the older woman who commits suicide because her love for a younger man is unrequited' and 'the woman poet as disembodied muse' (Marks, 1979: 356). Shades of the Sappho/Phaeon legend inflect the relationship between Viviette Constantine and the young, golden-haired astronomer Swithin St Cleeve in *Two on a Tower*.
5. On arriving at the Great House, the groom draws Cytherea's attention to the sound of the waterfall which is 'enough to drive anybody mad', and to the dismal house itself, 'standing too low down in the hollow to be healthy'. It is, says the groom, 'just the house for a nice ghastly hair-on-end story, that would make the parish religious'. Later that night, as she imprisons the young girl in her arms, Miss Aldclyffe complains to her: 'I [...] have been sipping at your mouth as if it were honey, because I fancied no wasting lover knew the spot' (83). Her passionate supplication of Cytherea Gray in the younger woman's bed is accompanied by the noise of the maddening waterfall and wheel in the engine house, which Cytherea imagines 'turning incessantly, labouring in the dark like a captive starving in a dungeon', illuminated by the 'attenuated and skeleton-like rays' of the

moon (87). Additional gothic ambience is lent by the noise of Miss Aldclyffe's father dying: 'a very soft gurgle or rattle – of a strange abnormal kind [...]either close outside the window, close under the floor, or close above the ceiling' (87) and the howling of his dog in the room below.

6. Hardy claimed to have read Swinburne's *Poems and Ballads* (1866), a volume suffused with Sappho, with excitement and intense pleasure. In 1910, shortly after Swinburne's death, Hardy wrote 'A Singer Asleep', while sitting next to Swinburne's grave at Bonchurch on the Isle of Wight, in which the older poet is referred to as the 'knowing' pupil of 'she the Lesbian, she the music-mother / Of all the tribe that feel in melodies; / Who leapt, love-anguished, from the Leucadian steep'. The poem's narrator imagines Sappho's spirit surfacing to greet Swinburne at the water's edge below the cliffs at Bonchurch' (Hynes, II: 31).

7. Sappho's life is 'bitter' with love for Anactoria, which is experienced palpably as 'blinding', 'burning' and keen: 'thy sharp sighs / Divide my flesh and spirit with soft sound, / And my blood strengthens, and my veins abound' (Swinburne, 2004: 93, lines: 2–5). Oxymoron and synaesthesia express the agony and pleasure of an unappeased desire that vents itself in the imagined murder of the beloved:

I would find grievous ways to have thee slain
Intense device, and superflux of pain;
Vex thee with amorous agonies, and shake
Life at thy lips, and leave it there to ache.

(lns: 27–30)

Denied consummation Sappho seeks instead to consume Anactoria: 'That I could drink thy veins as wine, and eat / Thy breasts like honey!' and imagines her flesh 'in my flesh [...] entombed' (Swinburne, 2004: 96, lls: 100–4).

8. In Swinburne's 'Laus Veneris' (Swinburne, 2004: 71–82) Tannhäuser describes Venus's 'sad kissed mouth' and how 'with blind lips I felt for you, and found / About my neck your hands and hair enwound' (lls: 314; 317–18), which echoes Miss Aldclyffe's exhortation to Cytherea to 'put your hair round mamma's neck and give me one good long kiss' (85).

9. Hardy uses 'rank' to describe the weeds that Sue wraps her pagan images in and the weeds in the garden through which Tess is drawn by Angel's harp music.

10. Elaine Marks claims that Sappho and the island of Lesbos are 'omnipresent in literature about women loving women, whatever the gender or sexual preference of the writer and whether or not Sappho and her island are explicitly named' (Marks, 1979: 356).

11. See Faderman (1978) and Prins (1999: 112–73).

12. Hardy claims to have 'rediscovered' Swinburne's rendition of a Sappho fragment in 'Thee, too, the years shall cover', probably in his 1895 edition of Wharton's Sappho. John Pentland Mahaffy's first and unexpurgated edition of *Social Life in Ancient Greece from Homer to Menander* (1874), which Hardy purchased after Horace Moule's suicide, refers to Sappho's love poems as 'precious fragments of burning complaint', a comment Hardy copied into his *Literary Notebook* (*LN*, I: 524).

13. Wharton is at pains to point to Athenaeus's 'testimony to the purity of [Sappho's] love for her girlfriends' (Wharton, 1885: 26). See also DeJean (1989); Reynolds (2000; 2003) and Prins (1999). However, some of the renditions and translations in Wharton adopt what Joan DeJean terms the 'evasively undefinable internal signature' (DeJean, 1989: 17), so the gender of the speaking subject of the fragments is not always clearly Sappho, or even female, which liberates them from an

ideologically constrained and conservative construction of the poet's life, thereby allowing not just for a wider erotic range, but also for a freer play of meaning.

14. Wharton's 1885 edition of *Sappho* was praised by 'Michael Field' in *Long Ago* (1889) as 'of the highest value by those who desire to obtain a vivid impression of the personality, the influence, and the environment of the poet' (see: Prins, 1999: 74).

15. See Rimmer (1998). Patricia Ingham notes that 'Cytherea' is an alternative name for Aphrodite, the Greek goddess of love and beauty and is linked to the island of Cythera where the goddess is said to have landed after being born from the sea foam (Ingham, 2003: nt. 7).

16. See also the 'throned Cytherean', i.e. Aphrodite goddess of love in Swinburne's 'Hymn to Proserpine': 'clothed round with the world's desire as with raiment, and fair as the foam' (McGann and Sligh, 2004: 103, l. 75).

17. This lack of specificity is also registered in 'Michael Field's' 1889 rendition of Fragment 63: 'Ah for Adonis! So / the virgins cry in woe: / Ah, for the Spring, the spring, / And all fleet blossoming', where 'fleet' suggests 'swift', 'nimble' or transitory (Wharton, 1895: 110).

18. A more detailed discussion of the relationship between the sexual and the erotic is undertaken in Chapter 4.

19. *The Mayor of Casterbridge* was published in 1886, in the same year as R. L. Stevenson's *The Strange Case of Dr Jekyll and Mr Hyde*. In both novels, the relationship between Elizabeth-Jane and Lucetta and Henchard and Donald Farfrae, demonstrate a similar interest in schizophrenia and demonic doubling.

20. The narrator describes Grace's look as 'expressing a tendency to wait for others' thoughts before uttering her own: possibly also to wait for others' deeds before her own doings'. She has 'a gentleness that might hinder sufficient self-assertion for her own good' (*TW*: 35).

21. Accidently intruding on the sleeping Fitzpiers, Grace turns towards the bell-pull: 'Approaching the chimney, her back was towards Fitzpiers, but she could see him in the glass. An indescribable thrill passed through her as she perceived that the eyes of the reflected image were open, gazing wonderingly at her' (115).

22. Although Felice dislikes the woods 'they had the advantage of being a place in which she could walk comparatively unobserved' (211).

23. On her return from her abortive visit to Angel's parents, Tess runs into a plantation of deciduous trees to escape the suggestive threat of the 'well-to-do boor' who was knocked down by Angel for his coarse remarks to Tess, and who is later revealed to be Farmer Groby. Once safely inside, she scrapes together the dead leaves 'into a sort of nest' into which she creeps. She is disturbed, however, by the noise of the wounded pheasants in the trees above her whose necks she breaks to shorten their suffering. The connection between the hounded Tess, and the pheasants shot by 'rough and brutal men' 'looking over hedges, or peering through bushes and pointing their guns; strangely accoutred, a bloodthirsty light in their eyes' (297) suggests the dangers that exist outside this 'provisional shelter'.

24. The narrator's reference to 73rd psalm of Asaph connects the unenviable situation of Felice and Suke Damson with that of the apparently prosperous sinners momentarily envied by the psalm's singer. Grace keeps her council because she recognises that the wife of a philanderer, however victimised, is more protected by the law than her rivals are.

25. See Thomas (1999: 96–112) for a fuller examination of Paula's laodiceanism.

26. Somerset's confident early exploration of one of the turrets of the great tower ends in a fall and imprisonment in the 'dry well' of the 'walled-up space' (64), from whence he is rescued by a dreary footman (66). Here, we later learn, is where 'the man fell in, years ago, and was starved to death!' This appears to have been one of Hardy's recurrent dreams, as he told Sydney Cockerell on 15 December 1919: 'My dreams are not so coherent as yours. They are more like cubist paintings & generally end by my falling down the turret stairs of an old church owing to steps being missing.' (Millgate, 2004: 511).
27. In response to Paula's declaration that she is not 'a medievalist' Somerset asks her: 'What are you' to which she replies 'I am a Greek' Later she claims to be 'an eclectic' (78).
28. See Thomas (1999: 105–6).
29. See Chapter 5 below.
30. Simon Gatrell notes how in the scene in which we see Paula in her pink flannel costume 'there is at least a hint that her gender-orientation is one of the things she sometimes sits on the fence about' (Gatrell, 2011: 151).
31. Garber's 'third space' is discussed in more detail in Chapter 5.
32. 'He always ends in one way – thanks to the knotted whipcord – in a level trot round the lunger with the regularity a horizontal wheel, and the loss for ever to his character of the bold contours which the fine hand of Nature gave it. Yet the process is considered to be the making of him' (6).
33. In the utopian theories of J. J. Bachofen, Sapphic love rises above the imperatives of class, social ambition, sexuality and reproduction and is cited as an example of an advanced stage of civilisation. For Bachofen, Sapphism, or 'the love of women for their own sex', was closely associated with Dionysian Orphism, in which ' "masculine loves" stood in opposition to the purely sensual and sexual desires aroused by women' and embraced 'a liberation from the dominion of matter, an ascent from the body to the soul, a transfiguration in which love rises above sexuality' (Bachofen, 1861; 1967: 204). Sappho's aim 'was to elevate and educate her sex':

    > She opposed and punished all hetaerism, every passion that disturbed the harmony of Orphic life, for her the chaste brow betokened chastity of the soul, which she regarded as woman's highest ornament. (205)

34. In 'George Egerton's' story 'Virgin Soil', published in *Discords* (1893), the central protagonist Florence also rails against the unequal terms of marriage 'in which a man demands from a wife as a right what he must sue from a mistress as a favour; until marriage becomes for many women a legal prostitution, a nightly degradation a hateful yolk under which they age, [...] until their love [...] the mystery, the crowning glory of their lives, is turned into a duty they submit to with distaste instead of a favour granted to a husband who must become a new lover to obtain it' (Egerton, 1983: 155). See Hardy's correspondence with Egerton (Mary Chavelita Clairmonte in *CL*, 2: 102).
35. Vicinus defines two major paradigmatic forms of lesbian behaviour, namely romantic friendship between women and an intimate, sexual connection defined by the adoption of 'butch-femme' roles, and concludes: 'women who love woman, who choose women to nurture and support and to create a living environment in which to work creatively and independently, are lesbians' (Vicinus, 1982: 470–1).
36. Although, as Marion Thain and Richard Dellamora remind us, Havelock Ellis defined the lesbian on the basis of gender rather than sexual inversion and

included only women of a specifically 'masculine' disposition in his definition of the 'female invert' (Thain, 2007: 46). See Stanley (1992) for women's reactions to Carpenter and Ellis.

37. This atavistic paganism is also attributed to Eustacia Vye and Barbara of the House of Grebe in Hardy's 1891 story of the same name (*ND*: 1912: 53–93). See (Thomas, 2010: 246–72).

38. Interestingly, Sue's father was responsible for 'all the wrought ironwork at St Silas' before he went away to London (*JO*: 100).

39. ' "Yes!" exclaimed Paula with tears of vexation in her eyes. "It isn't every man who gets a woman of my position to run after him on foot, and alone, and he ought to have looked round!" ' (*AL*: 352).

40. Kate Thomas suggests that the novel's ending is not 'an unmitigated heterosexual resolution'. Paula's final words show that 'she herself is haunted by desire and desires to be haunted'. Paula's desire remains 'a queer desire [. . .] and the yearned-for spectral presence is Charlotte' (Thomas, 2012: 134).

3 Sexual Desire and the Lure of the Erotic

1. Although, see Chapter 2 of this study where I suggest the lost 'sapphic' possibilities of her encounter with Grace Melbury.

2. In Chapter 4 of *Two on a Tower* the narrator expatiates on 'Love between man and woman, which in Homer, Moses, and other early exhibitors of life, is mere desire' (1999: 215).

3. Indeed, it is often the specifically sensual knowledge of the female characters displayed by Hardy's omniscient narrators that makes them both palpable and problematic for the reader. For instance, the narrator knows that Eustacia Vye is 'soft to the touch as a cloud', that 'her temper could always be softened by stroking [her tresses] down', and describes her passing and re-passing 'a prickly tuft of the large Ulex Europaeus' in order to enjoy the sensation of having her hair brushed by it (*RoN*, 2005: 66). See Boumelha (1982) and Morgan (1988) on this. John Goode (1979) discusses the erotic interplay between character and reader as mediated by the narrator in 'Sue Bridehead and the New Woman'.

4. Simon Gatrell notes how the fringes and ribbons of Elfride's dress are 'figure[d] with desire as tasting and feeling with the sensitivity of tongues the texture of her dress, touching her as intimately as such dress will allow, much more intimately than he can, save with his eyes in the archetypal male gaze, mediated through Victorian convention, so that for Knight her dress and her hair act as he wishes (subconsciously) to act' (Gatrell, 2011: 77).

5. Hardy was extremely susceptible to the affecting power of music expertly played. He describes listening to his father playing tunes on the violin and being moved to tears as a child (*LW*: 19).

6. The term 'reels' here perfectly suggests both the repetitive dance of desire and its giddying, unsettling motion.

7. See also Simon Gatrell's chapter 'Hardy's Dance' (Gatrell, 1993: 24–41) for an extended study of the erotics of dance in Hardy's texts.

8. Andrew Radford describes the dance as 'a revel sustained by the modulations of erotic delirium, inducing self-forgetfulness and euphoric trance, thus affording transient release from the inexorable forward motion of mechanical time and the lumpishness of daily labour'. However, Eustacia is unable to re-enter this

'primal condition of existence' because she embodies through her selfishness 'a destructive emasculating force' (2003: 88–9).

9. See Chapter 4 below for an examination of how, through cross-dressing, Eustacia seeks to satisfy her proscribed desires.

10. See Radford (2003: 77–94) for an interesting examination of paganism in *The Return of the Native*.

11. See Thomas (2010) for the significance of buried ancient classical statues in later Victorian literature including Hardy's 'Barbara of the House of Grebe'.

12. The awakening of Tess's conscience is reminiscent of the scene depicted in Holman Hunt's 'The Awakening Conscience' (1853) exhibited at the Royal Academy in 1854 and praised by Ruskin in a letter to the *Times* in the same year (see Prettejohn, 2005: 111–13).

13. Tess frustrates Angel by her refusal to name their wedding day, thereby delaying indefinitely the moment of sexual consummation: 'Tess's desire seemed to be for a perpetual betrothal, in which everything should remain as it was then' (218). While this in part stems from the fear and guilt of her earlier sexual experiences with Alec d'Urberville there may be something else operative: perhaps the desire for a permanent courtship, or to maintain that detachment from the bodily, indeed from her own body, that she describes to Dairyman Crick.

14. This passage surely refutes Judith Mitchell's rather bald assertion that 'it makes little sense to question the degree of [Tess's] erotic subjectivity; quite simply, she has none' (1994: 194).

15. Judith Butler notes the 'double-alienation' of woman which is, in effect, a 'double alienation from desire itself': 'the woman learns to embody the promise of a return to a preoedipal pleasure, and to limit her own desire to those gestures that effectively mirror his desire as absolute' (1987; 1999: 203).

16. In this respect, Angel's erotic investment in Tess echoes Henry Knight's identification with Elfride as 'untouched' and emotionally, as well as physically, intact.

17. '[Angel] had come as to a place from which as from a screened alcove he could calmly view the absorbing world without, and, apostrophizing it with Walt Whitman – Crowd of men and women attired in the usual costumes, How curious you are to me! – resolved upon a plan for plunging into that world anew' (*Td'U*: 1998; 2003: 153).

18. See Chapter 1, note 15, for my comment on the implications of the word 'gleam'.

19. Forced to confront the revival of Alec's sexual desire for her, Tess experiences 'the wretched sentiment which had often come to her before, that in inhabiting the fleshly tabernacle with which Nature had endowed her, she was somehow doing wrong' (*Td'U*, 1983; 2005: 329).

20. Writing to the radical bisexual aristocrat and poet Roden Noel concerning the addition of the subtitle 'A pure woman faithfully presented' to the first edition of the novel, Hardy lamented that 'the parochial British understanding knocks itself against this word like a humblebee against a wall, not seeing that "paradoxical morality" may have a very great deal to say for itself, especially in a work of fiction' (*CL*, 1: 267). See Thomas, 2007 for the possible significance of this for Noel himself.

21. J. Hillis Miller notes how Tess seems trapped in her own destiny: her life is simply 'a new version of a life which has been lived over and over again by her ancestors, as if she were no more than a puppet of history or an actor in a play already performed a thousand times' (Miller, 1970: 103).

22. Christine Brooke-Rose states: 'Knowledge is desire and Christminster is clearly female [...] or female fused with God the Father' (2000: 122). Marjorie Garson

explores the 'strong links between Jude's desire for Sue and his desire for Christminster [...]. Desiring in her not only the woman but the cultivation she embodies...Jude attributes to her many of the values which he has attributed to the city, imagining them both as bodiless, visionary presences' (Garson, 1991: 152–3). Jude feminises Christminster as his 'Alma Mater' and at the start of the novel, as the orphaned boy apparently abandoned by his school teacher, gazes at the moon-like shining disc of water at the bottom of the ancient well, the mouth of which is lined by green moss near the top 'and nearer still the hart's-tongue fern' (5). Like Angel Clare before him, he seems almost to be envisioning a return to the maternal plenitude that he has been alienated from.

23. Terry Wright notes how, in the first edition of the novel, the pig's penis played an even more central part in their first meeting than in later versions. It is a token of exchange between Jude and Arabella before she hangs it on the rail of the bridge where, 'by a species of mutual curiosity, they both turned, and regarded it' (Wright, 1989: 122).

24. Interestingly, Jude later compares the 'light' of his intellect to Sue's as that of a 'benzoline lamp' compared to 'a star' (*JO*: 422).

25. Hardy describes the 'fresh harrow lines' in the field as seeming 'to stretch like the channelings in a piece of new corduroy, lending a meanly utilitarian air to the expanse' (*JO*: 1998: 8). The use of the term 'a new channel' to describe Jude's sexual interest in Arabella suggests that this will trap him even more firmly in his current condition.

26. http://ebooks.adelaide.edu.au/v/voltaire/dictionary/chapter311.html

27. See Grosz (1990) for a full exploration of the gender implications of Lacan's theory of desire.

28. There is evidence that Hardy's description of Sue may have been influenced by Havelock Ellis's pamphlet *Sexual Inversion in Women* which Ellis sent to him on 29 July 1895 (*CL*, 2: 83).

29. Venus Urania represents spiritual and intellectual rather than sexual love. Sue's use of desire here seems to relate to what the narrator of *Two on a Tower* refers to as 'mere desire': desire subjugated to its purely sexual expression.

30. As Marjorie Garson notes, *Jude* is not a convincing analysis of the contractual obligations of marriage as 'the divorces it depicts are so readily obtained' (Garson, 1991; 161). See also Ingham (1976: 164).

31. Much earlier in the narrative, Jude claims, with some justification given his experience with Arabella, that men suffer equally to women but that women fail to see this 'and instead of protesting against the conditions they protest against the man, the other victim [...] when he is only the helpless transmitter of the pressure put upon him' (*JO*: 301).

32. John Hughes also notes how 'Jude's obscurity is most fully to be accounted for in terms of the unrecognizable forms of life which his experience anticipates, the times yet to come to which the text recurrently signals' (Hughes, 1997: 90).

4 Poor Men and Ladies: Aspirational Desire

1. In 'The Subject and the Other: Alienation', Lacan defines the 'Other' as 'the locus in which is situated the chain of the signifier that governs whatever may be made present of the subject – it is the field of that living being in which the subject has to appear' (1977: 203).

2. Hardy may have been drawn to Smith's analysis of the poor man's son because, in many respects, it was remarkably appropriate to his own case.

3. Jude Fawley is Hardy's quintessential Poor Man: his paternal origins are yet another aspect of the 'obscurity' of his short life.
4. Laura Green has demonstrated how 'cultivated' society was 'putatively a sphere of female power' administered by upper class women and that one way for a man to enter this female realm was to marry into the class above him (Green, 1995).
5. Elizabeth Langland has discussed the ways in which the Poor Man reads (or misreads) the Lady as a sign or embodiment of what he lacks, or has lost and aspires to (Langland, 1993).
6. See Ebbatson (2004) for a contextual analysis of Hardy and class.
7. Pamela Dalziel regards 'An Indiscretion in the Life of an Heiress' as 'absolutely central to the tracing and understanding of Hardy's development as a fiction writer because of its closeness to his first unpublished novel *The Poor Man and the Lady* (1867–68)' (Dalziel, 1994: xx).
8. Norman Page has noted the similarities between this vision of Fancy: 'a young girl framed as a picture by the window architrave' and Dante Gabriel Rossetti's painting 'The Blessed Damozel'. Hardy is unlikely to have seen Rossetti's painting, which was executed during the period 1875–79, but he would have read Rossetti's poem of the same name, which was first published in 1850, in which the lady is imagined by her earthly lover 'whose likeness with thy soul / was but its love for thee' as 'one of God's choristers' who yearns for him to join her. The poem reappears as an intriguing intertext in Hardy's 'Poor Man and Lady' novels.
9. Despite her love for Dick, Fancy is aware of 'those times when you look silly and don't seem quite good enough for me' (132), and she accepts Maybold's proposal because of her love of refinement of mind and manners and what she calls her, or any woman's, fascination with more elegant and fashionable surroundings than she is accustomed to.
10. However, Frances Ferguson has suggested, that Wordsworth's 'Fancy' is predicated upon 'the illusion of stable "affinities" between the human mind and nature' (Ferguson, 1977: 55). It is a faculty which wantonly 'misconstrues' the 'reality of nature', allowing the poet to give alternative and indeed contradictory significations to the objects of the material world, thus demonstrating the slipperiness of the relationship between object and meaning, signifiers and signifieds (58). Ferguson demonstrates how 'The interchange between the human fancy and natural objects appears as a natural structure of desire', affording a measure of stability to 'man's disordered fortunes' through their association with the order of Nature (Ferguson, 1977: 63).
11. See also Stephen J. Spector (1988) for further discussion of the significance of Fancy's name.
12. This play on Fancy's name is repeated by old William in response to speculation concerning Maybold's attraction to her:

> 'I could fancy last night that we should have some trouble wi' that young man,' said the tranter [...] looking towards the unconscious Mr Maybold in the pulpit. '*I* fancy,' said old William, rather severely, 'I fancy there's too much whispering going on to be of any spiritual use to gentle or simple.' (46)

13. The narrator tells us that 'Dick implied that such a remark was rather to be tolerated than admired; though deliberateness in speech was known to have, as a rule, more to do with the machinery of the tranter's throat than with the matter enunciated' (40).

14. For a detailed analysis of the erotic significance of Fancy's clothes and boots see Gatrell (2011: 113–18), although he does not discuss this particular episode.
15. The description of the new horse and Dick's trade as printed on the card suggests the commodification of Fancy herself. Earlier in the novel, in reference to Dick's removal of Fancy and her household goods from her father's cottage to the school house, Reuben Dewey enquires of his son 'Th'st hauled her back I suppose?'
16. Hardy's choice of surname for his Poor Man may have been an homage to the well-known Professor of Architecture at the Royal Institute of British Architects, Thomas Roger Smith, whom he had assisted in designing schools for the London School Board (*LW*: 89). Smith had contacted Hardy with an offer of work while he was completing the manuscript of *A Pair of Blue Eyes* and was 'surprised and amused' when Hardy confessed that he was now writing novels, 'and thus was severed to [Hardy's] great regret an extremely pleasant if short professional connection with an able and amiable man' (94). However, as Alan Manford suggests in his notes to the Oxford World's Classics edition of the novel, 'it is probably wise to take with a pinch of salt many of Hardy's statements in *Life*' concerning the details of the novel.
17. See Dellamora (1990: 454) for a discussion of Jude's initially erotic fixation on Phillotson.
18. See: Childers (1981); Boumelha (1982: 32–3); Beegel (1987); Morgan (1988); and Mitchell (1994: 162–74). For a persuasive riposte to conventional feminist readings of Bathsheba and Gabriel's relationship, see Shires (1991).
19. The 'load' or 'lodestar' is the pole star, the literal and metaphorical guiding star.
20. Bonozzi Gozzi is probably a veiled reference to Benozzo Gozzoli 1421–97, an Italian Renaissance painter from Florence, a contemporary and pupil of Fra Angelico.
21. We are told that 'in wishing her fiction to appear like a real narrative of personal adventure' Ethelberta 'did wisely to make Defoe her model' who, according to one 'modern critic' had 'the most amazing talent on record for telling lies' (119).
22. It is appropriate that the young Ethelberta attempts to educate herself by hiding under the bookcase of the library of the mansion where her father is employed as a footman with a view to staying there all night to read.
23. My chapter on *The Hand of Ethelberta* (Thomas, 1999: 85–95) explores this in some depth.
24. Christopher tells his sister Faith that he feels 'moved around like a puppet in the hands of a person who legally can be nothing to me; and I cannot make up my mind whether I like it or not' (44).
25. In the 1895 and later editions Viviette simply signs with her married name (Shuttleworth, 1999).
26. As Sally Shuttleworth notes, Hardy may have taken this idea from Mahaffy's *Social Life in Greece from Homer to Menander*, which he quotes in his *Literary Notes*, I, entry 545. See Shuttleworth (1999, note, 5: 282).

5 As You Like It: Cross-Dressing and the Gendered Expression of Desire

1. The examples of cross-dressing I discuss here are also discussed in Gatrell's comprehensive study *Thomas Hardy Writing Dress* (2011), but not from the point of view of desire.

2. See Lacan's 'Seminar of 21 January, 1975', reprinted in Mitchell and Rose (1985 162–71: 168).
3. For a resumé of feminist reactions to Lacan, see Grosz (1990: 19–23) and Mitchell and Rose (1985).
4. Hollander (1978) cited in Gatrell (2011: 13).
5. The term 'transvestism' was coined by Magnus Hirschfeld in 1910 in *Die Transvestiten: Eine Untersuchung über den erotischen Verkleidungstrieb mit umfangreichem casuistischen und historischem Material* (Alfred Pulvermacher: Berlin), who regarded it as the outward manifestation of what we now call gender dysmorphia.
6. Sometime around 1890, Hardy translated a line from the preface to the 1845 Paris edition of *Mademoiselle de Maupin* and noted it: 'Virginity, mysticism, melancholy...diseases brought in by the Christ' (*LN*, 2: 1842). In March 1911 he 'readily agreed' to allow his name to be added to the 'Committee for honouring Theophile Gautier on his approaching centenary' (*LW*: 382). In addition to Gautier's novel, Hardy was also interested in Gautier as a symbolist and a Parnassian poet (see *LN*, 2: 2514).
7. 'Stranger still are waters charged with power to change men's minds as well as bodies. All the world has heard of the obscene [spring of] Salmacis' (Ovid, *Metamorphoses* (1977: 15.316).
8. In an interview with William Archer, Hardy reminisces about the Christmas Mummers' performances of *The Play of St George* in the Dorchester area, confirming that women did not take part in the performances: 'the Fair Sabra was always played by a boy. But the character was often omitted' (Ray, 2007: 31–2). See also Orgel (1996).
9. Mummers were originally actors in a dumb show. Eustacia's mumming/mumbling is thus a poor contrivance for the articulation of her desire.
10. See note 9.
11. The story is set between 1825 and 1830 (notes, *Wessex Tales* (1989: 242)).
12. The vicar is also willing to turn a blind eye to the villagers' illegal activities being, as Owlett informs Stockdale, 'as good a customer as we have got this side o' Warm'll' (208).
13. Latimer refers to the impossibility of finding anything 'by this owl's light' (202).
14. See note 12.
15. 'Trimming' describes the practice of 'inclining to each of two opposite sides as interest dictates' (OED). The *OED* also glosses 'trimmer' as 'to modify one's attitude in order to stand well with opposite parties' with a later meaning being 'to modify according to expediency'. Indeed, it cites a sentence from 'A Distracted Preacher' as an authority for this use of the term.
16. See Gatrell (2011) for an account of the significant changes Hardy made to Lizzy's adoption of male dress from the first published version of the story in the *New Quarterly Magazine* to its appearance in *Wessex Tales* in 1888, where Lizzy appears 'unmistakably male to the eye' (148), although, as I argue, her gait gives her away to Stockwell as female.
17. See Hardy's note of May 1912, at the end of the story (*WT*: 1998: 223).
18. 'An Imaginative Woman' was written in 1893 and first published in the *Pall Mall Magazine* in April 1894. It was originally collected in *Wessex Tales* in 1896 but was transferred to *Life's Little Ironies* for the Wessex Edition of 1912 (*LLI*, notes: 231–2).
19. Women's use of masculine or gender-neutral pseudonyms was an attempt to have their poetry judged objectively by the standards of the time (Leighton, 1992: 202).

20. Roger Ebbatson suggests that Ella's masculine pseudonym demonstrates the 'parasitic and self-destructive' nature of her relationship with the elusive Trewe (Ebbatson, 1993: 87). I read the story as Ella's attempt to arrogate to herself what she regards as the masculine role of the subject of desire which is signified by the elusive poet. Trewe's status for her is purely imaginary, his presence as an 'appropriate' object of desire depends on his absence as a physical being.

21. In this respect Ella's child fulfils a similar function to little Carrie in 'The Fiddler of the Reels' as discussed in Chapter 2.

22. 'The mantle of Elijah' is the mantle of prophesy that fell from Elijah to be taken up by his servant Elisha who prayed that upon his master's death 'a double portion of thy spirit be upon me" (2, Kings 2: 8). Ebbatson suggests that the overcoat is 'identified in Freudian dream-symbolism with the male sexual organ' and represents the 'hysterical woman seeking to obliterate her otherness' (Ebbatson, 1993: 88).

23. According to F. B. Pinion, the character of Robert Trewe was in part inspired by Dante Gabriel Rossetti 'and the idealization of his lady in *The House of Life*' (Pinion, 1968; 1976: 457–61).

24. Richard Dellamora examines Jude's sensuous identification with the schoolteacher and the radical alternatives he appears to offer (see Dellamora, 1990).

25. The term 'harlican' is Dorset dialect for an impish child and is probably derived from 'Harlequin', the name of the masked character of French and Italian light comedy or the mute, invisible clown of English pantomime. Harold Peake, in an article entitled 'Horned Deities', mentions that 'an anonymous writer in the *Quarterly Review*, No. 392 (1902): 462–82, contributed a suggestive article entitled "The Evolution of Harlequin", whom, we must remember, is always a masked character'. He cites an illustration in 'Arlequiniana, &c.' (Paris, 1694), of Harlequin with a black mask concealing his face, but suggests that the name is much older, appearing in Italy as Arlecchino about the middle of the sixteenth century, and is probably derived from the older form 'alichino', which occurs as the name of one of the ten demons in Dante's Inferno. Similar names attached to evil spirits are widespread; they crop up in France under the forms of herlequin, herlekin, hierlekin, hellequin. I am indebted to Simon Gatrell for this information. Compare this incident with how Jude is 'aroused from the woes of Dido by the stoppage of his cart and the voice of some old woman crying, "Two to-day, baker, and I return this stale one" ' (29).

26. Jude's vision of Christminster from the roof of the weather-beaten barn suggests the vision of the New Jerusalem given to John of Patmos in verse 3:12 and 21:2 of the Book of Revelations with the river of the water of life running through it.

27. See Higonnet (1993: 1–13) for a feminist discussion of Jude's term 'sense of sex'.

28. In relation to Sue's 'androgynous nature', Garson declares 'she "tries on" male styles of thought as opportunistically as she dons Jude's clothing, or as she uses the arguments of the dead student whose lover she refused to become' (Garson, 1991: 163).

29. The *OED* glosses 'epicene' as a term in Latin and Greek grammar 'said of nouns which without changing their grammatical gender may denote either sex' and, more generally as 'demonstrating the characteristics of both sexes'. Hardy also uses the term in *The Hand of Ethelberta*. Hardy saw Ben Jonson's *Epicœne: or The Silent Woman* (1609) in London in 1905 (Hardy, 1984: 349). It had disappeared from the stage in 1784, and was originally revived in Harvard in 1895 (Holdsworth, 1983: xxii).

30. For instance, *Punch's* 1891 review of Oscar Wilde's *The Picture of Dorian Gray* uses the term 'Ganymede-like' to refer to Dorian (Sinfield, 1994: 104). Carolyn Oulton notes that Hardy's use of the term 'an epicure in emotions' to describe Sue is a 'telling echo of *Wilde's* Dorian Gray' (Oulton, 2007: 120). The term 'catamite' derives from the Latin term 'Catamitus', the Latin form of the Greek 'Ganymedes', and for anguished and crusading homosexuals such as John Addington Symonds, with whom Hardy had been in affectionate correspondence since 1889 (see Thomas, 2007), suggested not only erotic, pederastic practices but also the ideal, asexual, worship of youthful male beauty. The rape of Ganymede is alluded to in the name of The Eagle and Child public house at 48 and 49 St Giles Street, Oxford.

31. Mitchell asserts that 'Sue has desires but they are significantly not sexual ones' (1994: 203) and wrongly, to my mind, insists that Sue 'reveals the limits of Hardy's ability to imagine a desiring adult female subjectivity' (202).

32. Hardy saw several performances of *As You Like It* and commented on the performances of actresses in the role of Rosalind, including Ada Rehan in June 1890 (Millgate, 1984: 238), Helen Faucit in November 1866 and Mrs Scott-Siddons (Millgate, 2004: 95). Hardy claimed that his poem 'The Two Rosalinds' 'was suggested by [Ada Rehan's] performance combined with some other; but there is no certainty about this, and dates and other characteristics do not quite accord' (*LW*, 1984: 239). Millgate speculates that Hardy's poem 'To an Impersonator of Rosalind' was inspired by Mrs Scott-Siddons's performance in the role and composed a few months later in late 1866 or early 1867 (Millgate, 2004: 95). Hardy was reading Shakespeare from 1863 onwards and took part in amateur readings at Wimbourne in 1881 (Millgate, 2004: 83). The title of *Under the Greenwood Tree* was taken from Amiens's song, and Hardy's *Studies and Specimens* notebook contains several references to *As You Like It*.

6   Art, Aesthetics and Masculine Desire: *The Well-Beloved* (1897)

1. Edward Neill suggests, persuasively, that Hardy 'almost seems to be toying with the possibility that 'little object "a"' is indeed 'a vice' ('Avice')' (Neill, 2004: 120–21).

2. J. Hillis Miller notes that the 'theory of signs' is presupposed in Hardy's novel in its obsession with the power and frustration of representation (Miller, 1982b: 149).

3. In this respect, Pierston is possessed of the belated self-awareness that characterises Adam Smith's 'poor man's son'.

4. J. Hillis Miller has discussed, in relation to *The Well-Beloved* how 'the discovery that the beloved is my twin, that I love myself in the beloved, shows the futility of the attempt to found the self by a displacement of its love for itself to the love of its image in a changed sex' (Miller, 1982b: 168).

5. Pierston and Avice are not, as Miller declares, 'close cousins' (Miller, 1982b: 149; 167).

6. The anthropomorphisation of the house, which we have noted in Hardy's 'domicilium' poems, is evident here. Pierston's childhood home seems to register in its very aspect the departure of Avice the Third from its precincts and from Pierston himself: 'On approaching he discovered that a strange expression which seemed to hang about the house-front that morning was more than a fancy, the gate, door, and two windows being open, though the blinds of other windows

were not drawn up, the whole lending a vacant, dazed look to the domicile, as of a person gaping in sudden stultification' (183).

7. See the British Archaeological Association (1849: 6–14) on archaeological artefacts found on Portland.

8. See my introduction to *The Well-Beloved* (Thomas, 2000) for discussion of ancient Dorset courtship rituals and their significance in this novel.

9. Miller offers a gendered model of the island. For him it is 'a somewhat epicene male emblem, contradictory in import, single and multiple at once, seeds and eggs together, dead and yet life-giving, the ocean into which the peninsular juts is the female counterpart. This model pits the masculine symbol against the feminine Other out of which it is generated (Miller, 1982b: 165).

10. Compare this with Hardy's poem 'The Two Houses' discussed in Chapter 1.

11. 'The Gods in Exile' was included in *Prose Miscellanies by Heinrich Heine*, translated by S. L. Feischman (J. B. Lippincott and Company, Philadelphia, 1876).

12. Alison Smith describes how Martha Mary Dalrymple, who, upon her marriage to Thomas Eustace Smith, Liberal MP for Tynemouth from 1868 to 1885, changed her name to Eustacia, liked to associate herself with the pagan goddesses in the paintings acquired by the couple who were noted patrons of the arts. I have not been able to ascertain whether this influenced Hardy in his choice of Eustacia Vye's name (Barringer and Prettejohn, 1999: 27).

13. John Addington Symonds's (1885) rendition of Sappho fragment 1 also refers to Aphrodite as 'Wile-weaving daughter of high Zeus' (Wharton, 1895: 60).

14. In April 1897 Hardy wrote to Swinburne thanking him for his 'kind note' about *The Well-Beloved*, 'my fantastic little tale which, if it can make, in its better parts, any faint claim to imaginative feeling, will owe something of such feeling to you, for I often thought of lines of yours during the writing; & indeed, was not able to resist the quotation of your words now & then' (*CL*, 2: 158). Gosse called *The Well-Beloved* the tragedy of a nympholept possibly, quoting Swinburne's poem of the same title and certainly referring to Swinburne's passionate advocacy of the creative imagination as the force that animates nature.

15. In the *Symposium*, Plato attributes two personalities to Aphrodite: the spiritual 'Heavenly Aphrodite' (Aphrodite Urania) and the 'Common Aphrodite' representing physical, erotic desire. Aphrodite is also associated with the universal natural cycle and the energy of desire. Geoffrey Miles quotes the Roman philosopher poet Lucretius, as translated by Dryden, to illustrate this:

> All nature is thy gift; earth, air, and sea;
> Of all that breathes, the various progeny,
> Stung with delight, is goaded on by thee.
>
> (Miles, 1999: 26).

perfectly capturing for our purposes the combined irresistible force of pain and pleasure that is the energy of being

16. Marcia's query as to whether he would ever be ARA suggests that her desire for him has a practical rather than a metaphysical base, making her a more cultivated but no less materialistic version of Arabella.

17. 'Unsight' is a typically Hardyian neologism signifying the negation or opposite of 'sight' – not 'blindness' but that which cannot be perceived or seen in material form.

18. See Edward Neill's witty comparison to 'corpsing' as, among other things, 'dramatising the death of [Pierston's] desire' (Neill, 2004: 114).

19. This links to the extract from Shakespeare's 'Sonnet LXXIII' that begins Section III. i of the novel: 'In me thou seest the glowing of such fire, / That on the ashes of his youth doth lie /As the death-bed whereon it must expire, / Consumed with that which it was nourished by'(*WB*: 138).

20. Others include 'At Waking' (Hynes, I: 274) and 'The Well-Beloved' (Hynes, I: 168).

21. Tennyson's lines read: 'Alas! for this gray shadow, once a man – / So glorious in his beauty and thy choice, / Who madest him thy chosen, that he seem'd / To his great heart none other than a God!' (*Poetical Works*, 1950; Globe: 96–97).

22. 'I Look Into My Glass' may have inspired or influenced Philip Larkin's poem 'Skin'.

23. See note on the significance of 'gleam' in Chapter 1.

24. Hardy noted John Addington Symonds's critique of Pater in *Essays Speculative and Suggestive* in relation to Pater's apparent denial of art's responsibilities 'to its subject or material', which was the basis of the *fin de siècle* belief in 'Art for Art's Sake' (*LN*, I: 1864).

25. Pierston is like Shakespeare's Caliban in hearing the 'sounds', 'sweet airs' and voices that give access to a dream world of riches beyond the clouds (*The Tempest*, 3, 2: 148–56, 2007: 1066).

26. For the critic Peter Widmer, music 'summons us out of self-consciousness' but only by 'pouring into the folds of abstract language'. It reaches for the ecstatic domain of human consciousness through sheer affect and aims to bring the realm beyond human mortality into the realm of knowledge. However, it ultimately fails to shake off its linguistic dimension and thus cannot provide unmediated access to the lost *jouissance* that is beyond the confines of the symbolic order (Apollon and Feldstein, 1995: 300).

27. See also 'To a Motherless Child' in which the speaker expresses a wish that if a child could be wholly her 'darling mother's' the mother would 'relive to me', but that 'niggard Nature' bars 'lest she overjoy, / Renewal of the loved on earth / save with alloy' (Hynes, I: 85).

28. Pierston says, of Ann Avice, to Somers that 'Behind the mere pretty island-girl (to the world) is, in my eye, the Idea, in Platonic phraseology – the essence and epitome of all that is desirable in this existence' (108).

7 'Scanned Across the Dark Space': Poetry, Desire and Aesthetic Fulfilment

1. In 1937 Pound wrote of Hardy's poetry: 'Now *there* is a clarity. There is the harvest of having written 20 novels first' (cited in Peck, 1972: 5). Concerning the poets of the 1890s, Eliot wrote to Pound in 1924, 'I am as blind to the merits of these people as I am to Thomas Hardy' (Locke, 2009: 450).

2. See Peck (1972) for an account of Hardy's reception by the new generation of modernist writers; F. R. Southerington (1972), for brief exploration of critical attitudes to Hardy's poetry from 1928 to 1972; Locke (2009) and Morgan (2009) for a more up to date resumé. The edition of *Agenda* magazine edited by Donald Davie in 1972 charts the beginning of a sustained and serious critical attention to Hardy's poetry (Davie, ed., 1972a).

3. *Satires of Circumstance* was published in September 1914; two months later Joyce sent the final instalments of *Portrait of the Artist* to *The Egoist*. On receiving the last pages, Pound, who was editing the volume, wrote immediately to Joyce that the book was 'hard, perfect, permanent, and comparable to Hardy and James, the

only other recent writers of value' (Ellman, 1976: 365). In a letter to W. H. Rouse in 1938 Pound wrote 'Nobody has taught me anything about writing since Hardy died' (Locke, 2009: 450).

4. Auden begins his homage: 'I cannot write objectively about Thomas Hardy because I was once in love with him' (1965: 135). He continues 'Hardy comforted me as an adolescent, and educated my vision as a human being, but I owe him another and, for me personally, an even more important debt, of technical instruction'. Hardy's ' "modern" rhetoric', by which Auden meant his 'direct colloquial diction', he found 'more fertile and adaptable to different themes than any of Eliot's gas-works and rat's feet which one could steal but never make one's own' (141–2).

5. Dennis Taylor (1993) suggests that 'Hardy used his poetry to explore in a more concentrated and confined way the type of language critics complained about in his novels' (cited Locke, 2009). Charles Locke (2009) insists that 'In the poetry, it is language, the words themselves, that do the work of unsettling the voice by denying the phrase or frustrating it' (455). Linda Shires concludes that Hardy's poetry 'should be seen [...] as an ambivalent echo, memorialising, adaptation, reversal and/or rejection of beliefs, ideologies and poetic strategies recorded in nineteenth-century poems he read' (Shires, 2004: 258). See also John Powell Ward (1994) for an examination of what he terms 'Hardy's aesthetic of imperfection'.

6. Taylor claims, not unreasonably, that 'the death of Emma [...] provided Hardy with the final clarification of his art' (Taylor, 1981: 24).

7. Gifford (1972); Davie (1972b); Miller (1970); Sacks (1985); Morgan (1974); and Sexton (1991). For a summary of the various positions of these critics see Armstrong (2009: 143). Henry Gifford notes that the three poems that precede 'Poems of 1912–13', 'Under the Waterfall', 'The Spell of the Rose,' and 'St. Launce's Revisited', 'also referred to Emma', whereas the last two, plus a poem from the first group of 'Lyrics and Reveries' are added to 'Poems of 1912–13' in the *Collected Poems* 1919 (Gifford, 1972: 136). In a letter to A. C. Benson in 1914, Hardy described his discomfort at the appearance of poems 'written at a later date when my thoughts had been set on quite another track by painful events' in the same volume as the 'Satires' (*CL*, 5: 72). Grouping these poems under a separate heading has the effect of insulating them from the rest of the volume (see also Gifford, 1972) on this.

8. Brunetière goes on to dismiss the Symbolist poets for their apparent transcendentalism, reminding his readers that 'if there is something beyond *nature*, we can only express it with nature's means' and that only through 'observation' can we 'correct [...], mend[...] and transform[...]' nature: 'Idealism, & even symbolism, are not possible without a little naturalism, which mingles with it to sustain it [...] to prevent it evaporating in cloud, & the cloud in nothing' (*LN*, I: 1640).

9. See also Catherine Maxwell's sensitive commentary on this poem (Maxwell, 2008: 200–5).

10. Wilde also claimed that 'the self-conscious aim of Life is to find expression, and that Art offers it certain beautiful forms through which it may realise that energy' (Wilde, 1989: 239).

11. Hardy's language is nowhere near as experimental as that of Joyce (whom Lacan admired), Pound or other avant-garde Modernists. Nevertheless, as Charles Locke suggests, it is significant that both of these much younger writers were admirers of Hardy's work. (see Notes 1 and 3). John Lucas has pointed out that Hardy may be regarded as ambiguous rather than antagonistic towards

free verse commenting in 1912: 'A style grows to perfection. Nothing more can be done in it. And no mere device for change, no irreverence or impatience, but a necessity of artistic development pushes poets & artists into new channels of expressions, new forms' (Lucas, 2000). However, Hardy was not drawn to the experimentation of free verse. See also Paul Volsik's interesting discussion of what he regards as Hardy's modern 'heterogeneous lexis' (Volsik, 2004).

12. See Volsik (2004) on Hardy's use of the phantom or ghost figure.

13. Following Henry Gifford, Melanie Sexton sees the 'Poems of 1912–13' as structured by a 'here/there' division, leading to a movement of recovery through which Hardy is able to 'figure' Emma (Sexton, 1991). For DeSales Harrison, however, the gap or space figures as 'an unbridgeable distance' and 'an immoveable obstacle to full presence' (Harrison, 2010: 420). The 'discomfort' of this space 'resists the assimilating work of elegy' (421). I will address this point later in the chapter.

14. In an interview with William Archer published in the *Pall Mall Gazette* on 23 April 1901, Hardy insisted that, though he had no belief in the existence of phantoms or ghosts, he was imaginatively drawn to 'the fascinating labyrinths' of the paranormal, not least because 'the material world is so uninteresting, human life is so miserably bounded, circumscribed, cabin'd, cribb'd, confined. I want another domain for the imagination to expatiate in' (Ray, 2007: 35).

15. Harrison does concede that the 'fold, rift, cleft or crease in the representational field of the poem' constitutes a ' "successful" impediment' that 'encrypt[s] – and thereby preserv[es] a hold upon – that which it cannot yield to and that this 'encryption' constitutes 'a fault' on the surface of the poem (Harrison, 2010: 422).

16. Hardy comes close to registering this in his adoption of Leslie Stephen's motto: 'The aim of the poet should be to touch our hearts by showing his own, and not to exhibit his learning, or his fine taste, or his skill in mimicking the notes of his predecessors' (*LW*: 131).

17. 'No doubt very few people understand the purely subjective character of the phenomenon that we call love, or how it creates, so to speak, a supplementary person, distinct from the person whom the world knows by the same name, a person most of whose constituent elements are derived from ourselves. Desire is excited, satisfies itself, disappears – and that is all. Thus the young girl who one marries is not the one with whom one has fallen in love' (Proust, 1913–1927; 1980: 505). Taylor suggests that the image of Hardy's early love for Emma 'had become a "phantom horsewoman", a *personne supplémentaire*, which had persisted long after the couple themselves had changed' (Taylor, 1981: 23).

18. At the same time, of course, these are elegies inspired by the death of a woman, so it is unsurprising that the realm of death and dissolution is feminised in this way.

19. Dennis Taylor's study is a notable exception to the biographicalist trend which nevertheless allows due importance to the circumstances that inspired these elegies (Taylor, 1993). See also Volsik (2004).

20. See Sacks (1985); Sexton (1991); Shaw (1994); Ramazani (1994); Zeiger (1997); Armstrong (2000); Kennedy (2007); and Maxwell (2008).

21. In a letter to the *Daily Chronicle* on 28 December 1899, Hardy wrote 'One's modern fantasy of a disembodied spirit – unless intentionally humorous – is that of an entity which has passed into a tenuous, impartial, sexless, fitful form of existence' (*PW*: 201).

22. In her 'Translator's Preface' to Derrida's *On Grammatology*, Gayatri Chakravorty Spivak describes '*sous rature*' as 'the strategy of using the only available language

while not subscribing to its premises, or "operat[ing] according to the vocabulary of the very thing that one delimits" ' (Spivak, 1976: xviii).

23. Tim Armstrong also recognises this poem as 'a turning point in the sequence', moving from Dorset to Cornwall and the landscape of memory and romance, and offers a summary of the biographical background to the poem (Armstrong, 2009: 160).

24. I am aware that Hardy did visit this area of Cornwall on 6 March 1913, almost exactly 43 years after he first met Emma there, but this information is extra to the poem.

25. In any case it is highly unlikely that the 74-year-old Hardy would be wandering up on Beeny cliff at dawn. Armstrong suggests that 'the poet hears the hollow voice of the cave' but this is unlikely to be literally true (2000: 142).

26. This meaning of 'scan' was coined in 1928, three years after John Logie Baird gave the first public demonstration of a prototype television in Selfridges store, London, on 25 March 1925, just less than a decade after the publication of the poem in September 1914.

27. I am aware of the biographical background to this poem in Hardy's discovery of Emma's bitter diary, which he destroyed.

28. This is reminiscent of Pierston's description of the 'Well-Beloved' turning from a radiant 'vitality to a relic' (1986: 40).

29. Tim Armstrong notes, with reference to Maurice Blanchot's notion of identity as gained in 'weakness, in the naked dispossession of self', that 'Hardy's [sic] assertion of selfhood has a similar weakness to it predicated on following a ghost and abandoning knowledge, "Up the cliff, down, till I'm lonely, lost, / [...] Where you will next be there's no knowing" ' (Armstrong, 2000: 144).

30. See also Harrison (2010), who notes 'What Narcissus encounters when he hears this voice is a version of what he encounters in his reflection, the belief that a representation of himself is in fact a separate person, capable of being approached and addressed, not as an image but as an other' (420).

31. We might also compare it to W. B. Yeats's 'The Everlasting Voice' published in *The Wind Among the Reeds* (1899), which Hardy listed among his favourite books from that year (Millgate, 2001: 156). 'The Everlasting Voice' was first published in the *New Review* in January 1896.

32. See Zeiger (1997) on this.

33. see Morgan (1974).

34. Catherine Maxwell also notes how, in not looking at her, 'Hardy's speaker' 'keeps her "alive", defended from rational objectifying scrutiny'. She asserts that 'The poem testifies to the recreative power of imaginative vision over and against the empirical proofs of optical sight'. She qualifies this, however, by asserting that the poem tantalises us 'with that space at the back of his head', which is 'a withheld vision which the speaker can see and which we can't and which allures us by being ever out of reach' (Maxwell, 2008: 226).

35. Tim Armstrong suggests that the reversed rhymed pairing of 'lack' and 'track' echo 'After a Journey' and that 'the old track' which shadows 'lack' here is that of Hardy's own work. He also notes how the vocabulary of the poem suggests the idea of verse itself (standing and *stanza*; the turn; the 'rhythmic swing' of the trees; the 'track' of rhyme), and that 'the printed text here is the shadow of a voice which is not present' (Armstrong, 2000: 165). My reading suggests that the poem dramatises the start of the process of turning grief into art. The narrator 'turns' away from the shadowy phantom 'to keep down grief' which is subtly expressed in the poem itself.

36. Davie approves J. I. M. Stewart's description of this poem as 'a splendid taunt hurled at oblivion by the imagination', and adds, 'the execution is equal to the conception'. He concludes: 'The poem ends on a note of sublime assurance, of exultation even' (Davie, 1972b: 151).

37. Catherine Maxwell notes how this 'is reminiscent of the physical sensation described by Pater in the Conclusion to *The Renaissance*: "the moment... of delicious recoil from the flood of water in summer heat" ' (Maxwell, 2008: 201).

38. See Hardy's sketch of the incident and Emma's account in *Some Recollections* (Hardy, Emma, 1961: 57).

39. Maxwell's otherwise excellent readings of these poems are an interesting case of having one's biographical cake and eating it, in that she repeatedly brings in biographical information only to dispense with it as hardly necessary: see her reading of 'The Shadow on the Stone' (Maxwell, 2008: 225–6). For an exploration of the intertextual deployment of the myth of Hermaphroditus, see Chapter 5 above.

40. See also 'She at His Funeral', 'Bereft', 'She Hears the Storm', 'The Woman in the Rye', 'She Thinks She Dreams', 'His Heart', 'The Pink Frock', 'The Nettles', 'An Upbraiding', 'The Dead and the Living One' – further evidence of Hardy's radical engagement with the genre.

41. Armstrong reads this epigraph in relation to the 'cinder' (*cendre*), Derrida's name for the indelible trace of an erased presence, and for the losses involved in signification, language falling away from a lost origin, but none the less carrying the freight of being (Armstrong, 2000: 136).

42. See Davie (1972b: 142); Armstrong (2000: 143); and Miller (1970: 248–9).

Bibliography

Amis, Martin (2011) *Philip Larkin Poems Selected by Martin Amis* (London: Faber and Faber)

Apollon, Willy and Richard Feldstein (eds.) (1995) *Lacan, Politics, Aesthetics* (New York: State University of New York Press).

Arata, Stephen (1996) *Fictions of Loss in the Victorian Fin de Siécle* (Cambridge: CUP).

The Archaeological Journal (1849) V (25) British Archaeological Association, Central Committee (London: Central Committee of the British Archaeological Association).

Armstrong, Tim (2000) *Haunted Hardy: Poetry, History, Memory* (Basingstoke and New York: Palgrave Macmillan).

Armstrong, Tim (ed.) (2009), *Thomas Hardy: Selected Poems* (Harlow: Pearson Education).

Auden, W. H. (1963) 'A Literary Transference', in ed. A. Guérard, *Hardy: A Collection of Critical Essays* (Upper Saddle River, NJ: Prentice Hall): 135–42.

Bachelard, Gaston (1958; trans. 1964; 1994) *The Poetics of Space* (Massachusetts: Beacon Press).

Bachofen, J. J. (1861; 1967) *Myth, Religion and Mother Right: Selected Writings*, trans. Ralph Manheim (London: Routledge and Kegan Paul).

Balmer, Josephine (1992) *Sappho: Poems and Fragments* (Newcastle: Bloodaxe).

Barringer, Tim and Elizabeth Prettejohn (eds.) (1999) *Frederick Leighton: Antiquity Renaissance Modernity* (New Haven & London: Yale University Press).

Barrow, Rosemary (1999) 'Drapery, Sculpture and the Praxitelean Ideal', in eds. T. Barringer and E. Prettejohn, *Frederick Leighton: Antiquity Renaissance Modernity* (New Haven, CT & London: Yale University Press): 49–65.

Beegel, Susan (1987) 'Bathsheba's Lovers, Male Sexuality in *Far From the Madding Crowd*', in ed. H. Bloom, *Thomas Hardy: Modern Critical Views* (New York, NY: Chelsea House): 202–26.

Belsey, Catherine (1994) *Desire: Love Stories in Western Culture* (Oxford: Blackwell).

Benvenuto, Bice and Roger Kennedy (1986) *The Works of Jacques Lacan: An Introduction* (London: Free Association Books).

Benziman, Galia (2012) 'The Self-Resisting: Hardy's Ambivalent Evocation of Romantic Childhood', in Grafe and Stephens (2012), 15–28.

Bersani, Leo (1976) *A Future for Astyanax: Character and Desire in Literature* (Boston: Little, Brown).

———— (1977) *Baudelaire and Freud* (Berkeley, CA: University of California Press).

Björk, Lennart A. (ed.) (1985; 1988) *The Literary Notebooks of Thomas Hardy*, I (London and Basingstoke: Macmillan).

———— (1985; 1988) *The Literary Notebooks of Thomas Hardy*, 2 (London and Basingstoke: Macmillan).

Bloom, H. (ed.) (1987) *Thomas Hardy: Modern Critical Views* (New York: Chelsea House).

———— (ed.) (1991) *Modern Critical Views of the Return of the Native* (New York: Chelsea House).

Boothby, Richard (1991) *Death and Desire: Psychoanalytic Theory in Lacan's Return to Freud* (New York and London: Routledge).

Borch-Jacobsen, Mikkel (1991) *Lacan: The Absolute Master*, trans. Douglas Brick (Stanford, CA: Stanford University Press).

Boumelha, Penny (1982) *Thomas Hardy and Women: Sexual Ideology and Narrative Form* (Sussex and New Jersey: Harvester; Barnes and Noble).

—— (ed.) (2000) *Jude the Obscure Contemporary Critical Essays* (London, Basingstoke and New York: Palgrave, Macmillan).

Bowie, Malcolm (1987) *Freud, Proust, Lacan: Theory as Fiction* (Cambridge: Cambridge University Press).

Brady, Kristin (1982) *The Short Stories of Thomas Hardy* (New York: St Martin's Press).

Breton, André (1924) *Manifesto of Surrealism* (accessed online at http://www.tcf.ua.edu/ Classes/Jbutler/T340/SurManifesto/ManifestoOfSurrealism.htm).

Bromwich, David (1987) 'Poetic Invention and the Self-Unseeing', *Grand Street*, vol. 7, no. 1 (Autumn, 1987): 115–129.

Bronfen, Elizabeth (1992) *Over Her Dead Body, Death, Femininity and the Aesthetic* (Manchester: MUP).

Brooke-Rose, Christine (1981) *A Rhetoric of the Unreal: Studies in Narrative and Structure, Especially of the Fantastic* (Cambridge: Cambridge University Press).

—— (2000) 'Ill Wit and Sick Tragedy: *Jude the Obscure*', in ed. P. Boumelha. *Jude the Obscure Contemporary Critical Essays* (London, Basingstoke and New York: Palgrave, Macmillan): 122–44.

Brooks, Jean (1971) *Thomas Hardy: The Poetic Structure* (Ithaca, NY: Cornell University Press).

Brooks, Peter (1984) 'Freud's Masterplot', in ed. P. Brooks, *Reading for the Plot: Design and Intention in Narrative* (Oxford: Clarendon Press): 90–112.

Bullen, J. B. (1986) *The Expressive Eye: Fiction and Perception in the Work of Thomas Hardy* (Oxford: Clarendon Press).

Butler, Judith (1987; 1999) *Subjects of Desire: Hegelian Reflections in Twentieth-Century France* (New York: Columbia University Press).

—— (1990) *Gender Trouble, Feminism and the Subversion of Identity* (New York and London: Routledge).

—— (1993) *Bodies That Matter: On the Discursive Limits of 'Sex'* (New York and London: Routledge).

—— (2004) *Undoing Gender* (New York and London: Routledge).

Casteras, Susan P. and Colleen Denney (eds.) (1996) *The Grosvenor Gallery: A Palace of Art in Victorian England* (New Haven and London: Yale University Press).

Castle, Terry (1993) *The Apparitional Lesbian: Female Homosexuality and Modern Culture* (New York: Columbia University Press).

Childers, Mary (1981) 'Thomas Hardy the Man who "Liked" Women ', *Criticism*, 23 (4): 317–34.

Cole, Jonathan (1999) 'On "Being Faceless": Selfhood and Facial Embodiment', in eds. S. Gallagher and Jonathan Shear, *Models of the Self* (Exeter: Imprint Academic): 301–18.

Colvin, Sydney (1869) Review of *The Earthly Paradise, Pall Mall Gazette*, 11 December: 26–7.

Copjec, Joan (1994) *Read My Desire: Lacan against the Historicists* (Cambridge, MA and London: MIT Press).

Cramer, Jeffrey S. (1986) 'The Spectre of the Real', *The Thomas Hardy Year Book*, 13: 6–34.

Culler, Jonathan (1983) *On Deconstruction: Theory and Criticism after Structuralism* (London, Melbourne and Henley: Routledge and Kegan Paul).

Daleski, H. M. (1997) *Thomas Hardy and Paradoxes of Love* (Columbia: University of Missouri Press).

Dallery, Arleen B. and Charles E. Scott (eds.) (1989) *Question of the Other: Essays in Contemporary Continental Philosophy* (New York: State University of New York Press).

Dalziel, Pamela (ed.) (1992) *Thomas Hardy: The Excluded and Collaborative Stories* (Oxford: OUP).

—— (ed.) (1994) *Thomas Hardy: An Indiscretion in the Life of an Heiress and Other Stories* (Oxford: OUP).

Dalziel, Pamela and Michael Millgate (eds.) (2009) *Thomas Hardy's 'Poetical Matter' Notebook* (Oxford: OUP).

Della Rocca, Michael (2008), *Spinoza* (The Routledge Philosophers) (Oxford: Routledge).

Davie, Donald (ed.) (1972a) *Agenda Thomas Hardy Special Issue* 10 (2–3) (London: Arts Council of Great Britain).

—— (1972b) 'Hardy's Virgilian Purples', in ed. D. Davie, *Agenda Thomas Hardy Special Issue* 10 (2–3): 137–56.

DeJean, Joan (1989) *Fictions of Sappho 1546–1937* (Chicago and London: University of Chicago Press).

De Kesel, Marc and Sigi Jottkandt (2009) *Eros and Ethics: Reading Jacques Lacan's Seminar VII* (New York: SUNY Press).

Deleuze, Gilles and Félix Guattari (1972) *Anti-Oedipus: Capitalism and Schizophrenia* (Minneapolis, MN: University of Minnesota Press).

Dellamora, Richard (1990) *Masculine Desire: The Sexual Politics of Victorian Aestheticism* (Carolina: University of North Carolina Press).

—— (2004) *Friendship's Bonds: Democracy and the Novel in Victorian England* (Philadelphia, PA: University of Pennsylvania Press).

Dolin, Tim (1997) *Thomas Hardy: The Hand of Ethelberta (Introduction)*, Penguin Classics (London: Penguin): xix–xli.

Dollimore, Jonathan (1998) *Death, Desire and Loss in Western Culture* (London: Allen Lane, Penguin).

Downing, Linda (2003) *Desiring the Dead: Necrophilia and Nineteenth-Century Literature* (Oxford: Legenda, European Humanities Research Centre, University of Oxford).

Ebbatson, Roger (1993) *The Margin of the Unexpressed* (Sheffield: Sheffield Academic Press).

—— (2004) 'Hardy and Class', in ed. Phillip Mallett, Palgrave *Advances in Thomas Hardy Studies* (Basingstoke and New York, NY: Palgrave Macmillan): 111–34.

—— (2005) *An Imaginary England: Nation, Landscape and Literature 1840–1920* (Aldershot and Burlington: Ashgate).

—— (2007) 'Prophetic Landscapes: Thomas Hardy and Richard Jefferies,' ed. C. Meredith, *Moment of Earth* (Aberystwyth: Celtic Study Publications): 114–34.

Egerton, George (1983) *Keynotes and Discords* with an introduction by Martha Vicinus (London: Virago Press).

Eliot, T. S. (1975) *The Complete Plays and Poems* (London: Book Club Associates).

Ellman, Richard (1976) *James Joyce* (Oxford: Oxford University Press).

Elster, Jon (ed.) (1986) *The Multiple Self* (Cambridge: Cambridge University Press).

Evans, Dylan (1996) *An Introductory Dictionary of Lacanian Psychoanalysis* (London and New York: Routledge).

Faderman, Lilian (1978) 'The Morbidification of Love between Women by Nineteenth-Century Sexologists,' *Journal of Homosexuality*, 4: 73–90.

Feischman, S. L. (trans.) (1876) *Prose Miscellanies by Heinrich Heine* (London and Philadelphia, PA: J. B. Lippincott and Company).

Feldman, Shoshana (ed.) (1981) *Literature and Psychoanalysis: The Question of Reading: Otherwise* (Baltimore, MD and London: The Johns Hopkins University Press).

Feldstein, Richard, Bruce Fink and Maire Jaanus (eds.) (1994) *Reading Seminar XI including the first English Translation of 'Position of the Unconscious' by Jacques Lacan* (New York: SUNY Press).

Ferguson, Frances (1977) *Wordsworth: Language as Counter Spirit* (New Haven, CT: Yale University Press).

Foucault, Michel (1967;2001) *Madness and Civilization: A History of Insanity in the Age of Reason* (Oxford: Routledge).

Freud, Sigmund (1964) *Standard Edition of the Complete Psychological Works of Sigmund Freud*, 24 vols. in ed. J. Strachey with Anna Freud (London: Hogarth Press).

Gagnier, Regenia (2000) *The Insatiability of Human Wants: Economics and Aesthetics in Market Society* (London and Chicago: University of Chicago Press).

Gallagher, Sean and J. Shear (eds.) (1999) *Models of the Self* (Exeter: Imprint Academic).

Garber, Marjorie (1992; 1997) *Vested Interests: Cross-Dressing and Cultural Anxiety* (New York: Routledge).

Garson, Marjorie (1991) *Hardy's Fables of Integrity: Woman, Body, Text* (Oxford: Clarendon Press).

Gatrell, Simon (1984) 'The Early Stages of Hardy's Fiction,' in ed. Norman Page, *Thomas Hardy Annual No 2* (London: Macmillan): 3–29.

—— (1993) *Thomas Hardy and the Proper Study of Mankind* (London and Basingstoke: Macmillan).

—— (1999) *Introduction* to Thomas Hardy's *Under the Greenwood Tree* (Oxford: Oxford World's Classics): xi–xxiii.

—— (2011) *Thomas Hardy Writing Dress* (Oxford and Bern: Peter Lang).

Gautier, Théophile (1835; 2005), *Mademoiselle de Maupin* (Harmondsworth: Penguin)

Gifford, Henry (1972) 'Hardy's Revisions (*Satires of Circumstance*),' in ed. D. Davie, *Agenda Thomas Hardy Special Issue* 10: 126–37.

Gifford, Paul (2005) *Love, Desire and Transcendence in French Literature: Deciphering Eros* (Aldershot: Ashgate).

Gilbert, Paul and K. Lennon (2005) *The World, the Flesh and the Subject: Continental Themes in Philosophy of Mind and Body* (Edinburgh: Edinburgh University Press).

Gill, Stephen and D. Wu (eds.) (1994) *William Wordsworth: A Selection of his Finest Poems* (Oxford: OUP).

Gilmartin, Sophie and R. Mengham (2007) *Thomas Hardy's Shorter Fiction* (Edinburgh: Edinburgh University Press).

Giordano Jr., Frank (1984) *'I'd Have My Life Unbe: Thomas Hardy's Self-Destructive Characters* (Alabama: University of Alabama Press).

Girard, René (1965) *Deceit, Desire, and the Novel: Self and Other in Literary Structure*, trans. Yvonne Freccero (Baltimore, MD: The Johns Hopkins Press).

Gittings, Robert (1975) *Young Thomas Hardy* (Harmondsworth: Penguin).

—— (1978) *The Older Hardy* (Harmondsworth: Penguin).

Goode, John (1979) 'Sue Bridehead and the New Woman', in ed. M. Jacobus, *Women Writing and Writing About Women* (London: Croom Helm): 100–13.

Grafe Adrian and Jessica Stephens (2012), *Lines of Resistance: Essays on British Poetry from Thomas Hardy to Linton Kwesi Johnson* (London: McFarland & Com, Inc.).

Grange, Joseph (1989) 'Lacan's "Other" and the Factions of Plato's Soul', in eds. Arleen B. Dallery and Charles E. Scott, *Question of the Other: Essays in Contemporary Continental Philosophy* (New York, NY: State University of New York Press): 157–17.

Green, Laura (1995) ' "Strange [in]Difference of Sex": Thomas Hardy, the Victorian Man of Letters, and the Temptations of Androgeny', *Victorian Studies*, 38 (4): 523–49.

Gregor, Ian (1974) *The Great Web: The Form of Hardy's Major Fiction* (London: Faber and Faber).

Grosz, Elizabeth (1990) *Jacques Lacan: A Feminist Introduction* (London: Routledge).

Guattari, Félix (1979) ' "A Liberation of Desire": An Interview by George Stambolian', in eds. Stamboulian George and Elaine Marks, *Homosexualities and French Literature: Cultural Contexts/Critical Texts* (Ithaca, NY and London: Cornell University Press): 56–69.

Guérard, Albert J. (ed.) (1963) *Hardy: A Collection of Critical Essays* (New Jersey: Prentice Hall).

Hardy, Emma (1961) *Some Recollections by Emma Hardy with Some Relevant Poems by Thomas Hardy* (Oxford: Oxford University Press).

Hardy, Thomas (1865) 'How I Built Myself a House', in ed. H. Orel, *Thomas Hardy's Personal Writings* (London: Macmillan): 159–68 and ed. P. Dalziel *Thomas Hardy: The Excluded and Collaborative Stories* (Oxford: OUP): 10–16.

Desperate Remedies (1871; 2003) edited with introduction and notes by Patricia Ingham (Oxford: Oxford World's Classics).

(1871; 1998) edited with introduction and notes by Mary Rimmer (London: Penguin).

Under the Greenwood Tree (1872; 1999) edited with introduction and notes by Simon Gatrell (Oxford: Oxford World's Classics).

A Pair of Blue Eyes (1873; 2005) edited with notes by Alan Manford, with a new introduction by Tim Dolin (Oxford: Oxford World's Classics).

(1873; 2005) edited with introduction and notes by Pamela Dalziel (London: Penguin Classics).

Far from the Madding Crowd (1874; 2002) edited with notes by Suzanne B. Falck-Yi, new introduction by Linda Shires (Oxford: Oxford World's Classics).

The Hand of Ethelberta (1876; 1997) edited with an introduction by Tim Dolin (London: Penguin Classics).

The Return of the Native (1878; 2005) edited Simon Gatrell, notes by Nancy Barrineau, with a new introduction by Margaret Higonnet (Oxford: Oxford World's Classics).

An Indiscretion in the Life of an Heiress (1878) ed. Pamela Dalziel, *Thomas Hardy: The Excluded and Collaborative Stories* (Oxford: OUP): 66–87.

An Indiscretion in the Life of an Heiress and Other Stories (1994) edited with an introduction and notes by Pamela Dalziel (Oxford: Oxford World's Classics).

A Laodicean (1881; 1997) edited with an introduction and notes by John Schad (London: Penguin Classics).

Two on a Tower (1882; 1999) edited with an introduction and notes by Sally Shuttleworth (London: Penguin Classics).

The Mayor of Casterbridge (1886; 2004) edited with notes by Dale Kramer, with a new introduction by Pamela Dalziel (Oxford: Oxford World's Classics).

The Woodlanders (1887; 2004) with introduction and notes by Phillip Mallett (Hertfordshire: Wordsworth Classics).

(1887; 2005) edited with notes by Dale Kramer, with a new introduction by Penny Boumelha (Oxford: Oxford World's Classics).

Wessex Tales (1888; 1912; 1989) edited with an introduction and notes by Kathryn R. King (Oxford: Oxford World's Classics).

Tess of the d'Urbervilles (1891; 2003) edited with notes by Tim Dolin, introduction by Margaret R. Higonnet (London: Penguin Classics).

(1891; 2007) edited by Juliet Grindle and Simon Gatrell, with a new introduction by Penny Boumelha, notes by Nancy Barrineau (Oxford: Oxford World's Classics).

A Group of Noble Dames (1891; 1912) London: Macmillan.

Life's Little Ironies (1894; 1999) edited by Alan Manford, with an introduction by Norman Page (Oxford: Oxford World's Classics).

Jude the Obscure (1896; 1998) edited with an introduction and notes by Patricia Ingham (Oxford: Oxford World's Classics).

The Well-Beloved (1897; 1986) edited with an introduction by Tom Hetherington (Oxford: Oxford World's Classics).

The Well-Beloved with The Pursuit of the Well-Beloved (1892; 2000) with an introduction and notes by Jane Thomas (Hertfordshire: Wordsworth).

The Complete Poems (1976) ed. James Gibson (London and Basingstoke: Macmillan).

The Complete Poetical Works of Thomas Hardy (1982–1995) ed. Samuel Hynes (Oxford: Clarendon Press).

Vol. 1 (1982): *Wessex Poems; Poems of the Past and Present; Time's Laughingstocks*.

Vol. II (1987): *Satires of Circumstance; Moments of Vision; Late Lyrics and Earlier*.

Vol. III (1985): *Human Shows; Winter Words; Uncollected Poems*.

Vol. IV (1995): *The Dynasts, Parts First and Second*.

Vol. V (1995): *The Dynasts, Part Third; The Famous Tragedy of the Queen of Cornwall; The Play of 'St George'; 'O Jan O Jan O Jan' Collected Letters of Thomas Hardy* (1978–1988) ed. Richard Little Purdy and Michael Millgate (Oxford: Clarendon Press), 1978–1988 in 7 vols (Vol. 1 (1978): 1840–1892; Vol. 2 (1980): 1893–1901; Vol. 3 (1982): 1902–1908; Vol. 4 (1984): 1909–1913; Vol. 5 (1985): 1914–1919; Vol. 6 (1987): 1920–1925; Vol. 7 (1988): 1926–1927).

Hardy, Thomas (1989) *The Life and Work of Thomas Hardy by Thomas Hardy*, ed. Michael Millgate (Basingstoke and London: Macmillan Press).

—— (1994) ' "Studies, Specimens &c." Notebook', in eds. Pamela Dalziel and Michael Millgate (Oxford: Clarendon Press).

Harrison, DeSales (2005), *The End of the Mind,The Edge of the Intelligible in Hardy, Stevens, Larkin, Plath and Glück* (Oxford: Routledge)

Harrison, DeSales (2010) 'Reading Absences in Hardy's Lyrics: Representation and Recognition', in ed. R. Morgan, *The Ashgate Research Companion to Thomas Hardy* (Surrey and Burlington: Ashgate): 403–26.

Heffernan, J. A. (1993) *Museum of Words: The Poetics of Ekphrasis from Homer to Ashbery* (Chicago: University of Chicago Press).

Heidegger, Martin (1978; 2007) *Martin Heidegger, Basic Writings from Being and Time (1927) to The Task of Thinking* (1964), ed. David Farrell Krell (London and New York: Routledge).

Heine, Heinrich (1876), *Prose Miscellanies by Heinrich Heine*, trans. S. L. Feischman (Philadelphia: J. B. Lippincott and Company).

Herring, Scott (2007) *Queering the Underworld: Slumming, Literature, and the Undoing of Lesbian and Gay History* (Chicago and London: University of Chicago Press).

Higonnet, Margaret R. (ed.) (1993) *The Sense of Sex: Feminist Perspectives on Thomas Hardy* (Illinois: University of Illinois Press).

Hill, Selima (1993) *A Little Book of Meat* (Newcastle: Bloodaxe Books).

Holdsworth, Roger V. ed (1983), *Epicoene, or The Silent Woman* (London: New Mermaids).

Hollander, Anne (1978) *Seeing Through Clothes* (Berkeley, CA, Los Angeles, CA and London: University of California Press).

Hollander, John (1995) *The Gazer's Spirit: Poems Speaking to Silent Works of Art* (Chicago and London: University of Chicago Press).

Hughes, John (1997) *Lines of Flight: Reading Deleuze with Hardy, Gissing, Conrad, Woolf* (Sheffield: Sheffield Academic Press).

Hunter, Lynette (1989) *Modern Allegory and Fantasy: Rhetorical Stances of Contemporary Writing* (Basingstoke: Macmillan).

Hunter, Richard (2004) *Plato's Symposium* (Oxford: OUP).

Hutcheon, Linda (1998) 'Irony, Nostalgia and the Postmodern', http://www.library. utoronto.ca/utel/criticism/hutchinp.html

Jaanus, Maire (1994) 'The Demontage of the Drive', in eds. Feldstein Fink and M. Jaanus, *Reading Seminar XI Including the First English Translation of 'Position of the Unconscious' by Jacques Lacan* (New York, NY: SUNY Press): 119–38.

Jackson, Rosemary (1981) *Fantasy: The Literature of Subversion* (London: Methuen).

Jacobus, Mary (1979) *Women, Writing, and Writing about Women* (London: Croom Helm).

James, Henry (1974; 1982) 'The Last of the Valerii', in *Selected Tales of Henry James* (Harmondsworth: Penguin): 13–42.

Johnson, S. R. (1993) 'Metamorphosis, Desire, and the Fantastic in Thomas Hardy's "The Withered Arm" ', *Modern Language Studies*, 23 (4): 131–41.

Johnson, Bruce (1987), 'The Perfection of Species. And Hardy's *Tess*', in ed. H. Bloom, *Modern Critical Approaches: Thomas Hardy's Tess of the d'Urbervilles* (New York, NY: Chelsea House): 25–43.

Kelly, Mary Ann (1982) 'Hardy's Reading in Schopenhauer: *Tess of the d'Urbervilles*', *Colby Library Quarterly*, 18 (3): 182–98.

Kennedy, David (2007) *Elegy* (London and New York: Routledge).

Keys, R. T. (1985) 'Hardy's Uncanny Narrative: A Reading of "The Withered Arm" , *Texas Studies in Literature and Language*, 27: 106–23.

Knoepflmacher, U. C. (1990) 'Hardy's Ruins: Female Spaces and Male Designs', *PMLA*, 5 (1): 1055–70.

Kolm, Serge-Christophe (1986) 'The Buddhist Theory of "No-Self" ', trans. Martin Thom, in ed. J. Elster, *The Multiple Self* (Cambridge: Cambridge University Press): 233–63.

Krafft-Ebing, Richard Von (1886 trans. 1901) *Psychopathia Sexualis* (Philadelphia, PA: F.A. Davis Company).

Lacan, Jacques (1977) *Ecrits: A Selection*, trans. Alan Sheridan (London: Tavistock Publications).

———— (1966; 2006) *Ecrits: The First Complete Edition in English*, trans. Bruce Fink in collaboration with Héloïse Fink and Russell Grigg (New York and London: W. W. Norton & Company).

———— (1977b) *The Four Fundamental Concepts of Psycho-Analysis*, in ed. Jacques-Alain Miller, trans. Alan Sheridan (London: The Hogarth Press and the Institute of Psycho-Analysis), first published (1973) as *Le Seminaire de Jacques Lacan, Livre XI, 'Les quatres concepts fondamentaux de la psychoanalyse* (Editions du Seuil).

———— (1981) 'Desire and the Interpretation of Desire in *Hamlet*', in ed. S. Feldman: 11–52.

──── (1988) *The Seminar of Jacques Lacan, Book II: The Ego in Freud's Theory and in the Technique of Psychoanalysis, 1954–55*, trans. Sylvana Tomaselli (Cambridge: Cambridge University Press). originally published (1978) as *Le Seminaire, Livre II: Le moi dans la theorie de Freud et dans la technique de la psychoanalyse, 1954–1955* by Les Editions du Seuil (Paris).

──── (1992 *The Seminar of Jacques Lacan*, (Book VII) *The Ethics of Psychoanalysis 1959–60*, trans. Jacques-Alain Miller (New York and London:W. W. Norton).

Lacquer, Thomas (1990) *Making Sex: Body and Gender from the Greeks to Freud* (Harvard: Harvard University Press).

Langland, Elizabeth (1993) 'Becoming a Man in *Jude the Obscure*' in Higonnet, Margaret R (1993), pp. 32–48.

Larkin, Philip (1983) *Required Writing: Miscellaneous Pieces 1955–1982* (London: Faber and Faber).

Latham, David (2003) *Haunted Texts: Studies in Pre-Raphaelitism* (Toronto, ON: University of Toronto Press).

Laycock, Steven W. (1999) 'Consciousness It/Self', in eds. S. Gallagher and J. Shear, *Models of the Self* (Exeter: Imprint Academic): 295–406.

Ledger, Sally (2003) *Introduction to Keynotes and Discords by George Egerton* (Birmingham: University of Birmingham Press): ix–xxvi.

Lee, Vernon (1892; 2006) 'In the Praise of Old Houses', in ed. Patrick Madden, *Quotidiana*, 27 October 2006. ‹http://essays.quotidiana.org/lee/praise_of_old_houses/› (accessed 22 February 2010).

Leighton, Angela (1992) *Victorian Women Poets: Writing Against the Heart* (Hemel Hempstead: Harvester Wheatsheaf).

Levinson, Marjorie (2006), 'Object-Loss and Object-Bondage: Economies of Representation in Hardy's Poetry', *ELH* (73/2), 549–80.

Lewis, Charlton T. and Charles Short (1879) *A Latin Dictionary founded on Andrews' Edition of Freund's Latin Dictionary* (Oxford: Clarendon Press).

Locke, Charles (2009) 'Inhibiting the Voice: Thomas Hardy and Modern Poetics', in ed. K. Wilson, *A Companion to Thomas Hardy* (West Sussex: Wiley-Blackwell): 450–64.

Lougy, Robert E. (2004) *Inaugural Wounds: The Shaping of Desire in Five Nineteenth-Century English Narratives* (Athens, OH: Ohio University Press).

Lucas, John (2000) 'Thomas Hardy and Free Verse', *PN Review*, 132 (26): 4, March–April, http://www.pnreview.co.uk/cgi-bin/scribe?itemid=554 (accessed 4 August 2012).

Lucero-Montano, Alfredo (2003) 'Spinoza's *Ethics*: Determinism and Freedom', *Philosophy Pathways*, 67, http://www.philosophos.com/philosophy_article_63.html (accessed 20 December 2011).

Mahaffy, John Pentland (1874) *Social Life in Greece from Homer to Menander* (London: Macmillan).

Mallett, Phillip (2004a) Palgrave *Advances in Thomas Hardy Studies* (Basingstoke and New York: Palgrave Macmillan).

──── (2004b) ' "The Immortal Puzzle": Hardy and Sexuality', in ed. P. Mallett, *Palgrave Advances in Thomas Hardy Studies* (Basingstoke and New York: Palgrave Macmillan): 181–202.

──── (2004c) *Introduction to The Woodlanders* (Hartfordshire: Wordsworth).

──── (2009) 'Hardy and Philosophy', in ed. K. Wilson: 22–35.

Marcus, Sharon (2007) *Between Women: Friendship, Desire and Marriage in Victorian England* (Princeton, NJ and Oxford: Princeton University Press).

Marks, Elaine (1979) 'Lesbian Intertextuality', in eds. G. Stamboulian and E. Marks, *Homosexualities and French Literature: Cultural Contexts/Critical Texts* (Ithaca, NY and London: Cornell University Press): 353–78.

Maxwell, Catherine (2008) *Second Sight: Visionary Imagination in Late Victorian Literature* (Manchester and New York: Manchester University Press).

McGann, Jerome and C. L. Sligh (eds.) (2004) *Algernon Charles Swinburne: Major Poems and Selected Prose* (New Haven, CT and London: Yale University Press).

Michie, Helena (1989) 'There is no Friend like a Sister: Sisterhood as Sexual Difference', *ELH*, 56 (2): 401–21.

Miles, Geoffrey (1999) *Classical Mythology in English Literature, A Critical Anthology* (London: Routledge).

Mill, John Stuart (1832–33) *On Marriage: The Collected Works of John Stuart Mill*, 33 vols, Volume XXI, *Essays on Equality, Law, and Education*, in ed. John M. Robson, Introduction by Stefan Collini (Toronto, ON and London: University of Toronto Press and Routledge and Kegan Paul, 1984). http://oll.libertyfund.org/title/255/21642 (accessed 24 March 2011).

Miller, Jacques-Alain (2008) 'Extimite', *The Symptom*, 9, http://www.lacan.com/symptom/?p=36

Miller, J. Hillis (1970) *Thomas Hardy: Distance and Desire* (Cambridge, MA and London: Harvard University Press and OUP).

—— (1982a) *Fiction and Repetition: Seven English Novels* (Cambridge, MA: Harvard University Press).

—— (1982b) '*The Well-Beloved*: the Compulsion to Stop Repeating', *Fiction and Repetition: Seven English Novels* (Cambridge, MA: Harvard University Press): 147–75.

Millgate, Michael (ed.) (1996) *Letters of Emma and Florence Hardy* (Oxford: Clarendon Press).

—— (2001) *Thomas Hardy's Public Voice, the Essays, Speeches, and Miscellaneous Prose* (Oxford: Clarendon Press).

—— (2004) *Thomas Hardy: A Biography Revisited* (Oxford: OUP).

Mitchell, Judith (1994) *The Stone and the Scorpion: The Female Subject of Desire in the Novels of Charlotte Brontë, George Eliot and Thomas Hardy* (Westport, CT: Greenwood Press).

Mitchell, Juliet (1985) 'Feminine Sexuality in Psychoanalytic Doctrine', in Mitchell, Juliet and Jacqueline Rose (eds) *Feminine Sexuality: Jacques Lacan and the ecole freudienne* (New York and London: W. W. Norton and Company): 123–136.

Mitchell, Juliet and Jacqueline Rose (eds) (1985) *Feminine Sexuality: Jacques Lacan and the ecole freudienne* (New York and London: W. W. Norton and Company).

Morgan, Rosemarie (1988) *Women and Sexuality in the Novels of Thomas Hardy* (London: Routledge).

—— (ed.) (2010) *The Ashgate Research Companion to Thomas Hardy* (Surrey and Burlington: Ashgate).

Morgan, William W. (1974) 'Form, Tradition, and Consolation in Hardy's "Poems of 1912–13"', *PMLA*, 89 (3): 496–505.

—— (2009) 'Hardy's Poems: The Scholarly Situation', in ed. K. Wilson, *A Companion to Thomas Hardy* (West Sussex: Wiley-Blackwell): 395–412.

Morley, John (1866), Unsigned Review of Swinburne's *Poems and Ballads* in the *Saturday Review*, 4 August, 1866, xxii: 145–7.

Mulvey, Laura (2000) 'Death Drives: Hitchcock's Psycho', *Film Studies*, 2 (2000): 5–14.

Neill, Edward. (2004) *The Secret Life of Thomas Hardy 'Retaliatory Fiction'* (Ashgate: Aldershot).

Nemesvari, Richard (2011) *Thomas Hardy, Sensationalism, and the Melodramatic Mode* (Basingstoke: Palgrave).

Orel, Harold (ed.) (1966; 1967) *Thomas Hardy's Personal Writings* (London: Macmillan).

Orgel, Stephen (1996) *Impersonations: The Performance of Gender in Shakespeare's England* (Cambridge: Cambridge University Press).

Osborne, John (2008) *Larkin, Ideology and Critical Violence: A Case of Wrongful Conviction* (Basingstoke: Palgrave).

Oulton, Carolyn (2007) *Romantic Friendships in Victorian Literature* (Aldershot: Ashgate).

Ovid (1977) *Metamorphoses*, translated and with an introduction by Mary M. Innes (London: Penguin).

Page, Norman (1977) *Thomas Hardy* (London: Routledge).

Parish, Christina M. (2006) *Gender Dissonance and the Bourgeois Woman in the Victorian Novel* (Michigan: University of Michigan UMI Dissertation Series).

Pater, Walter (1868) 'Poems by William Morris', *Westminster Review*, 90: 300–12.

—— (1877) 'The School of Giorgione', *Fortnightly Review*, 22 (1877): 526–528.

—— (1878) 'Imaginary Portraits, 1: The Child in the House', *Macmillan's Magazine*, 38 (August): 313–21.

Peck, John (1972) 'Pound and Hardy', in ed. Davie Donald, *Agenda Thomas Hardy Special Issue* 10 (2–3): 3–10.

Peterson, Carla L. (1986) *'Jude the Obscure*; The Return of the Pagan', in ed. P. Boumelha, *Jude the Obscure Contemporary Critical Essays* (London, Basingstoke and New York, NY: Palgrave, Macmillan): 75–94.

Pickering, John (1999), 'The Self is a Semiotic Process' in ed. S. Gallagher and J. Shear *Models of the Self* (Exeter: Imprint Academic): 63–79.

Pierce, David (ed.) (2000) *Irish Writing in the Twentieth Century: A Reader* (Cork: Cork University Press).

Pinion, F. B. (1968; 1976) *A Hardy Companion* (London: Macmillan).

Preminger, A. (ed.); Franke J. Warnke and O. B. Hardison, Jr, assoc. (eds.) (1975) *Princeton Encyclopedia of Poetry and Poetics*, Enlarged Edition (London and Basingstoke: Macmillan).

Prettejohn, Elizabeth (2005) *Beauty and Art, 1750–2000* (Oxford: OUP).

Prins, Yopie (1999) *Victorian Sappho* (Princeton, NJ: Princeton University Press).

Proust, Marcel (1913–1927; 1980) *Remembrance of Things Past*, trans. C. K. Scott Moncrieff and Terence Kilmartin (London: Chatto and Windus).

Purdy, Richard Little (1954) *Thomas Hardy: A Bibliographical Study* (Oxford: Clarendon Press).

Radford, Andrew (2003) *Thomas Hardy and the Survivals of Time* (Aldershot: Ashgate).

Ramazani, Jahan (1994) *Poetry of Mourning: the Modern Elegy from Hardy to Heaney* (Chicago and London: University of Chicago Press).

Ray, Martin (ed.) (2007) *Thomas Hardy Remembered* (Hampshire and Burlington: Ashgate).

Reynolds, Margaret (2000) *The Sappho Companion* (London: Chatto and Windus).

—— (2003) *The Sappho History* (Basingstoke: Palgrave).

Rilke, Rainer Maria (1993*) Letters to a Young Poet*, trans. M. D. Herter Norton (London: W. W. Norton and Co).

Rimmer, Mary (1998) Introduction to *Desperate Remedies* (London: Penguin).

—— (2009) 'Hardy's "Novels of Ingenuity" *Desperate Remedies, The Hand of Ethelberta*, and *A Laodicean*: Rare Hands at Contrivances', in ed. K. Wilson, *A Companion to Thomas Hardy* (West Sussex: Wiley-Blackwell): 267–80.

Ruskin, John (1849; 1903) *The Seven Lamps of Architecture*, in eds. E. T. Cook and Alexander Wedderburn, *The Complete Works of John Ruskin*, 39 vols (vol. 8) (London: Allen, Longmans, Green and Co).

Rutland, William K. (1938) *Thomas Hardy: A Study of His Writings and Their Background* (Oxford: Blackwell).

Sacks, Peter M. (1985) *The English Elegy: Studies in the Genre from Spenser to Yeats* (Baltimore, MD and London: The Johns Hopkins University).

Saldívar, Ramón (1983) '*Jude the Obscure*: Reading and the Spirit of the Law', *ELH*, 50 (3): 607–25.

Schad, John (1997) Introduction to Thomas Hardy's *a Laodicean or The Castle of the De Stancys* (London: Penguin Books): xvii–xxxvi.

Schmidt, Michael (1998) *The Lives of the Poets* (London: Weidenfeld and Nicholson).

Schopenhauer, Arthur (1851; 1970) *Arthur Schopenhauer: Essays and Aphorisms*, trans. R. J. Holligdale (London: Penguin).

Sexton, Melanie (1991) 'Phantoms of His Own Figuring: The Movement towards Recovery in Hardy's "Poems of 1912–13" ', *Victorian Poetry*, 29 (3): 209–26.

Shakespeare, William (2007) *The Arden Shakespeare Complete Works* (London: Thomas Nelson and Sons).

Shaw, W. David (1994) *Elegy and Paradox, Testing the Conventions* (Baltimore, MD and London: Johns Hopkins University Press).

Shires, Linda (1991) 'Narrative, Gender, and Power in *Far From the Madding Crowd*', *Novel: A Forum on Fiction*, 24 (2): 162–77.

——— (2004) 'Hardy and Nineteenth-Century Poetry', in ed. P. Mallett, *Palgrave Advances in Thomas Hardy Studies* (Basingstoke and New York, NY: Palgrave Macmillan): 255–78.

Shuttleworth, Sally (1999) Introduction and Notes to Thomas Hardy's *Two on a Tower* (London: Penguin Classics): xvi–xxxiv and 263–96.

Simpson, Peter (1979) 'Hardy's "The Self-Unseeing" and the Romantic Problem of Consciousness', *Victorian Poetry*, 17 (1–2), *The Poetry of Thomas Hardy: A Commemorative Issue* (Spring-Summer): 45–50.

Sinfield, Alan (1994) *The Wilde Century: Effeminacy, Oscar Wilde and the Queer Moment* (New York: Columbia U P).

Smith, Adam (1759) *The Theory of Moral Sentiments* in *Adam Smith: Selected Philosophical Writings* (2004) edited and introduced by James R. Otteson (Exeter: Imprint Academic): 11–87.

Smith, Alison (1999) 'Nature Transformed: Leighton, the Nude and the Model', in eds. Tim Barringer and Elizabeth Prettejohn, *Frederick Leighton: Antiquity Renaissance Modernity* (New Haven, CT & London: Yale University Press): 19–44.

Southerington, F. R. (1972) 'Lives, Letters, and the Failure of Criticism, 1928–72', in ed. D. Davie, *Agenda Thomas Hardy Special Issue* 10 (2–3): 11–18.

Spector, Stephen J. (1988) 'Flights of Fancy: Characterization in Hardy's *Under the Greenwood Tree*', *ELH*, 55 (2): 469–85.

Spinoza, Baruch (1677; 1998), *Ethics*, trans. Shirley, S (Indianapolis: Hackett Publishing).

Spivak, Gayatri Chakravorti (trans. 1976) *Jacques Derrida: Of Grammatology* (Baltimore, MD: The Johns Hopkins University Press).

Stamboulian, George and Elaine Marks (eds.) (1979) *Homosexualities and French Literature: Cultural Contexts/Critical Texts* (Ithaca, NY and London: Cornell University Press).

Stanley, Liz (1992) 'Romantic Friendship? Some Issues in Researching Lesbian History and Biography', *Women's History Review*, 1 (2): 198–209.

Staten, Henry (1995) *Eros in Mourning: Homer to Lacan* (Baltimore, MD and London: Johns Hopkins University Press).

Stone, Donald D. (1984) 'House and Home in Thomas Hardy' (check), *Nineteenth-Century Fiction*, 39 (3): 292–304.

Sullivan, Jack (1978) *Elegant Nightmares: The English Ghost Story from Le Fanu to Blackwood* (Athens, OH and Georgia: Ohio University Press).

Suthrell, Charlotte (2004) *Unzipping Gender: Sex, Cross-Dressing and Culture* (Oxford and New York: Berg).

Swinburne, Algernon (2004) *Major Poems and Selected Prose*, eds. Jerome McGann and Charles L. Sligh (New Haven, CT and London: Yale University Press).

Symonds, John Addington (1890) *Essays Speculative and Suggestive* (London: Chapman Hall).

Taylor, Charles (1989) *Sources of the Self: The Making of Modern Identity* (Cambridge: Cambridge University Press).

Taylor, Dennis (1981) *Hardy's Poetry, 1860–1928* (London and Basingstoke: Macmillan).

—— (1988) *Hardy's Metres and Victorian Prosody* (Oxford: Clarendon Press).

—— (1993) *Hardy's Literary Language and Victorian Philology* (Oxford: Clarendon Press).

Tennyson, Alfred (1950) *Poetical Works* (London: Macmillan).

Thain, Marion (2007) *'Michael Field': Poetry, Aestheticism and the Fin de Siécle* (Cambridge: Cambridge University Press).

Thomas, J. (1999) *Thomas Hardy, Femininity and Dissent: Reassessing the 'Minor' Novels* (Basingstoke and London: Palgrave Macmillan).

—— (2000) 'Introduction' to *The Well Beloved, with 'The Pursuit of the Well-Beloved'* (Hertfordshire: Wordsworth): ix–xxvii.

—— (2006) 'Thomas Hardy and Desire: From Sappho to the Stranglers', *The Thomas Hardy Journal*, XXII (Autumn): 129–42.

—— (2007) 'Thomas Hardy, *Jude the Obscure* and "Comradely Love"', *Literature and History*, 16 (2): 1–15.

—— (2009) 'Hardy's "Romances and Fantasies": *A Pair of Blue Eyes, The Trumpet Major, Two on a Tower*, and *The Well-Beloved*: Experiments in Metafiction', in ed. K. Wilson, *A Companion to Thomas Hardy* (West Sussex: Wiley-Blackwell): 281–98.

—— (2010) 'Icons of Desire: The Classical Statue in Later Victorian Literature', *Yearbook of English Literature*, 40 (1–2): 246–72.

Thomas, Kate (2012), *Postal Pleasures: Sex, Scandal and Victorian Letters* (Oxford: OUP).

Tiffany, Grace (1995) *Erotic Beasts and Social Monsters: Shakespeare, Jonson, and Comic Androgyny* (Newark: University of Delaware Press).

Todorov, Tzvetan (1973) *The Fantastic: A Structural Approach to a Literary Genre*, trans. Richard Howard (Cleveland: The Press of Case Western Reserve University).

Vicinus, Martha (1982) 'Sexuality and Power: A Review of Current Work in the History of Sexuality', *Feminist Studies*, 8: 133–56.

—— (1992) ' "They Wonder to Which Sex I Belong": The Historical Roots of the Modern Lesbian Identity', *Feminist Studies*, 18 (3): 467–97.

Volsik, Paul (2004) ' "A Phantom of His Own Figuring": The Poetry of Thomas Hardy', *Etudes Anglaises*, 57 (2004/1): 103–16.

Ward, J. P. (1994) 'Hardy's Aesthetics and Twentieth-Century Poetry', in ed. P. Mallett, *Palgrave Advances in Thomas Hardy Studies* (Basingstoke and New York, NY: Palgrave Macmillan): 279–302.

Weber, Carl (1965) *Hardy of Wessex: His Life and Literary Career* (New York: Columbia University Press).

Wharton, Henry Thornton (1885) *Sappho: Memoir, Text, Selected Renderings, and a literal Translation by Henry Thornton Wharton* (London: John Lane).

——— (1895) *Sappho: Memoir, Text, Selected Renderings, and a literal Translation by Henry Thornton Wharton* (London: John Lane), Hardy's own copy in the Dorset County Museum.

White, Chris (ed.) (1999) *Nineteenth-Century Writings on Homosexuality: A Sourcebook* (London: Routlege).

Widdowson, Peter (1989) *Hardy in History: A Study in Literary Sociology* (London and New York: Routledge).

——— (2007) *Thomas Hardy* (Devon: Northcote House).

Widmer, P. (1996) 'Orpheus and Eurydice: Muses of Music', in eds. W. Apollon and R. Feldstein, *Lacan, Politics, Aesthetics* (New York, NY: State University of New York Press): 297–304.

Wigley, M. (1993) *The Architecture of Deconstruction: Derrida's Haunt* (Cambridge, MA: MIT Press).

Wilde, Oscar (1989) *The Major Works* (Oxford: Oxford World's Classics).

Williams, Linda Ruth (1995) *Critical Desire: Psychoanalysis and the Literary Subject* (London: Edward Arnold).

Wilson, Keith (ed.) (2009) *A Companion to Thomas Hardy* (West Sussex: Wiley-Blackwell).

Winterson, Jeanette (2011) *Why Be Happy When You Could Be Normal* (London: Jonathan Cape).

Wolfreys, Julian (2009) *Thomas Hardy* (Basingstoke: Palgrave Macmillan).

Wright, Terry (1989) *Thomas Hardy and the Erotic* (Basingstoke: Macmillan).

Wright, W. F. (1967) *The Shaping of the Dynasts: A Study in Thomas Hardy* (Lincoln, NE: University of Nebraska Press).

Yeats, W. B. (1907) 'Ideas of Good and Evil', in ed. D. Pierce, *Irish Writing in the Twentieth Century: A Reader* (Cork: Cork University Press): 57–9.

——— (1994) *W.B. Yeats: The Poems*, ed. Daniel Albright (London: Everyman).

Yeazell, Ruth Bernard (2008) *Art of the Everyday: Dutch Painting and the Realist Novel* (Princeton, NJ and Oxford: Princeton University Press).

Zeiger, Melissa (1997) *Beyond Consolation: Death, Sexuality, and the Changing Shape of Elegy* (Ithaca, NY and London: Cornell University Press).

Žižek, Slavoj (2006) *How to Read Lacan* (London: Granta Books).

Index

Printed and bound in Great Britain by
CPI Antony Rowe, Chippenham and Eastbourne